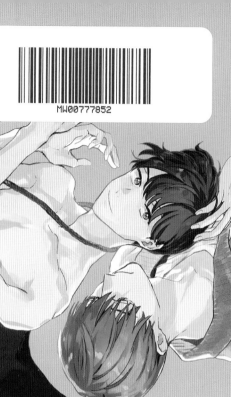

BUKURO YAMADA PRESENTS

YOU ARE MY HAPPINESS

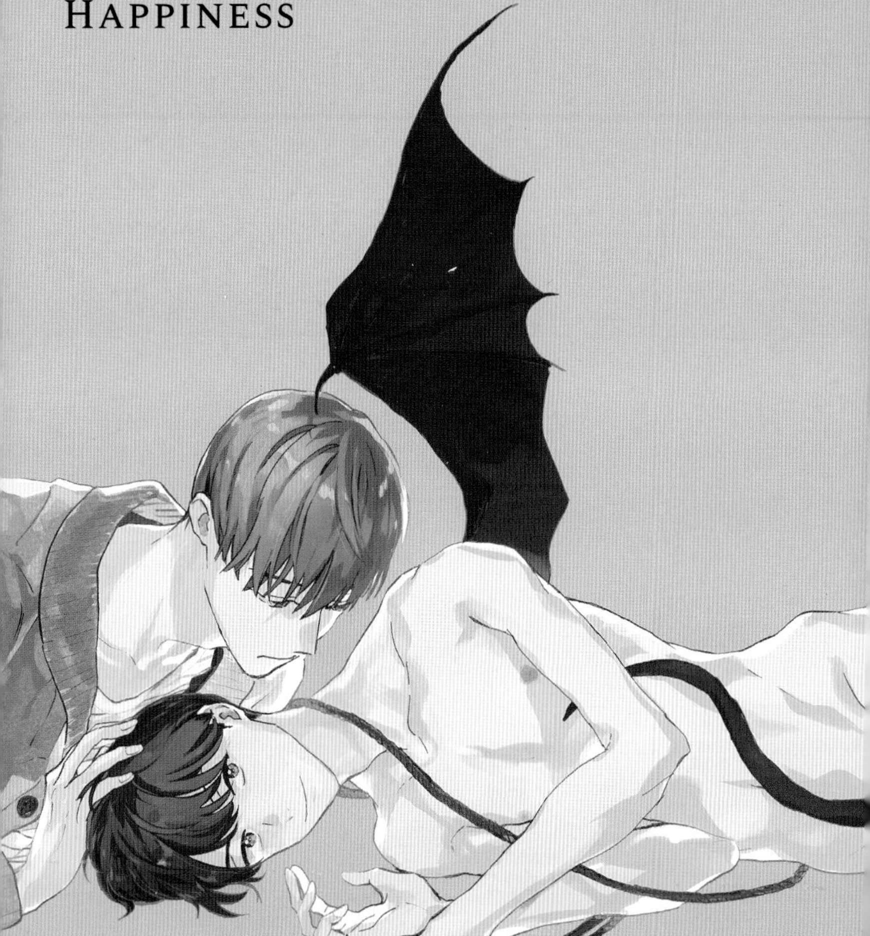

CONTENTS

Chapter 1

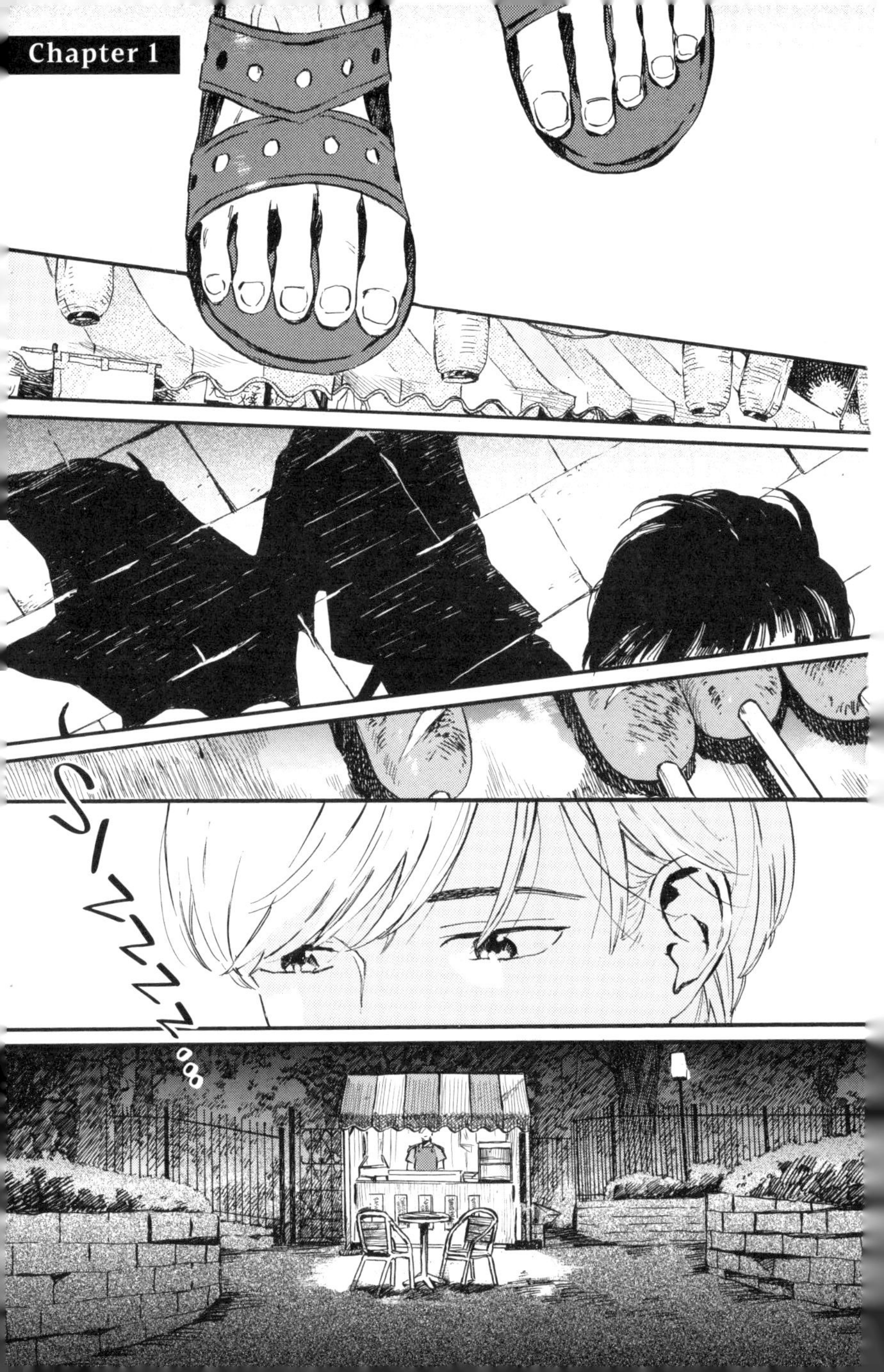
S—ZZZZ

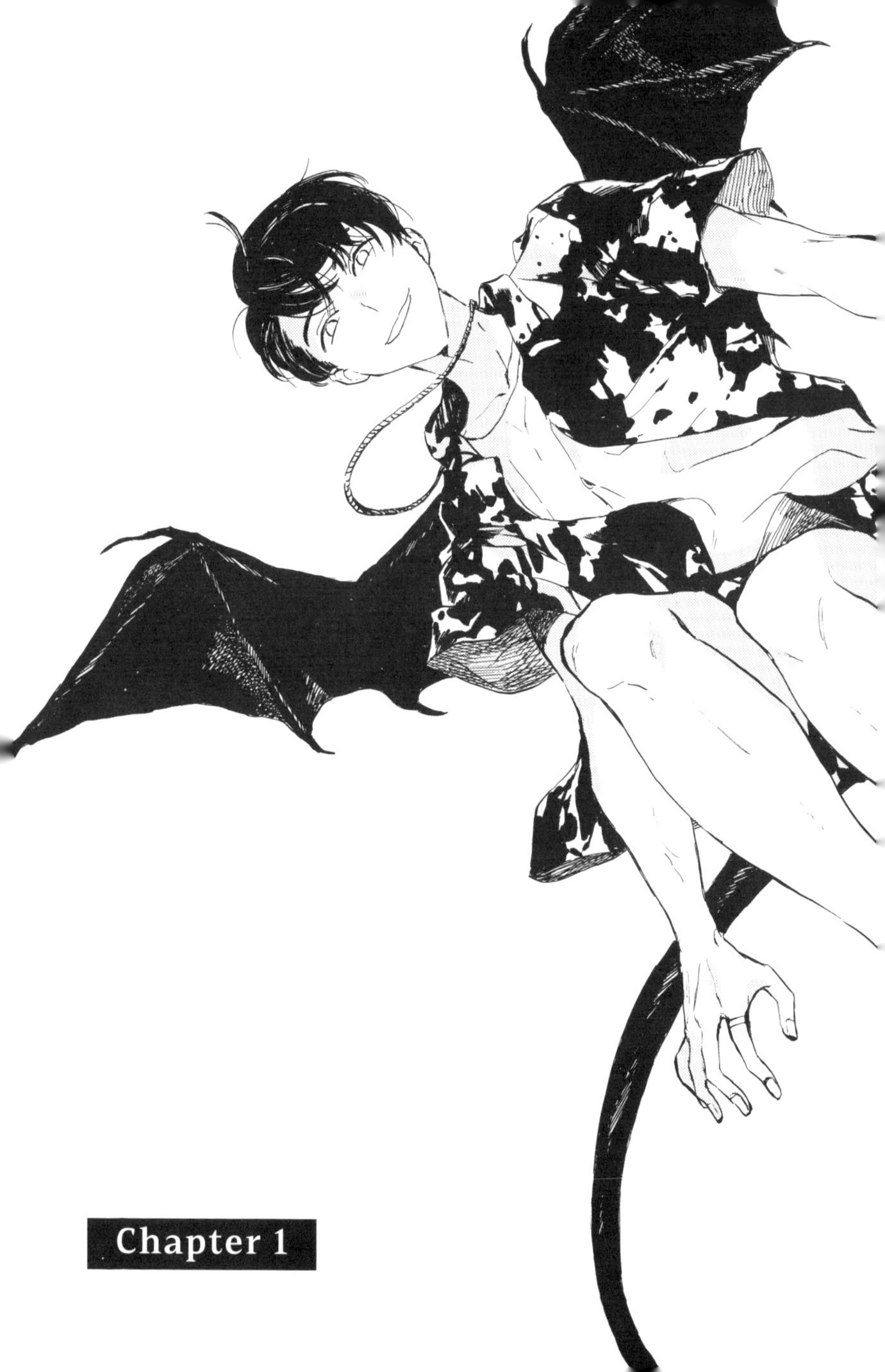

Chapter 1

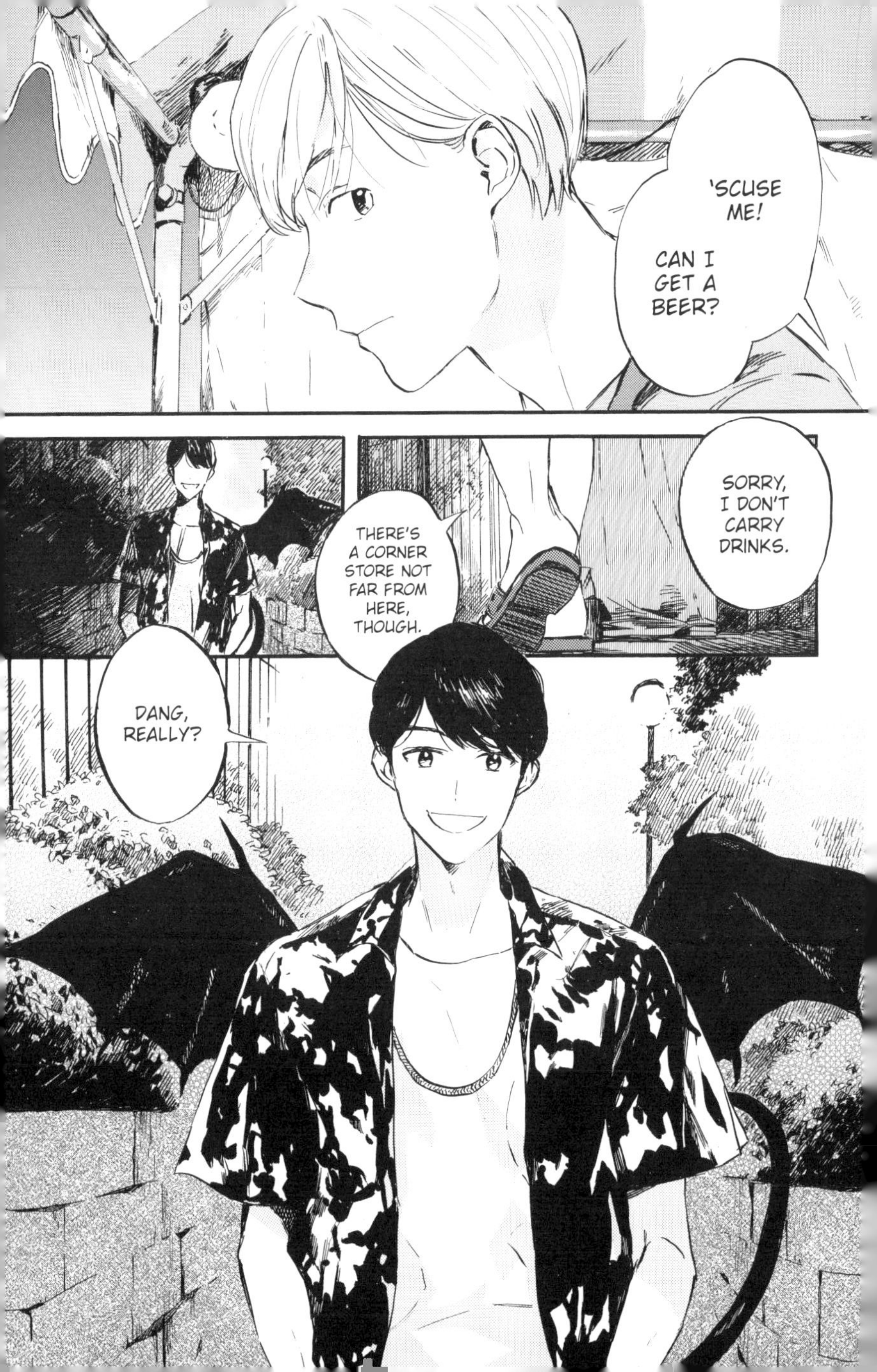
'SCUSE ME!
CAN I GET A BEER?
SORRY, I DON'T CARRY DRINKS.
THERE'S A CORNER STORE NOT FAR FROM HERE, THOUGH.
DANG, REALLY?

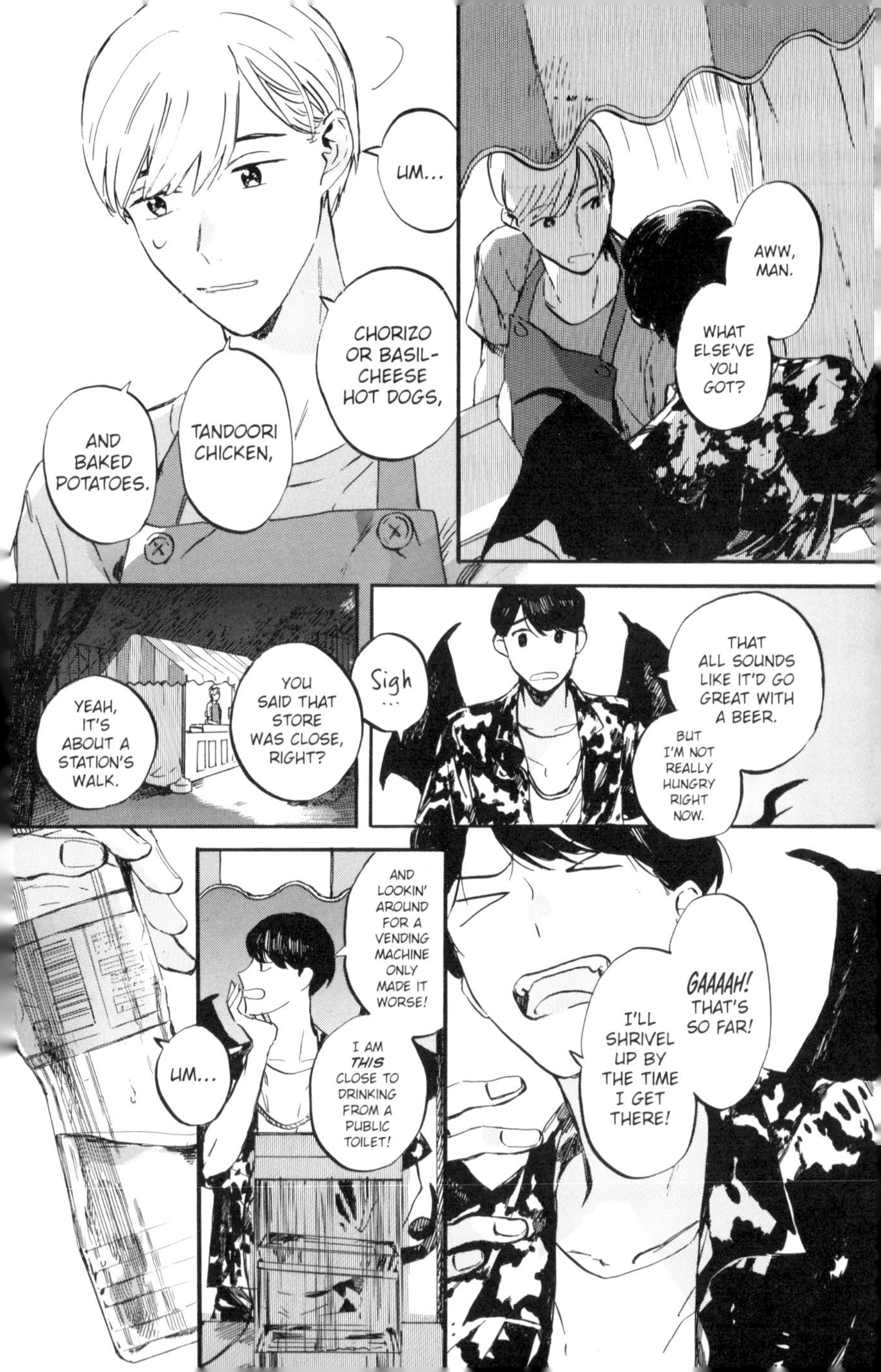
AWW, MAN.
WHAT ELSE'VE YOU GOT?
UM...
CHORIZO OR BASIL-CHEESE HOT DOGS,
TANDOORI CHICKEN,
AND BAKED POTATOES.
THAT ALL SOUNDS LIKE IT'D GO GREAT WITH A BEER.
BUT I'M NOT REALLY HUNGRY RIGHT NOW.
Sigh...
YOU SAID THAT STORE WAS CLOSE, RIGHT?
YEAH, IT'S ABOUT A STATION'S WALK.
GAAAAH! THAT'S SO FAR!
I'LL SHRIVEL UP BY THE TIME I GET THERE!
AND LOOKIN' AROUND FOR A VENDING MACHINE ONLY MADE IT WORSE!
I AM *THIS* CLOSE TO DRINKING FROM A PUBLIC TOILET!
UM...

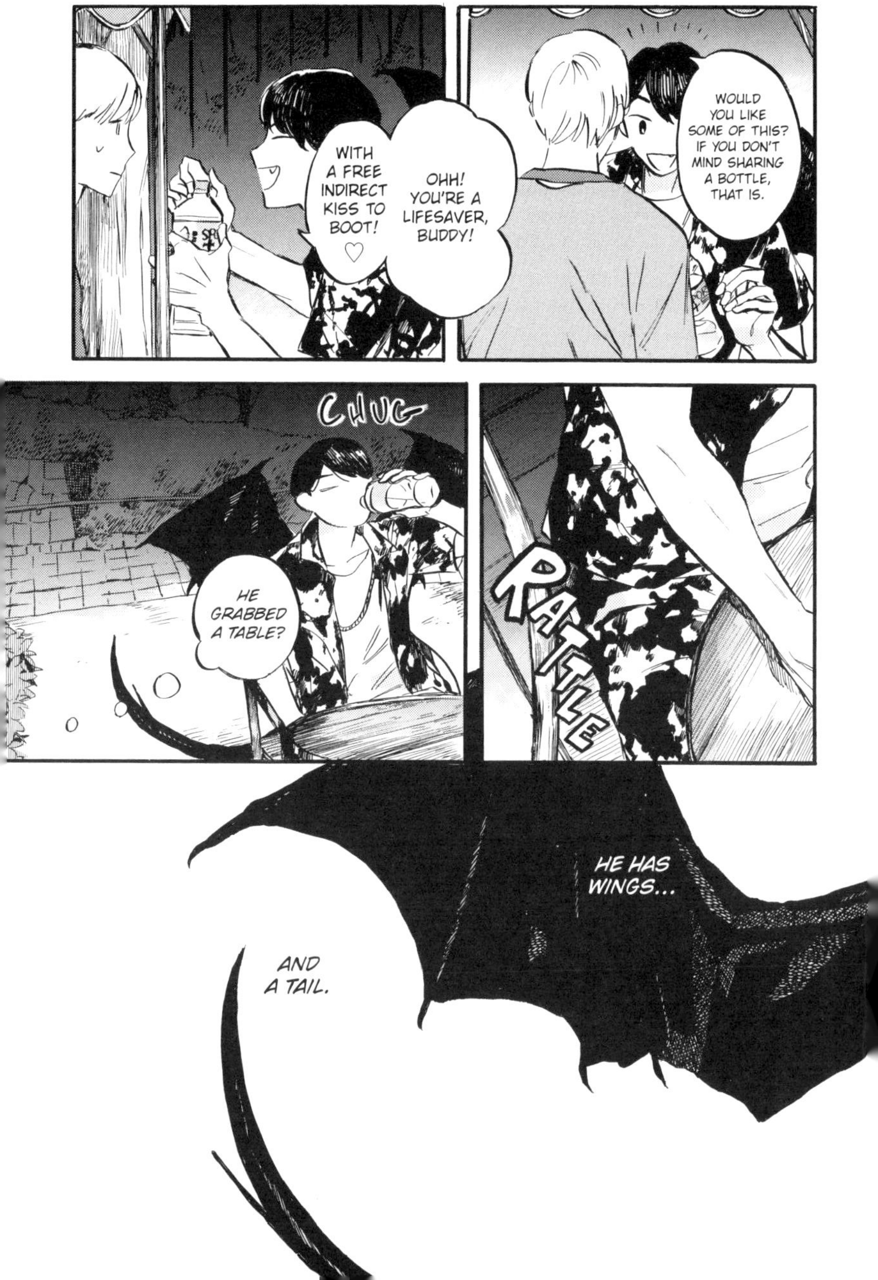
WOULD YOU LIKE SOME OF THIS? IF YOU DON'T MIND SHARING A BOTTLE, THAT IS.
OHH! YOU'RE A LIFESAVER, BUDDY!
WITH A FREE INDIRECT KISS TO BOOT! ♡
RATTLE
CHUG
HE GRABBED A TABLE?
HE HAS WINGS...
AND A TAIL.

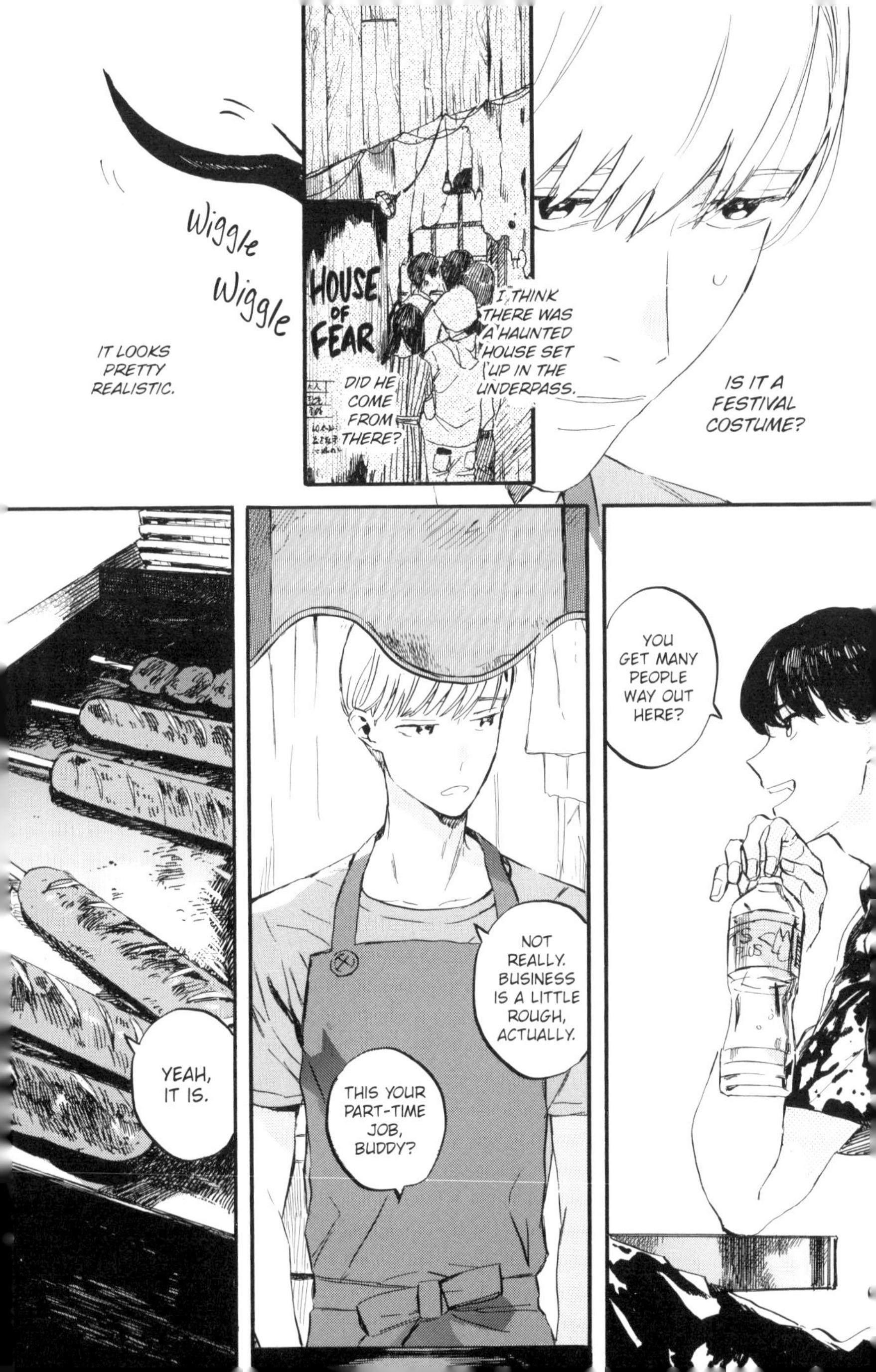
IS IT A FESTIVAL COSTUME?
I, THINK THERE WAS A HAUNTED HOUSE SET UP IN THE UNDERPASS.
DID HE COME FROM THERE?
HOUSE OF FEAR
Wiggle Wiggle
IT LOOKS PRETTY REALISTIC.
YOU GET MANY PEOPLE WAY OUT HERE?
NOT REALLY. BUSINESS IS A LITTLE ROUGH, ACTUALLY.
THIS YOUR PART-TIME JOB, BUDDY?
YEAH, IT IS.

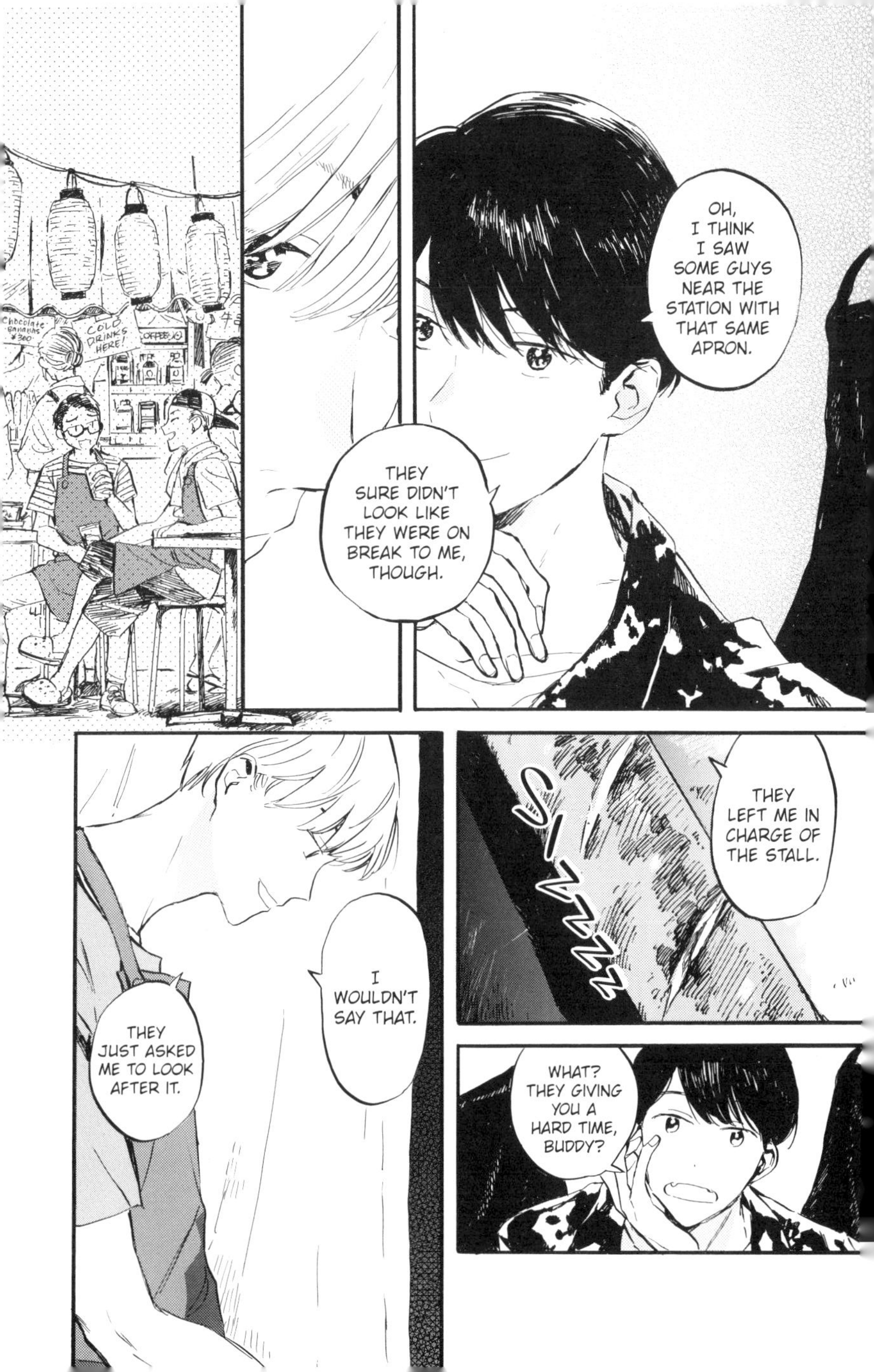
OH, I THINK I SAW SOME GUYS NEAR THE STATION WITH THAT SAME APRON.
THEY SURE DIDN'T LOOK LIKE THEY WERE ON BREAK TO ME, THOUGH.
Chocolate Bananas ¥300
COLD DRINKS HERE!
COFFEE
THEY LEFT ME IN CHARGE OF THE STALL.
S-NZZ
WHAT? THEY GIVING YOU A HARD TIME, BUDDY?
I WOULDN'T SAY THAT.
THEY JUST ASKED ME TO LOOK AFTER IT.

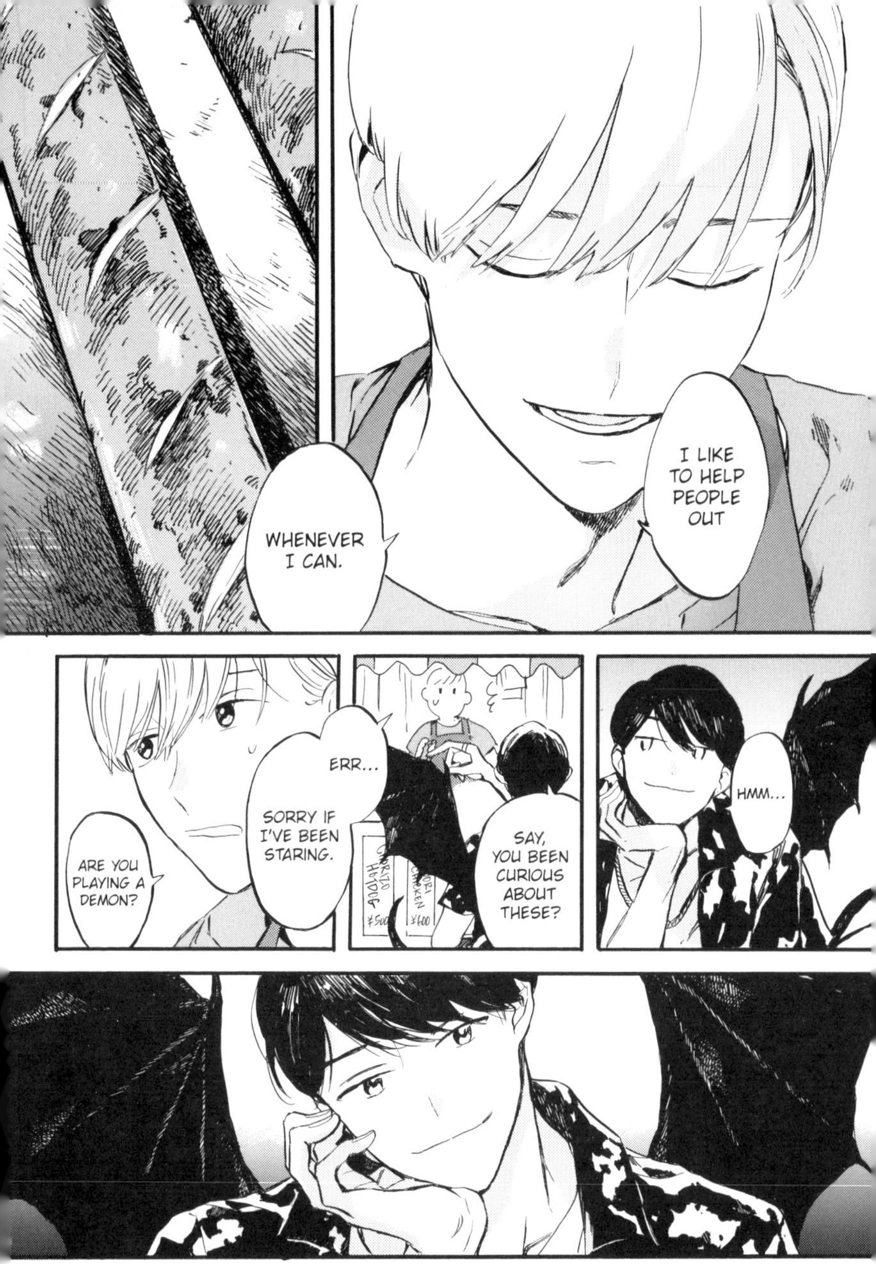
I LIKE TO HELP PEOPLE OUT
WHENEVER I CAN.
HMM...
SAY, YOU BEEN CURIOUS ABOUT THESE?
ERR...
SORRY IF I'VE BEEN STARING.
ARE YOU PLAYING A DEMON?

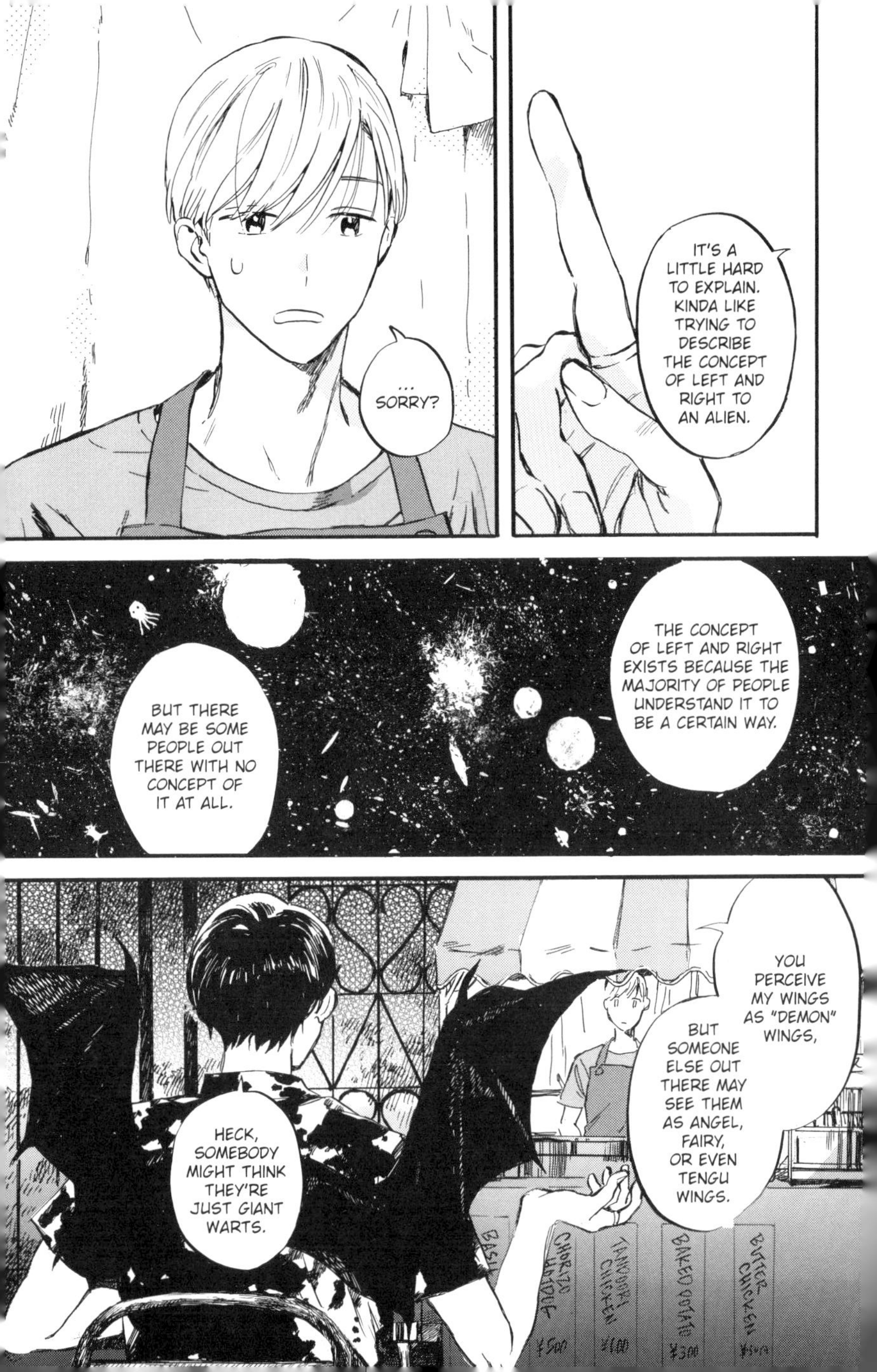
IT'S A LITTLE HARD TO EXPLAIN. KINDA LIKE TRYING TO DESCRIBE THE CONCEPT OF LEFT AND RIGHT TO AN ALIEN.
... SORRY?
THE CONCEPT OF LEFT AND RIGHT EXISTS BECAUSE THE MAJORITY OF PEOPLE UNDERSTAND IT TO BE A CERTAIN WAY.
BUT THERE MAY BE SOME PEOPLE OUT THERE WITH NO CONCEPT OF IT AT ALL.
YOU PERCEIVE MY WINGS AS "DEMON" WINGS,
BUT SOMEONE ELSE OUT THERE MAY SEE THEM AS ANGEL, FAIRY, OR EVEN TENGU WINGS.
HECK, SOMEBODY MIGHT THINK THEY'RE JUST GIANT WARTS.
BUTTER CHICKEN
BAKED POTATO
TANDOORI CHICKEN
CHORIZO
BASI

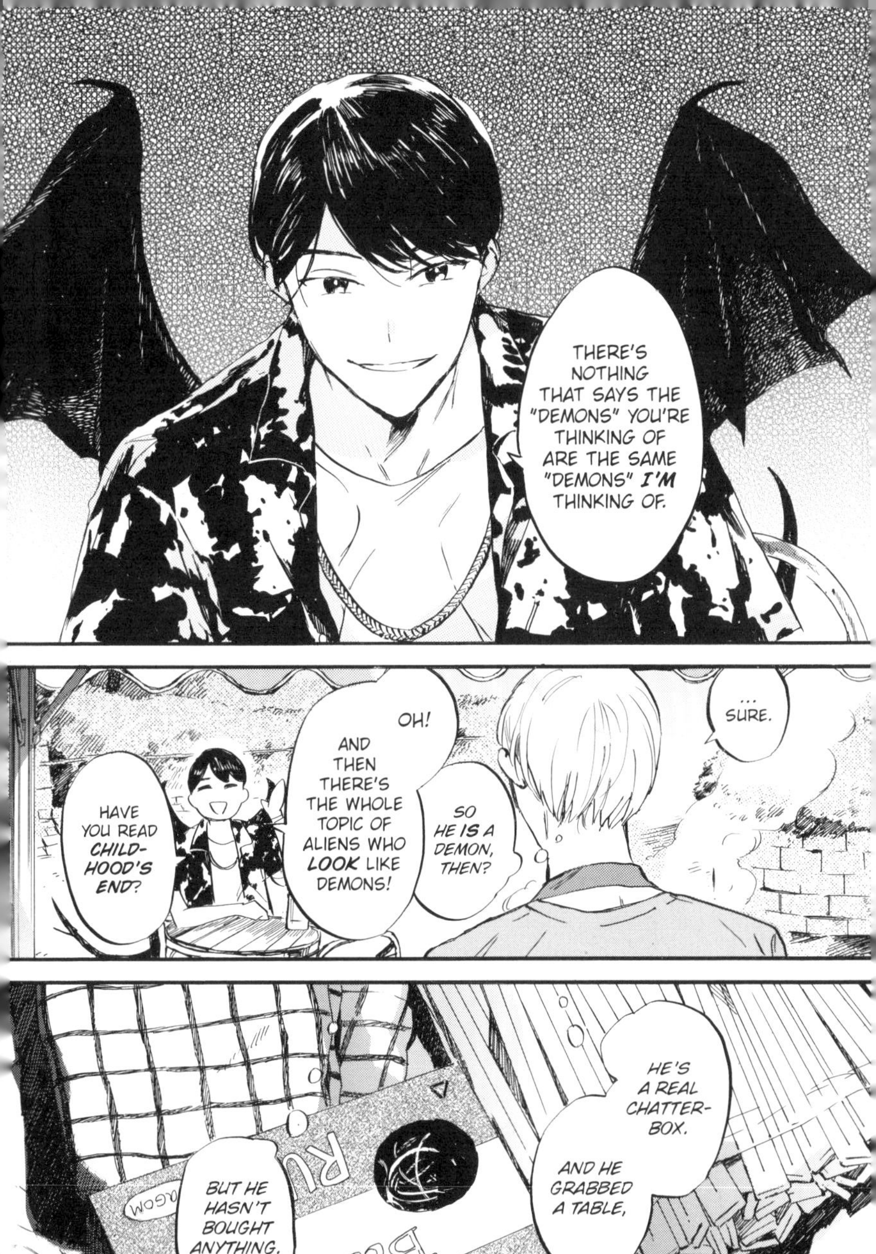
THERE'S NOTHING THAT SAYS THE "DEMONS" YOU'RE THINKING OF ARE THE SAME "DEMONS" ***I'M*** THINKING OF.
... SURE.
SO HE ***IS*** A DEMON, THEN?
OH!
AND THEN THERE'S THE WHOLE TOPIC OF ALIENS WHO ***LOOK*** LIKE DEMONS!
HAVE YOU READ ***CHILDHOOD'S END***?
HE'S A REAL CHATTER-BOX.
AND HE GRABBED A TABLE,
BUT HE HASN'T BOUGHT ANYTHING.

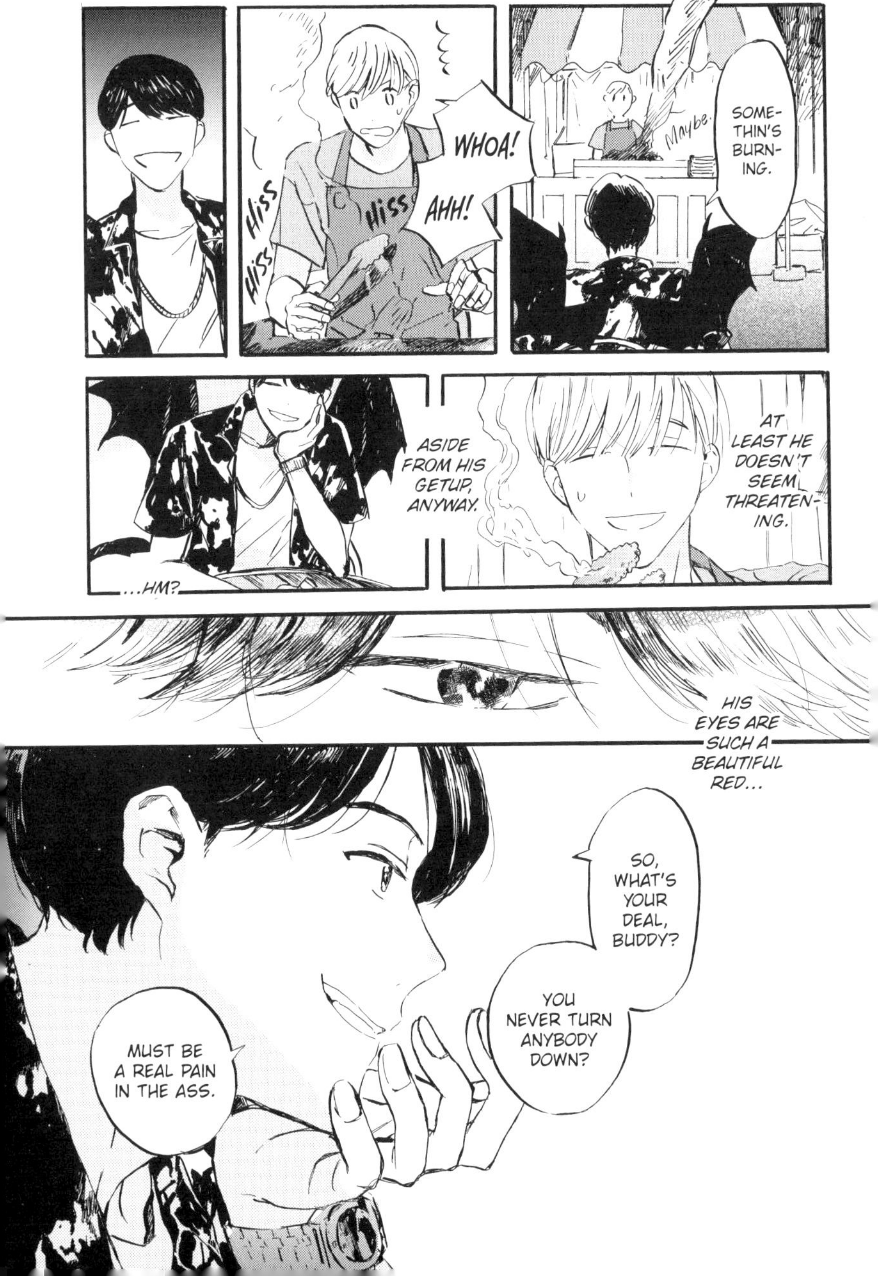
SOME-THIN'S BURN-ING.
Maybe.
WHOA!
AHH!
HISS
HISS
HISS
AT LEAST HE DOESN'T SEEM THREATEN-ING.
ASIDE FROM HIS GETUP, ANYWAY.
...HM?
HIS EYES ARE SUCH A BEAUTIFUL RED...
SO, WHAT'S YOUR DEAL, BUDDY?
YOU NEVER TURN ANYBODY DOWN?
MUST BE A REAL PAIN IN THE ASS.

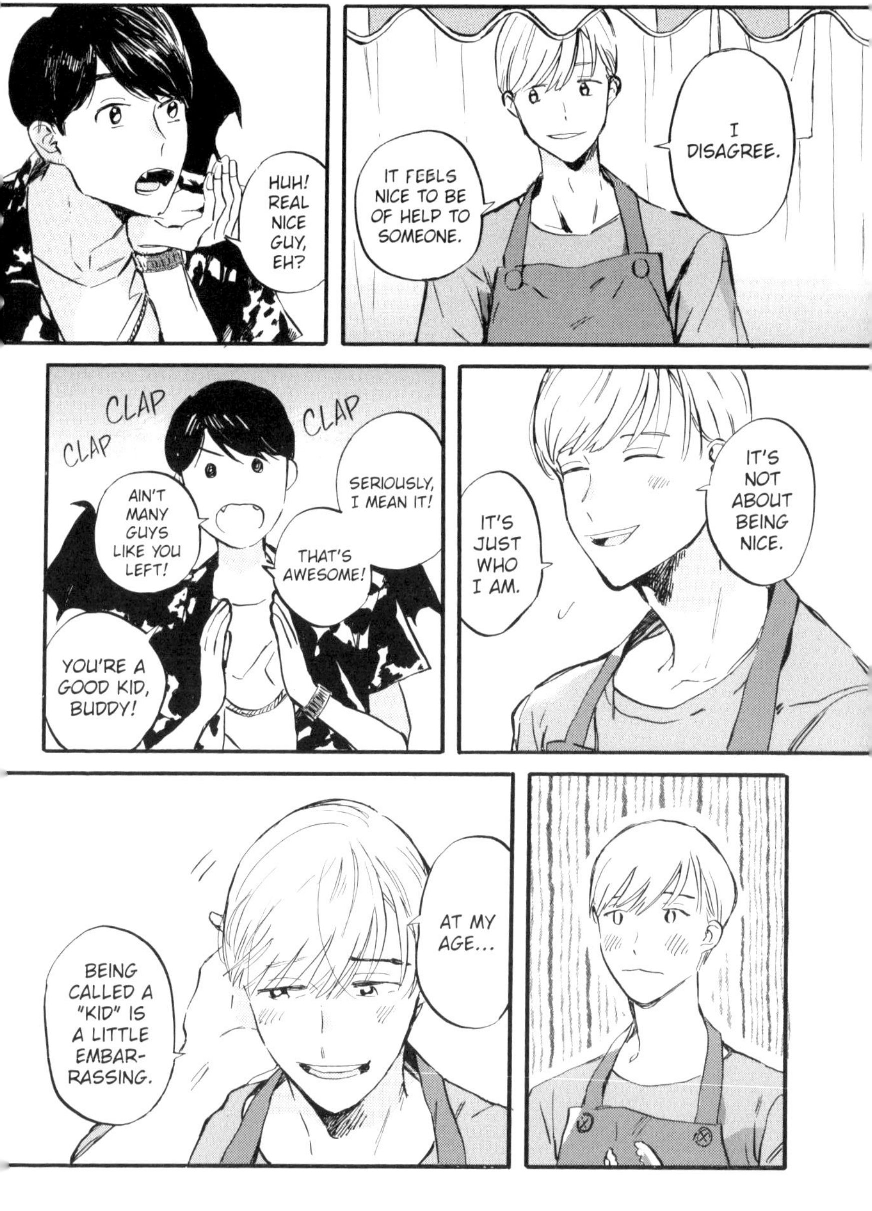
I DISAGREE.
IT FEELS NICE TO BE OF HELP TO SOMEONE.
HUH! REAL NICE GUY, EH?
IT'S NOT ABOUT BEING NICE.
IT'S JUST WHO I AM.
CLAP
CLAP
SERIOUSLY, I MEAN IT!
THAT'S AWESOME!
CLAP
AIN'T MANY GUYS LIKE YOU LEFT!
YOU'RE A GOOD KID, BUDDY!
AT MY AGE...
BEING CALLED A "KID" IS A LITTLE EMBAR-RASSING.

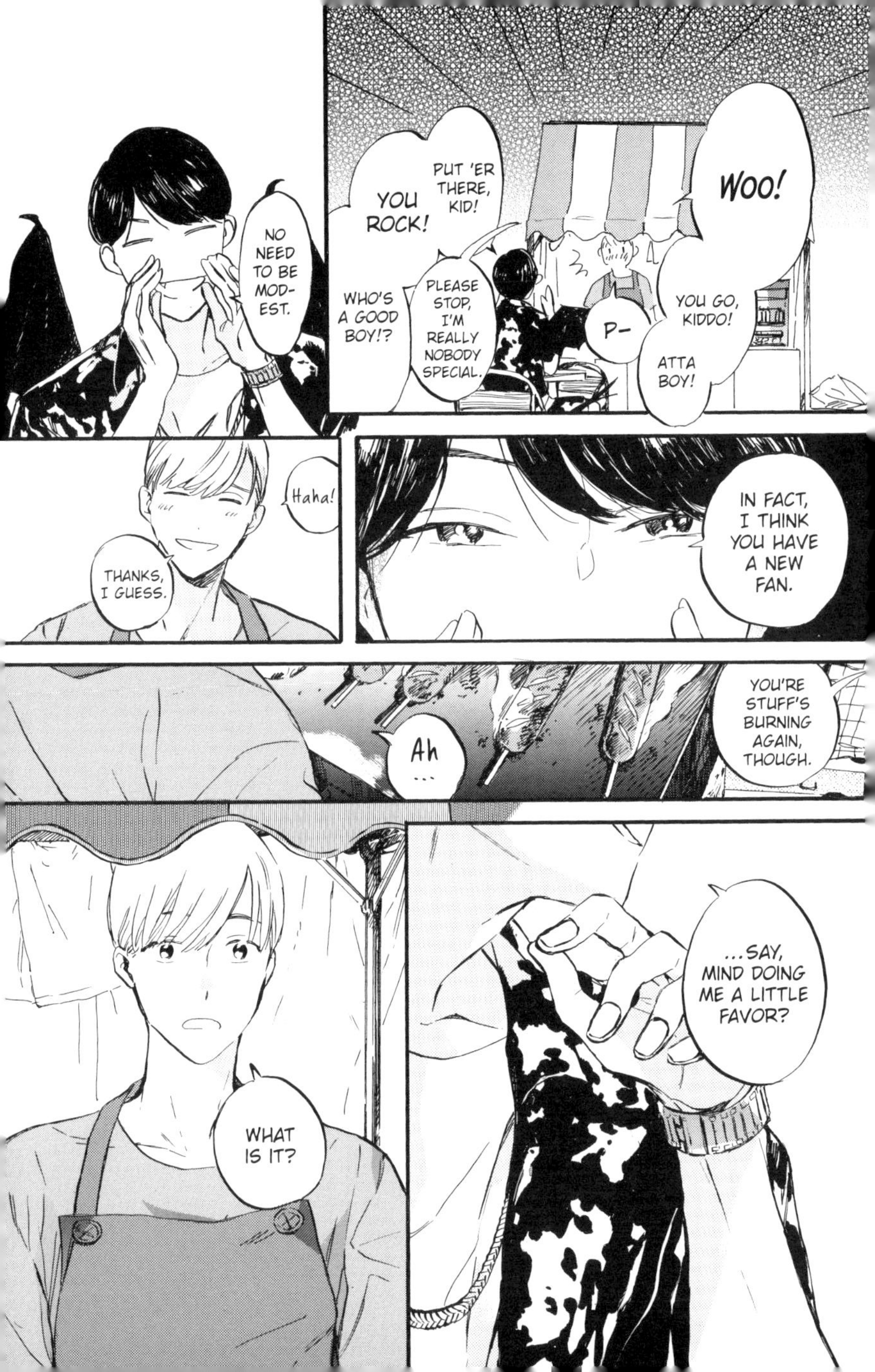
WOO!
YOU GO, KIDDO!
ATTA BOY!
P-
PUT 'ER THERE, KID!
YOU ROCK!
PLEASE STOP, I'M REALLY NOBODY SPECIAL.
WHO'S A GOOD BOY!?
NO NEED TO BE MOD-EST.
IN FACT, I THINK YOU HAVE A NEW FAN.
Haha!
THANKS, I GUESS.
YOU'RE STUFF'S BURNING AGAIN, THOUGH.
Ah ...
...SAY, MIND DOING ME A LITTLE FAVOR?
WHAT IS IT?

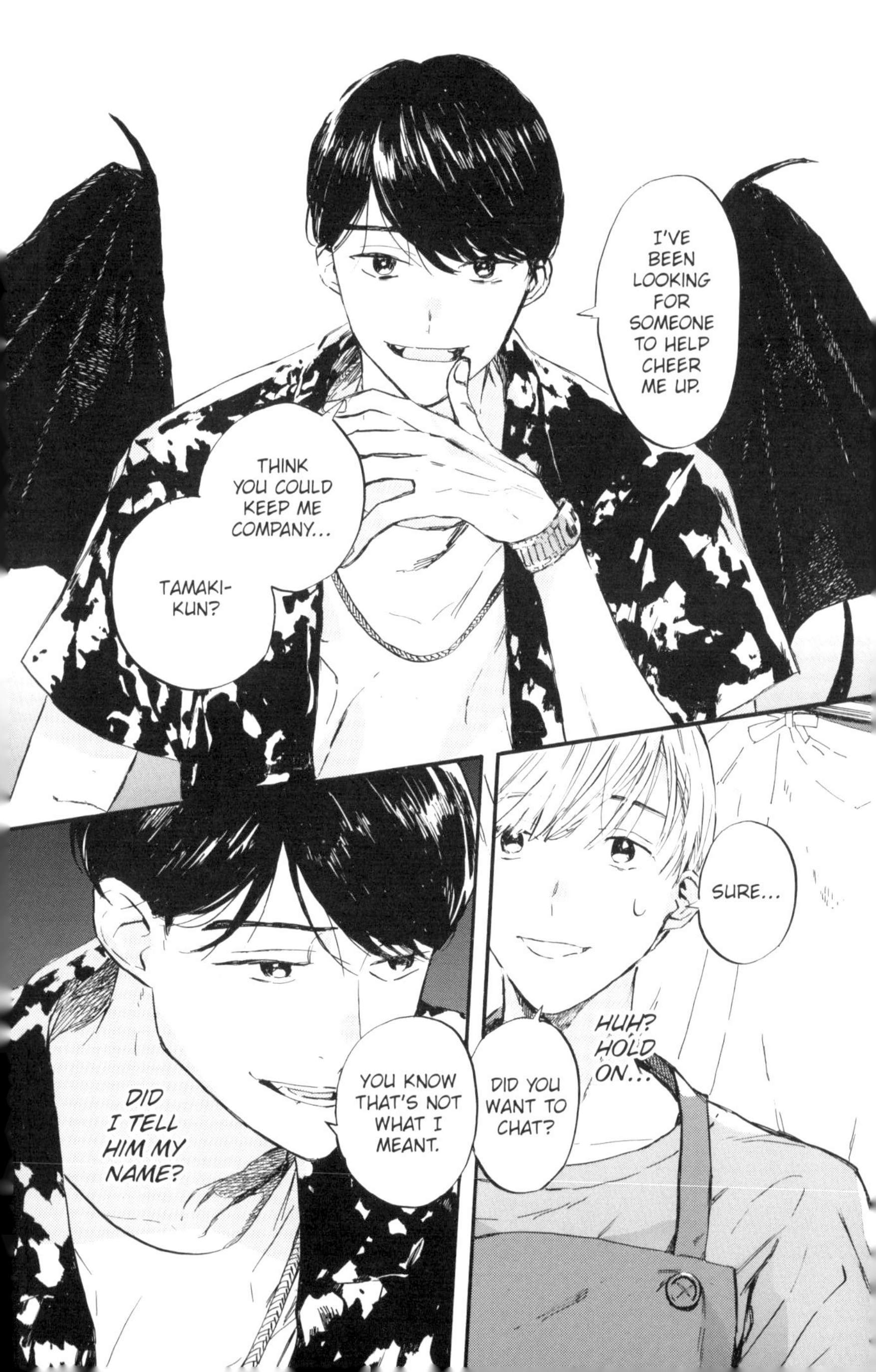
I'VE BEEN LOOKING FOR SOMEONE TO HELP CHEER ME UP.
THINK YOU COULD KEEP ME COMPANY...
TAMAKI-KUN?
SURE...
HUH? HOLD ON...
DID YOU WANT TO CHAT?
YOU KNOW THAT'S NOT WHAT I MEANT.
DID I TELL HIM MY NAME?

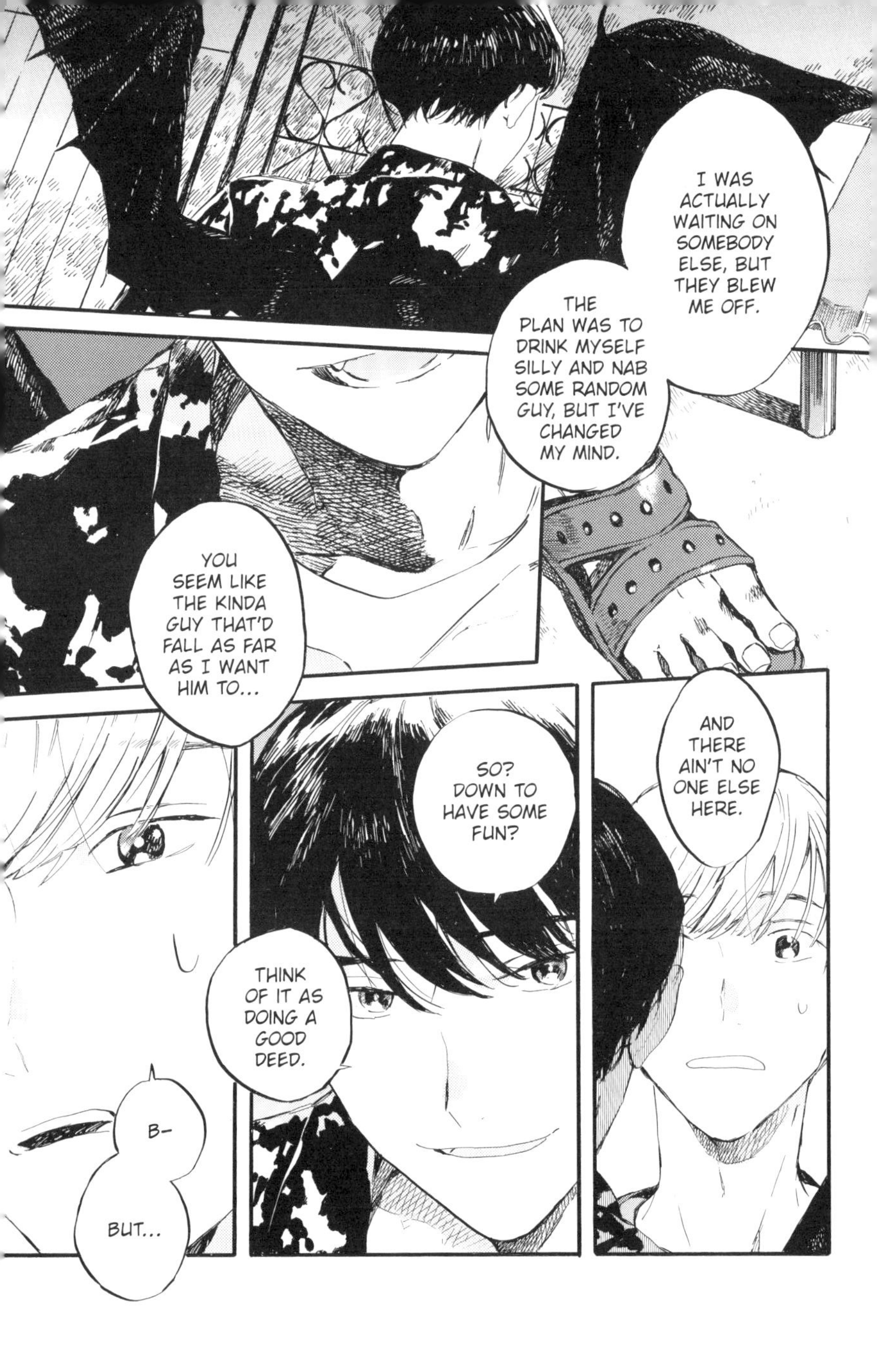
I WAS ACTUALLY WAITING ON SOMEBODY ELSE, BUT THEY BLEW ME OFF.
THE PLAN WAS TO DRINK MYSELF SILLY AND NAB SOME RANDOM GUY, BUT I'VE CHANGED MY MIND.
YOU SEEM LIKE THE KINDA GUY THAT'D FALL AS FAR AS I WANT HIM TO...
AND THERE AIN'T NO ONE ELSE HERE.
SO? DOWN TO HAVE SOME FUN?
THINK OF IT AS DOING A GOOD DEED.
B-
BUT...

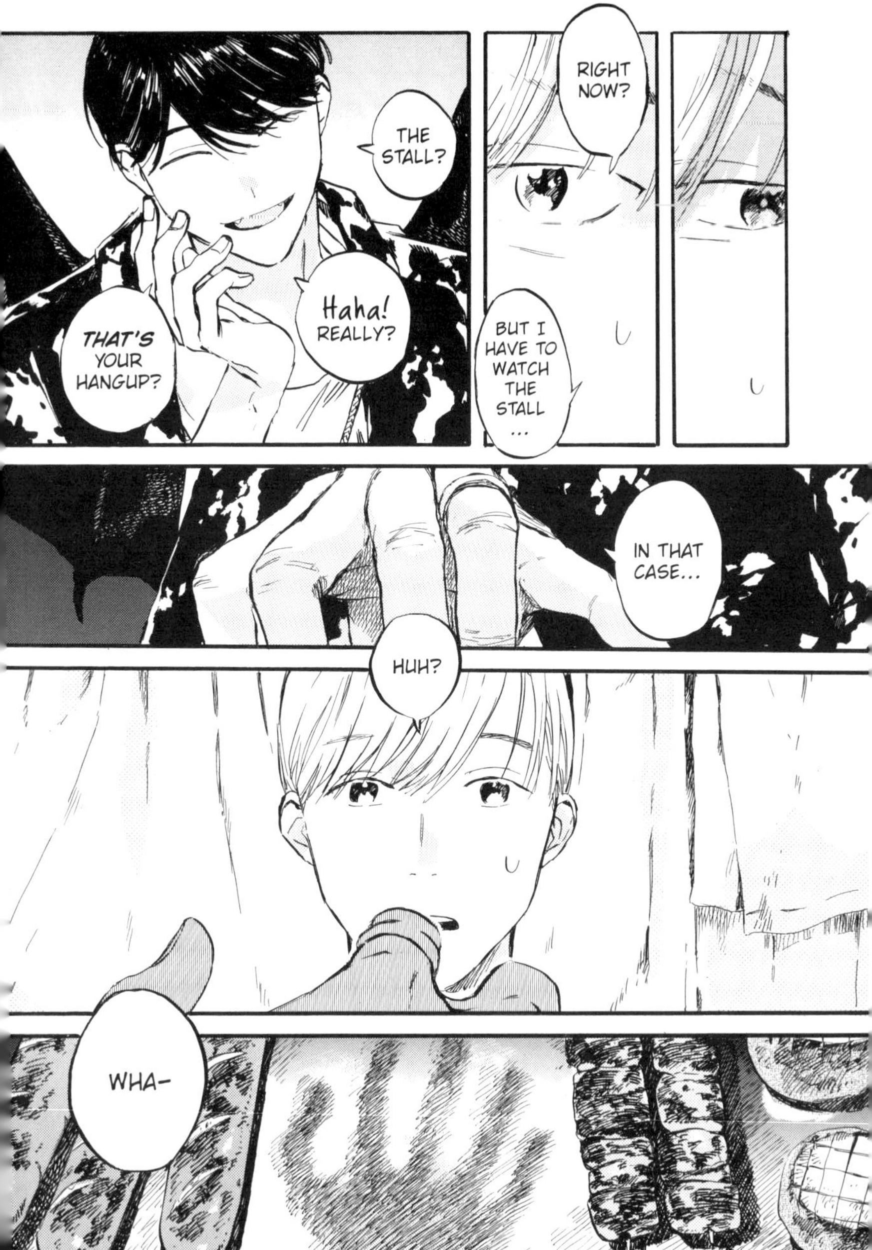
RIGHT NOW?
BUT I HAVE TO WATCH THE STALL...
THE STALL?
Haha! REALLY?
THAT'S YOUR HANGUP?
IN THAT CASE...
HUH?
WHA-

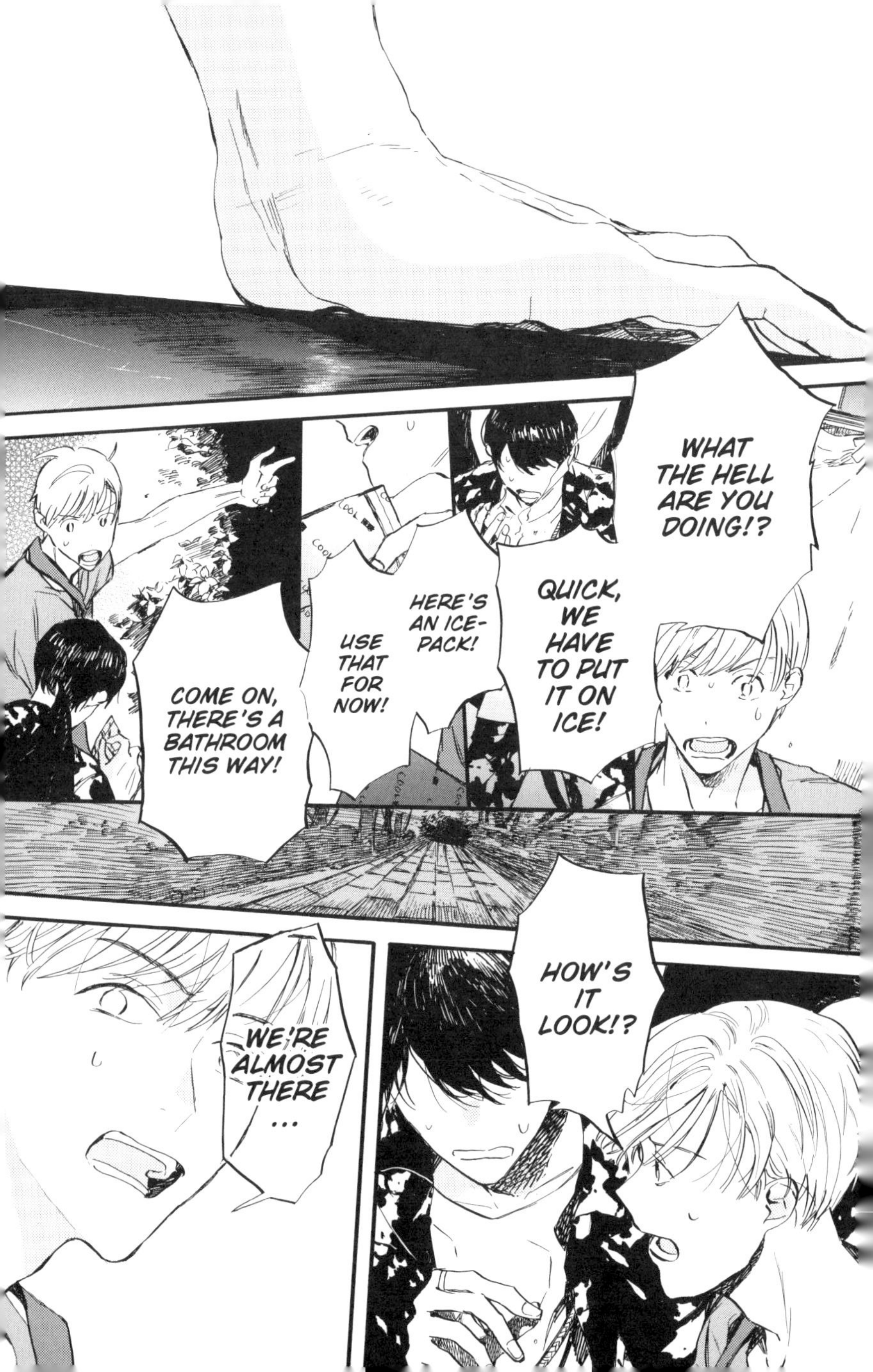
WHAT THE HELL ARE YOU DOING!?
QUICK, WE HAVE TO PUT IT ON ICE!
HERE'S AN ICE-PACK!
USE THAT FOR NOW!
COME ON, THERE'S A BATHROOM THIS WAY!
HOW'S IT LOOK!?
WE'RE ALMOST THERE ...

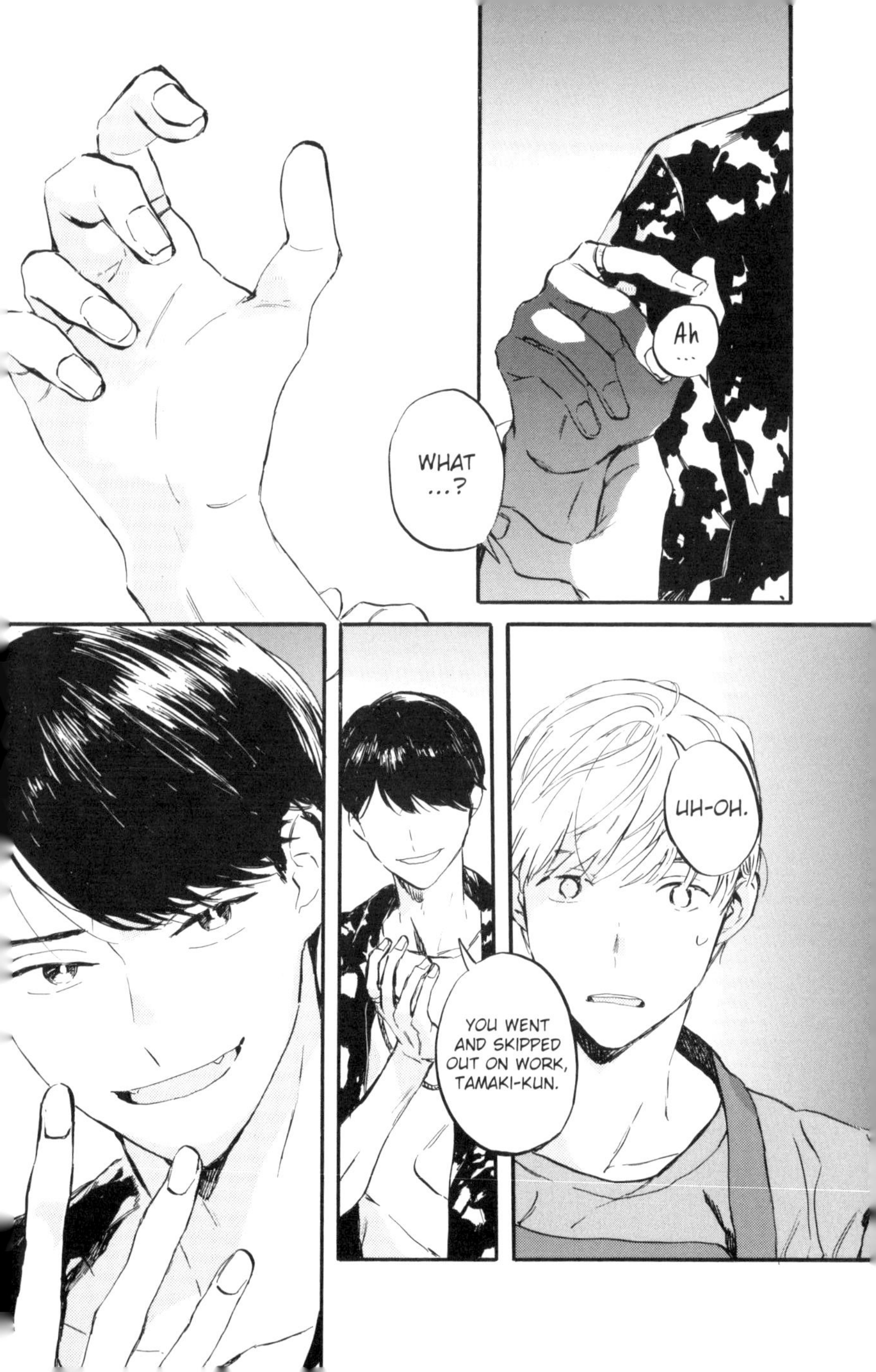
Ah ...
WHAT ...?
UH-OH.
YOU WENT AND SKIPPED OUT ON WORK, TAMAKI-KUN.

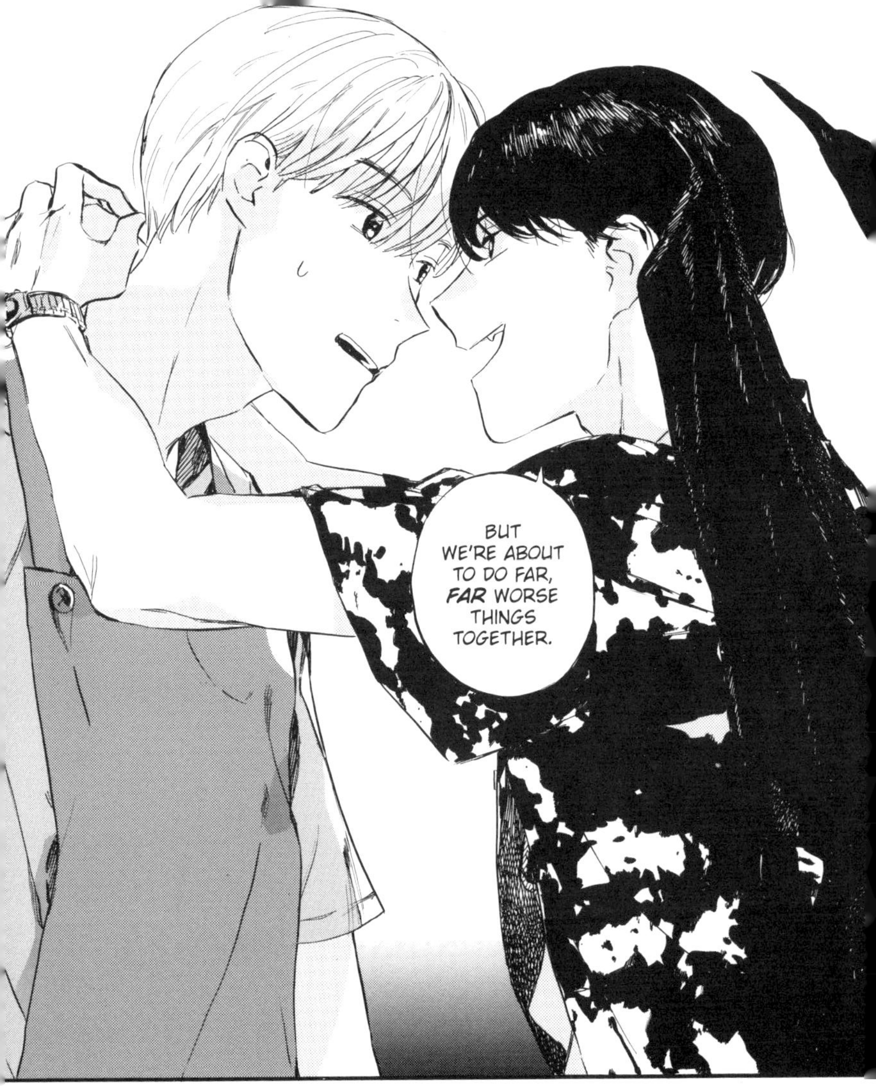
BUT WE'RE ABOUT TO DO FAR, **FAR** WORSE THINGS TOGETHER.

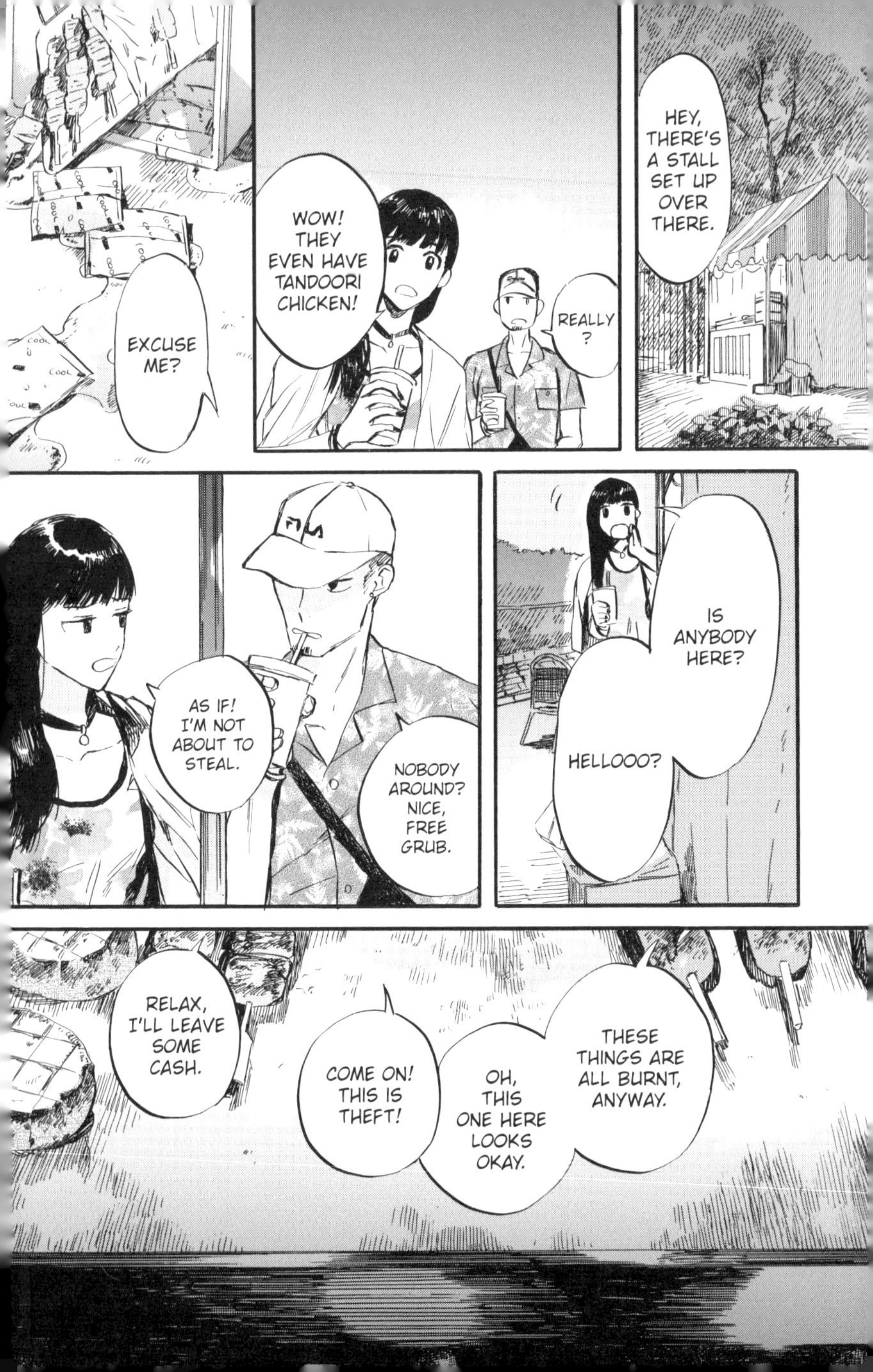
HEY, THERE'S A STALL SET UP OVER THERE.
REALLY?
WOW! THEY EVEN HAVE TANDOORI CHICKEN!
EXCUSE ME?
IS ANYBODY HERE?
HELLOOO?
NOBODY AROUND? NICE, FREE GRUB.
AS IF! I'M NOT ABOUT TO STEAL.
THESE THINGS ARE ALL BURNT, ANYWAY.
OH, THIS ONE HERE LOOKS OKAY.
COME ON! THIS IS THEFT!
RELAX, I'LL LEAVE SOME CASH.

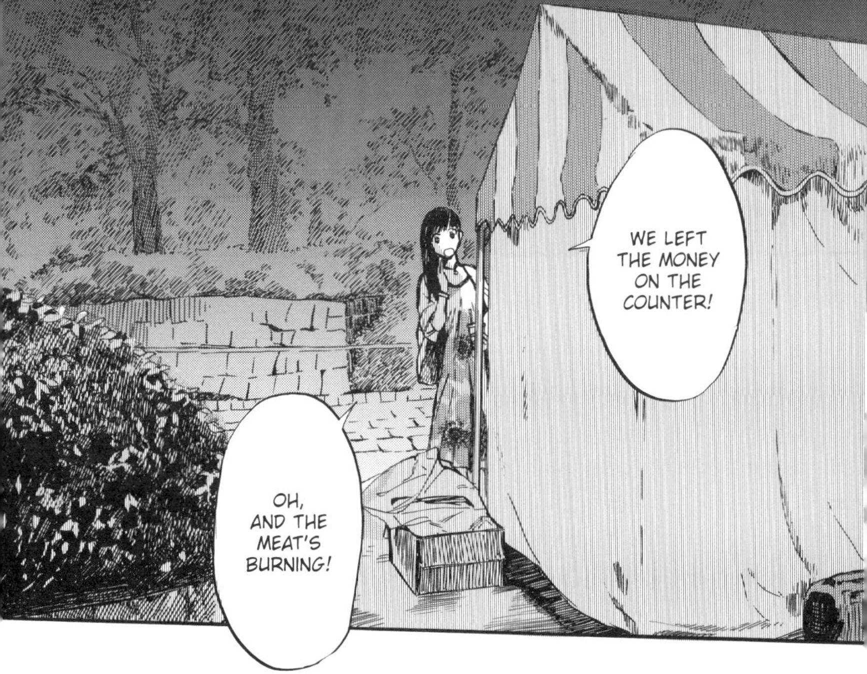
WE LEFT THE MONEY ON THE COUNTER!
OH, AND THE MEAT'S BURNING!
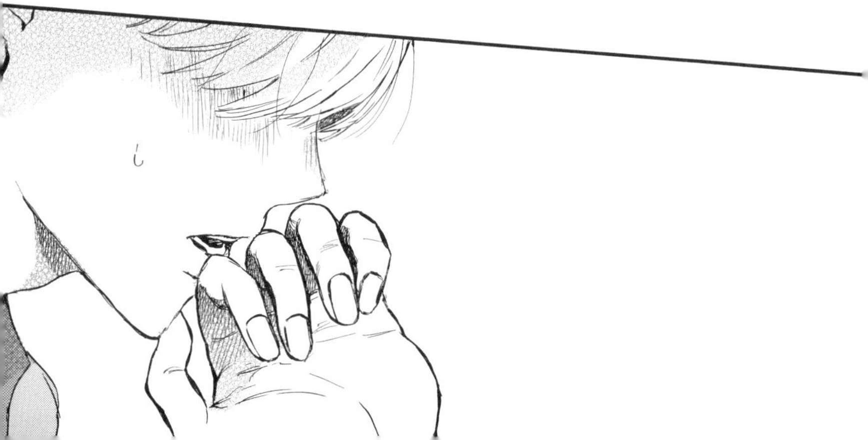

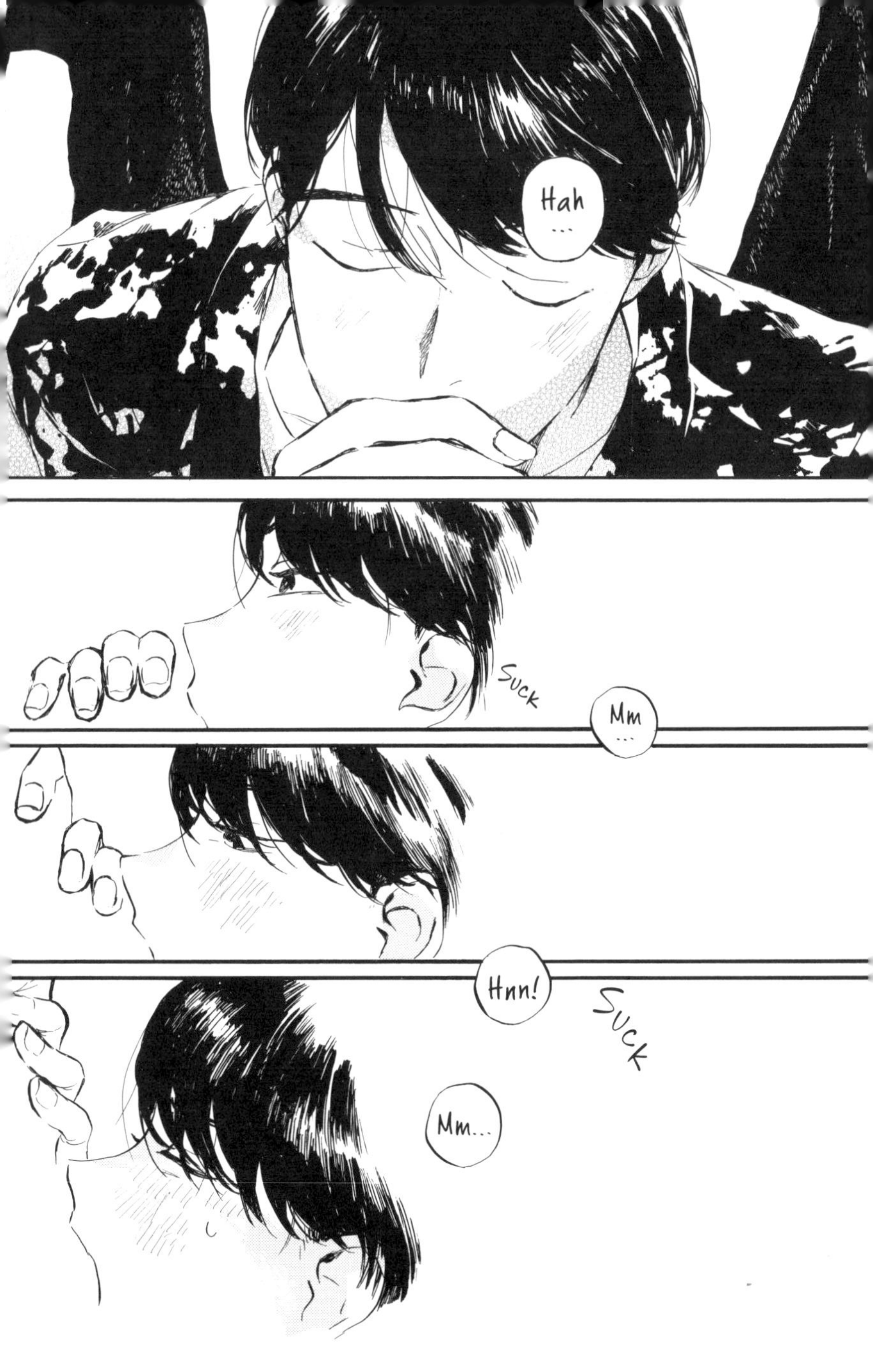
Hah ...
Mm ...
Suck
Hnn!
Suck
Mm...

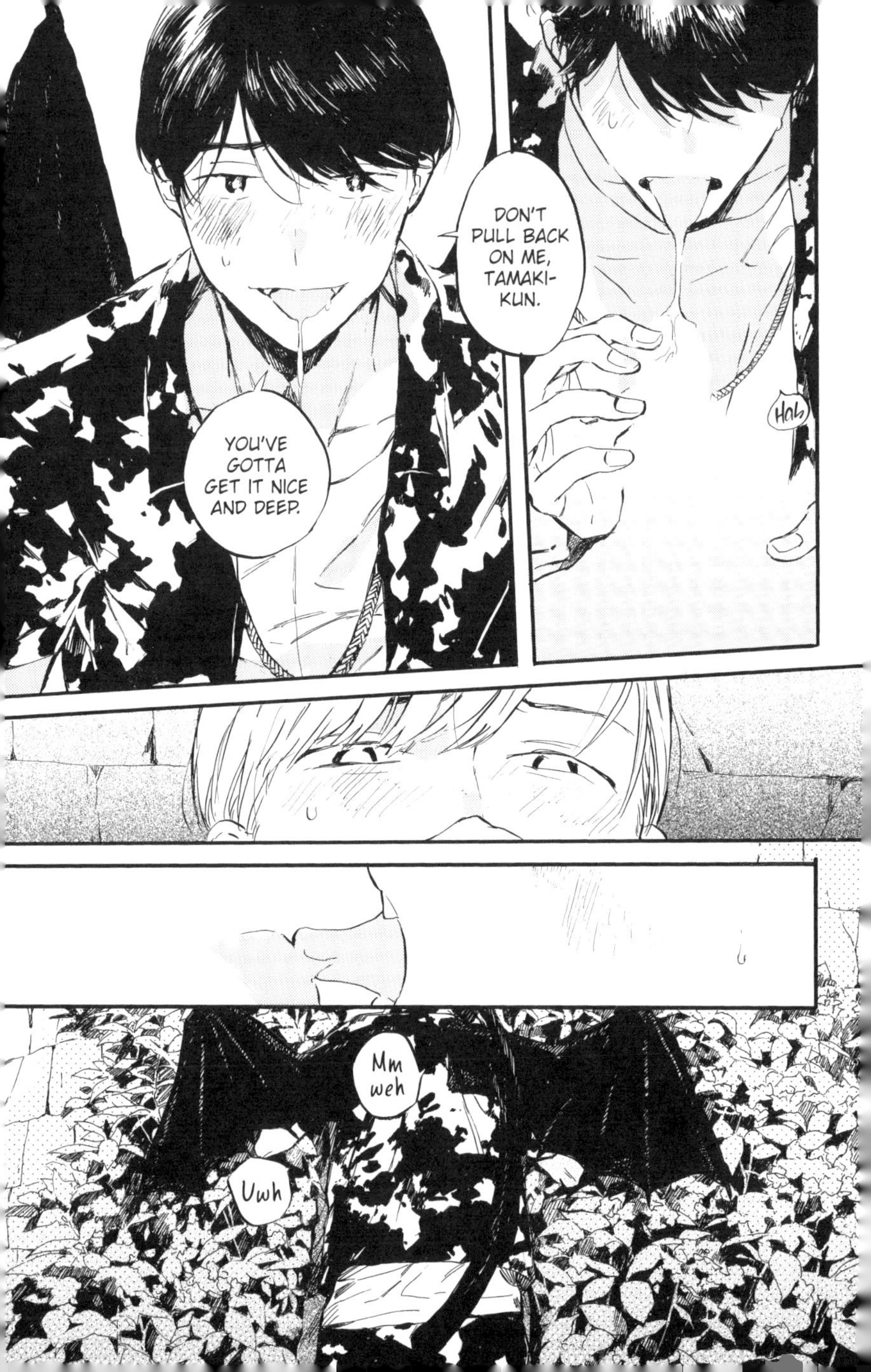
Hah
DON'T PULL BACK ON ME, TAMAKI-KUN.
YOU'VE GOTTA GET IT NICE AND DEEP.
Mm weh
Uwh

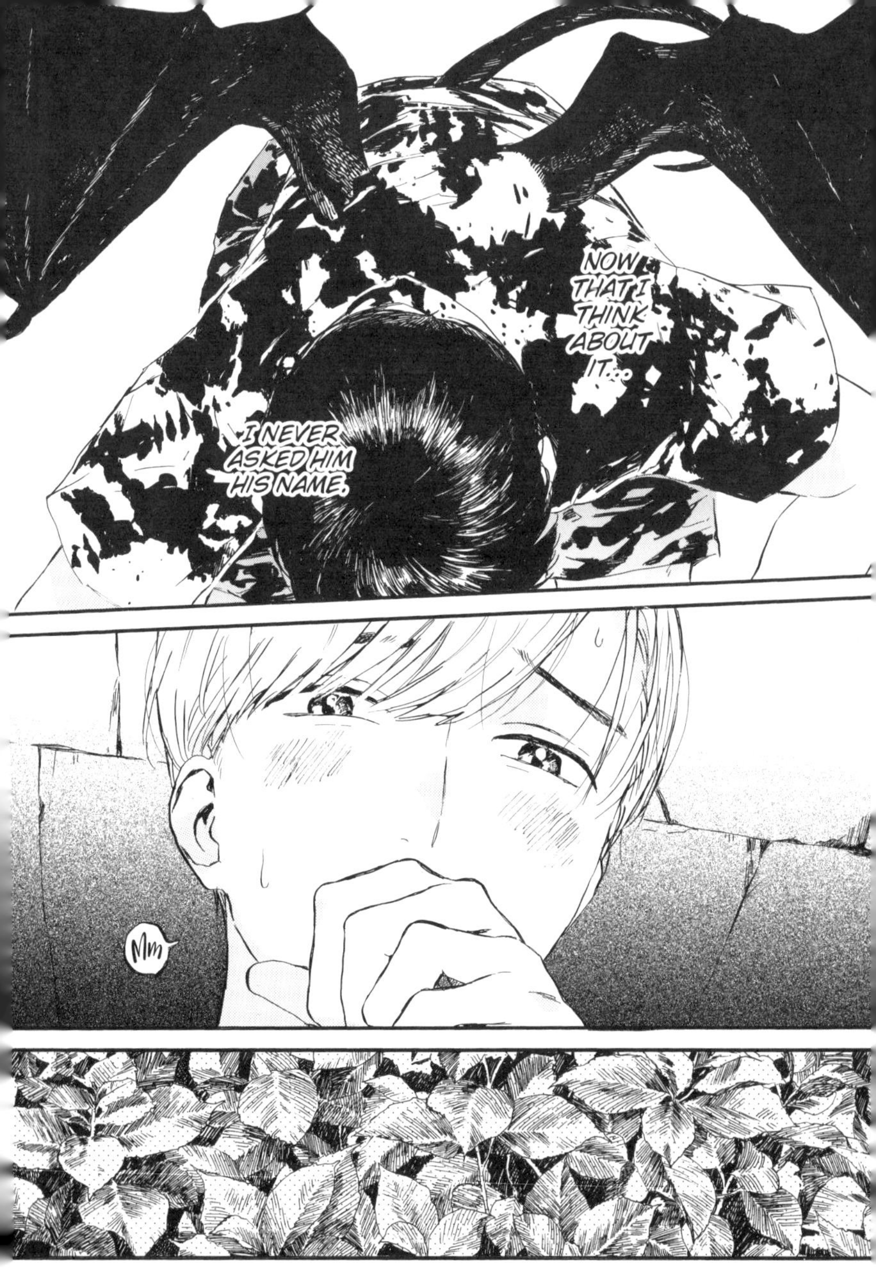
NOW THAT I THINK ABOUT IT...
I NEVER ASKED HIM HIS NAME.
Mm

Chapter 1 End

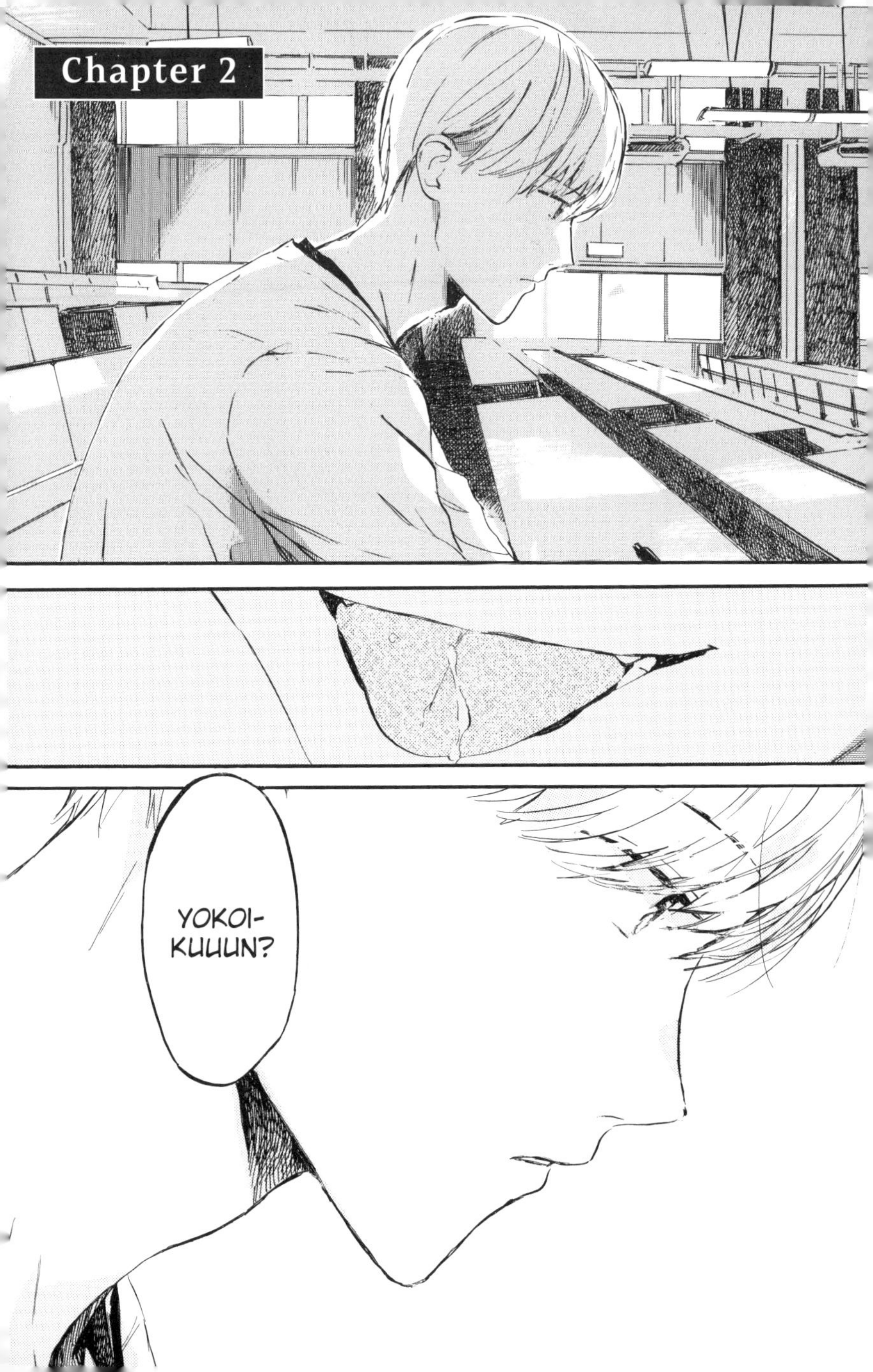
Chapter 2
YOKOI-KUUUN?

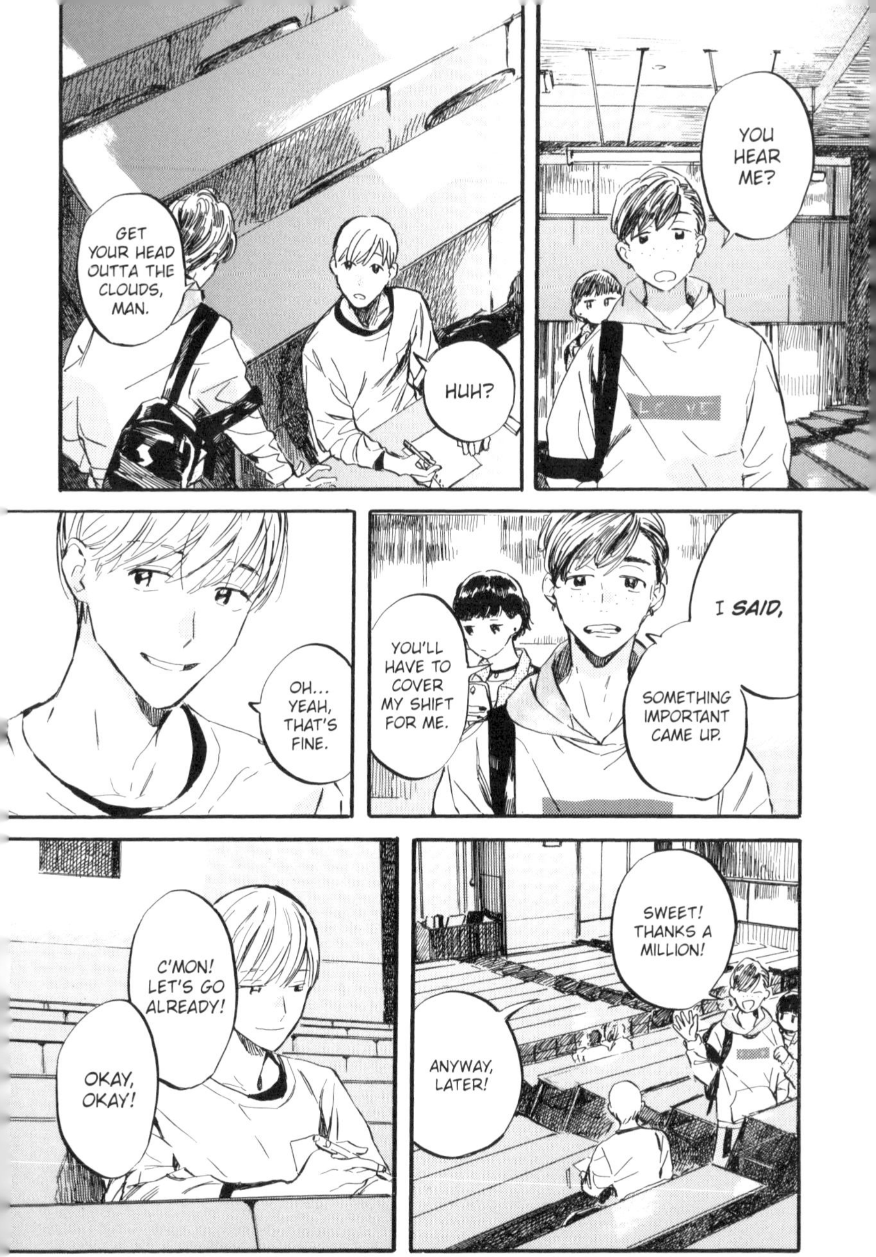
YOU HEAR ME?
GET YOUR HEAD OUTTA THE CLOUDS, MAN.
HUH?
I SAID,
SOMETHING IMPORTANT CAME UP.
YOU'LL HAVE TO COVER MY SHIFT FOR ME.
OH... YEAH, THAT'S FINE.
SWEET! THANKS A MILLION!
ANYWAY, LATER!
C'MON! LET'S GO ALREADY!
OKAY, OKAY!

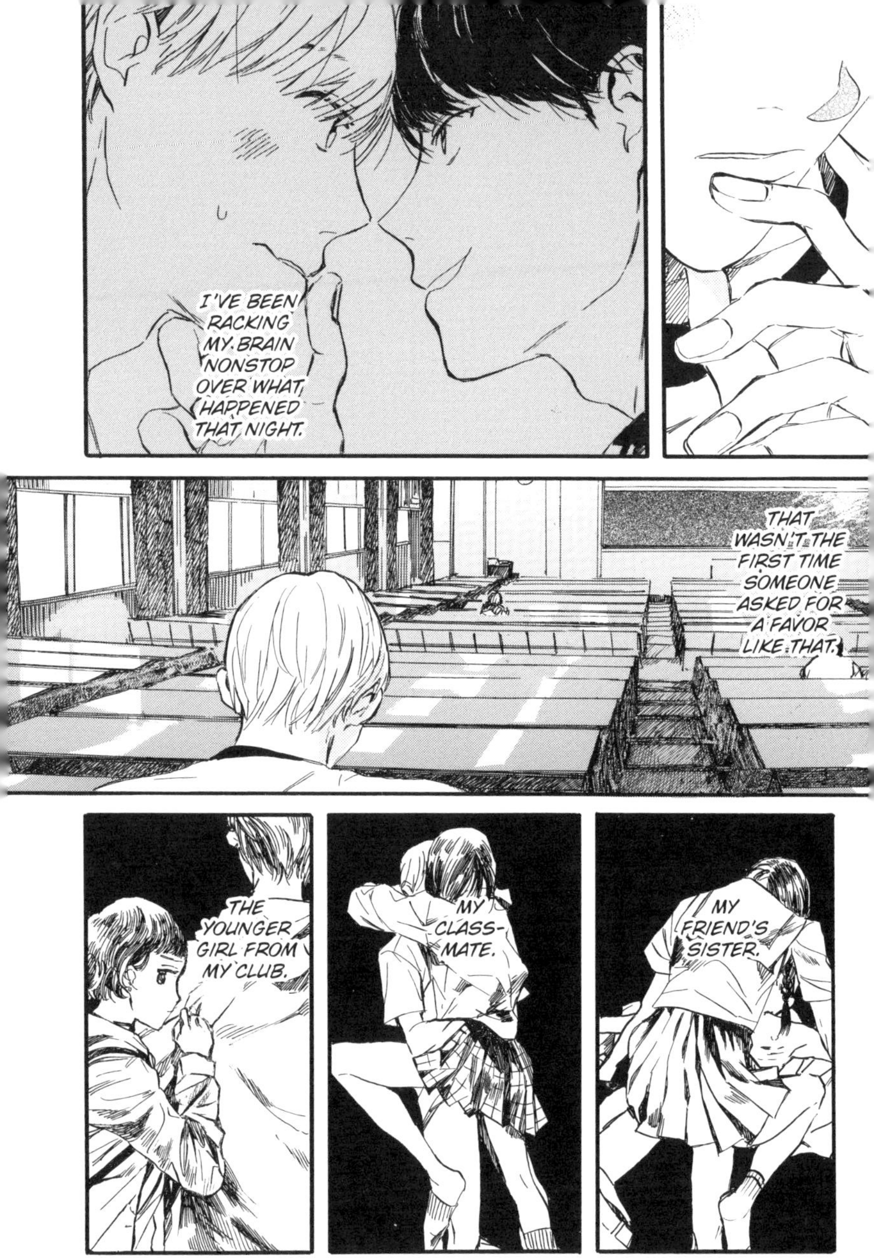
I'VE BEEN RACKING MY BRAIN NONSTOP OVER WHAT HAPPENED THAT NIGHT.
THAT WASN'T THE FIRST TIME SOMEONE ASKED FOR A FAVOR LIKE THAT.
MY FRIEND'S SISTER.
MY CLASS-MATE.
THE YOUNGER GIRL FROM MY CLUB.

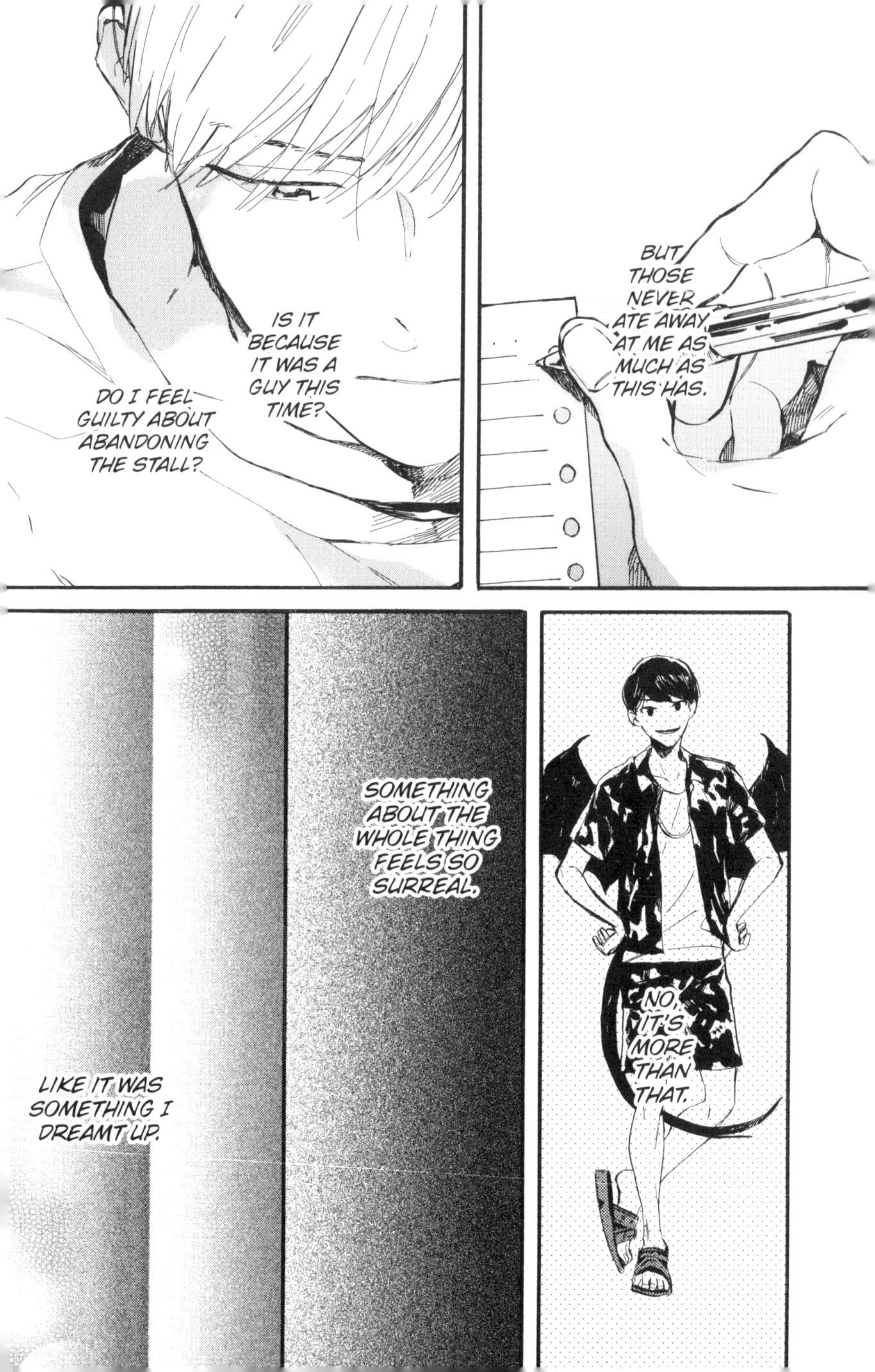
BUT THOSE NEVER ATE AWAY AT ME AS MUCH AS THIS HAS.
IS IT BECAUSE IT WAS A GUY THIS TIME?
DO I FEEL GUILTY ABOUT ABANDONING THE STALL?
NO, IT'S MORE THAN THAT.
SOMETHING ABOUT THE WHOLE THING FEELS SO SURREAL.
LIKE IT WAS SOMETHING I DREAMT UP.

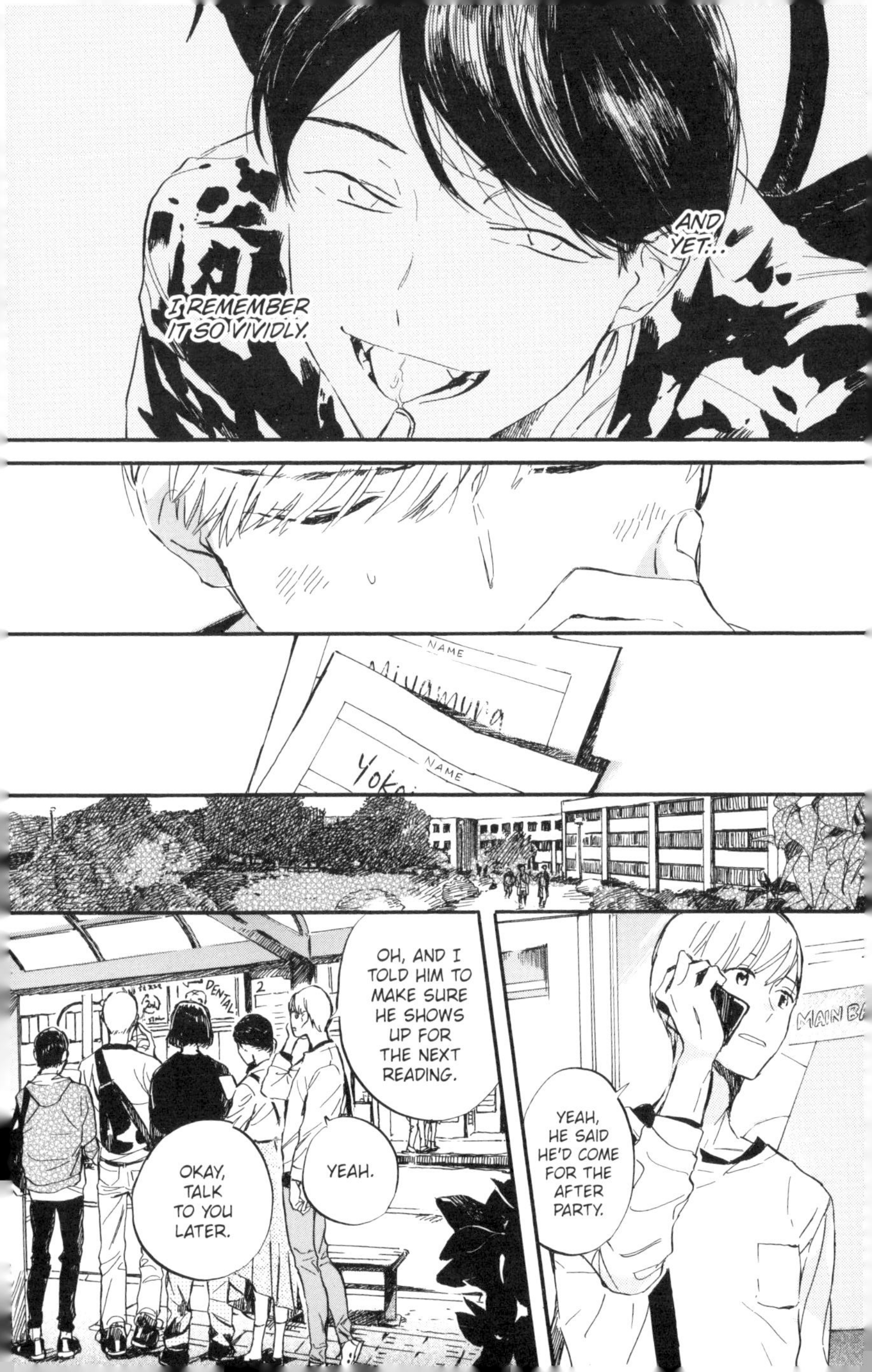
AND YET...
I REMEMBER IT SO VIVIDLY.
NAME
Miyamura
NAME
Yoko
YEAH, HE SAID HE'D COME FOR THE AFTER PARTY.
OH, AND I TOLD HIM TO MAKE SURE HE SHOWS UP FOR THE NEXT READING.
YEAH.
OKAY, TALK TO YOU LATER.
MAIN B
DENTAL

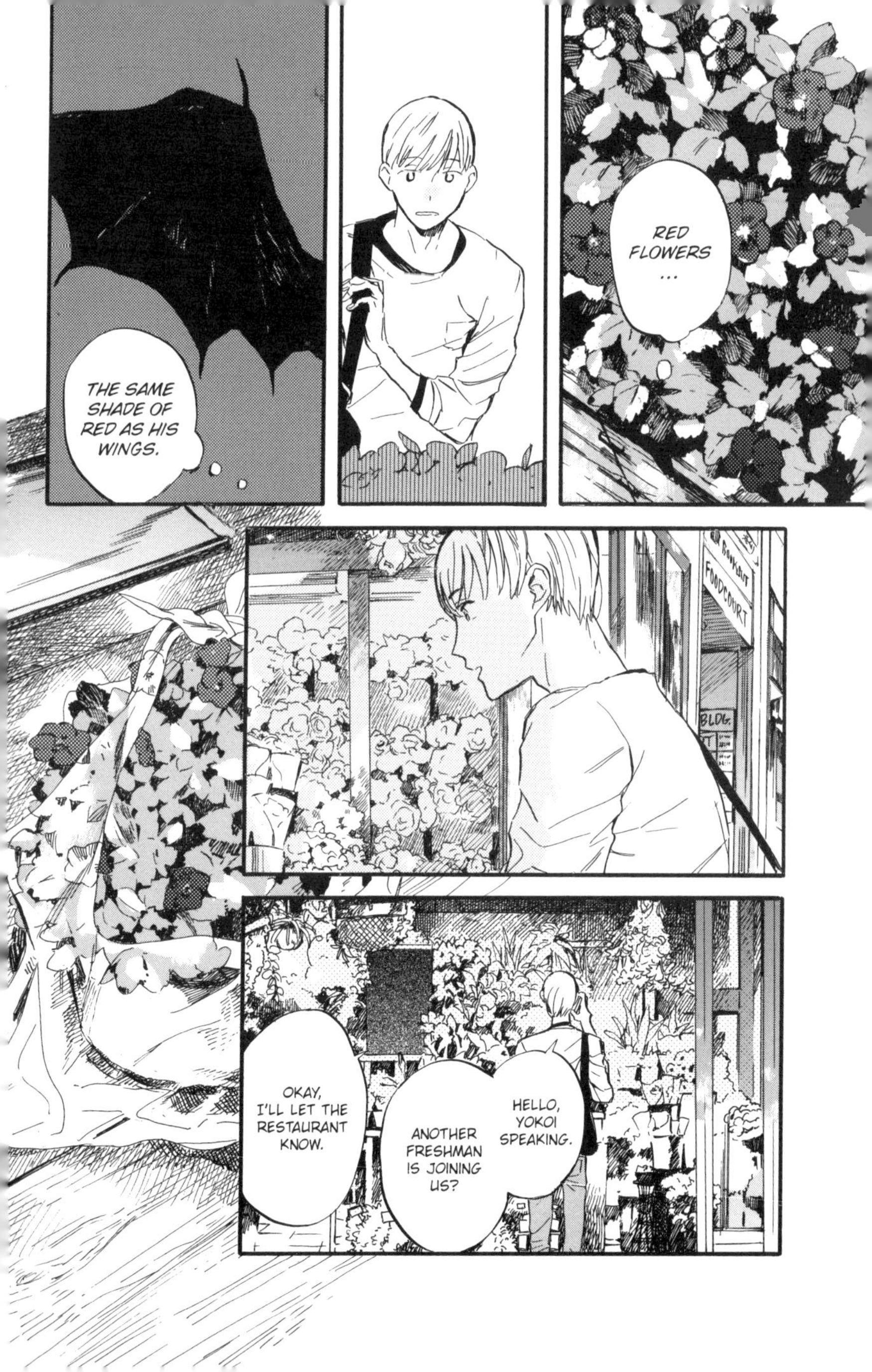
RED FLOWERS ...
THE SAME SHADE OF RED AS HIS WINGS.
FOODCOURT
BLDG.
HELLO, YOKOI SPEAKING.
ANOTHER FRESHMAN IS JOINING US?
OKAY, I'LL LET THE RESTAURANT KNOW.

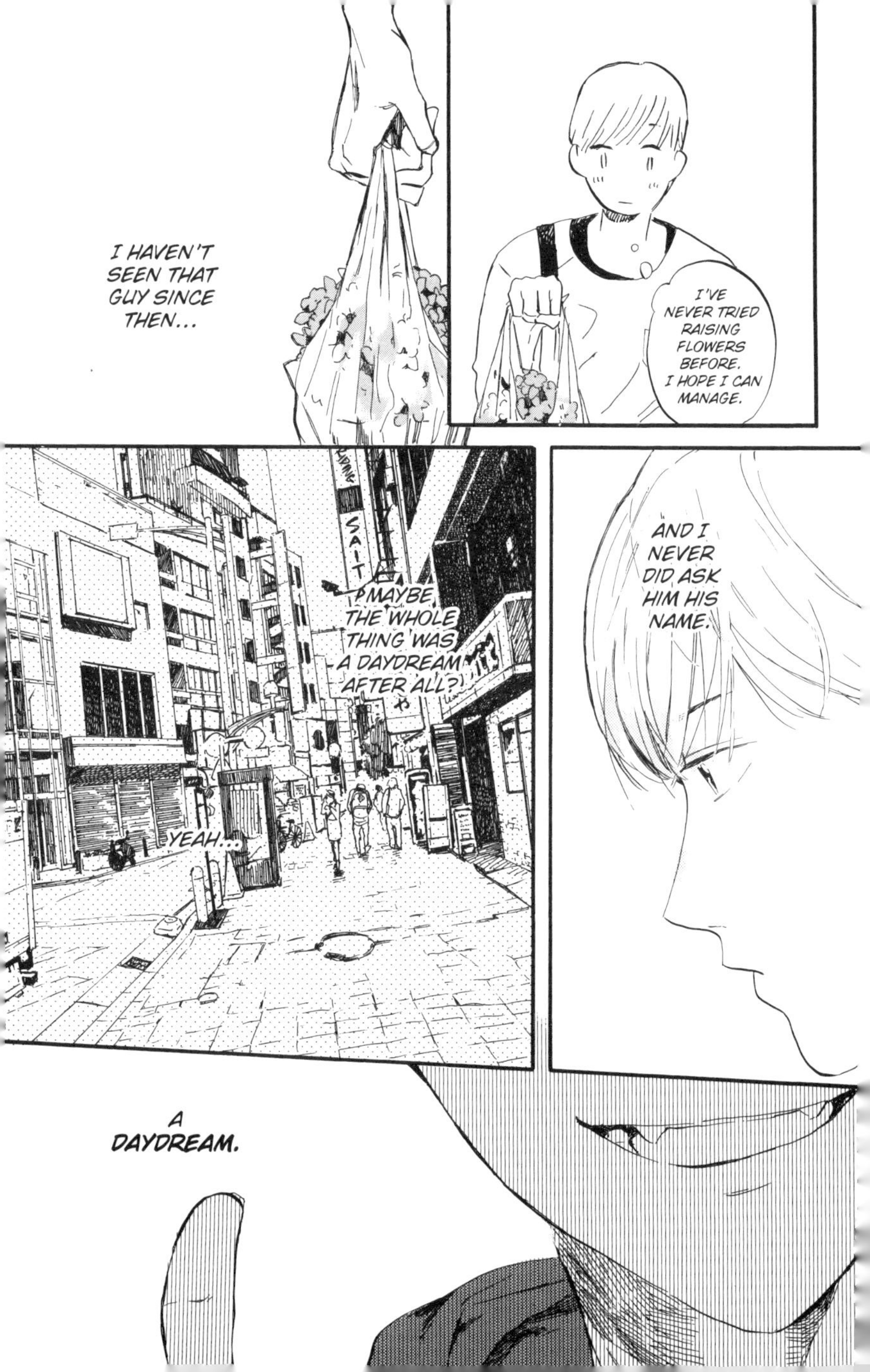
I'VE NEVER TRIED RAISING FLOWERS BEFORE. I HOPE I CAN MANAGE.
I HAVEN'T SEEN THAT GUY SINCE THEN...
AND I NEVER DID ASK HIM HIS NAME.
MAYBE THE WHOLE THING WAS A DAYDREAM AFTER ALL?
YEAH...
SAIT
A DAYDREAM.

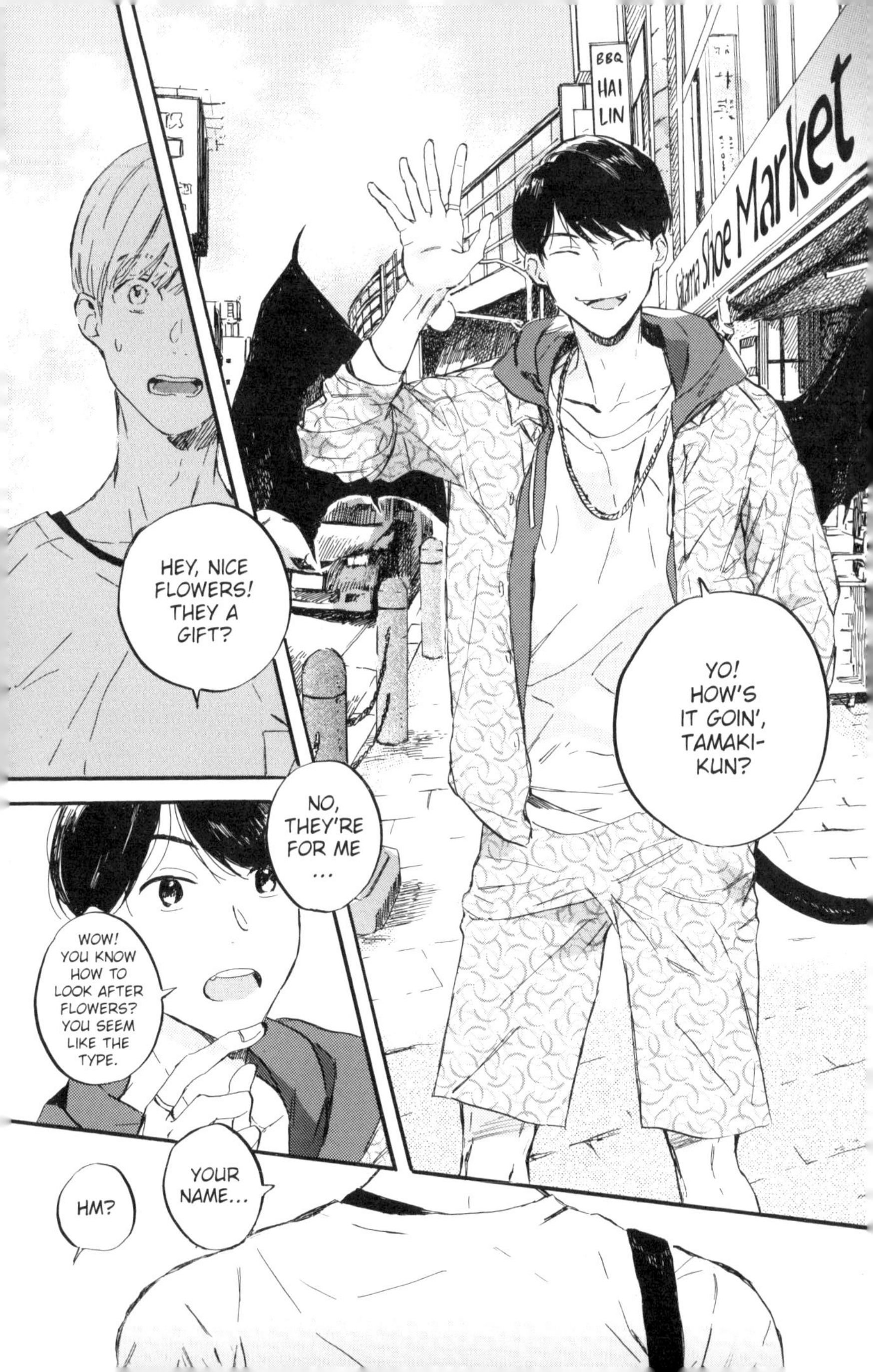
Saitama Shoe Market
BBQ HAI LIN
YO! HOW'S IT GOIN', TAMAKI-KUN?
HEY, NICE FLOWERS! THEY A GIFT?
NO, THEY'RE FOR ME ...
WOW! YOU KNOW HOW TO LOOK AFTER FLOWERS? YOU SEEM LIKE THE TYPE.
YOUR NAME...
HM?

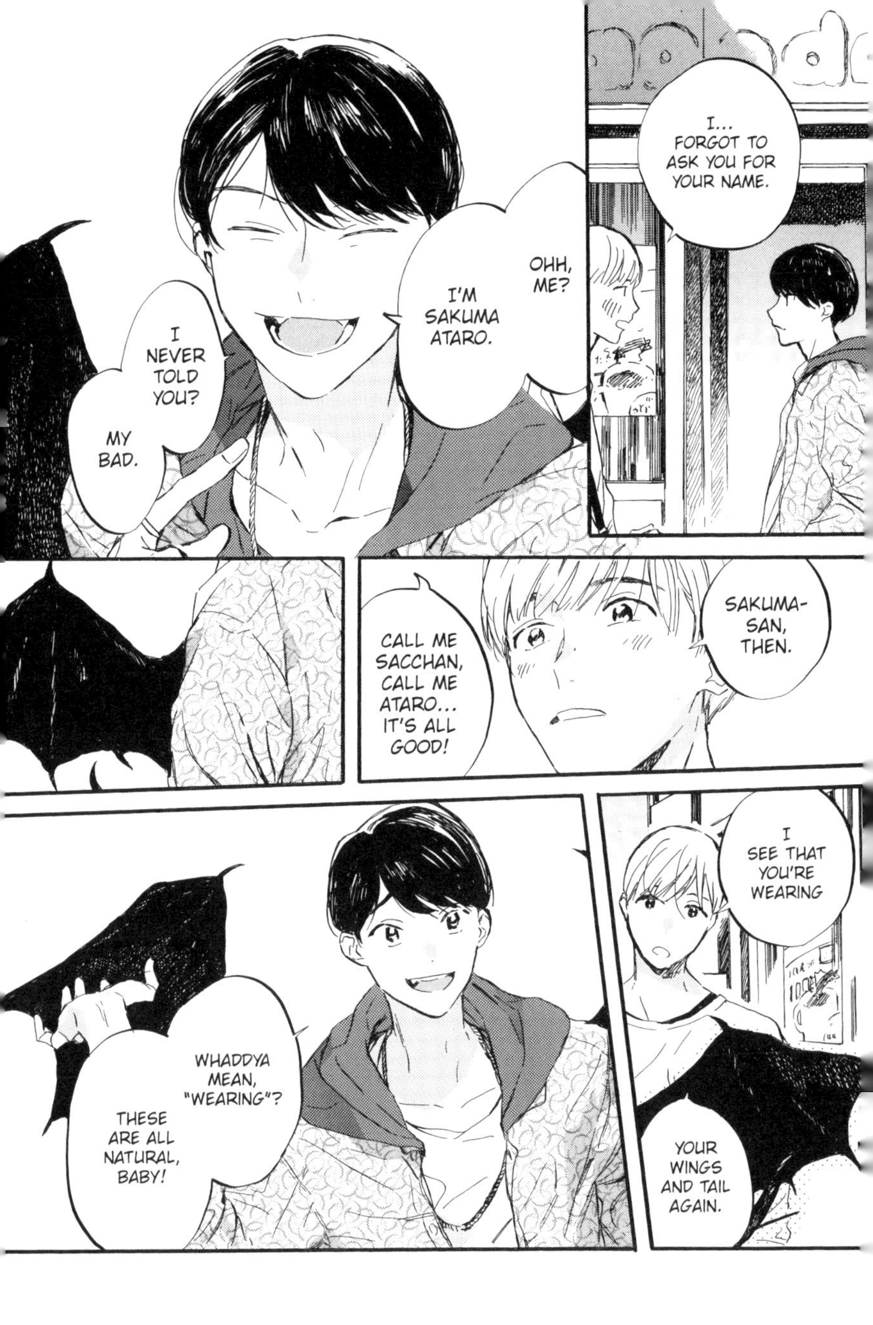
I... FORGOT TO ASK YOU FOR YOUR NAME.
OHH, ME?
I'M SAKUMA ATARO.
I NEVER TOLD YOU?
MY BAD.
SAKUMA-SAN, THEN.
CALL ME SACCHAN, CALL ME ATARO... IT'S ALL GOOD!
I SEE THAT YOU'RE WEARING
YOUR WINGS AND TAIL AGAIN.
WHADDYA MEAN, "WEARING"?
THESE ARE ALL NATURAL, BABY!

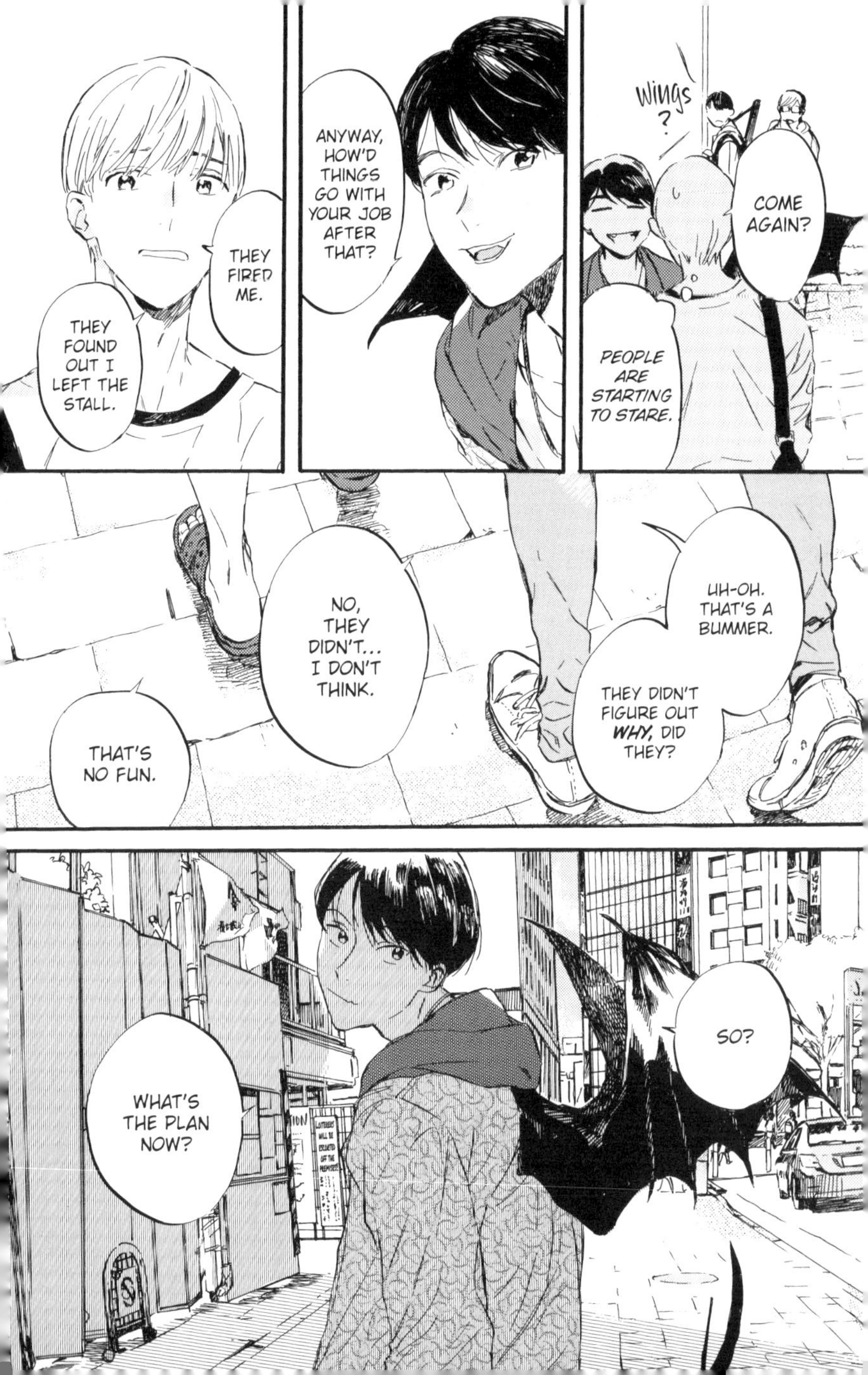
COME AGAIN?
wings?
PEOPLE ARE STARTING TO STARE.
ANYWAY, HOW'D THINGS GO WITH YOUR JOB AFTER THAT?
THEY FIRED ME.
THEY FOUND OUT I LEFT THE STALL.
UH-OH. THAT'S A BUMMER.
THEY DIDN'T FIGURE OUT **WHY**, DID THEY?
NO, THEY DIDN'T... I DON'T THINK.
THAT'S NO FUN.
SO?
LOITERERS WILL BE ESCORTED OFF THE PREMISES
WHAT'S THE PLAN NOW?

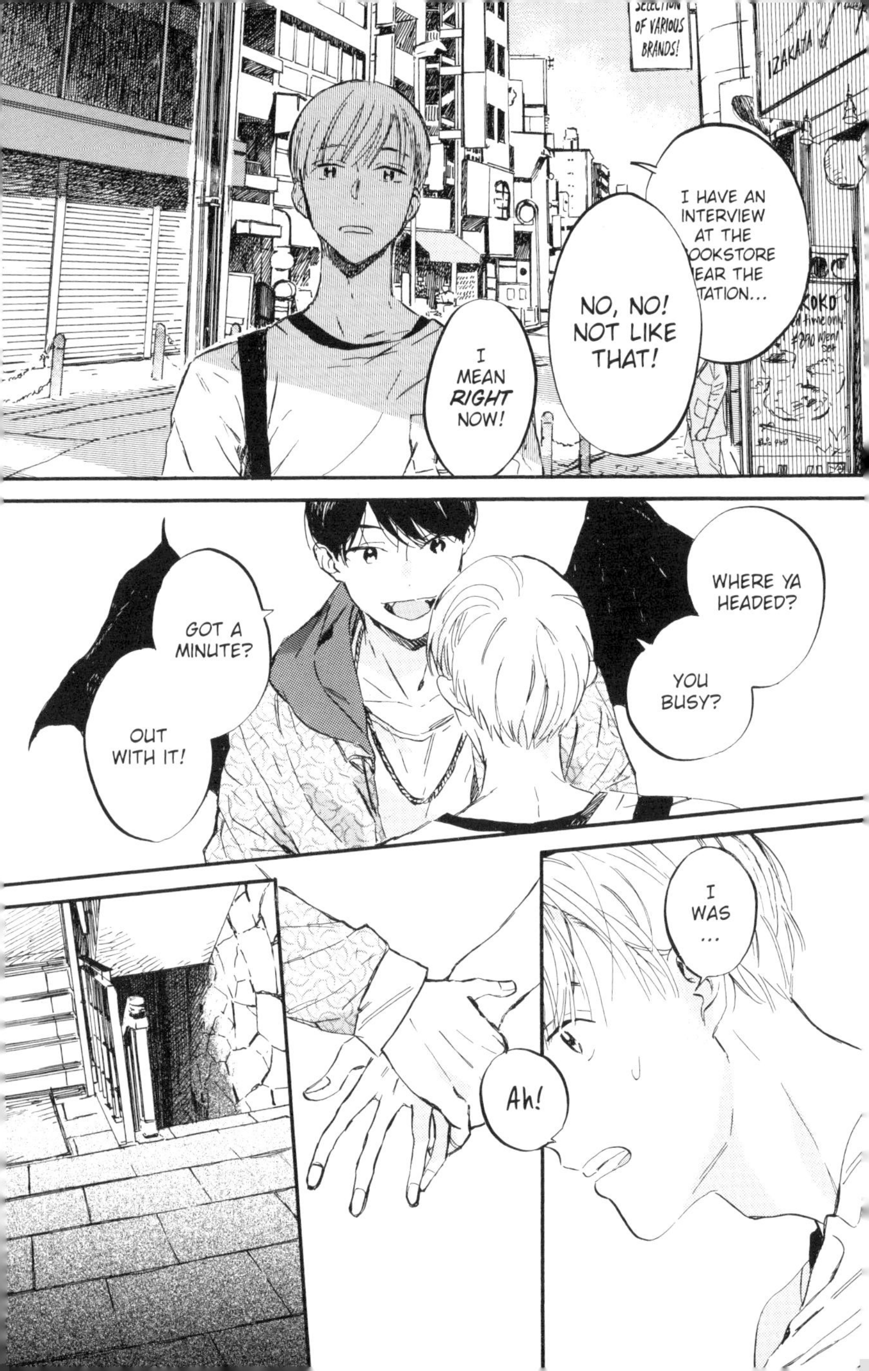
SELECTION OF VARIOUS BRANDS!
IZAKAYA
I HAVE AN INTERVIEW AT THE BOOKSTORE NEAR THE STATION...
NO, NO! NOT LIKE THAT!
I MEAN RIGHT NOW!
WHERE YA HEADED?
YOU BUSY?
GOT A MINUTE?
OUT WITH IT!
I WAS ...
Ah!

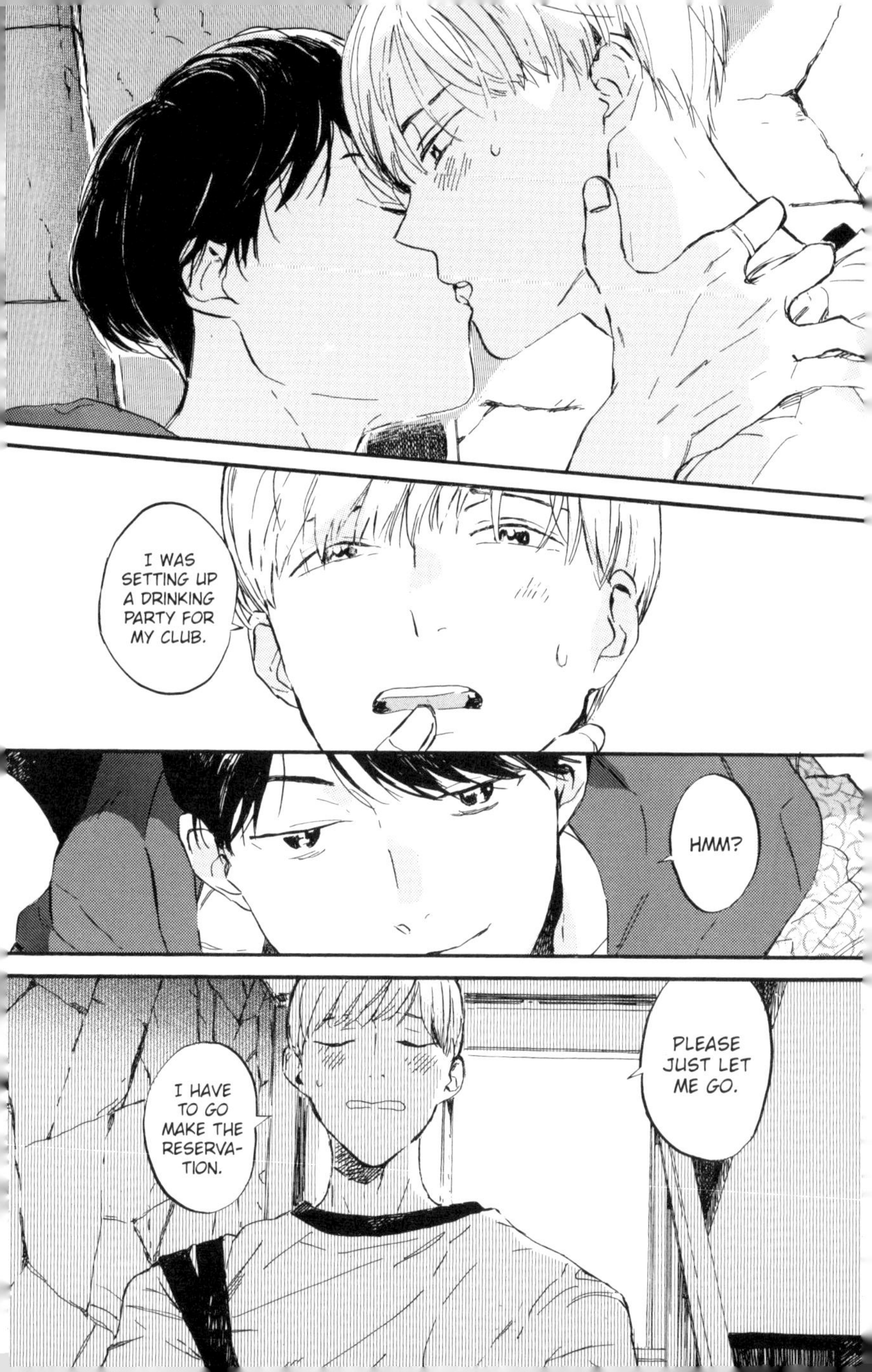
I WAS SETTING UP A DRINKING PARTY FOR MY CLUB.
HMM?
PLEASE JUST LET ME GO.
I HAVE TO GO MAKE THE RESERVA-TION.

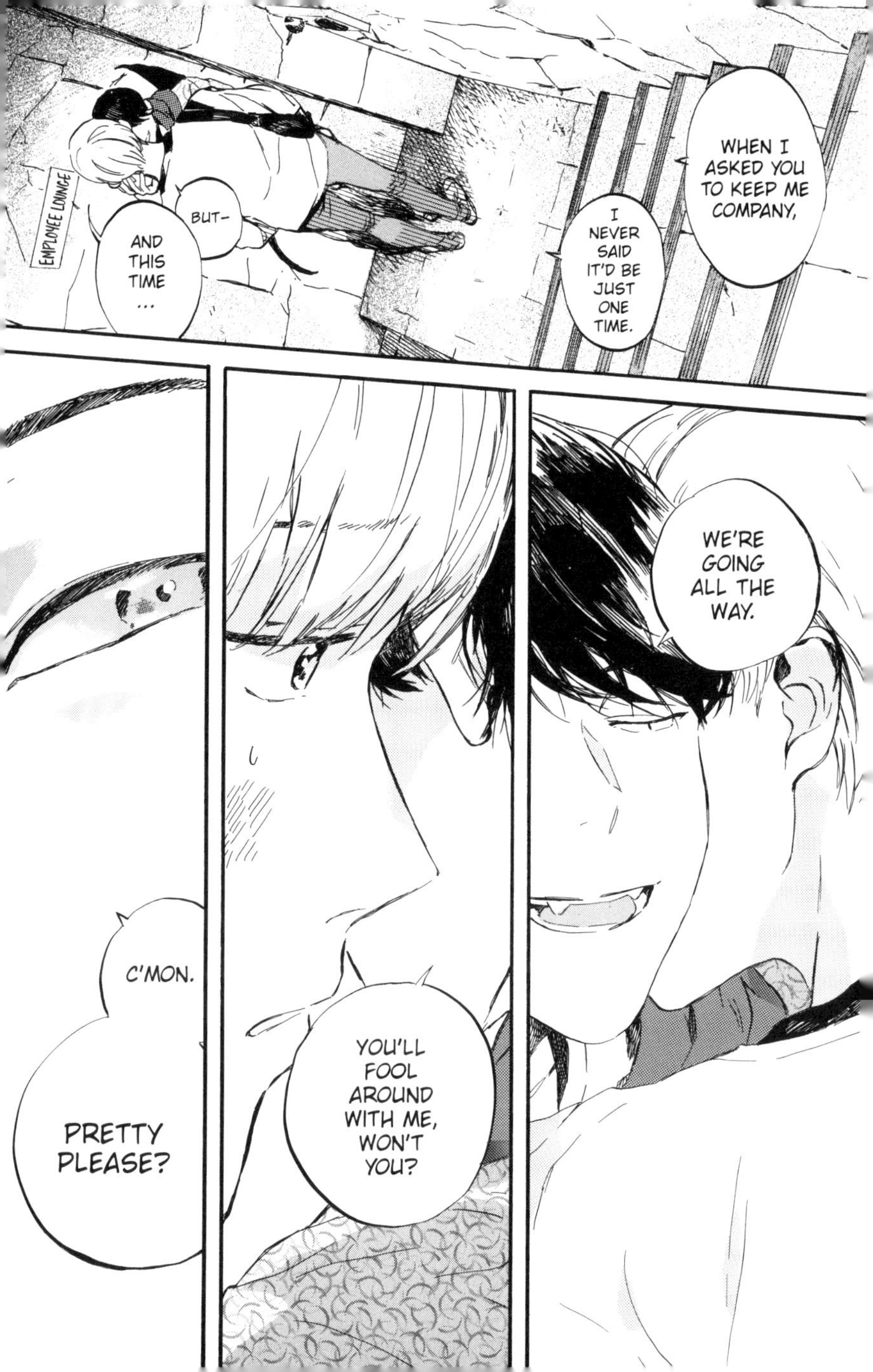
WHEN I ASKED YOU TO KEEP ME COMPANY,
I NEVER SAID IT'D BE JUST ONE TIME.
BUT-
AND THIS TIME ...
EMPLOYEE LOUNGE
WE'RE GOING ALL THE WAY.
YOU'LL FOOL AROUND WITH ME, WON'T YOU?
C'MON.
PRETTY PLEASE?

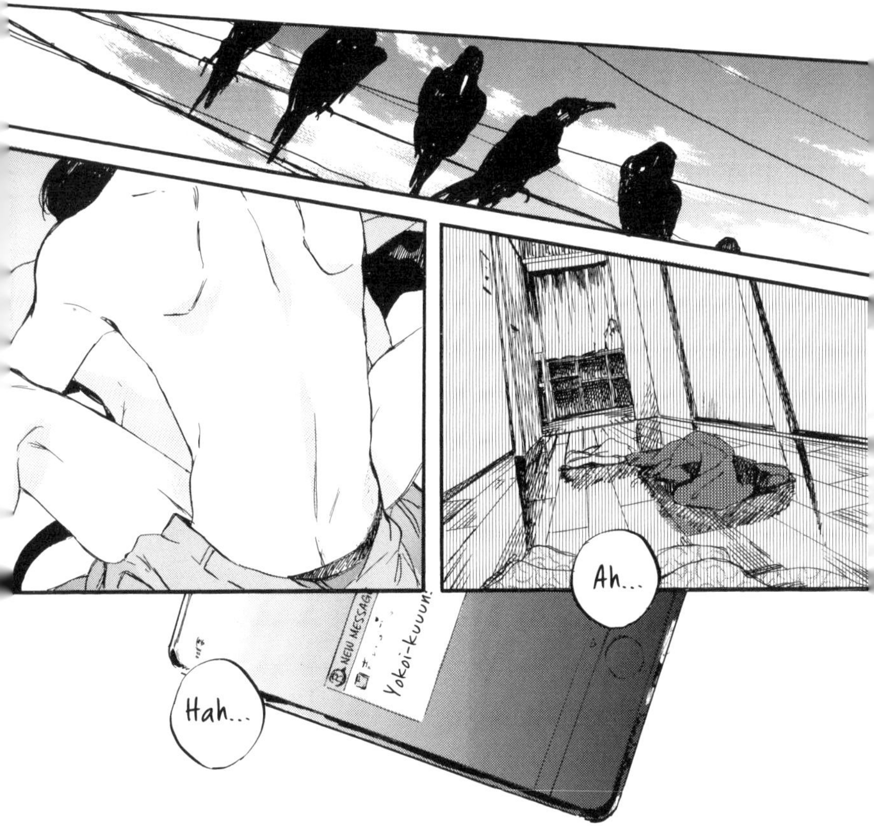
Ah...
NEW MESSAG
Yokoi-kuuun!
Hah...

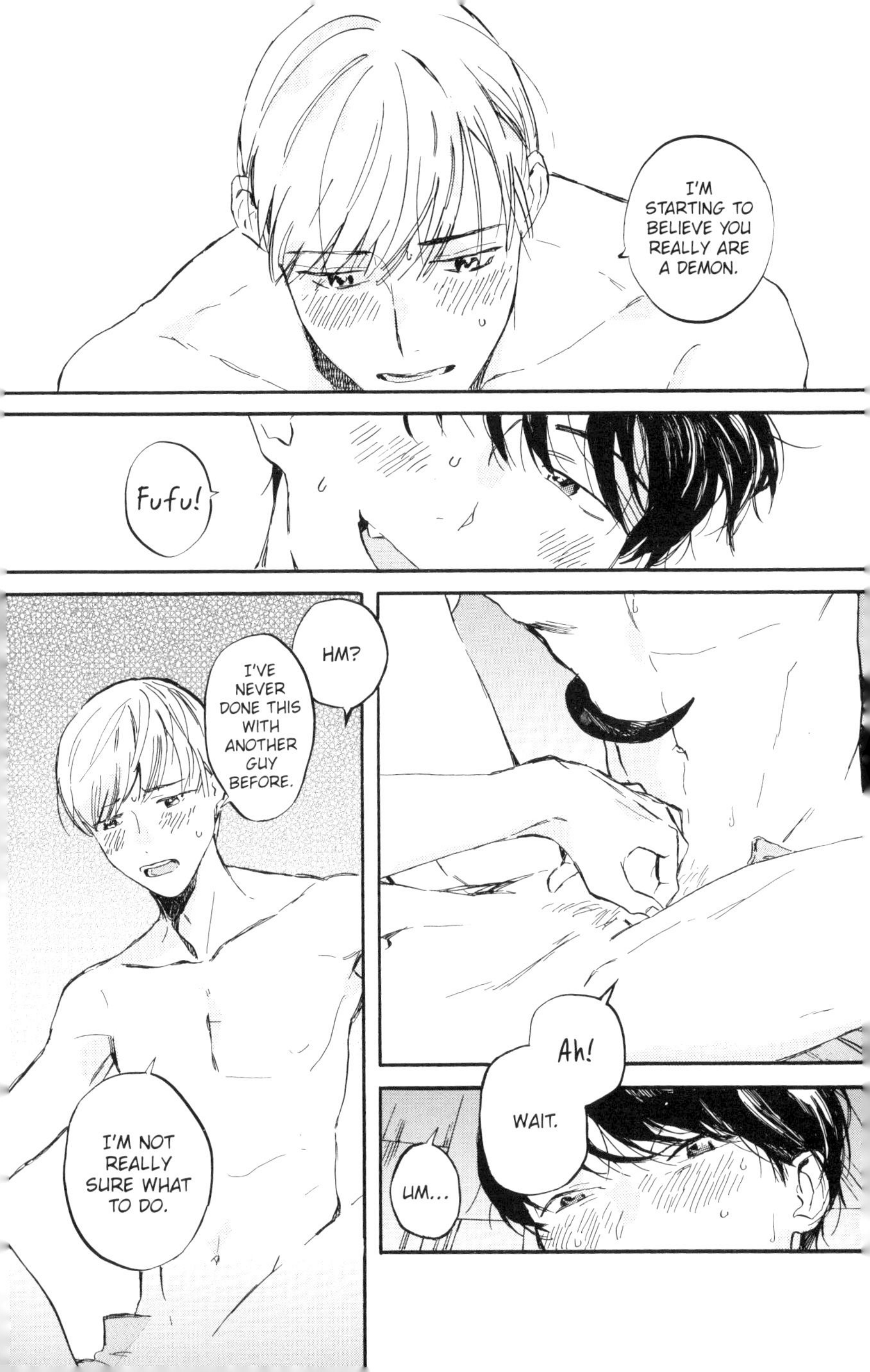
I'M STARTING TO BELIEVE YOU REALLY ARE A DEMON.
Fufu!
Ah!
WAIT.
UM...
HM?
I'VE NEVER DONE THIS WITH ANOTHER GUY BEFORE.
I'M NOT REALLY SURE WHAT TO DO.

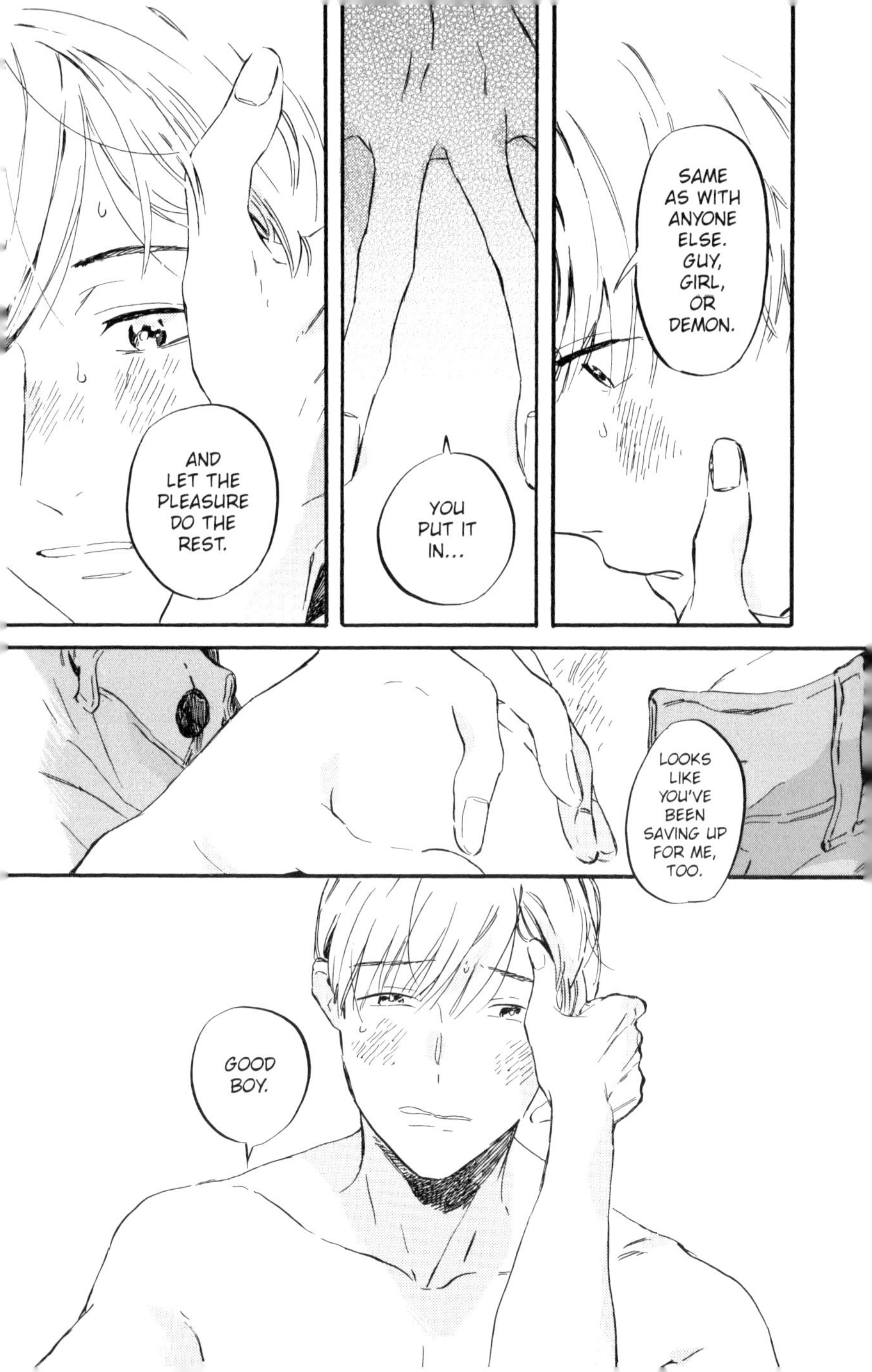
SAME AS WITH ANYONE ELSE. GUY, GIRL, OR DEMON.
YOU PUT IT IN...
AND LET THE PLEASURE DO THE REST.
LOOKS LIKE YOU'VE BEEN SAVING UP FOR ME, TOO.
GOOD BOY.

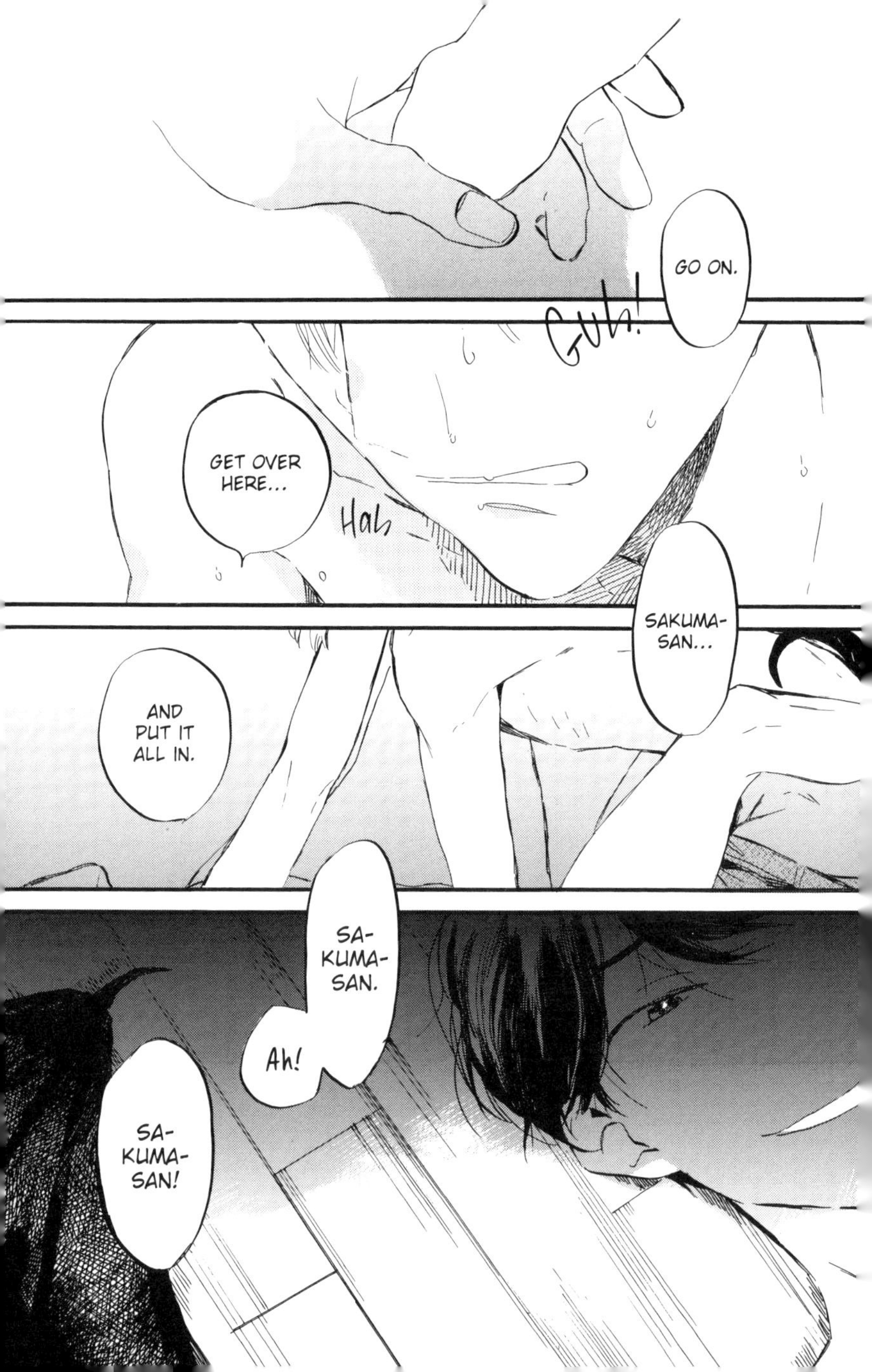
GO ON.
Guh!
GET OVER HERE...
Hah
SAKUMA-SAN...
AND PUT IT ALL IN.
SA-KUMA-SAN.
Ah!
SA-KUMA-SAN!

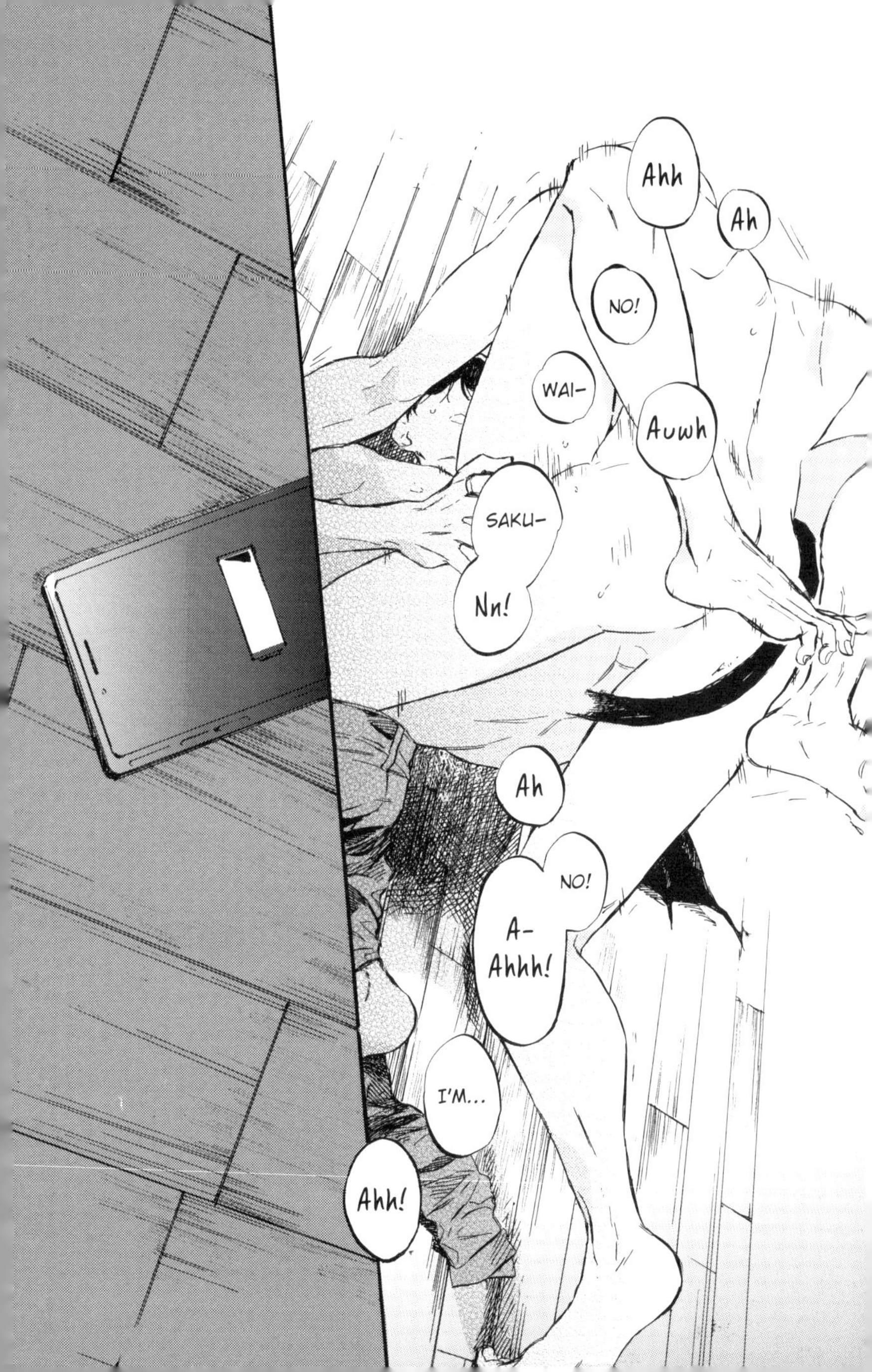
Ah
Ahh
NO!
Auwh
WAI-
SAKU-
Nn!
Ah
NO!
A-
Ahhh!
I'M...
Ahh!

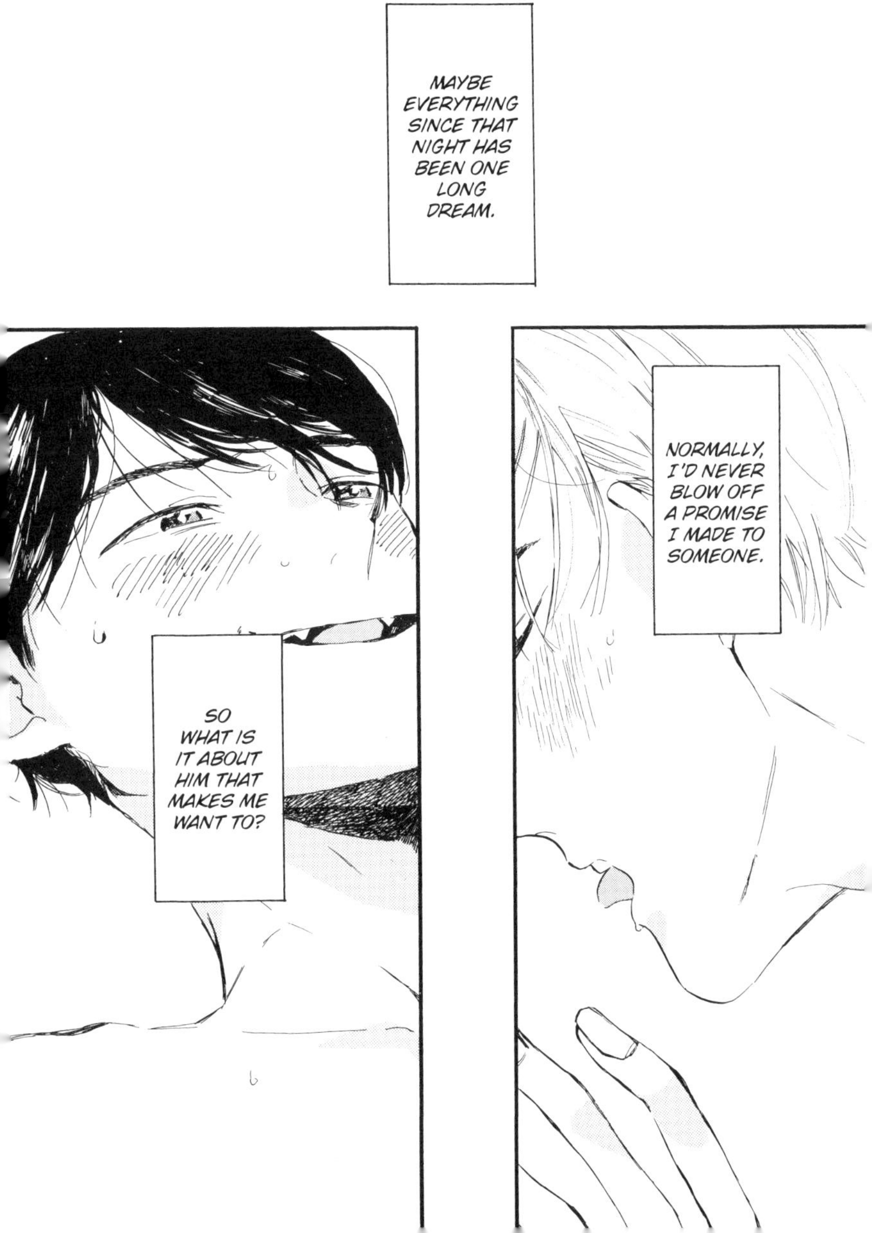
MAYBE EVERYTHING SINCE THAT NIGHT HAS BEEN ONE LONG DREAM.
NORMALLY, I'D NEVER BLOW OFF A PROMISE I MADE TO SOMEONE.
SO WHAT IS IT ABOUT HIM THAT MAKES ME WANT TO?

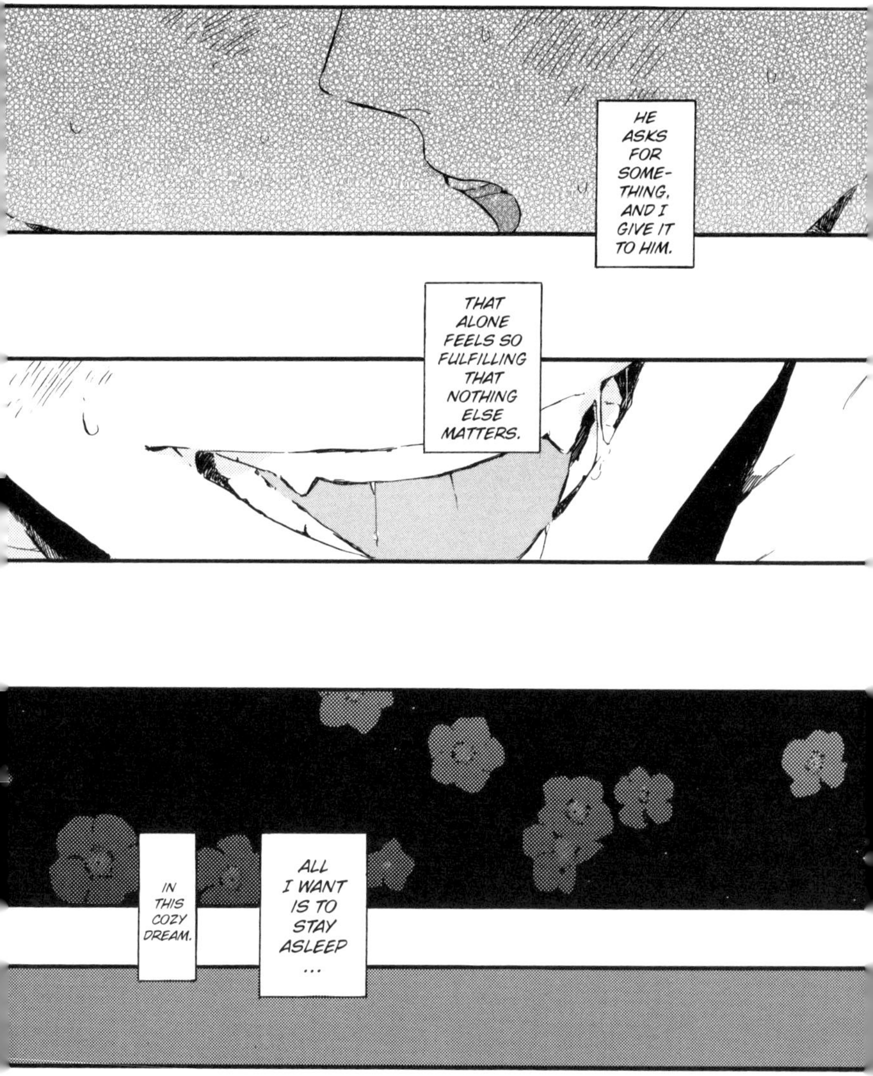
HE ASKS FOR SOME-THING, AND I GIVE IT TO HIM.
THAT ALONE FEELS SO FULFILLING THAT NOTHING ELSE MATTERS.
ALL I WANT IS TO STAY ASLEEP ...
IN THIS COZY DREAM.

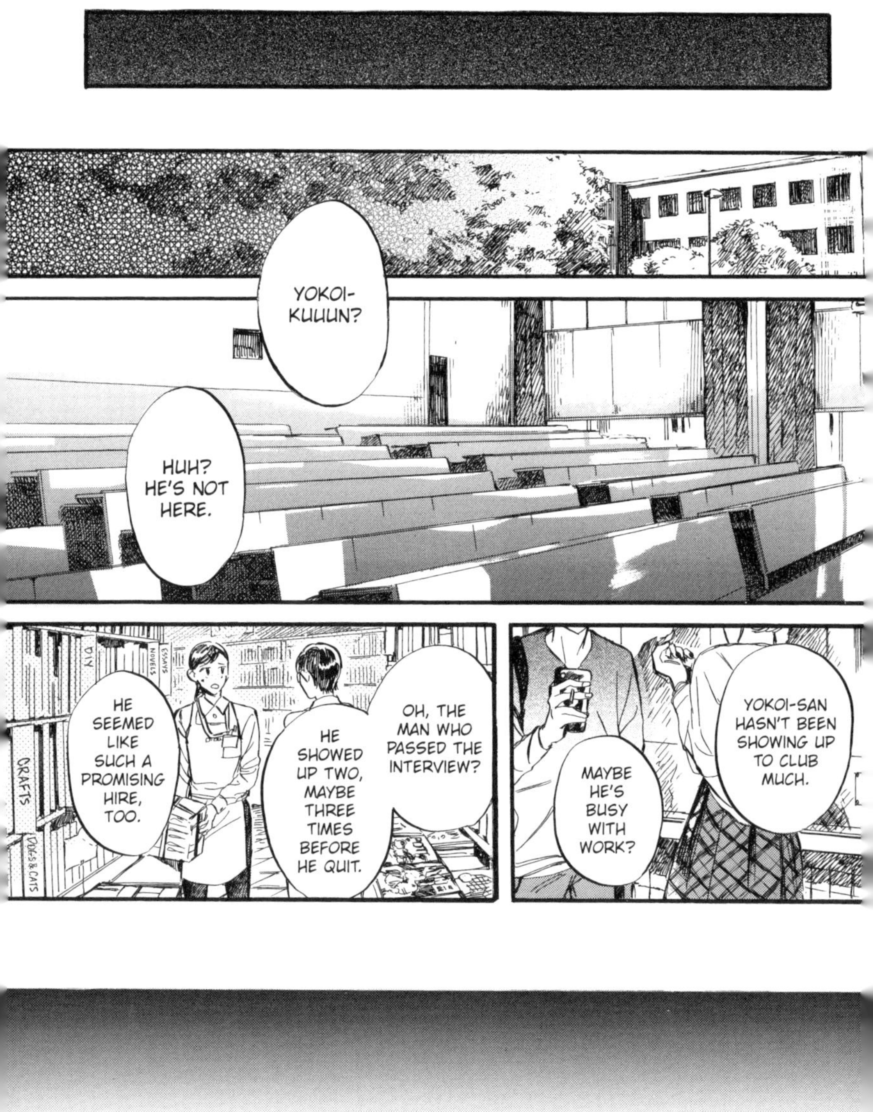
YOKOI-KUUUN?
HUH? HE'S NOT HERE.
YOKOI-SAN HASN'T BEEN SHOWING UP TO CLUB MUCH.
MAYBE HE'S BUSY WITH WORK?
OH, THE MAN WHO PASSED THE INTERVIEW?
HE SHOWED UP TWO, MAYBE THREE TIMES BEFORE HE QUIT.
HE SEEMED LIKE SUCH A PROMISING HIRE, TOO.
ESSAYS
NOVELS
DIY
CRAFTS
DOGS & CATS

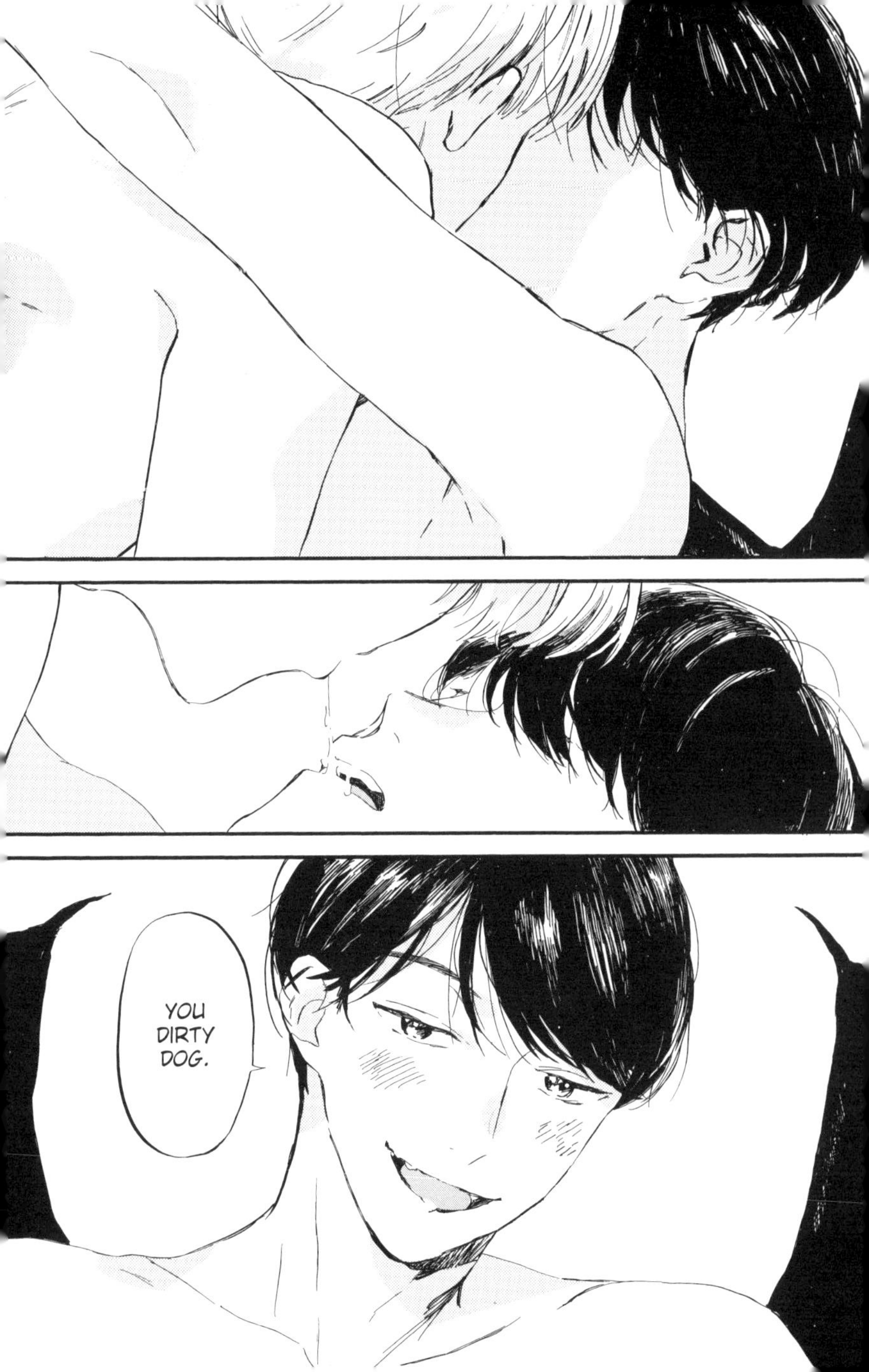
YOU DIRTY DOG.

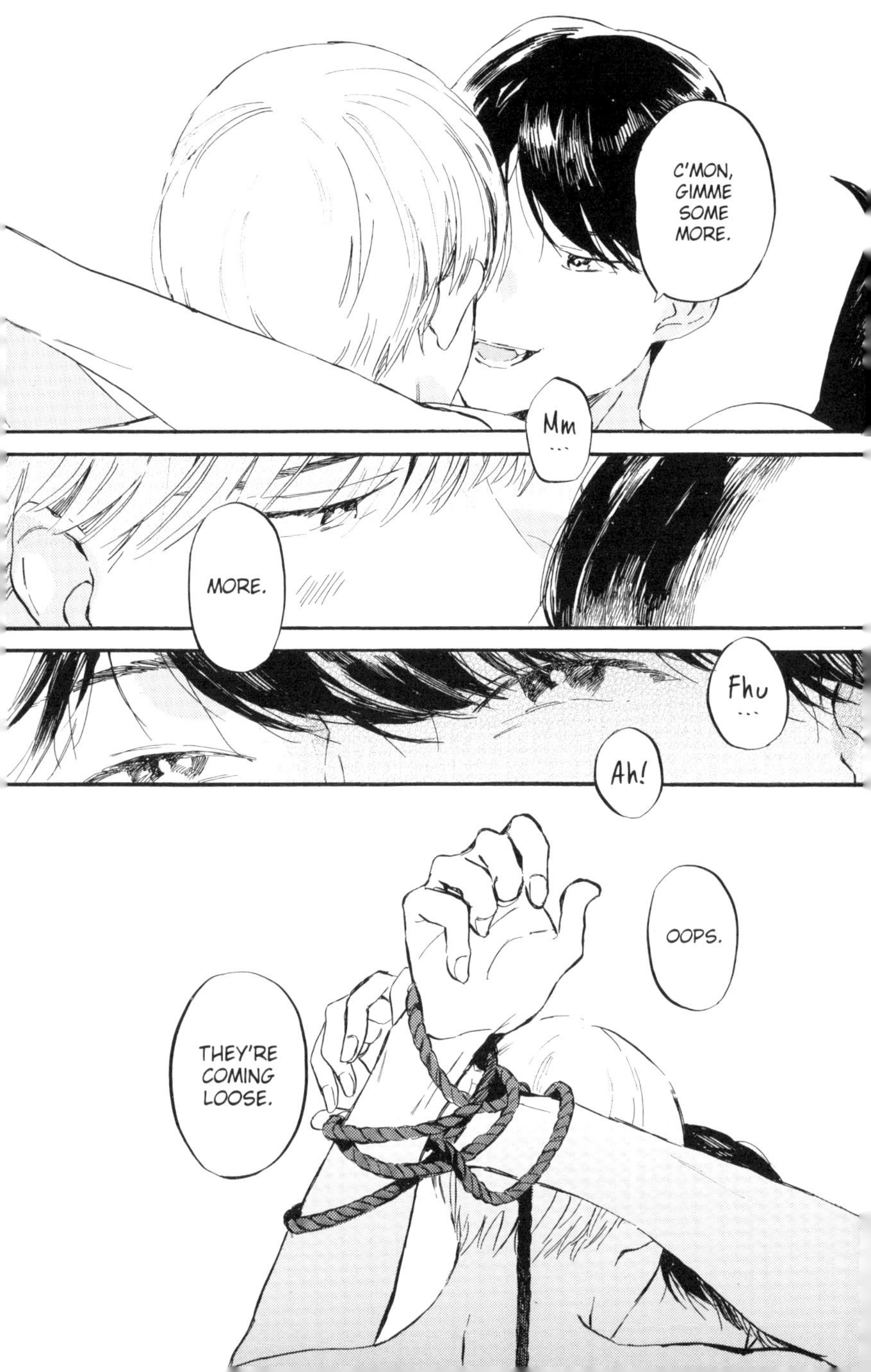
C'MON, GIMME SOME MORE.
Mm ...
MORE.
Fhu ...
Ah!
OOPS.
THEY'RE COMING LOOSE.

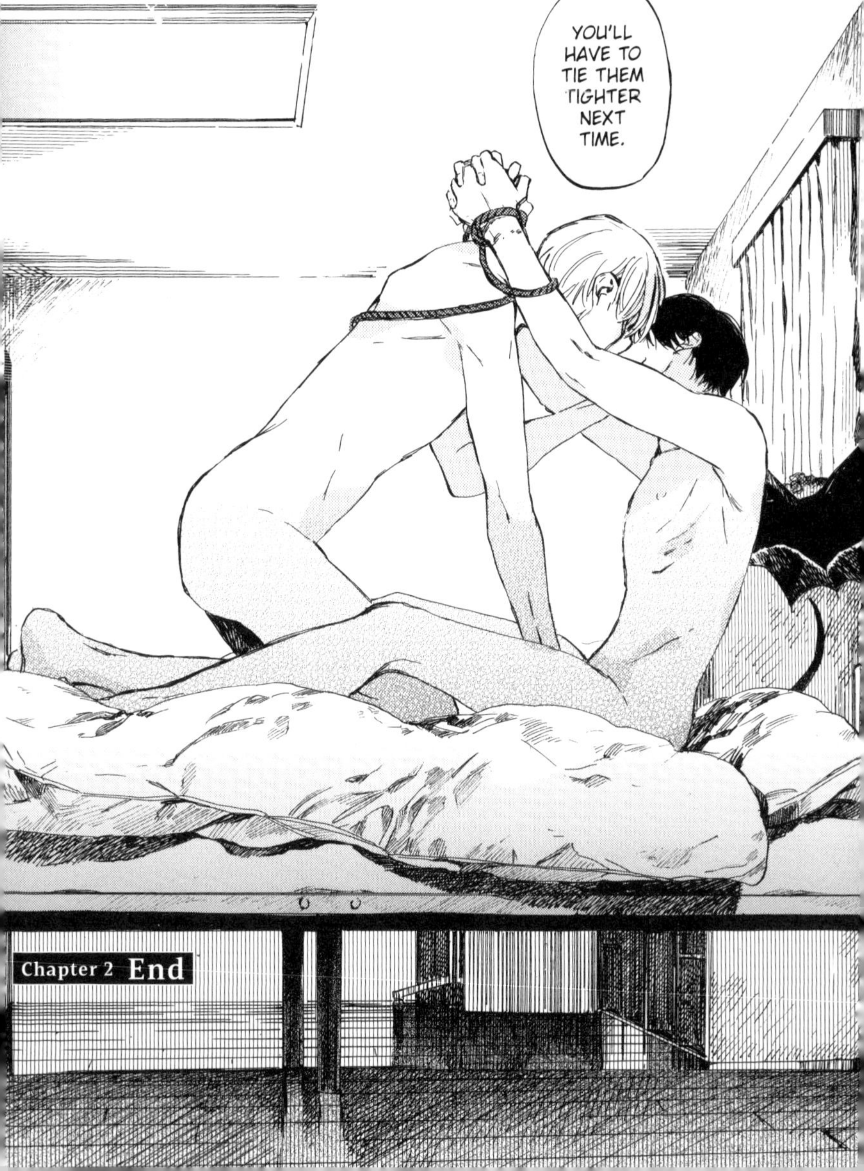
YOU'LL HAVE TO TIE THEM TIGHTER NEXT TIME.
Chapter 2 End

Chapter 3

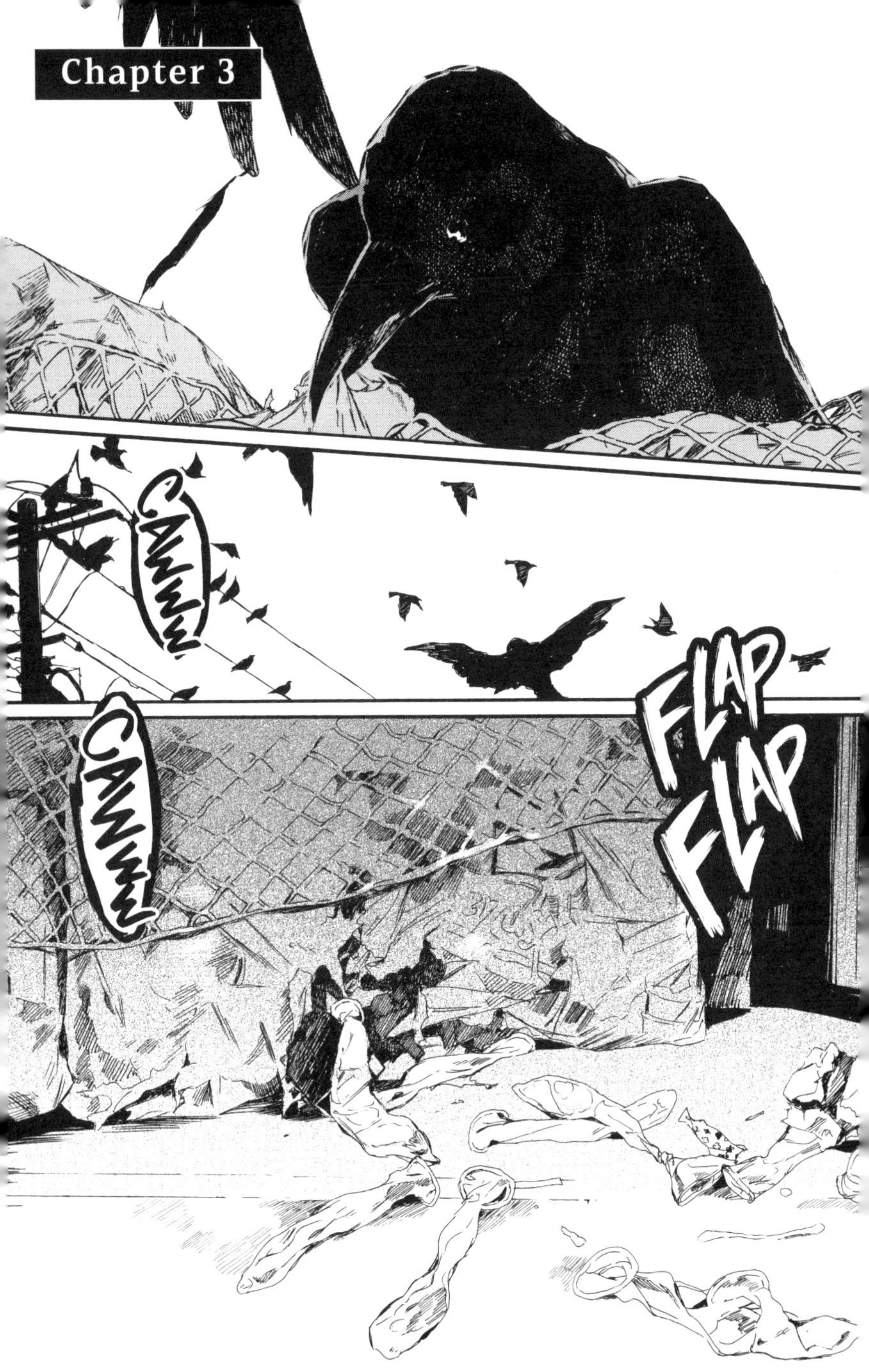
CAWWW
FLAP FLAP
CAWWW

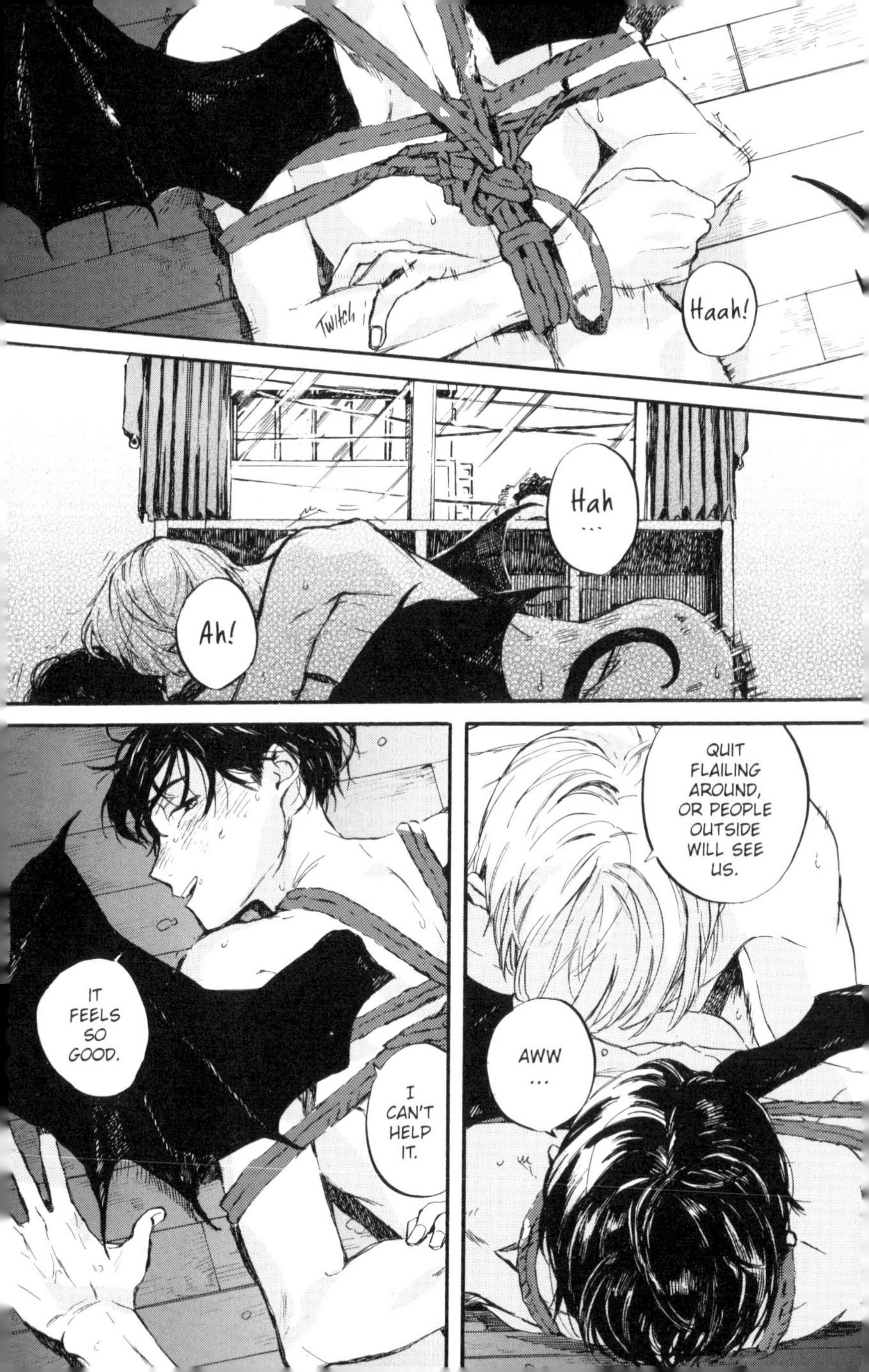
Haaah!
Twitch
Hah
...
Ah!
QUIT FLAILING AROUND, OR PEOPLE OUTSIDE WILL SEE US.
AWW
...
IT FEELS SO GOOD.
I CAN'T HELP IT.

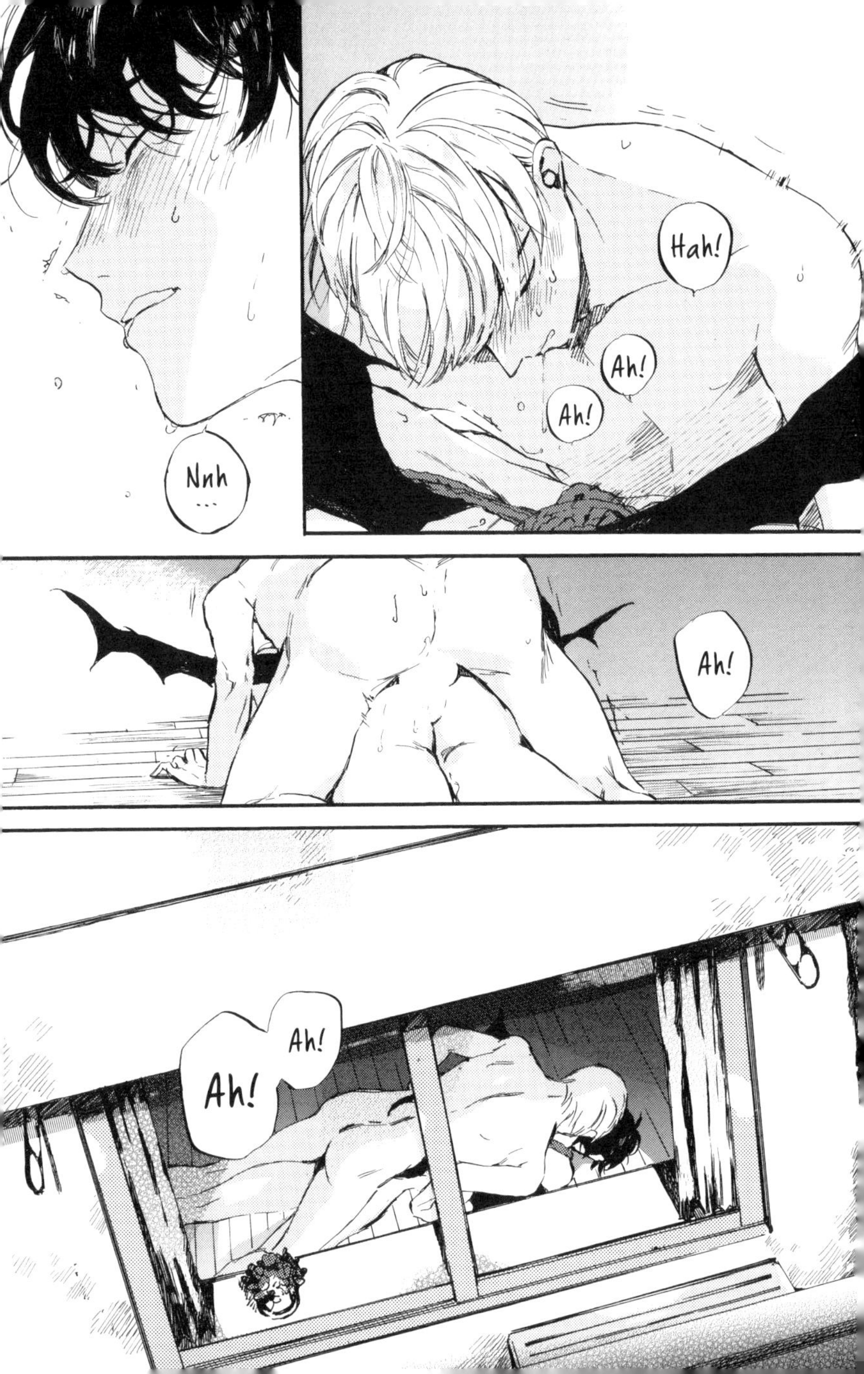
Hah!
Ah!
Ah!
Nnh
...
Ah!
Ah!
Ah!

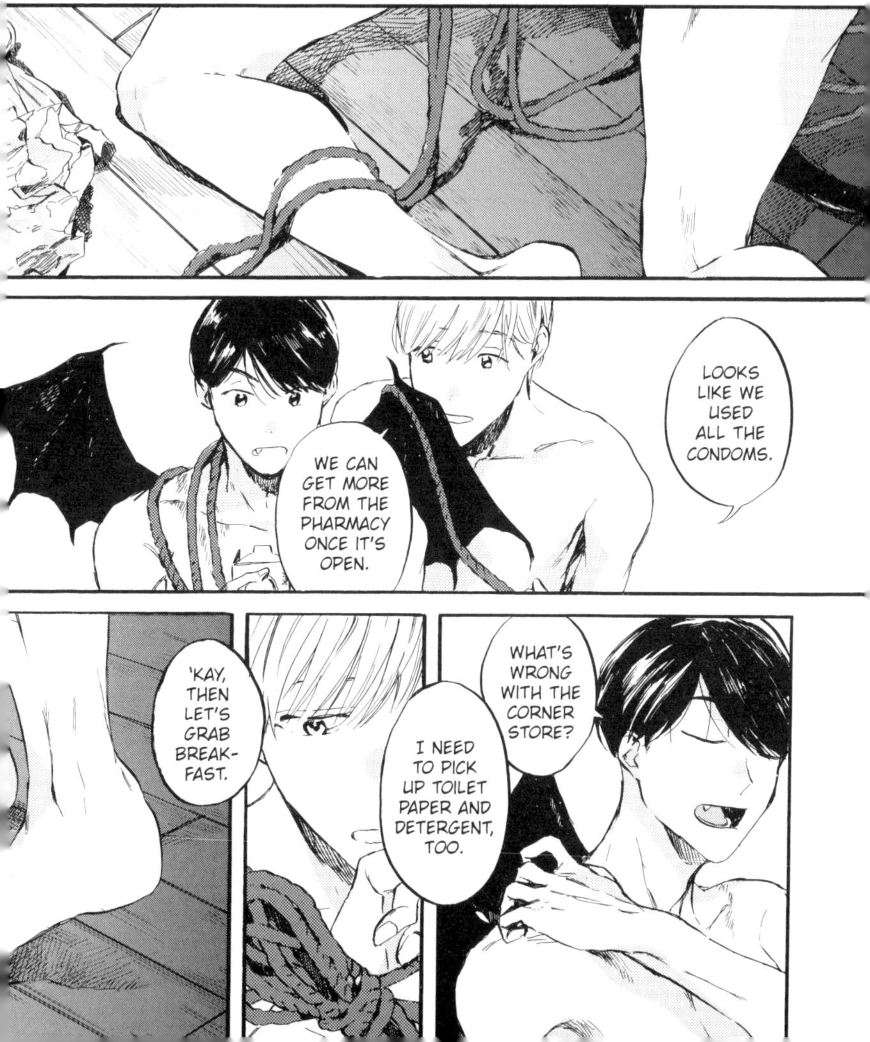
LOOKS LIKE WE USED ALL THE CONDOMS.
WE CAN GET MORE FROM THE PHARMACY ONCE IT'S OPEN.
WHAT'S WRONG WITH THE CORNER STORE?
I NEED TO PICK UP TOILET PAPER AND DETERGENT, TOO.
'KAY, THEN LET'S GRAB BREAK-FAST.

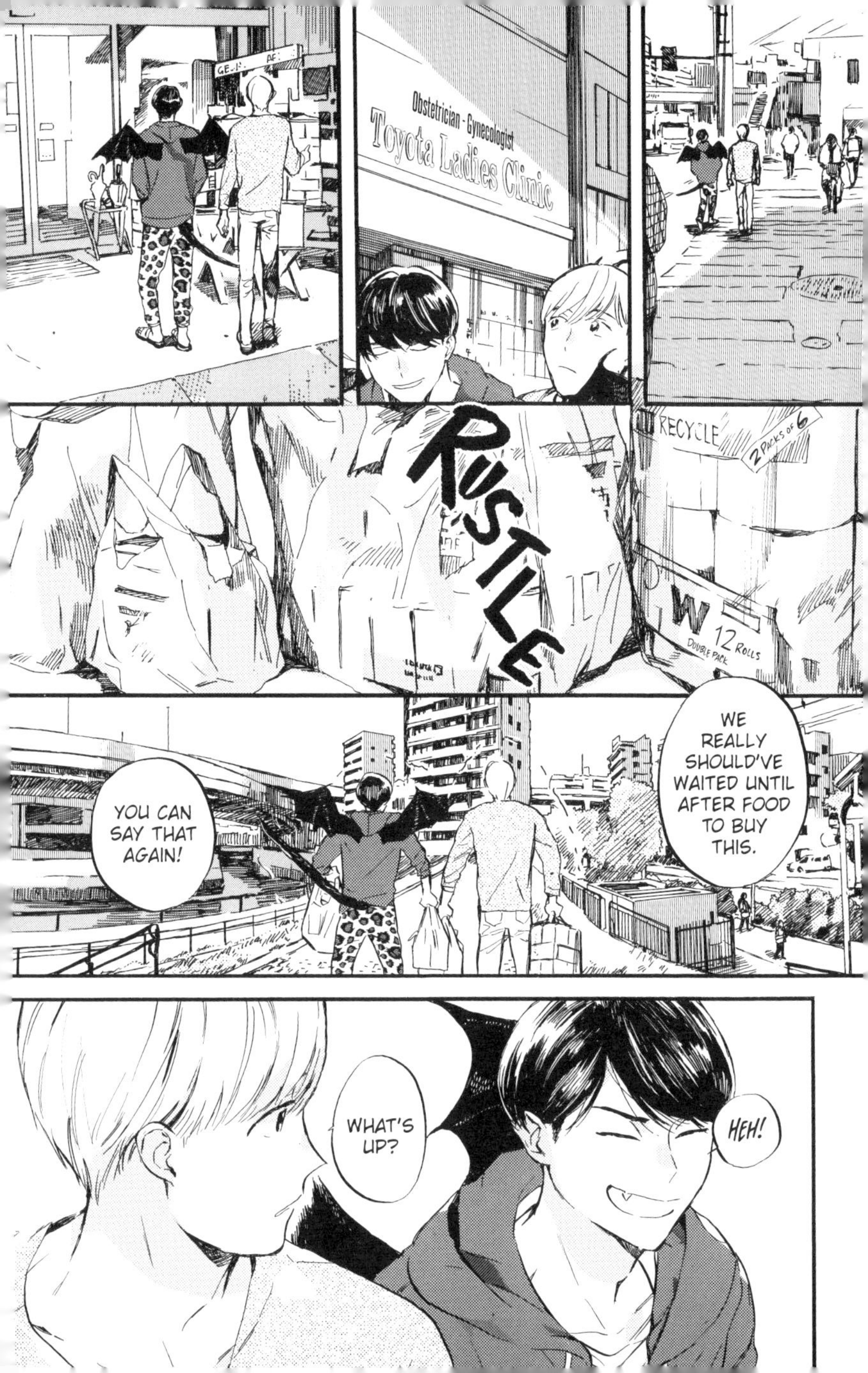
Obstetrician - Gynecologist
Toyota Ladies Clinic
RECYCLE
2 Packs of 6
W
12 Rolls
DOUBLE PACK
RUSTLE
WE REALLY SHOULD'VE WAITED UNTIL AFTER FOOD TO BUY THIS.
YOU CAN SAY THAT AGAIN!
HEH!
WHAT'S UP?

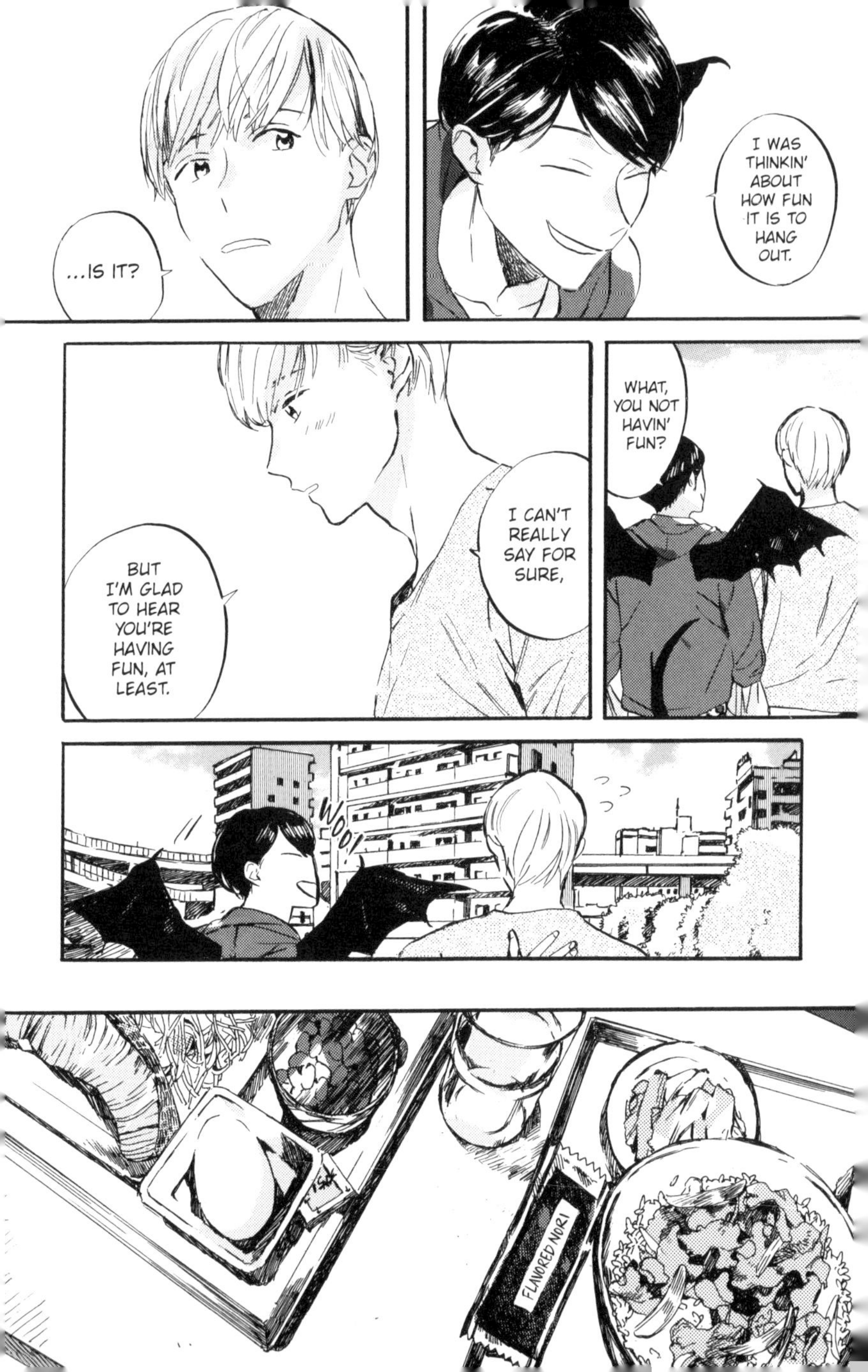
I WAS THINKIN' ABOUT HOW FUN IT IS TO HANG OUT.
...IS IT?
WHAT, YOU NOT HAVIN' FUN?
I CAN'T REALLY SAY FOR SURE,
BUT I'M GLAD TO HEAR YOU'RE HAVING FUN, AT LEAST.
WOO!
FLAVORED NORI

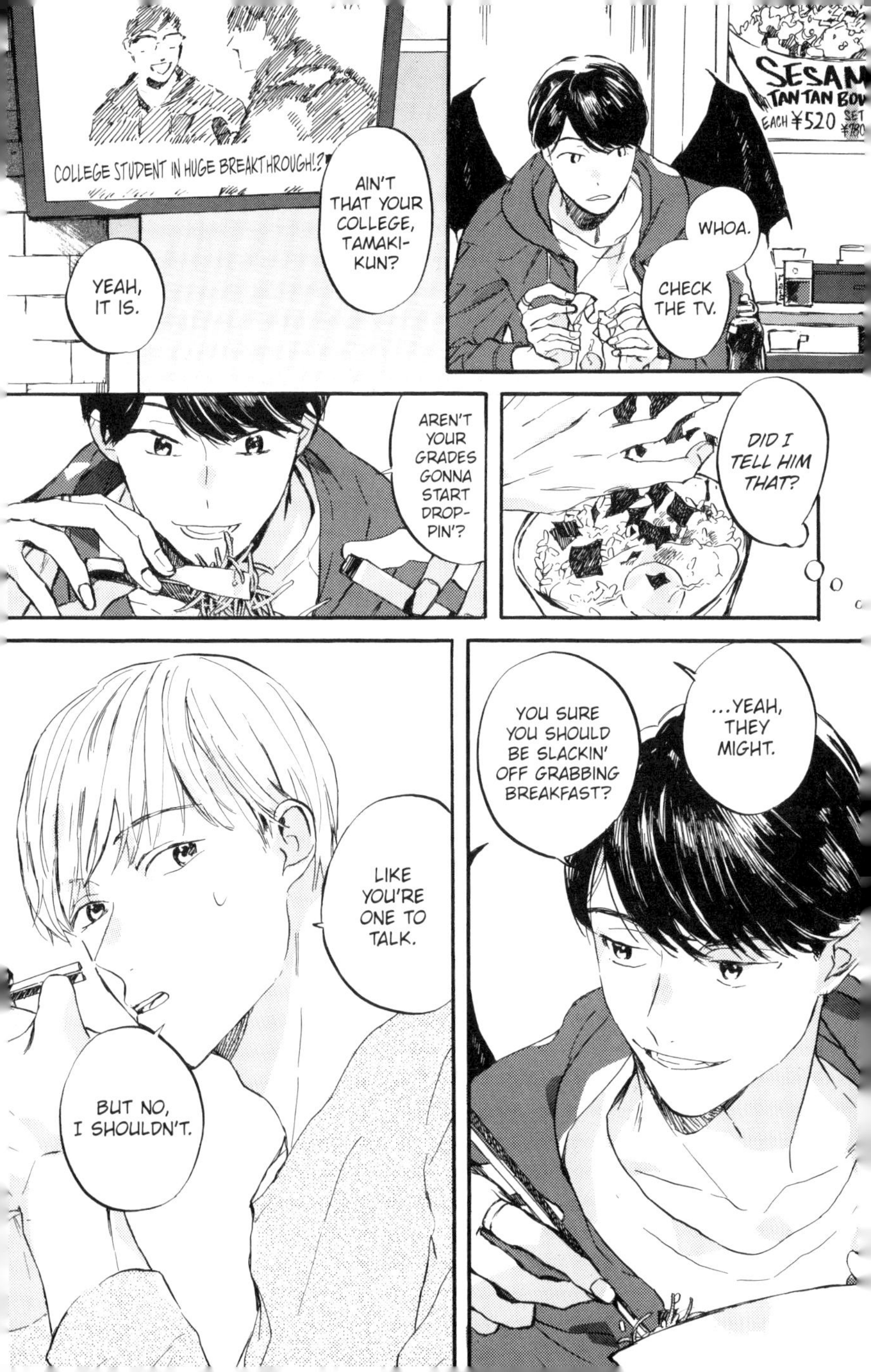
SESAM
TAN TAN BOW
EACH ¥520 SET ¥780
WHOA.
CHECK THE TV.
COLLEGE STUDENT IN HUGE BREAKTHROUGH!?
AIN'T THAT YOUR COLLEGE, TAMAKI-KUN?
YEAH, IT IS.
DID I TELL HIM THAT?
AREN'T YOUR GRADES GONNA START DROP-PIN'?
YOU SURE YOU SHOULD BE SLACKIN' OFF GRABBING BREAKFAST?
...YEAH, THEY MIGHT.
LIKE YOU'RE ONE TO TALK.
BUT NO, I SHOULDN'T.

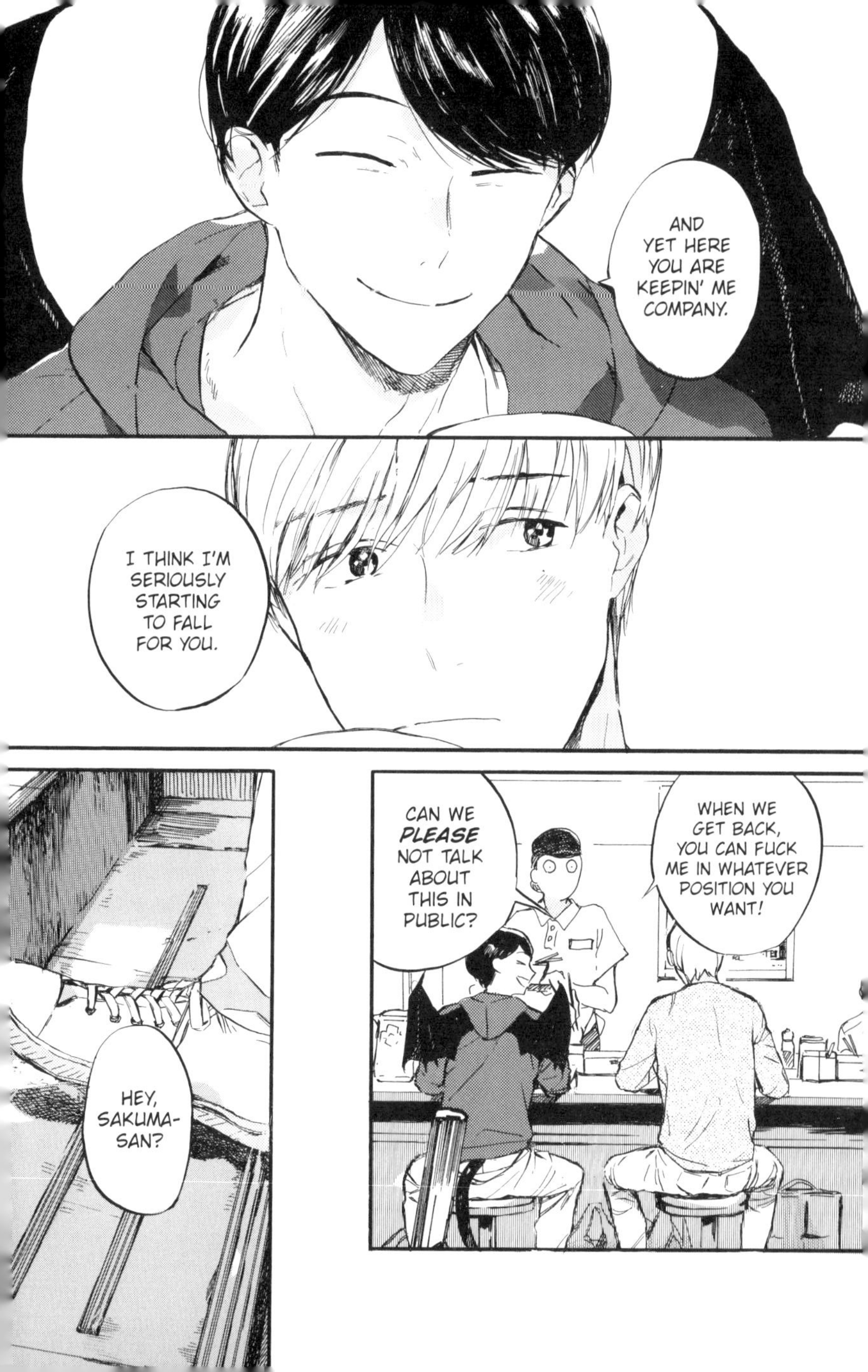
AND YET HERE YOU ARE KEEPIN' ME COMPANY.
I THINK I'M SERIOUSLY STARTING TO FALL FOR YOU.
WHEN WE GET BACK, YOU CAN FUCK ME IN WHATEVER POSITION YOU WANT!
CAN WE *PLEASE* NOT TALK ABOUT THIS IN PUBLIC?
HEY, SAKUMA-SAN?

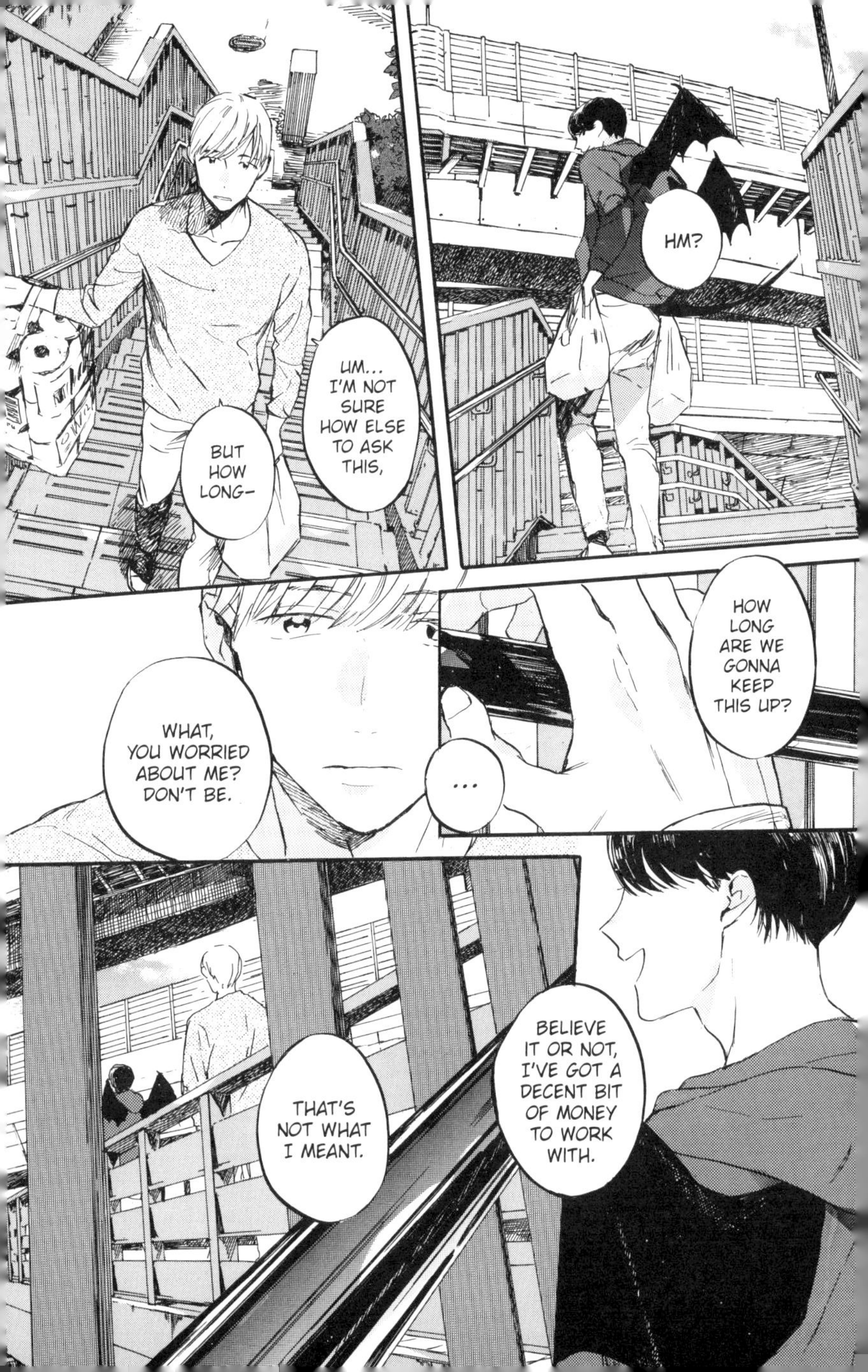
HM?
UM... I'M NOT SURE HOW ELSE TO ASK THIS,
BUT HOW LONG-
HOW LONG ARE WE GONNA KEEP THIS UP?
...
WHAT, YOU WORRIED ABOUT ME? DON'T BE.
BELIEVE IT OR NOT, I'VE GOT A DECENT BIT OF MONEY TO WORK WITH.
THAT'S NOT WHAT I MEANT.

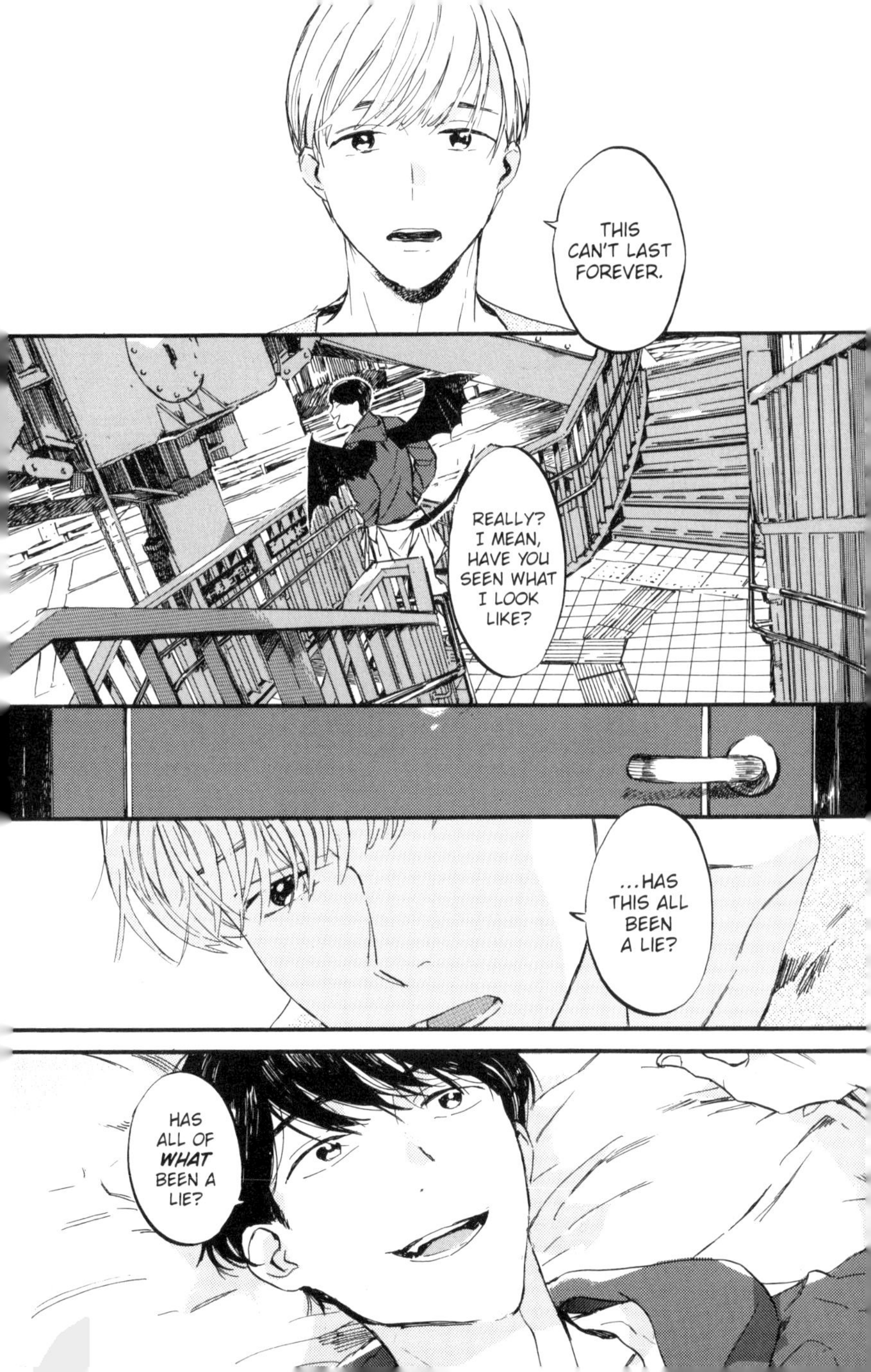
THIS CAN'T LAST FOREVER.
REALLY? I MEAN, HAVE YOU SEEN WHAT I LOOK LIKE?
...HAS THIS ALL BEEN A LIE?
HAS ALL OF ***WHAT*** BEEN A LIE?

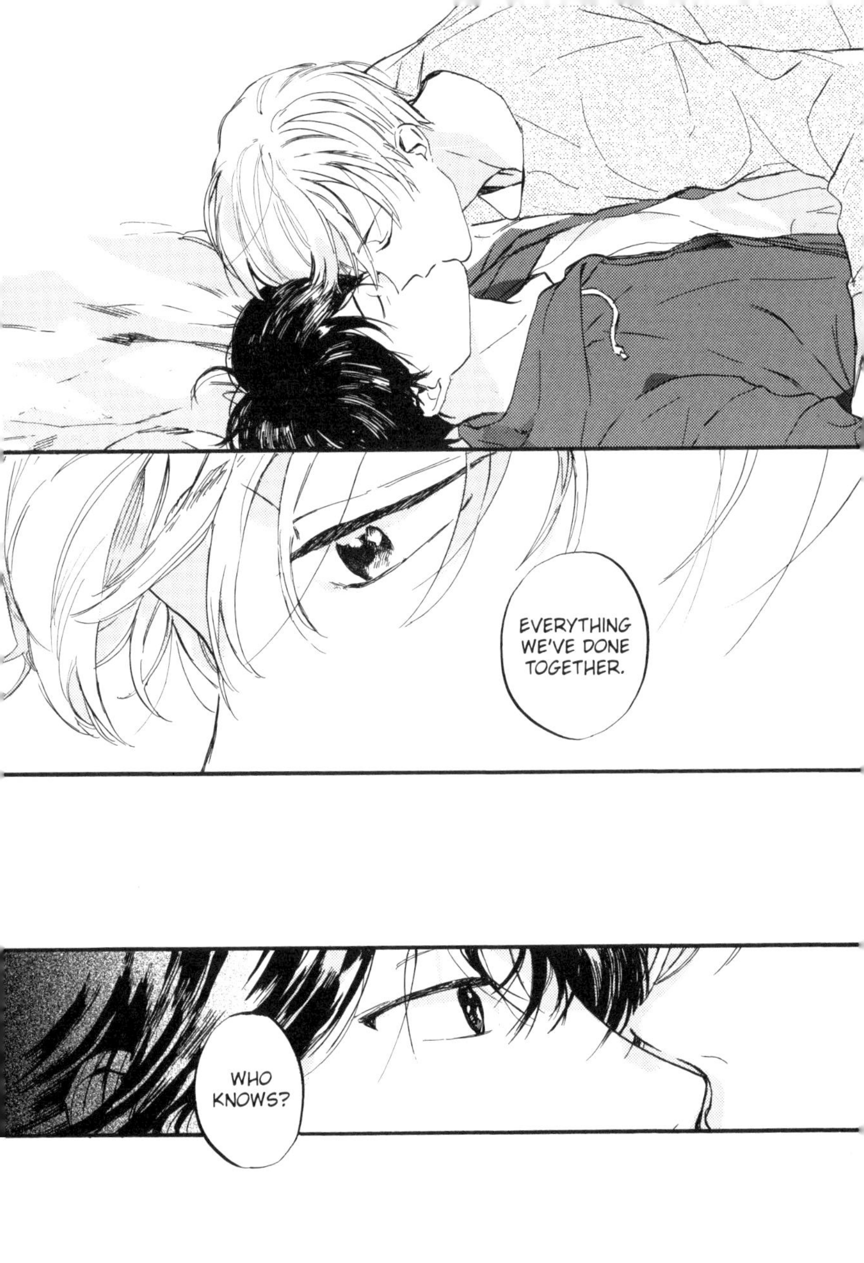
EVERYTHING WE'VE DONE TOGETHER.
WHO KNOWS?

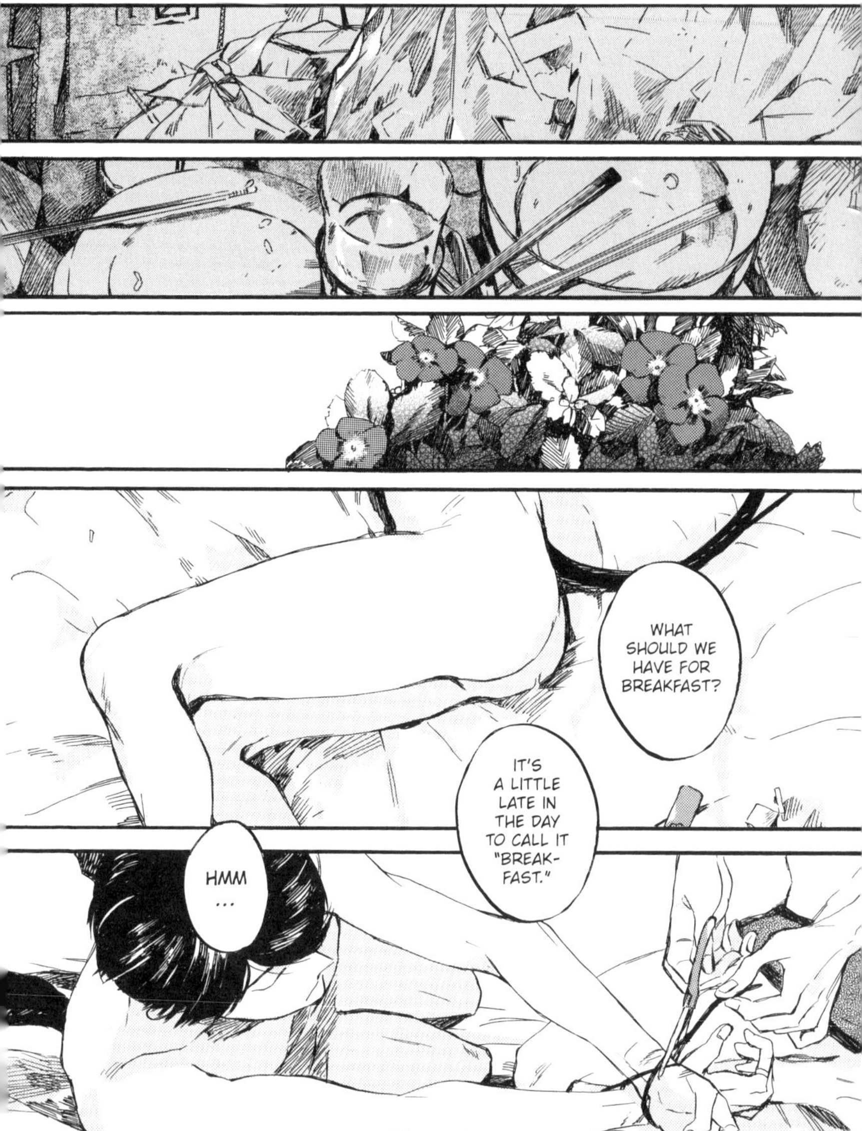
WHAT SHOULD WE HAVE FOR BREAKFAST?
IT'S A LITTLE LATE IN THE DAY TO CALL IT "BREAK-FAST."
HMM ...

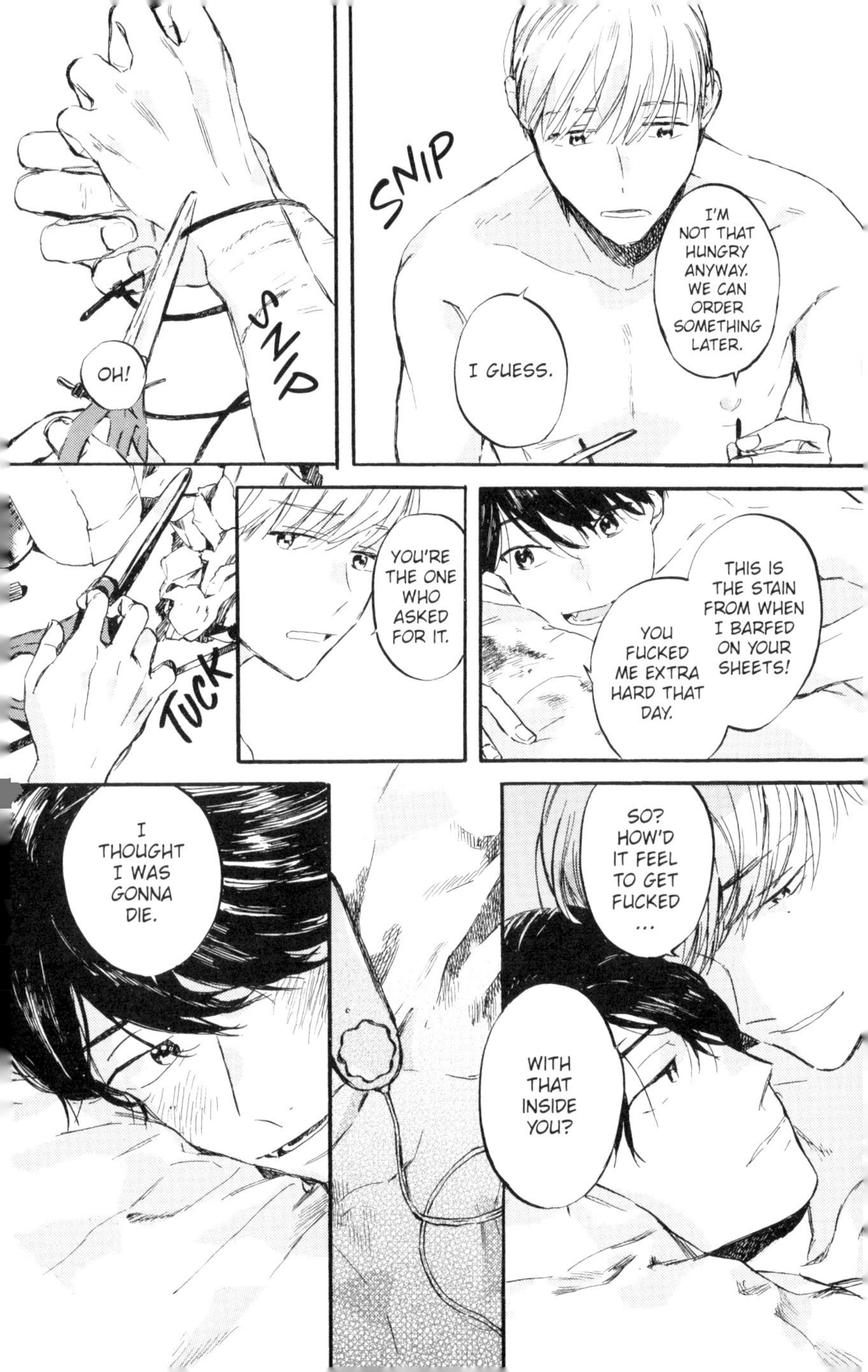
I'M NOT THAT HUNGRY ANYWAY. WE CAN ORDER SOMETHING LATER.
I GUESS.
SNIP
SNIP
OH!
THIS IS THE STAIN FROM WHEN I BARFED ON YOUR SHEETS!
YOU FUCKED ME EXTRA HARD THAT DAY.
YOU'RE THE ONE WHO ASKED FOR IT.
TUCK
SO? HOW'D IT FEEL TO GET FUCKED ...
WITH THAT INSIDE YOU?
I THOUGHT I WAS GONNA DIE.

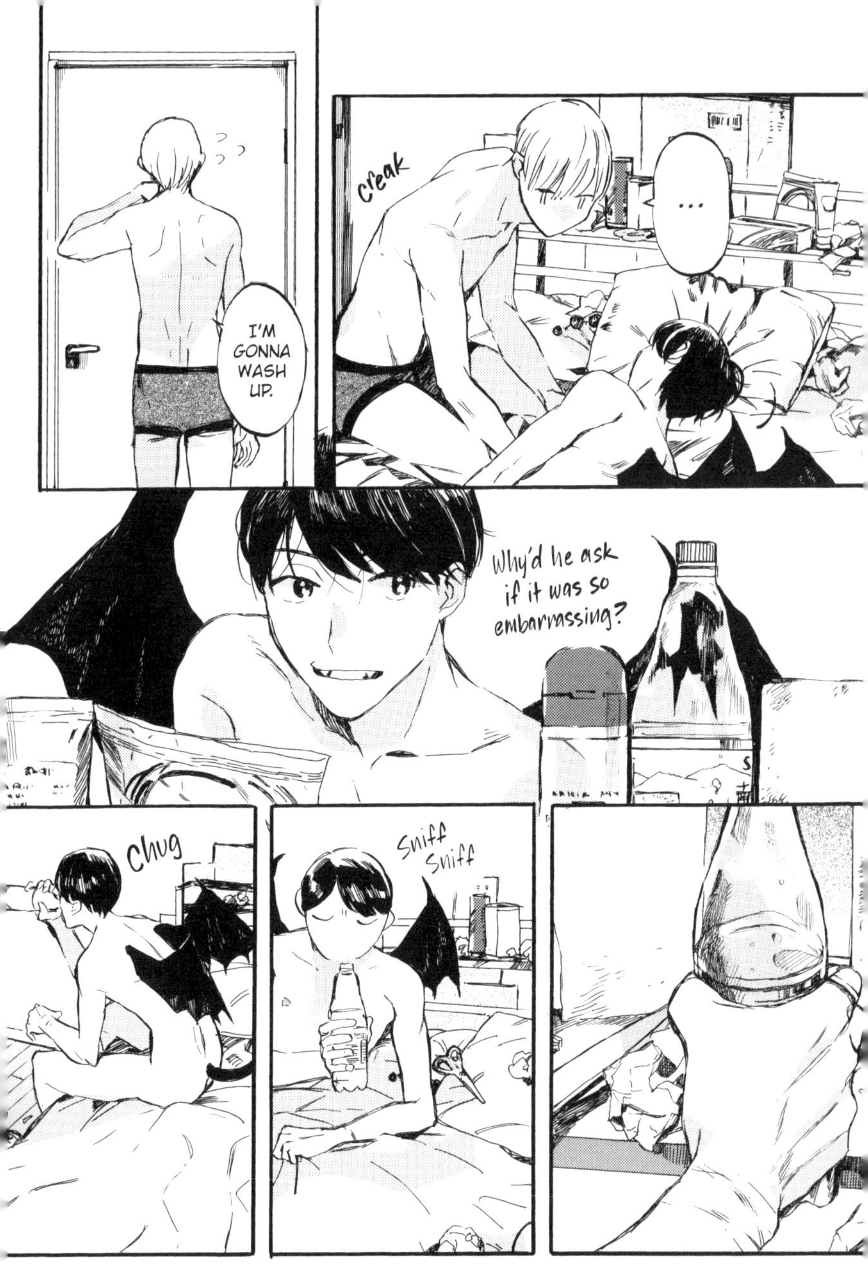
Creak
...
I'M GONNA WASH UP.
Why'd he ask if it was so embarrassing?
Sniff Sniff
Chug

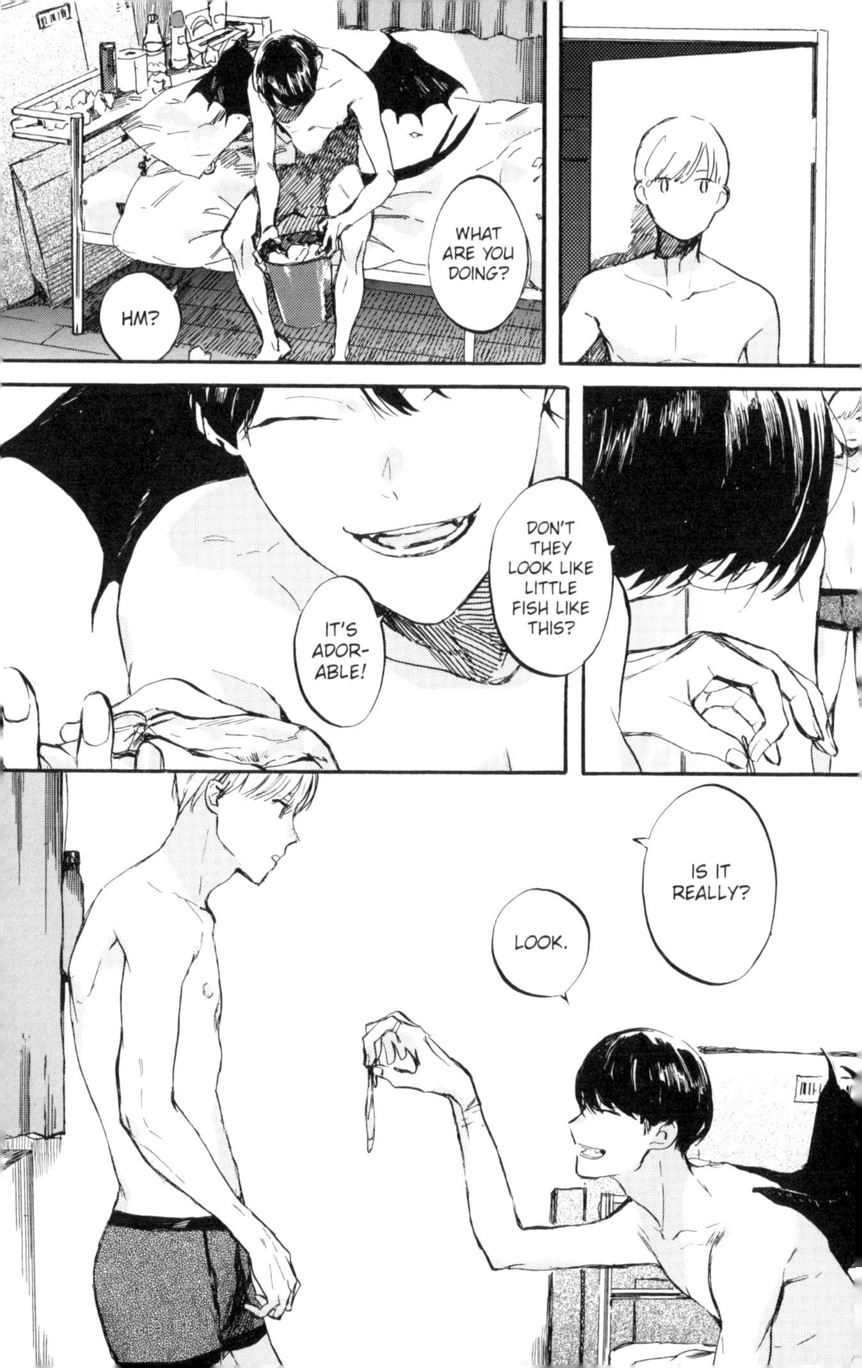
WHAT ARE YOU DOING?
HM?
DON'T THEY LOOK LIKE LITTLE FISH LIKE THIS?
IT'S ADOR-ABLE!
IS IT REALLY?
LOOK.

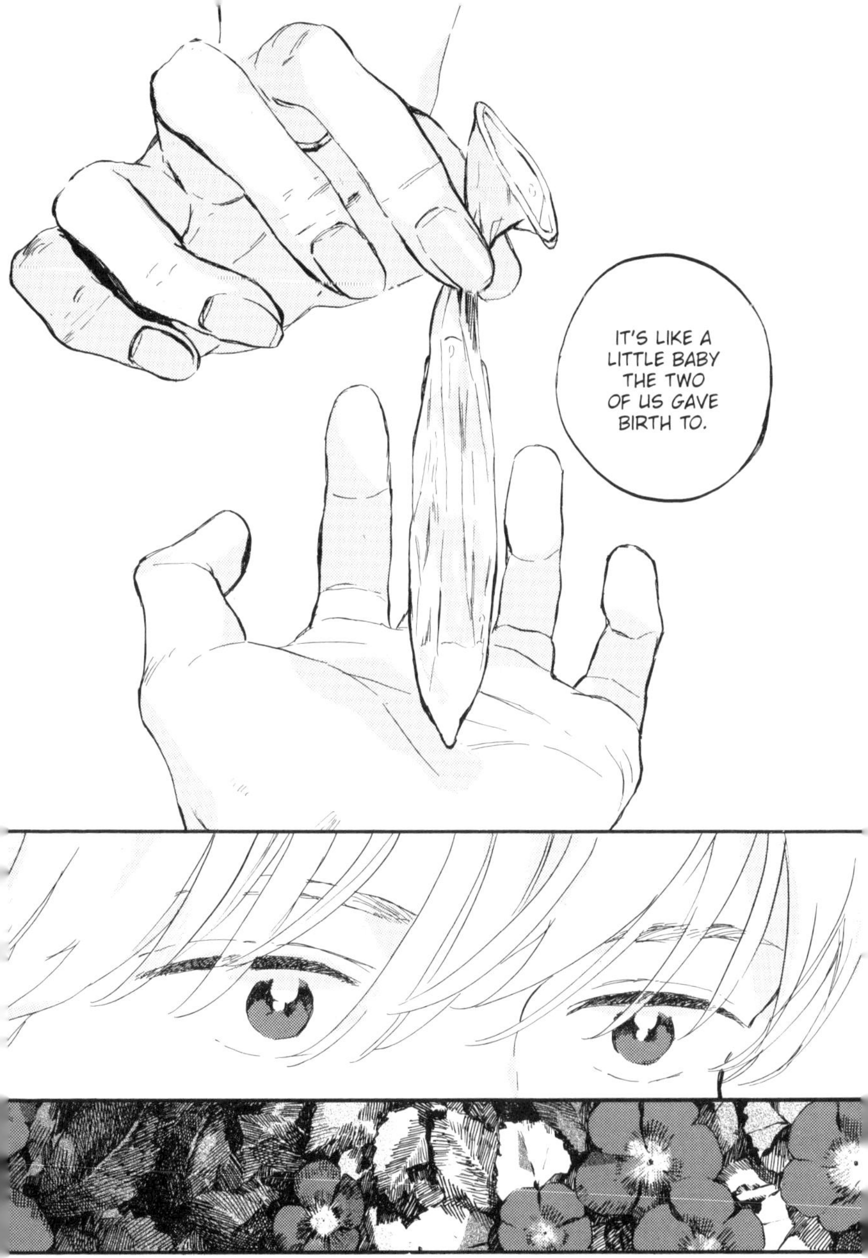
IT'S LIKE A LITTLE BABY THE TWO OF US GAVE BIRTH TO.

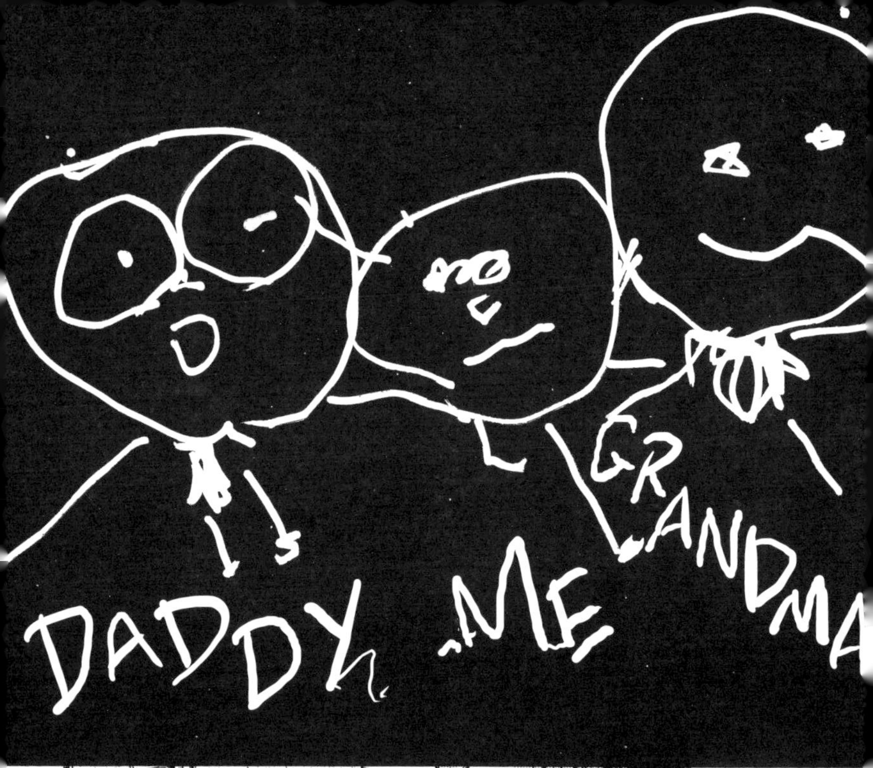
GRANDMA
ME
DADDY

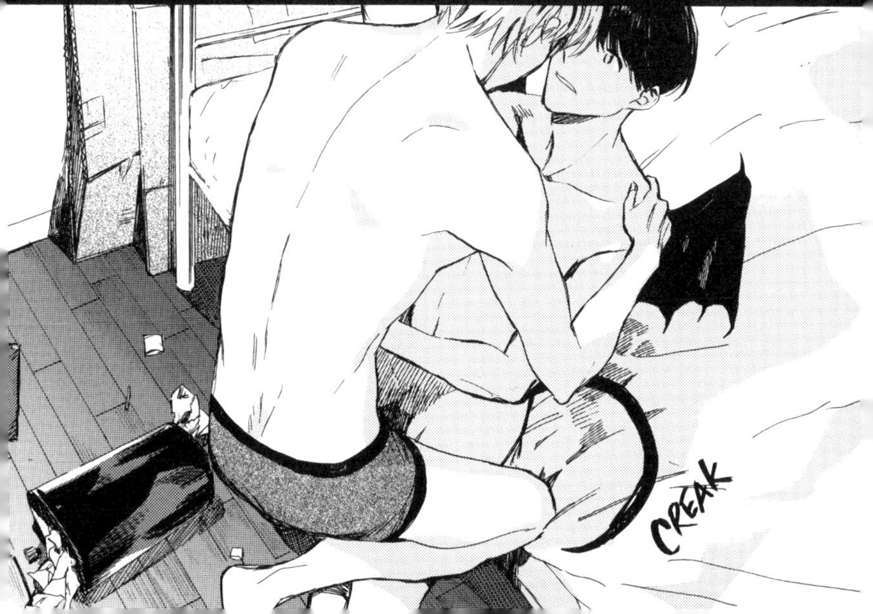
CREAK

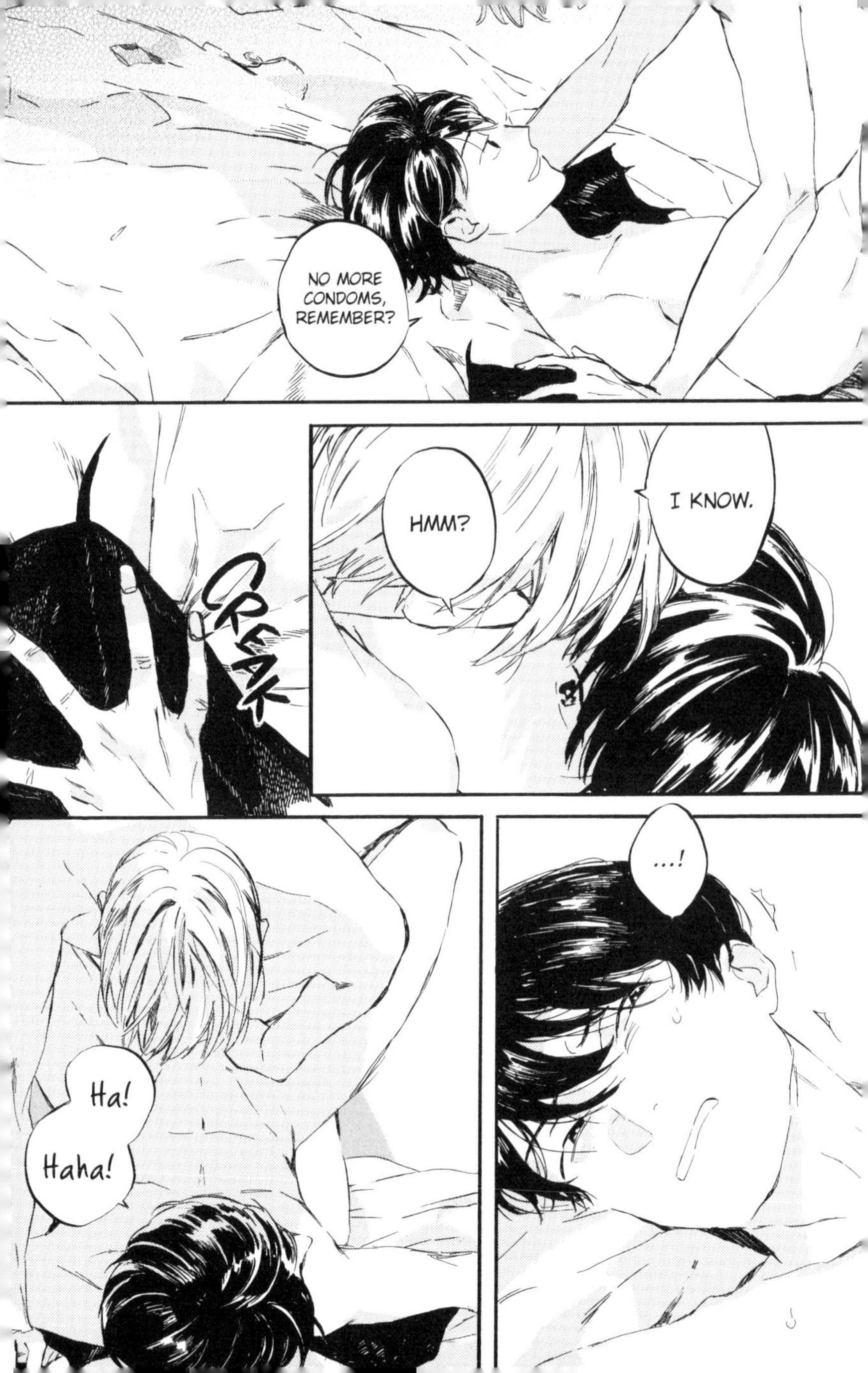
NO MORE CONDOMS, REMEMBER?
I KNOW.
HMM?
CREAK
...!
Ha!
Haha!

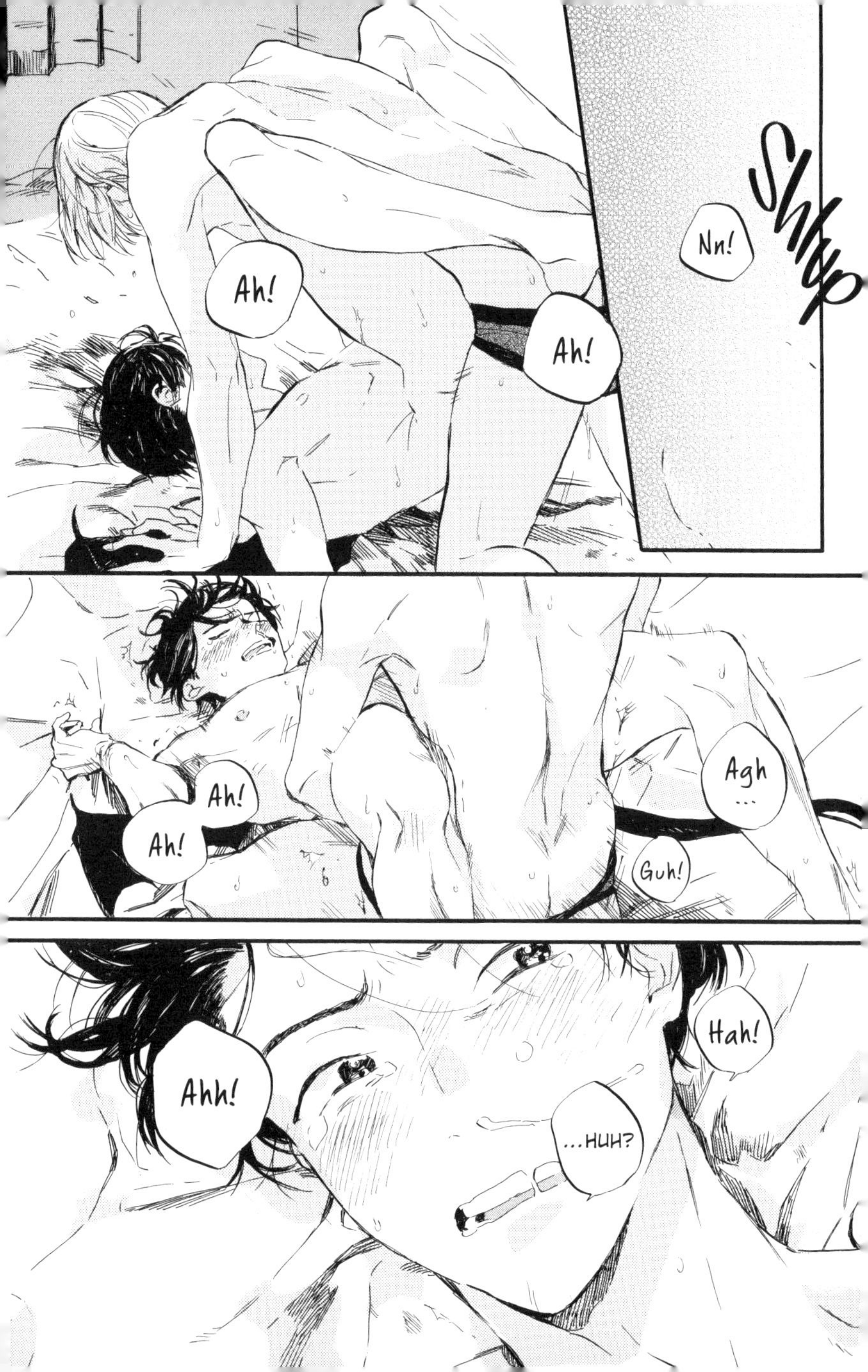
Shlup
Nn!
Ah!
Ah!
Agh ...
Guh!
Ah!
Ah!
Hah!
...HUH?
Ahh!

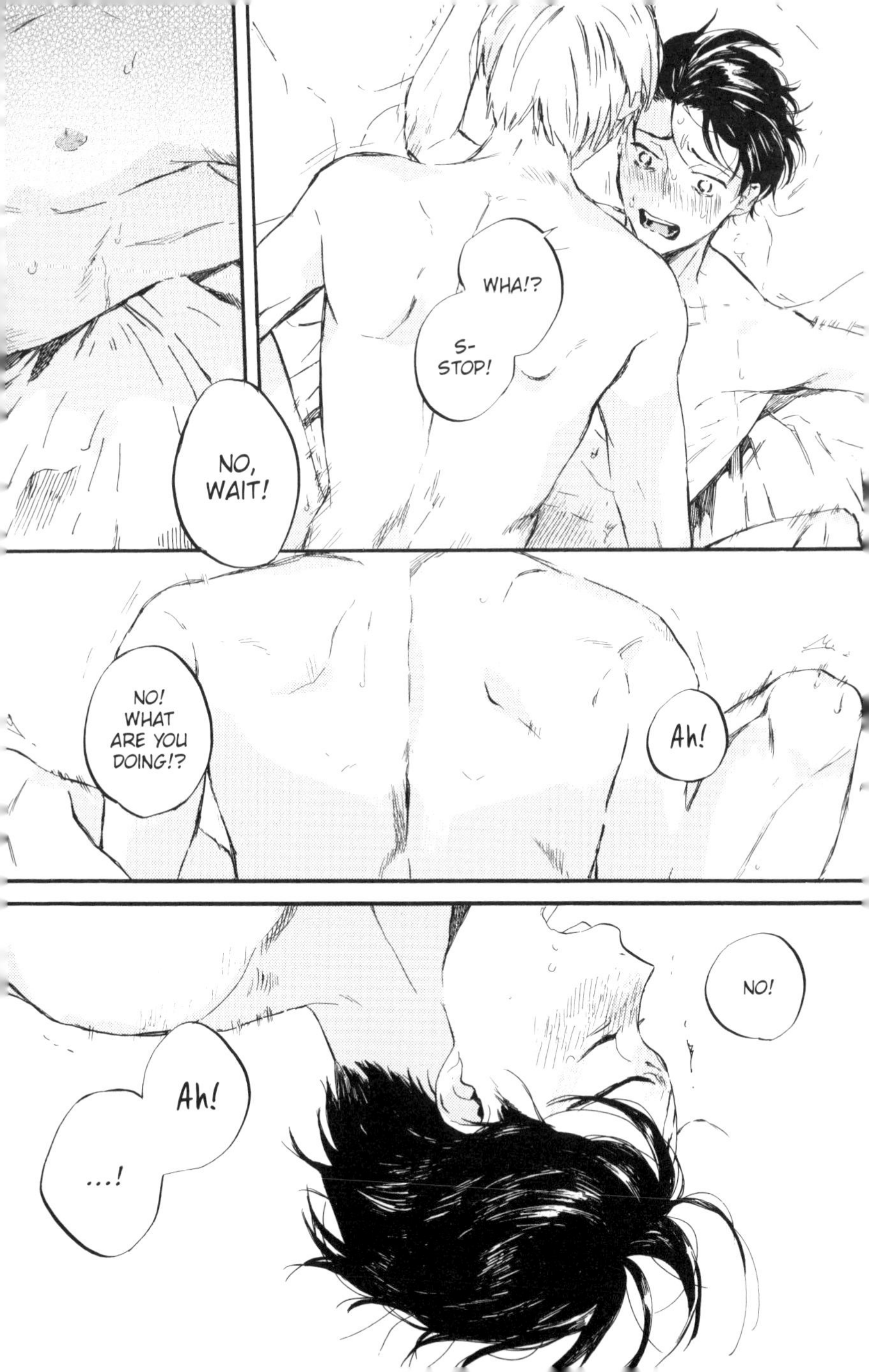
WHA!? S-STOP!
NO, WAIT!
Ah!
NO! WHAT ARE YOU DOING!?
NO!
Ah! ...!

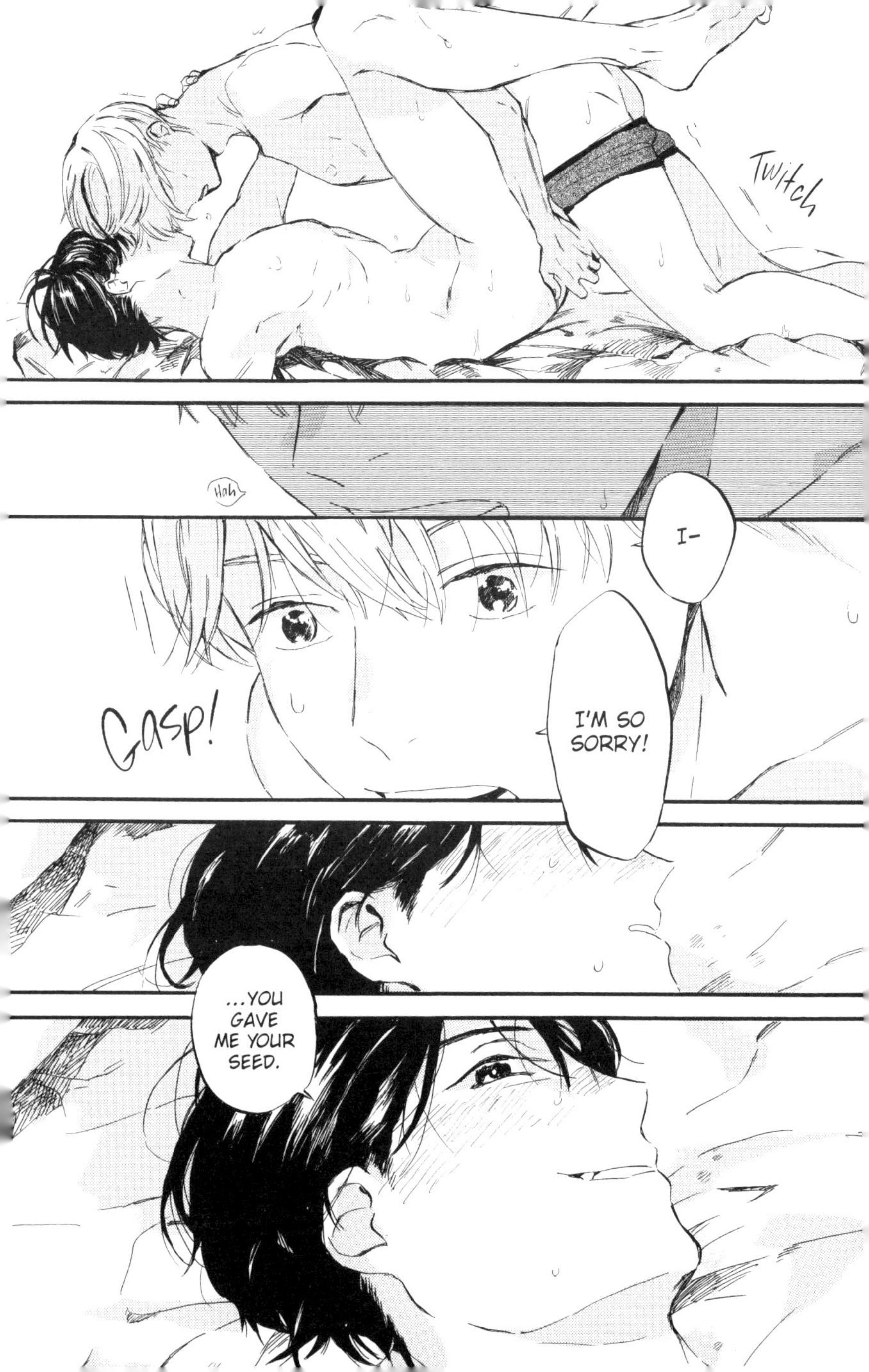
Twitch
Hah
I-
I'M SO SORRY!
Gasp!
...YOU GAVE ME YOUR SEED.

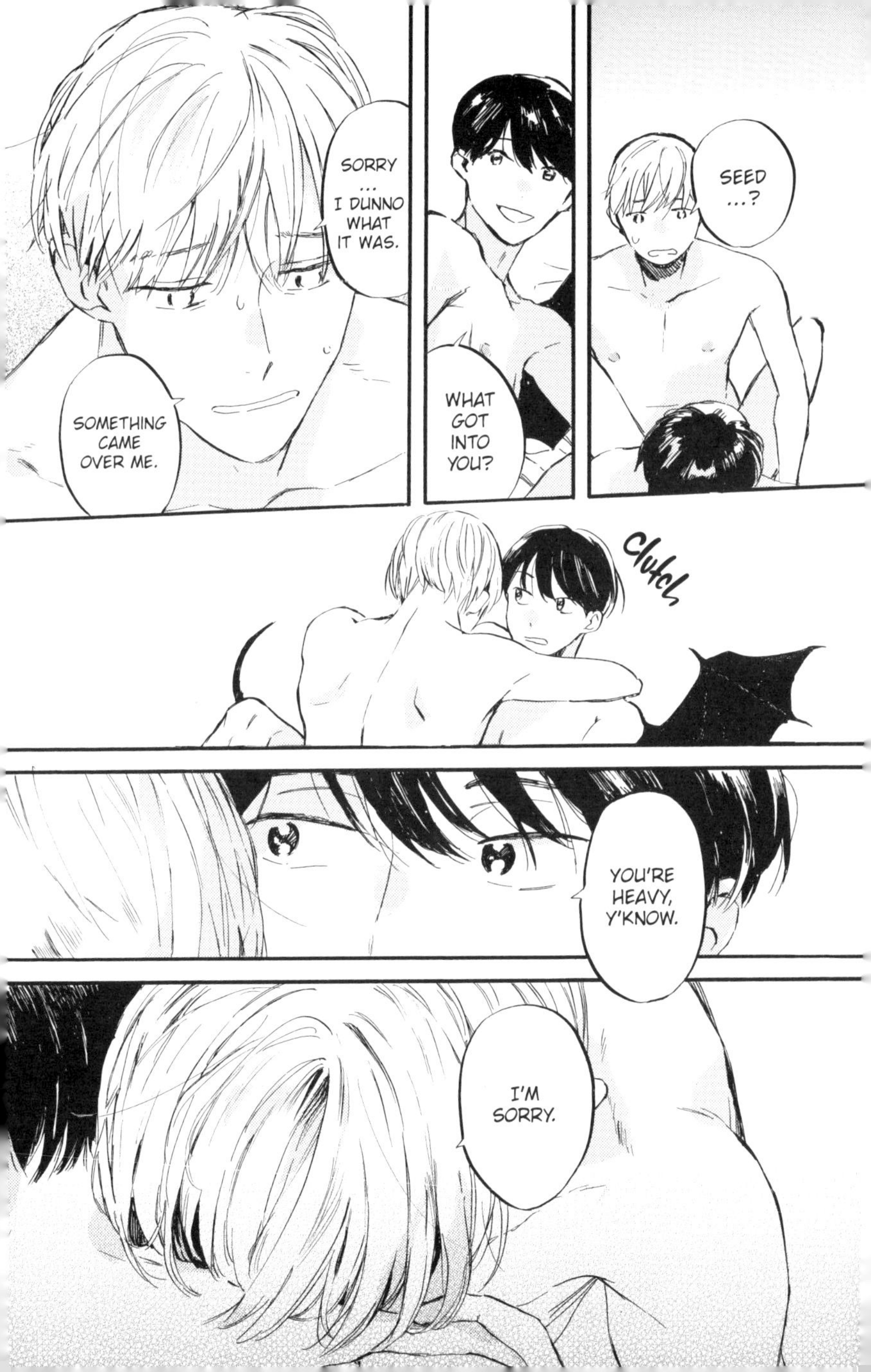
SEED ...?
WHAT GOT INTO YOU?
SORRY ... I DUNNO WHAT IT WAS.
SOMETHING CAME OVER ME.
Clutch
YOU'RE HEAVY, Y'KNOW.
I'M SORRY.

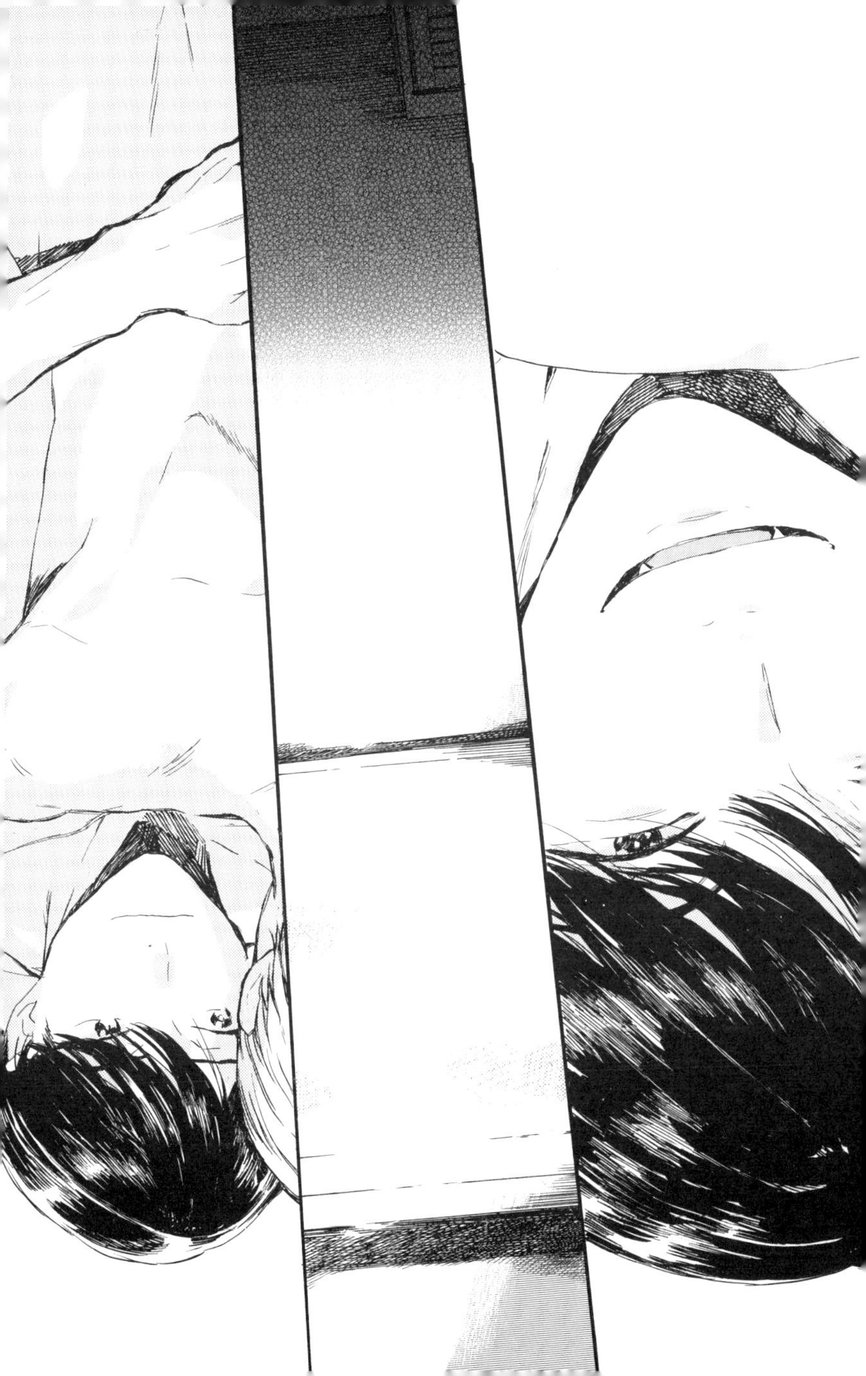

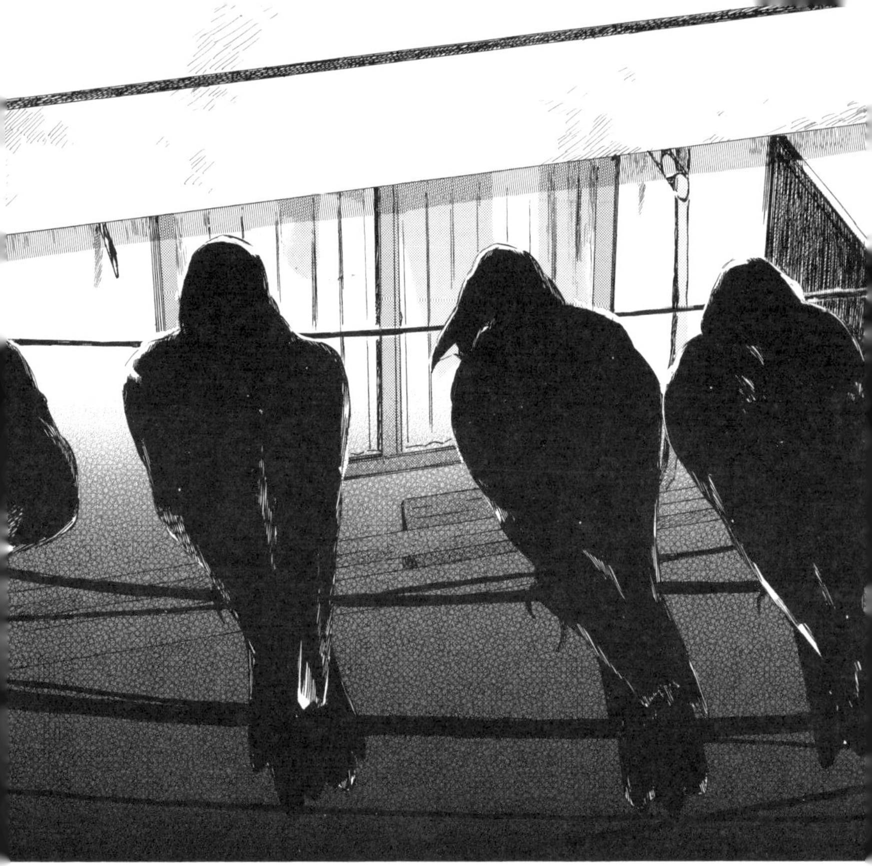

Chapter 3 End

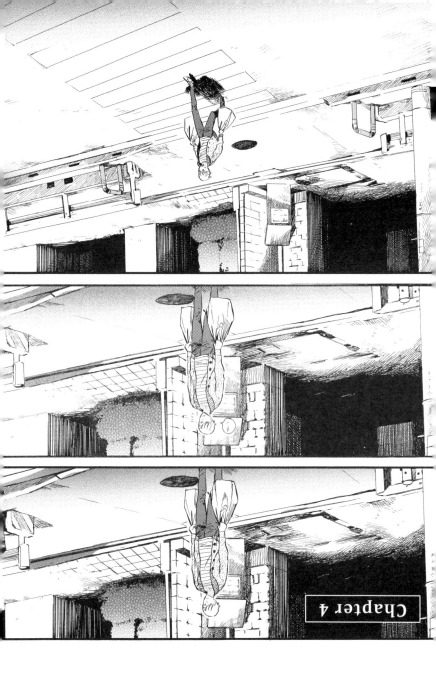

Chapter 4

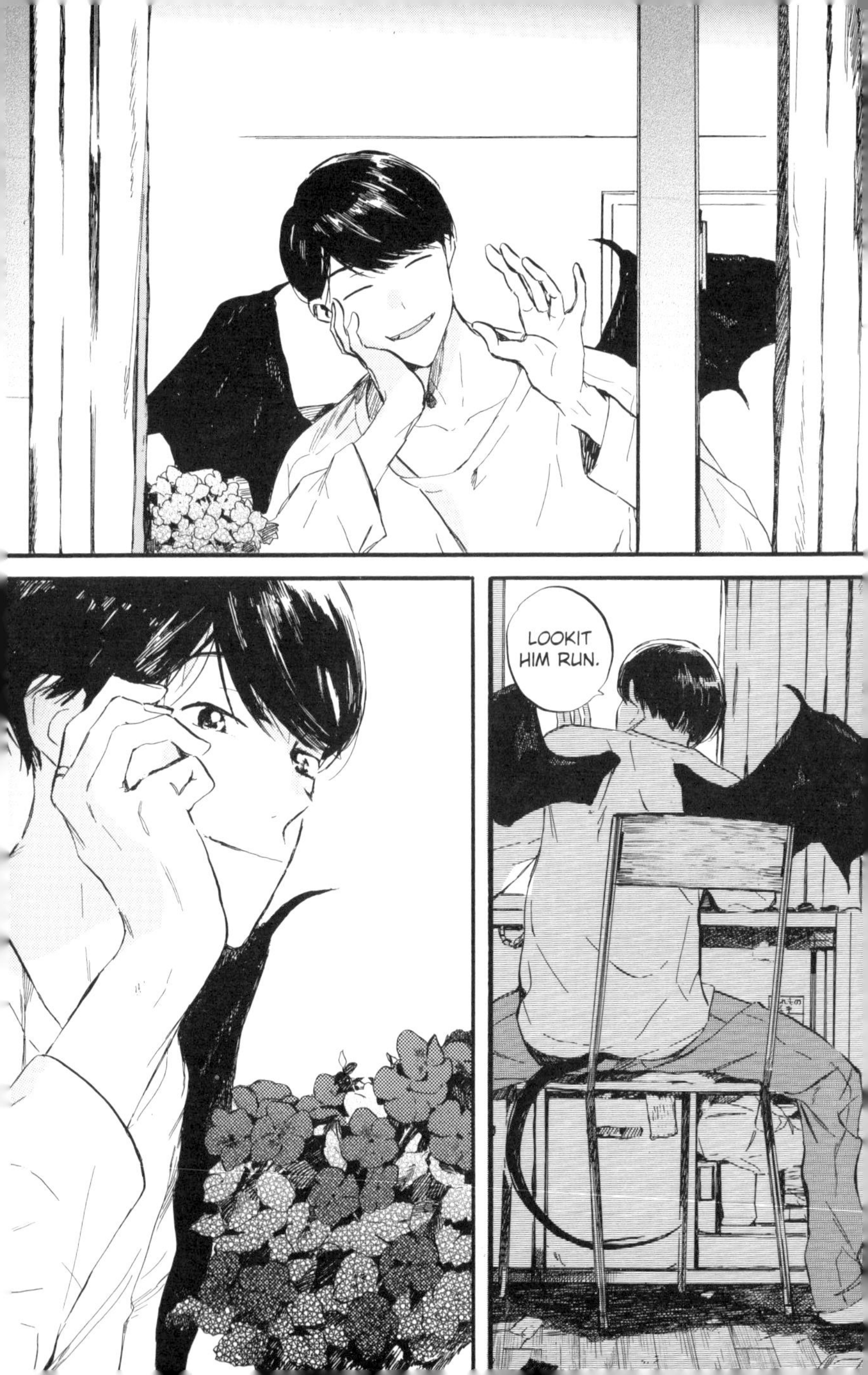
LOOKIT
HIM RUN.

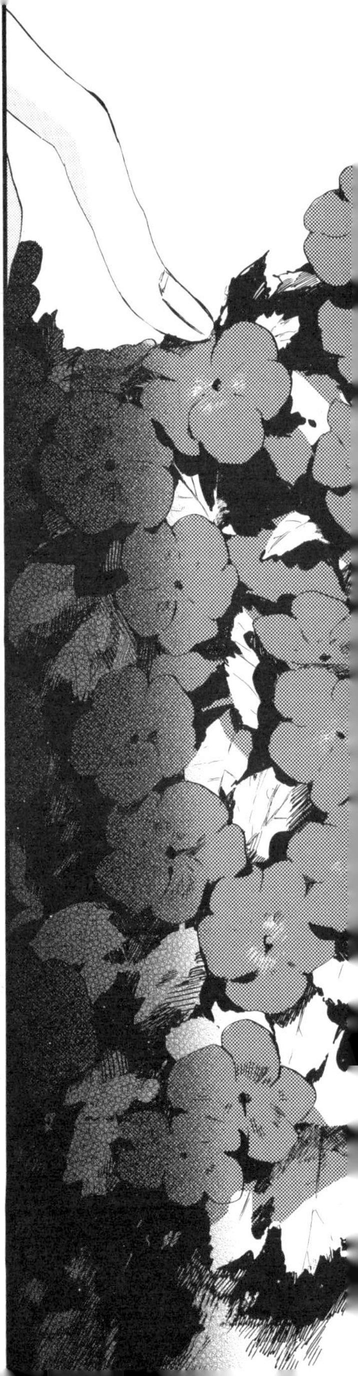

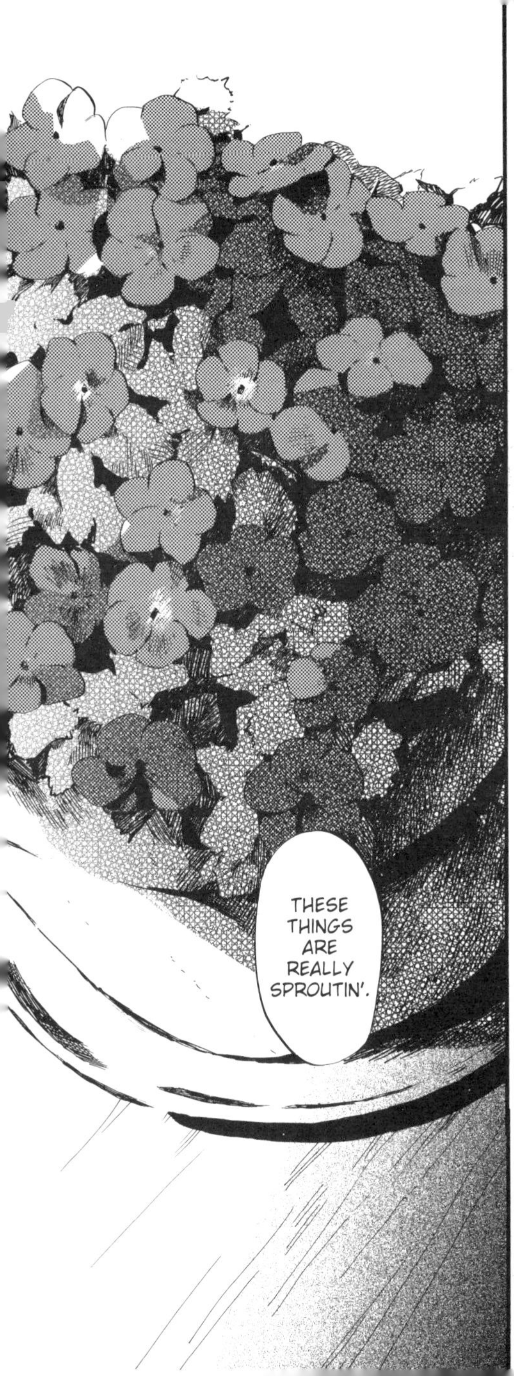
THESE THINGS ARE REALLY SPROUTIN'.

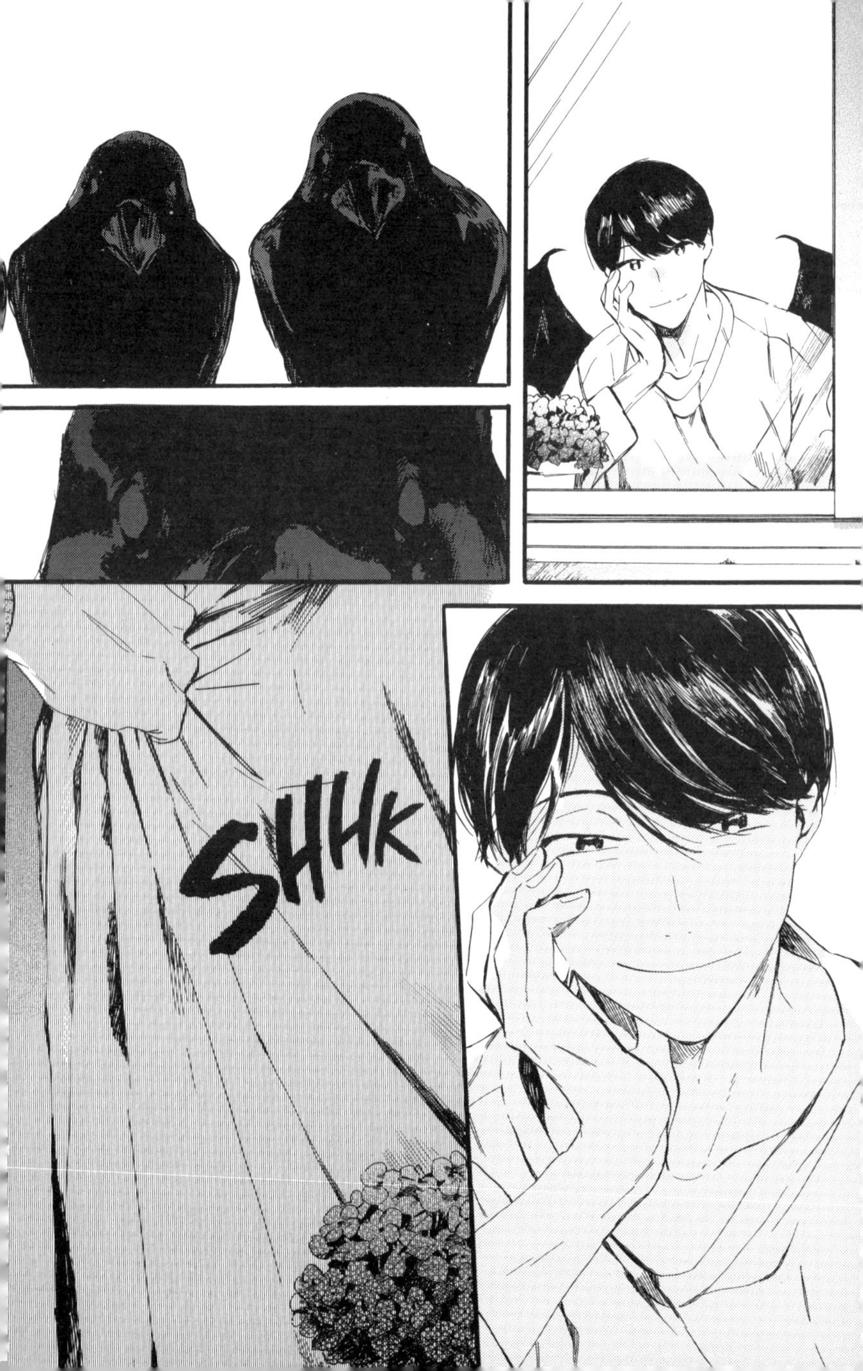
SHHK

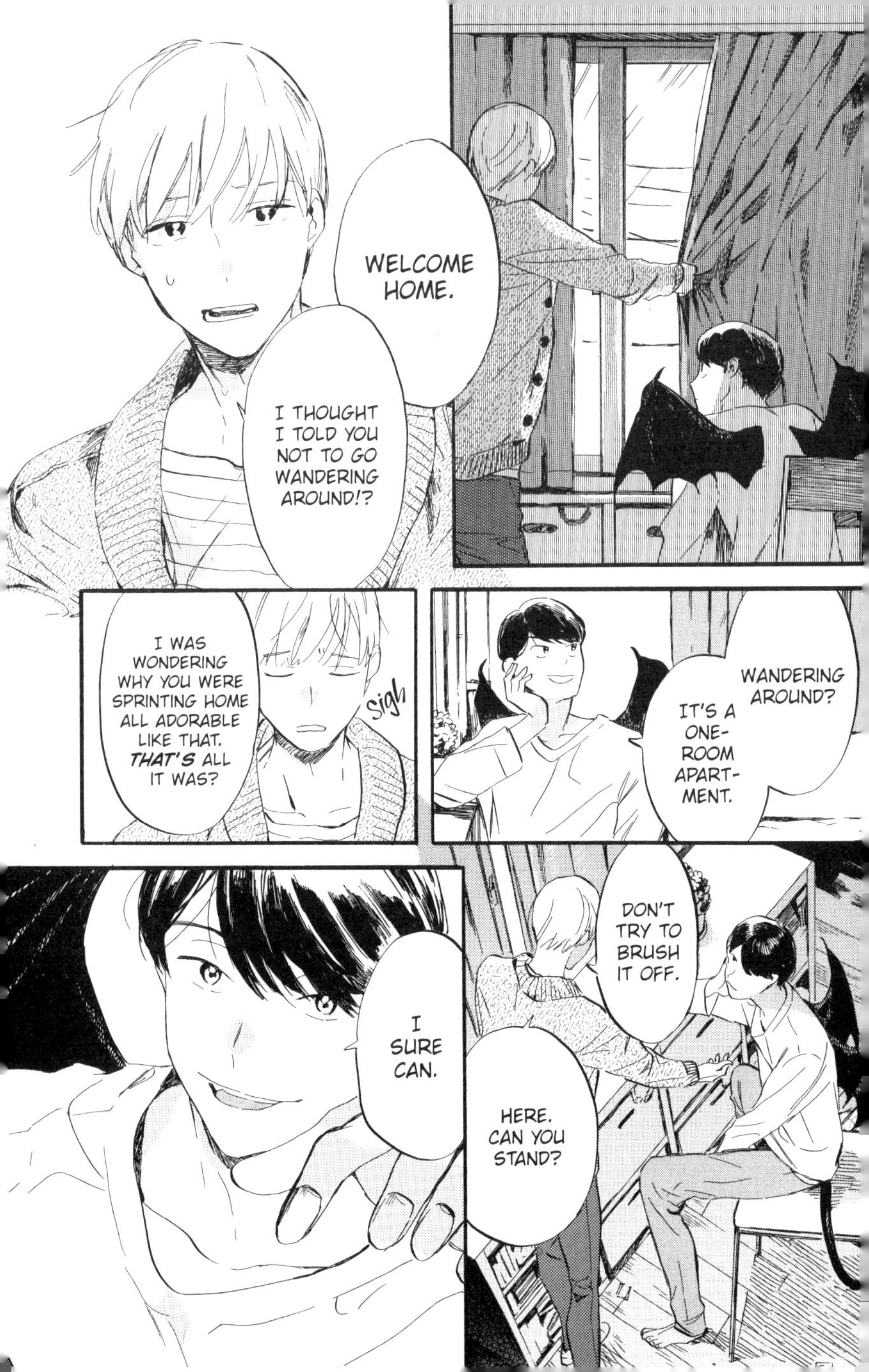
WELCOME HOME.
I THOUGHT I TOLD YOU NOT TO GO WANDERING AROUND!?
WANDERING AROUND?
IT'S A ONE-ROOM APARTMENT.
I WAS WONDERING WHY YOU WERE SPRINTING HOME ALL ADORABLE LIKE THAT. *THAT'S* ALL IT WAS?
Sigh
DON'T TRY TO BRUSH IT OFF.
HERE. CAN YOU STAND?
I SURE CAN.

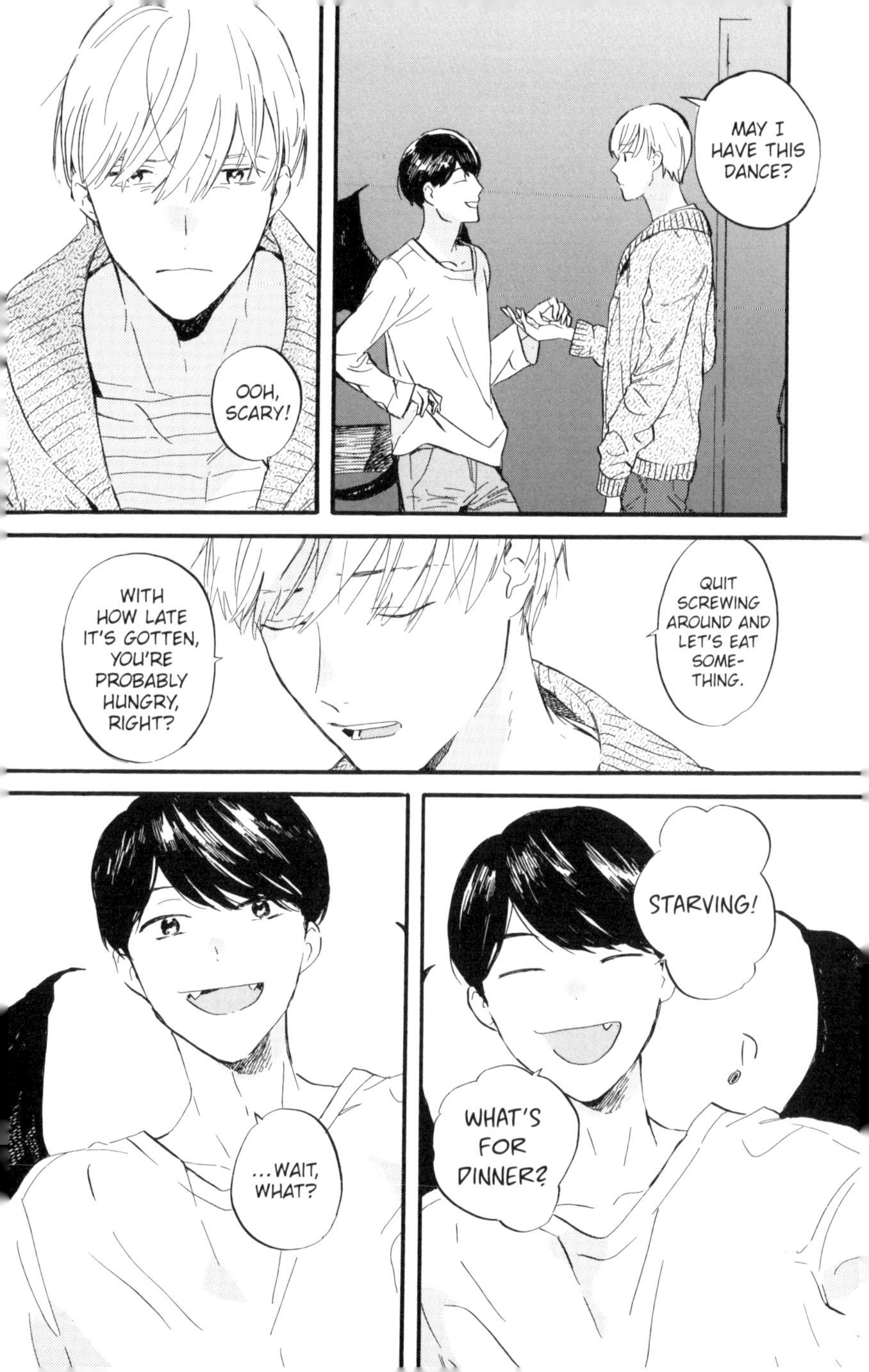
MAY I HAVE THIS DANCE?
OOH, SCARY!
QUIT SCREWING AROUND AND LET'S EAT SOME-THING.
WITH HOW LATE IT'S GOTTEN, YOU'RE PROBABLY HUNGRY, RIGHT?
STARVING!
WHAT'S FOR DINNER?
...WAIT, WHAT?

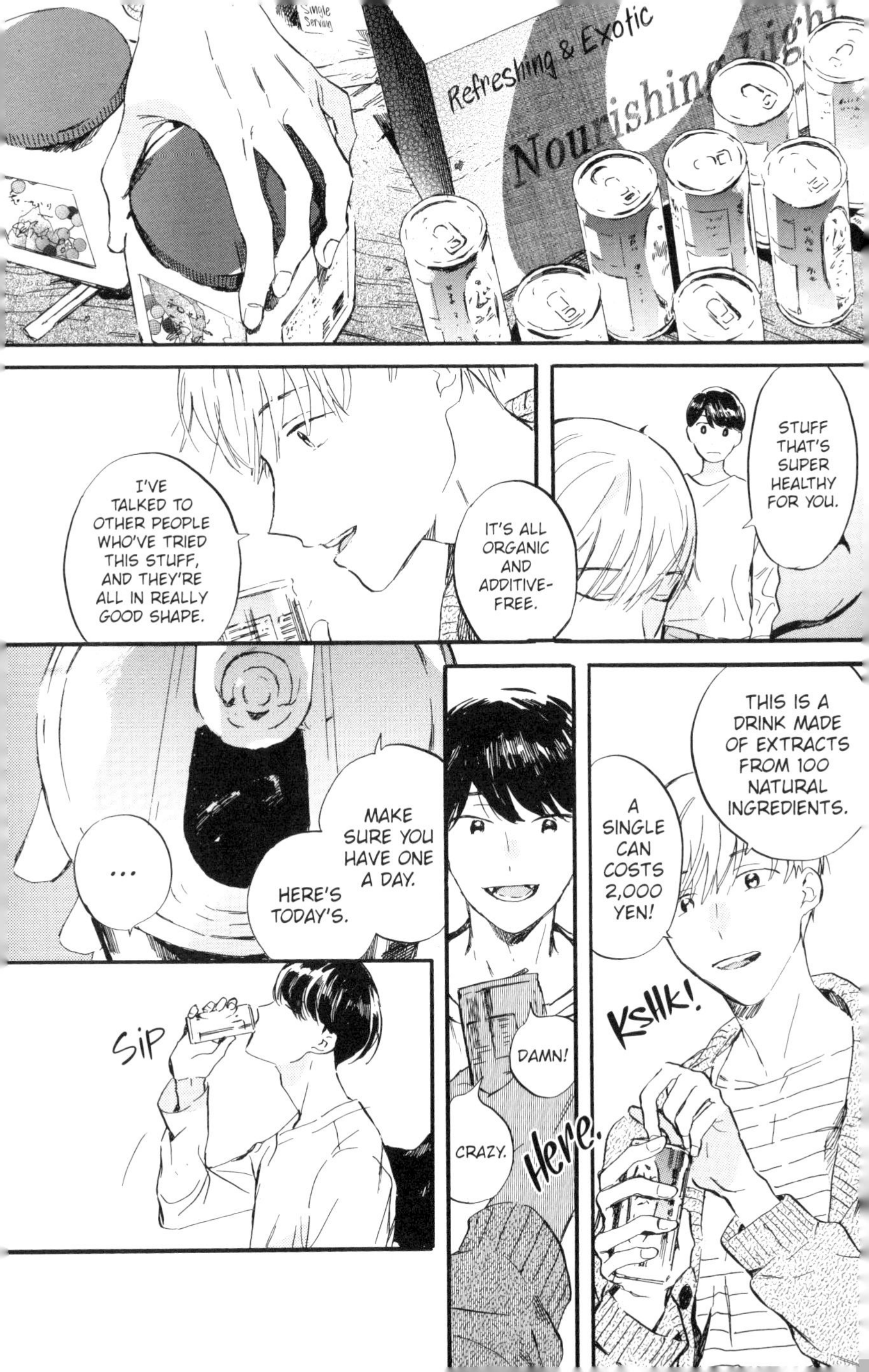
Single Serving
Refreshing & Exotic
Nourishing
STUFF THAT'S SUPER HEALTHY FOR YOU.
IT'S ALL ORGANIC AND ADDITIVE-FREE.
I'VE TALKED TO OTHER PEOPLE WHO'VE TRIED THIS STUFF, AND THEY'RE ALL IN REALLY GOOD SHAPE.
THIS IS A DRINK MADE OF EXTRACTS FROM 100 NATURAL INGREDIENTS.
A SINGLE CAN COSTS 2,000 YEN!
KSHK!
Here.
DAMN!
CRAZY.
MAKE SURE YOU HAVE ONE A DAY.
HERE'S TODAY'S.
...
SIP

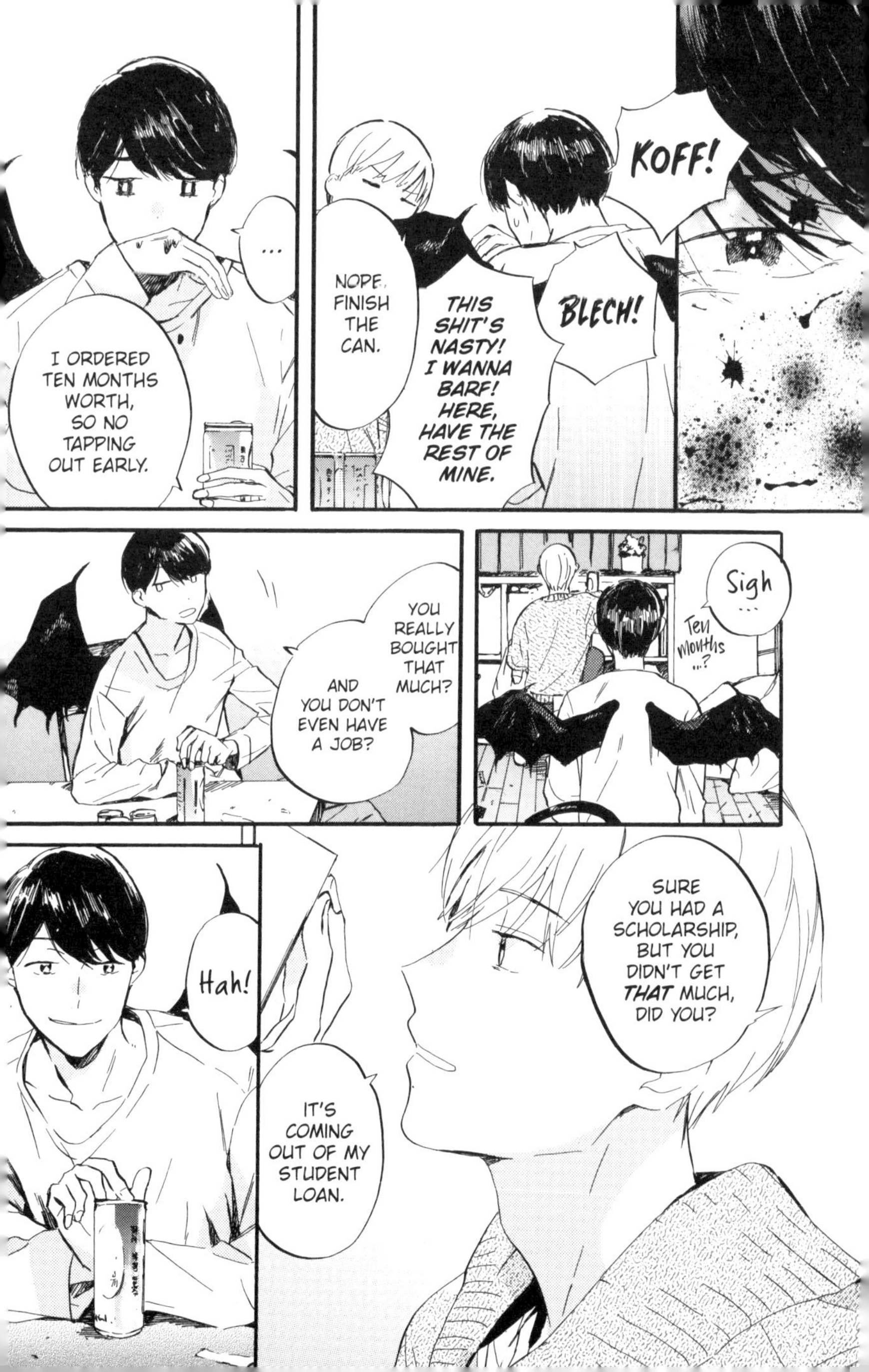
KOFF!
BLECH!
THIS SHIT'S NASTY! I WANNA BARF! HERE, HAVE THE REST OF MINE.
NOPE. FINISH THE CAN.
...
I ORDERED TEN MONTHS WORTH, SO NO TAPPING OUT EARLY.
Sigh ...
Ten months ...?
YOU REALLY BOUGHT THAT MUCH?
AND YOU DON'T EVEN HAVE A JOB?
SURE YOU HAD A SCHOLARSHIP, BUT YOU DIDN'T GET THAT MUCH, DID YOU?
IT'S COMING OUT OF MY STUDENT LOAN.
Hah!

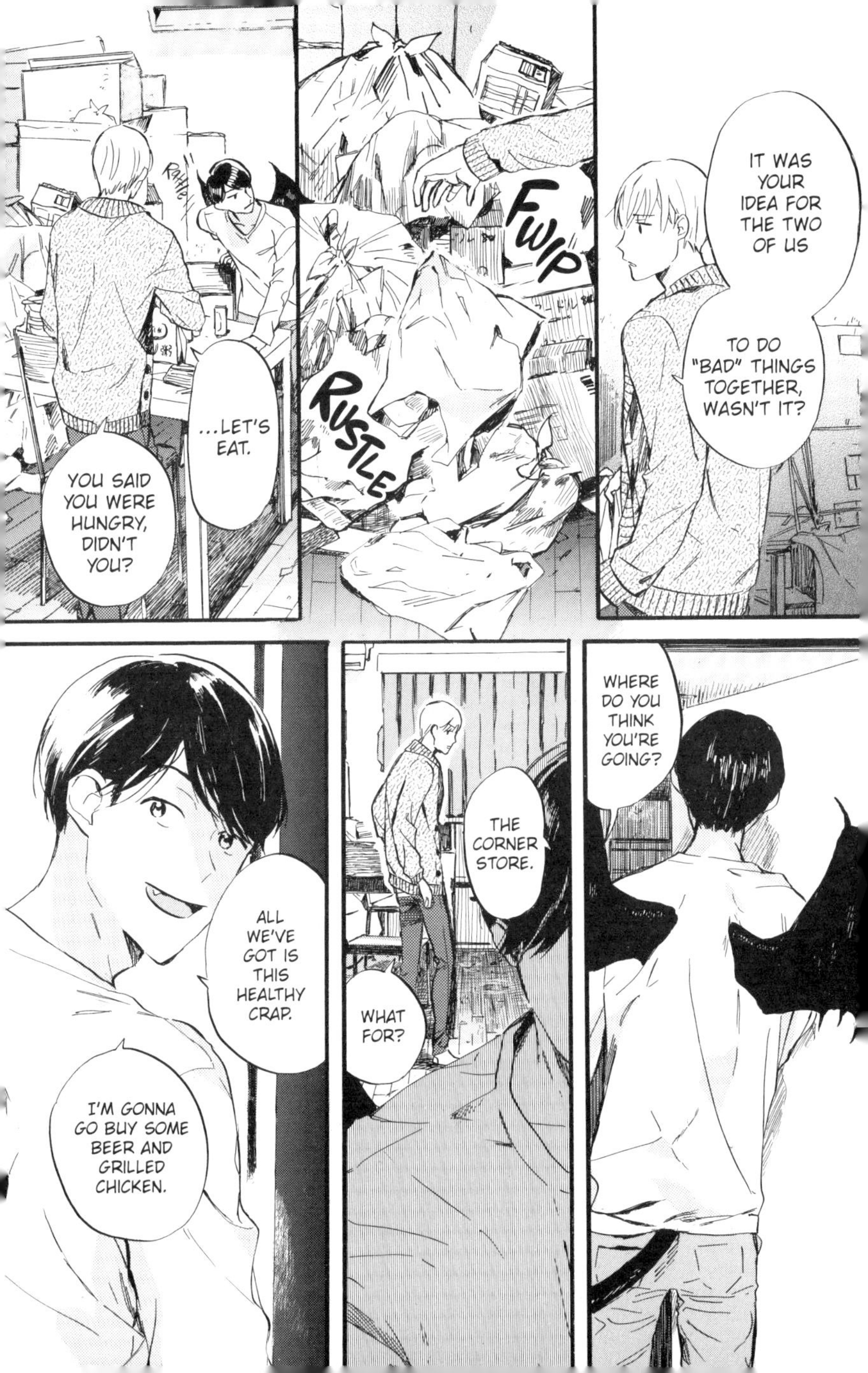
IT WAS YOUR IDEA FOR THE TWO OF US
TO DO "BAD" THINGS TOGETHER, WASN'T IT?
FWIP
RUSTLE
...LET'S EAT.
YOU SAID YOU WERE HUNGRY, DIDN'T YOU?
RATTLE
WHERE DO YOU THINK YOU'RE GOING?
THE CORNER STORE.
WHAT FOR?
ALL WE'VE GOT IS THIS HEALTHY CRAP.
I'M GONNA GO BUY SOME BEER AND GRILLED CHICKEN.

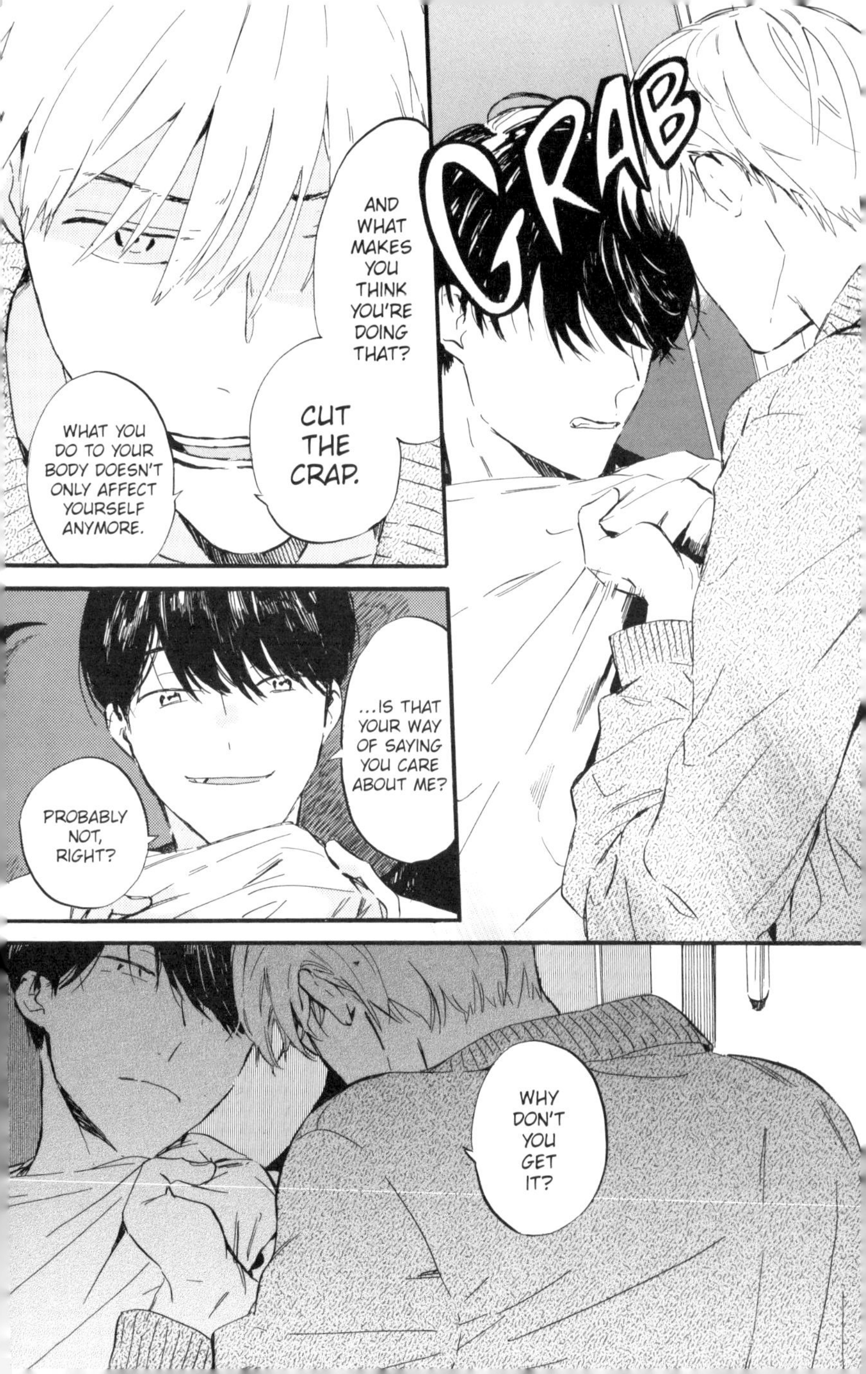
GRAB
AND WHAT MAKES YOU THINK YOU'RE DOING THAT?
CUT THE CRAP.
WHAT YOU DO TO YOUR BODY DOESN'T ONLY AFFECT YOURSELF ANYMORE.
...IS THAT YOUR WAY OF SAYING YOU CARE ABOUT ME?
PROBABLY NOT, RIGHT?
WHY DON'T YOU GET IT?

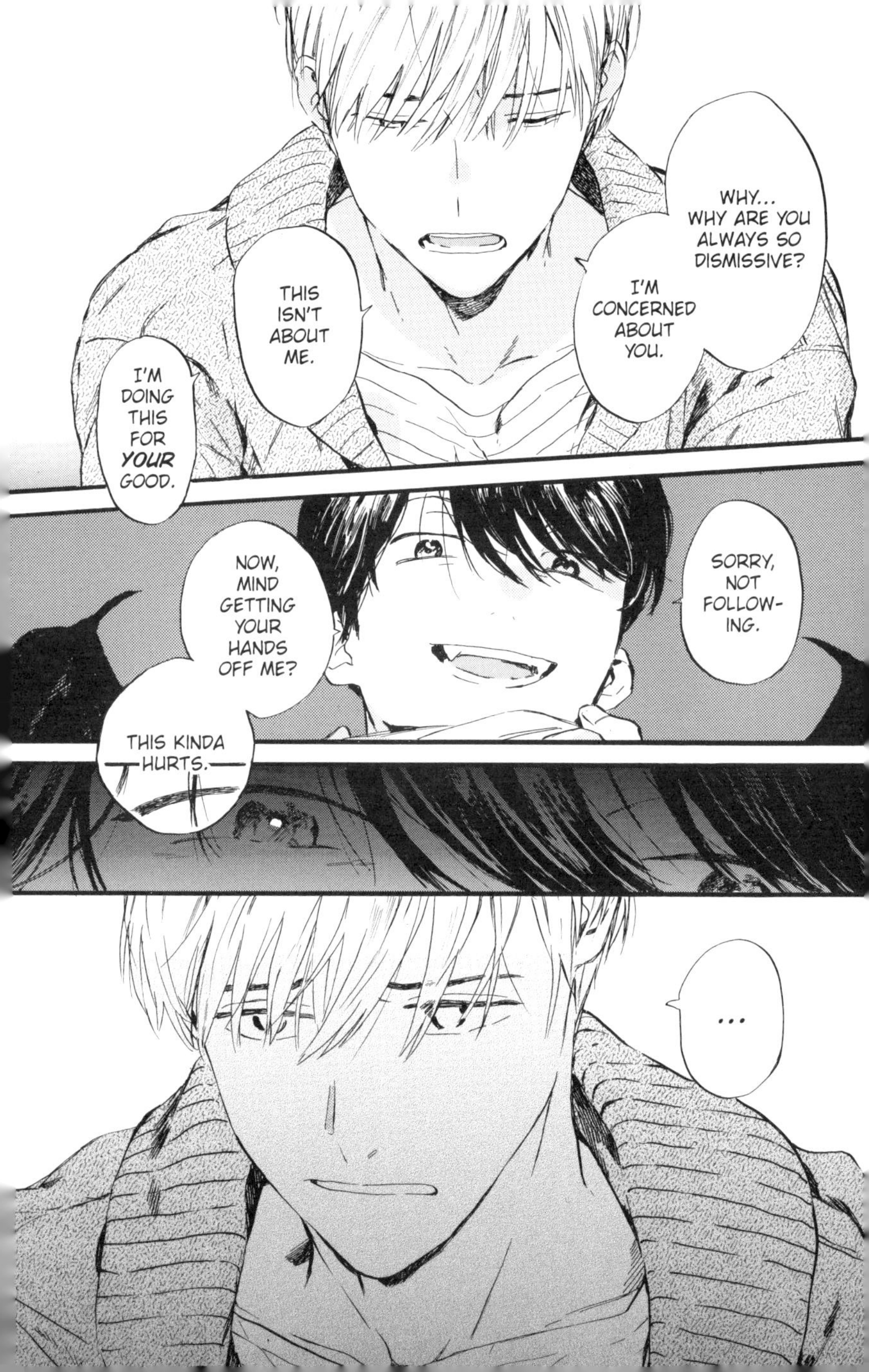
WHY... WHY ARE YOU ALWAYS SO DISMISSIVE?
I'M CONCERNED ABOUT YOU.
THIS ISN'T ABOUT ME.
I'M DOING THIS FOR **YOUR** GOOD.
SORRY, NOT FOLLOW-ING.
NOW, MIND GETTING YOUR HANDS OFF ME?
THIS KINDA HURTS.
...

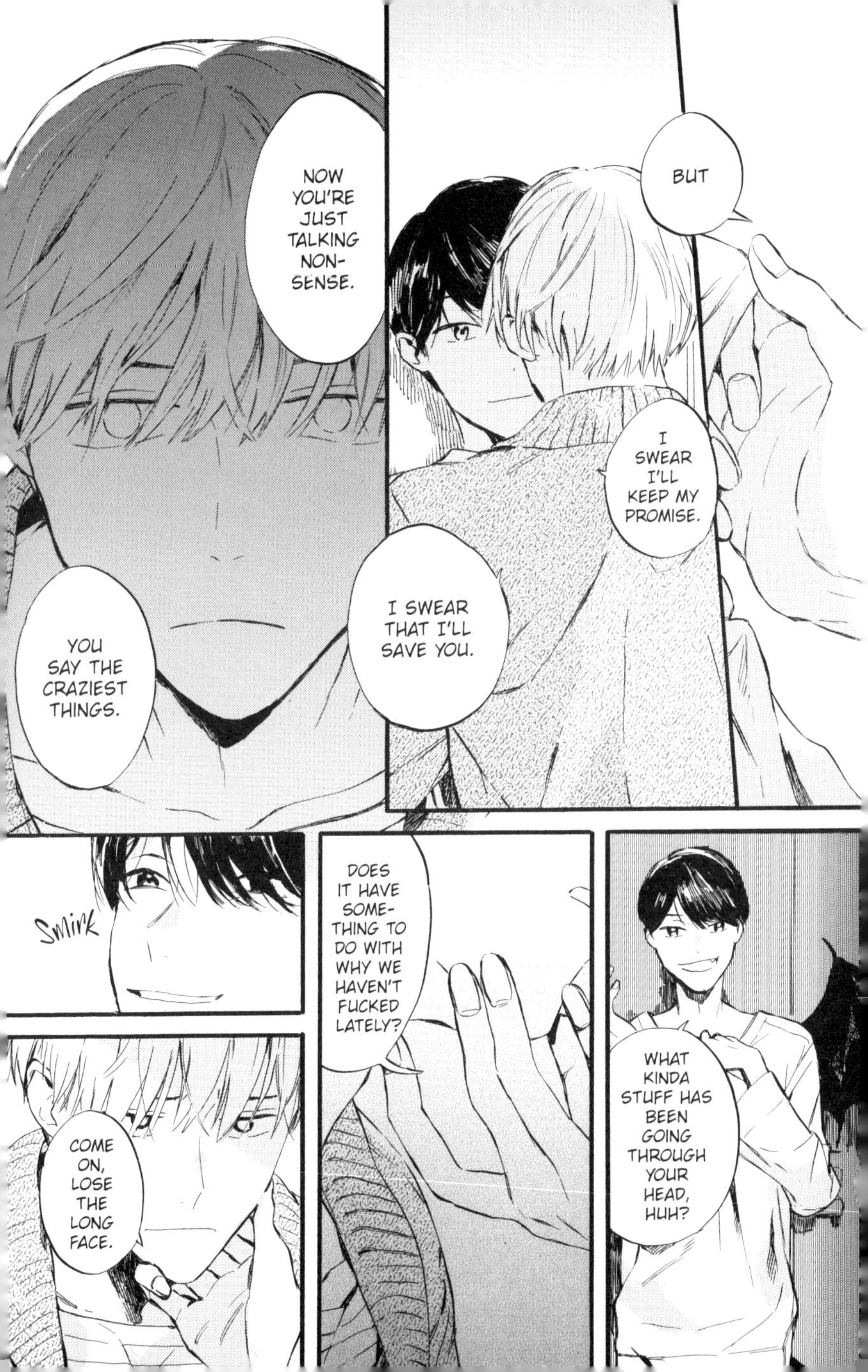
BUT
I SWEAR I'LL KEEP MY PROMISE.
I SWEAR THAT I'LL SAVE YOU.
NOW YOU'RE JUST TALKING NON-SENSE.
YOU SAY THE CRAZIEST THINGS.
WHAT KINDA STUFF HAS BEEN GOING THROUGH YOUR HEAD, HUH?
DOES IT HAVE SOME-THING TO DO WITH WHY WE HAVEN'T FUCKED LATELY?
Smirk
COME ON, LOSE THE LONG FACE.

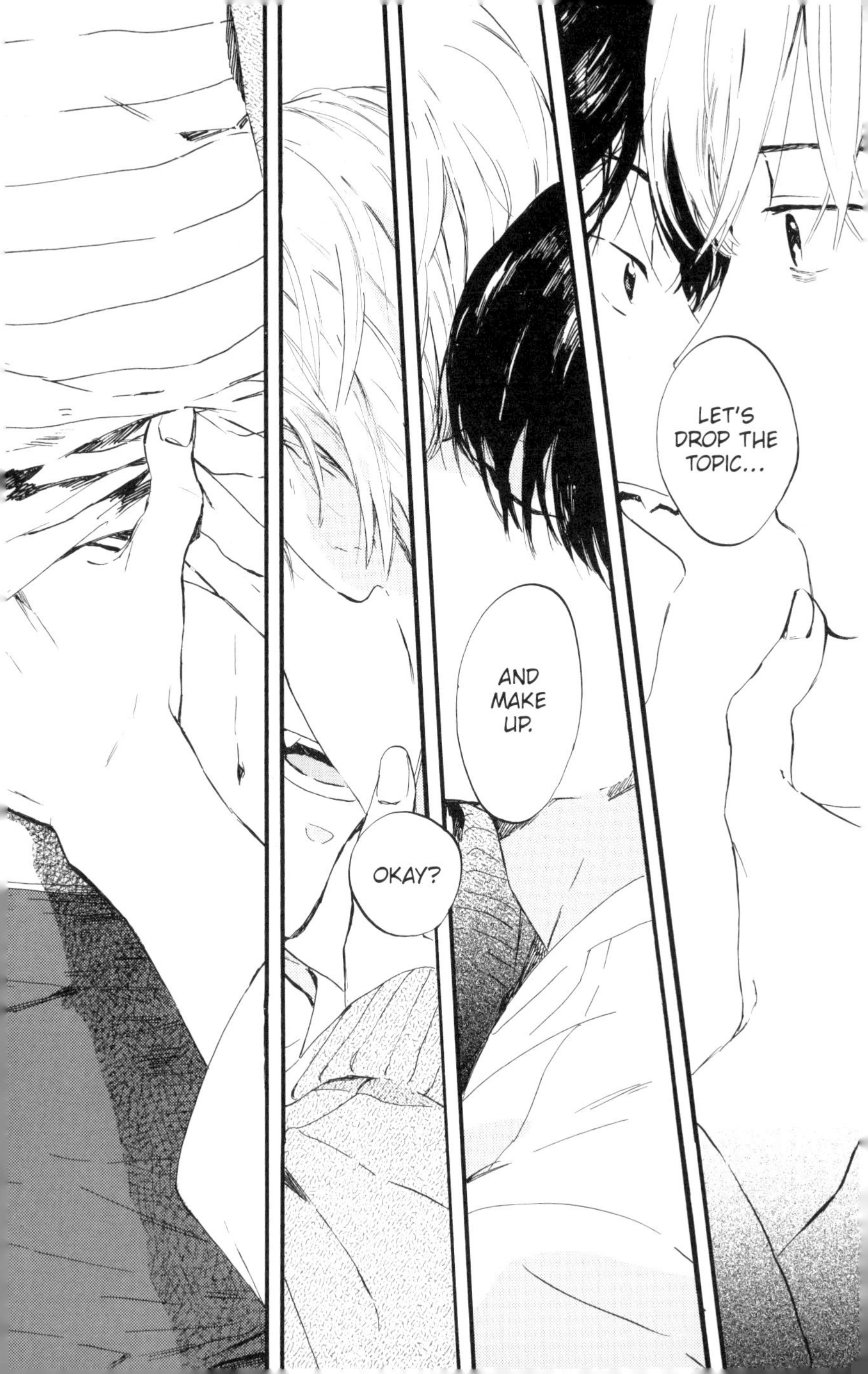
LET'S DROP THE TOPIC...
AND MAKE UP.
OKAY?

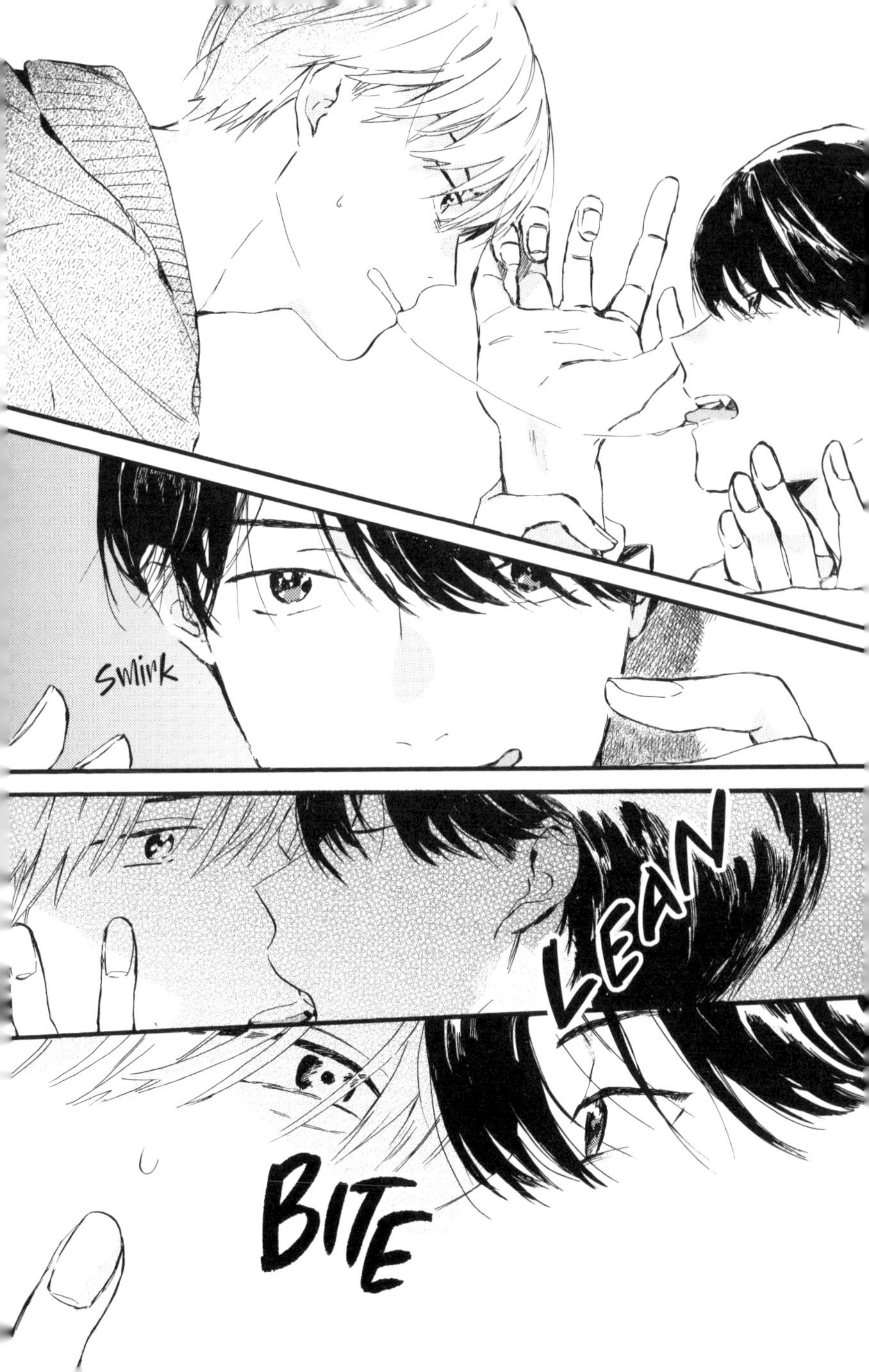
swirk
LEAN
BITE

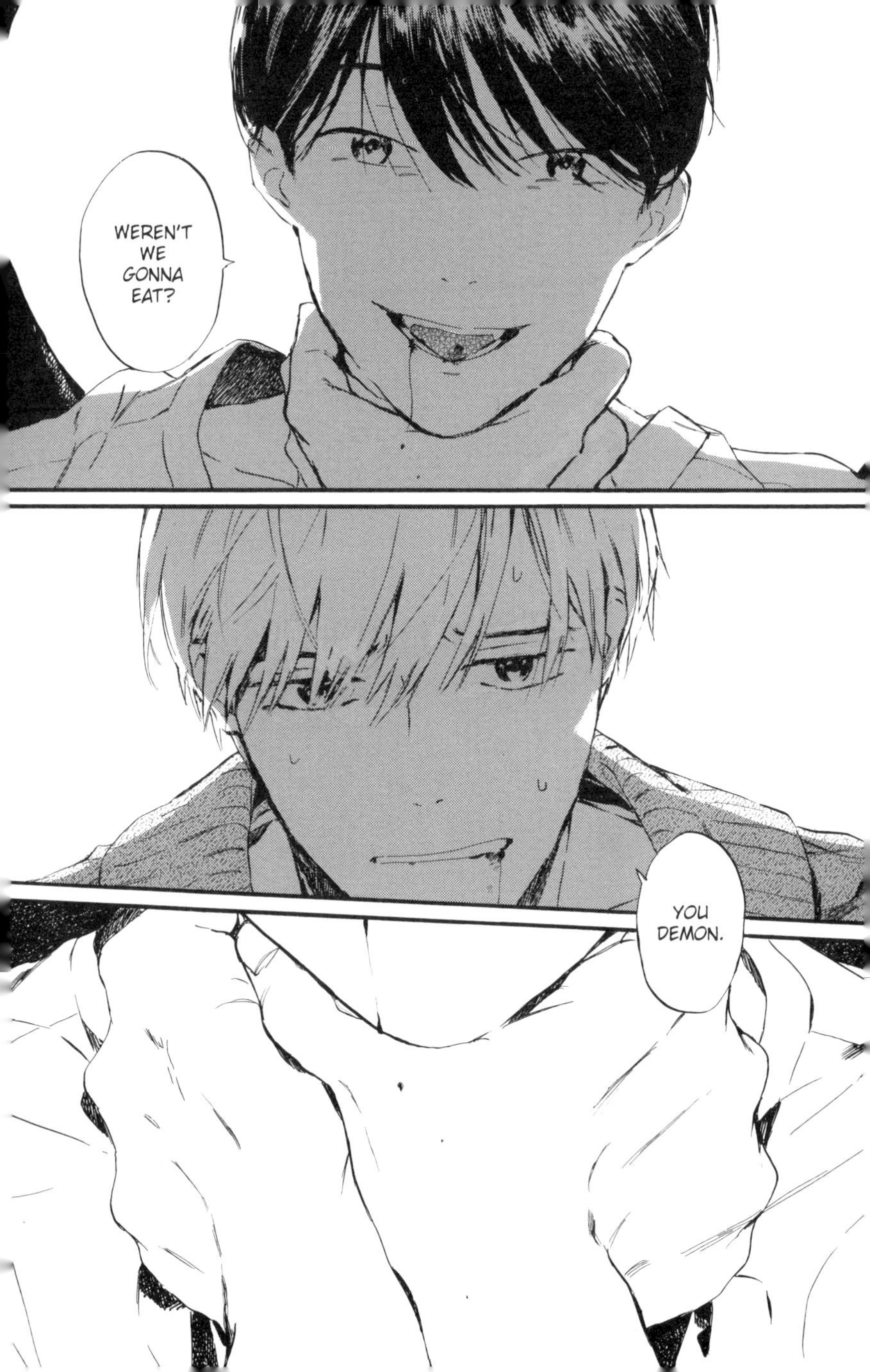
WEREN'T WE GONNA EAT?
YOU DEMON.

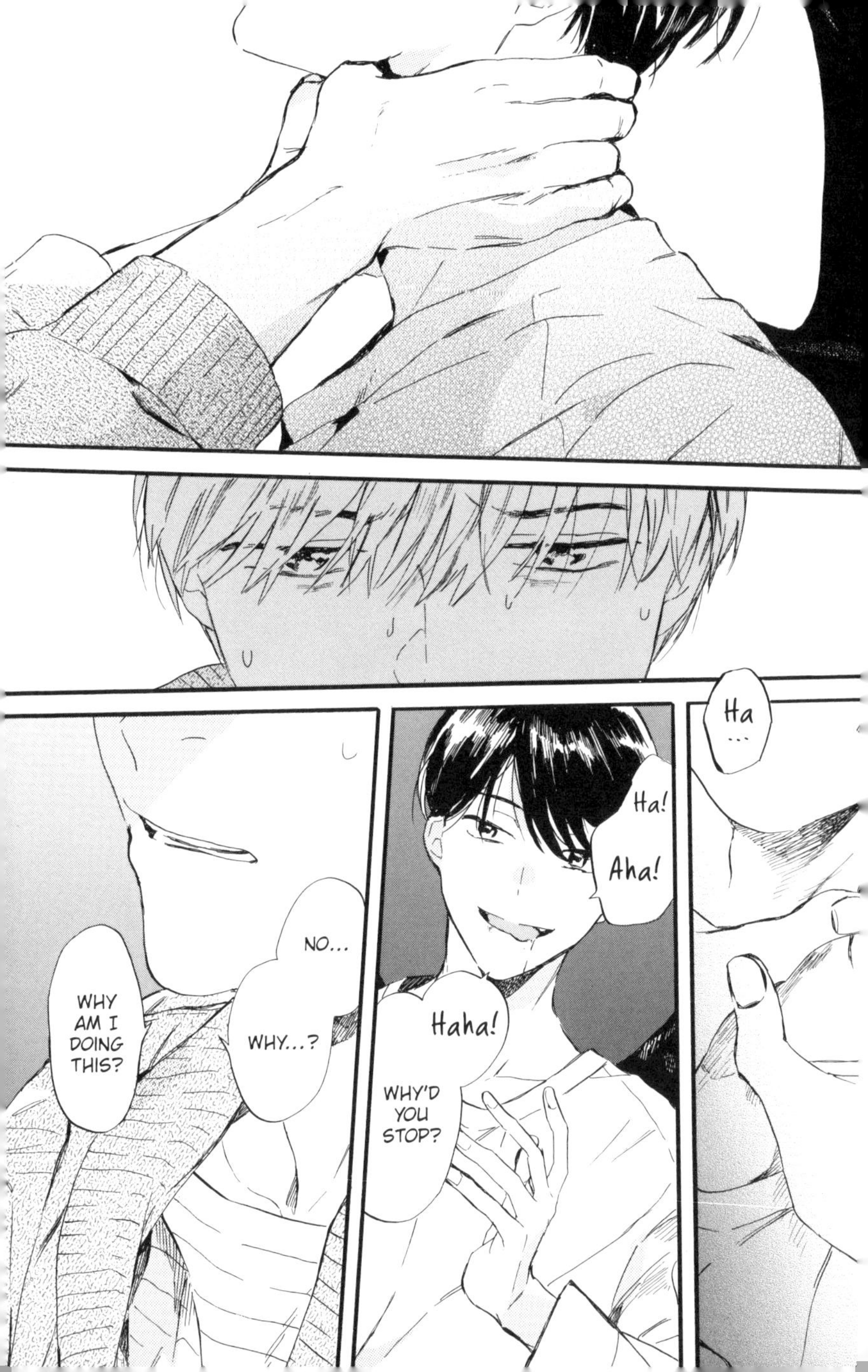
Ha...
Ha!
Aha!
Haha!
WHY'D YOU STOP?
NO...
WHY...?
WHY AM I DOING THIS?

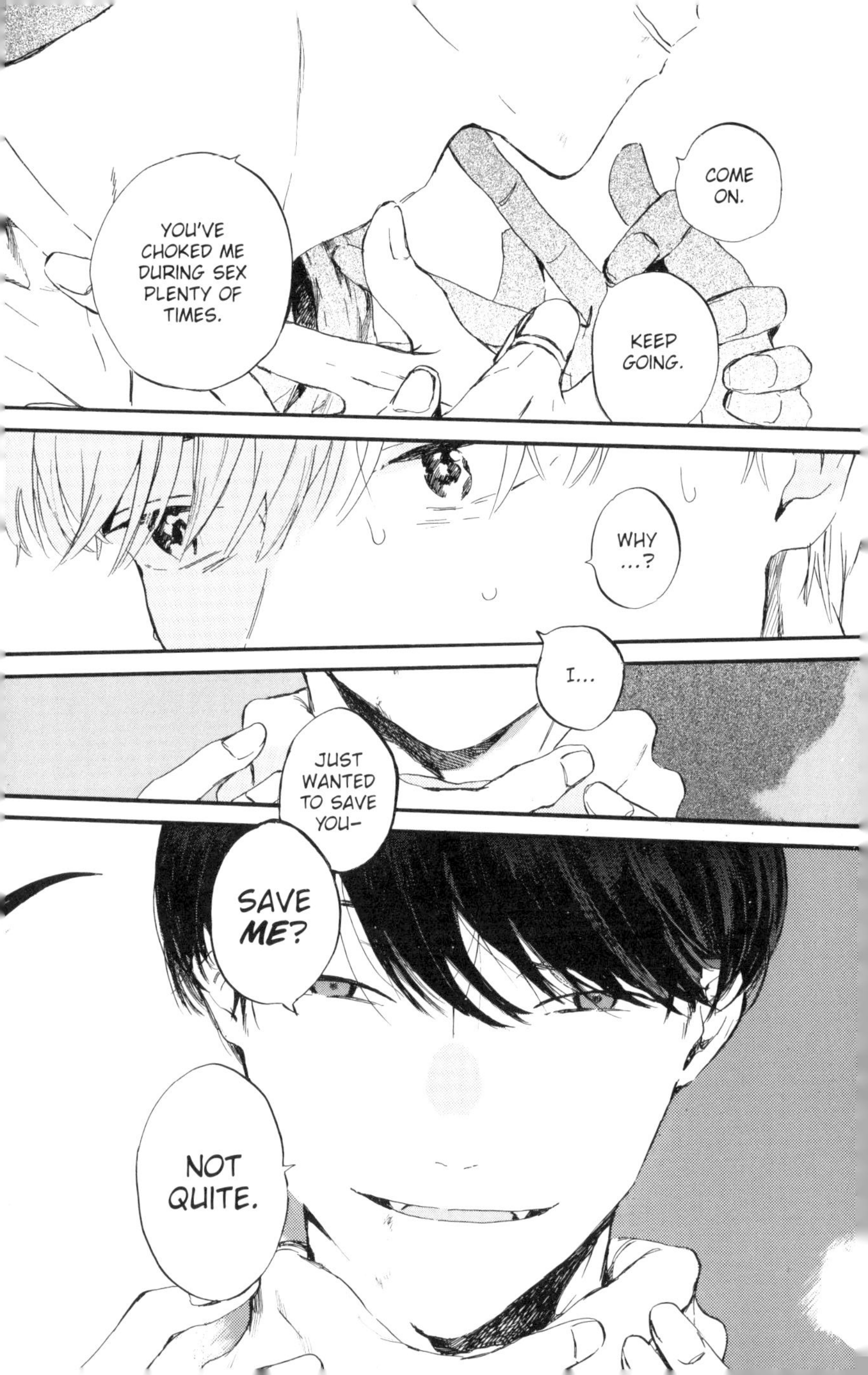
COME ON.
KEEP GOING.
YOU'VE CHOKED ME DURING SEX PLENTY OF TIMES.
WHY ...?
I...
JUST WANTED TO SAVE YOU–
SAVE *ME*?
NOT QUITE.

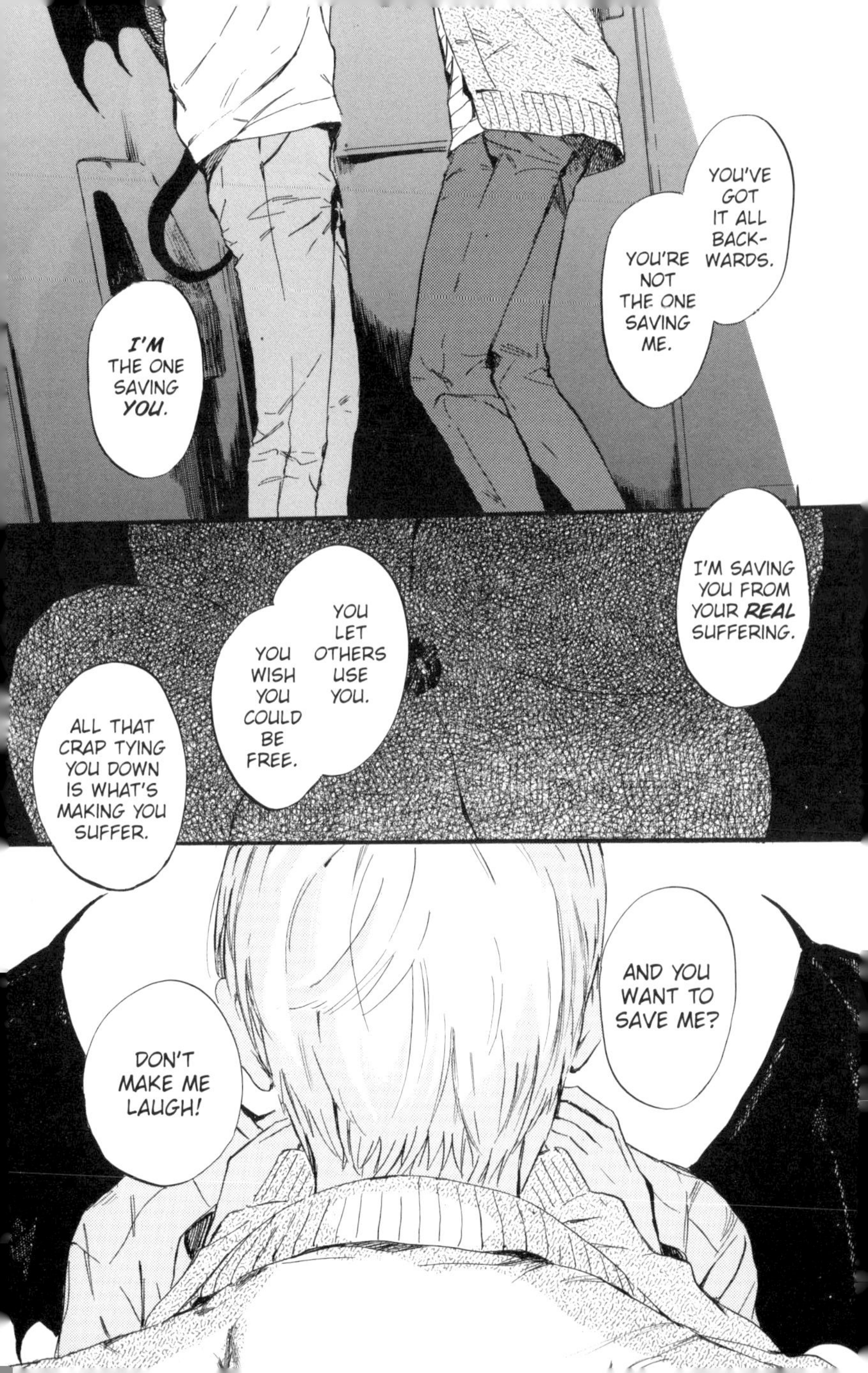
YOU'VE GOT IT ALL BACK-WARDS.
YOU'RE NOT THE ONE SAVING ME.
I'M THE ONE SAVING *YOU*.
I'M SAVING YOU FROM YOUR ***REAL*** SUFFERING.
YOU LET OTHERS USE YOU.
YOU WISH YOU COULD BE FREE.
ALL THAT CRAP TYING YOU DOWN IS WHAT'S MAKING YOU SUFFER.
AND YOU WANT TO SAVE ME?
DON'T MAKE ME LAUGH!

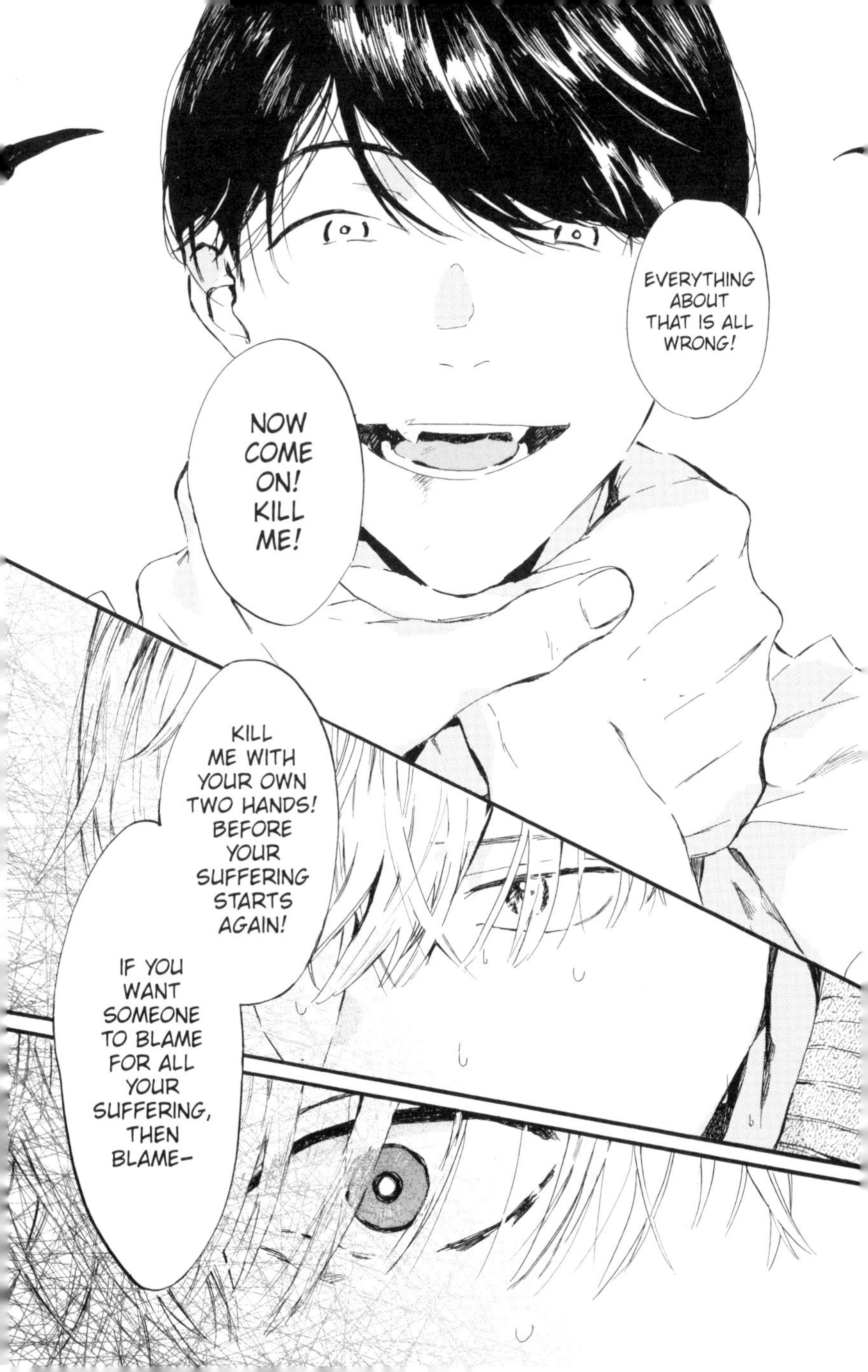
EVERYTHING ABOUT THAT IS ALL WRONG!
NOW COME ON! KILL ME!
KILL ME WITH YOUR OWN TWO HANDS! BEFORE YOUR SUFFERING STARTS AGAIN!
IF YOU WANT SOMEONE TO BLAME FOR ALL YOUR SUFFERING, THEN BLAME-

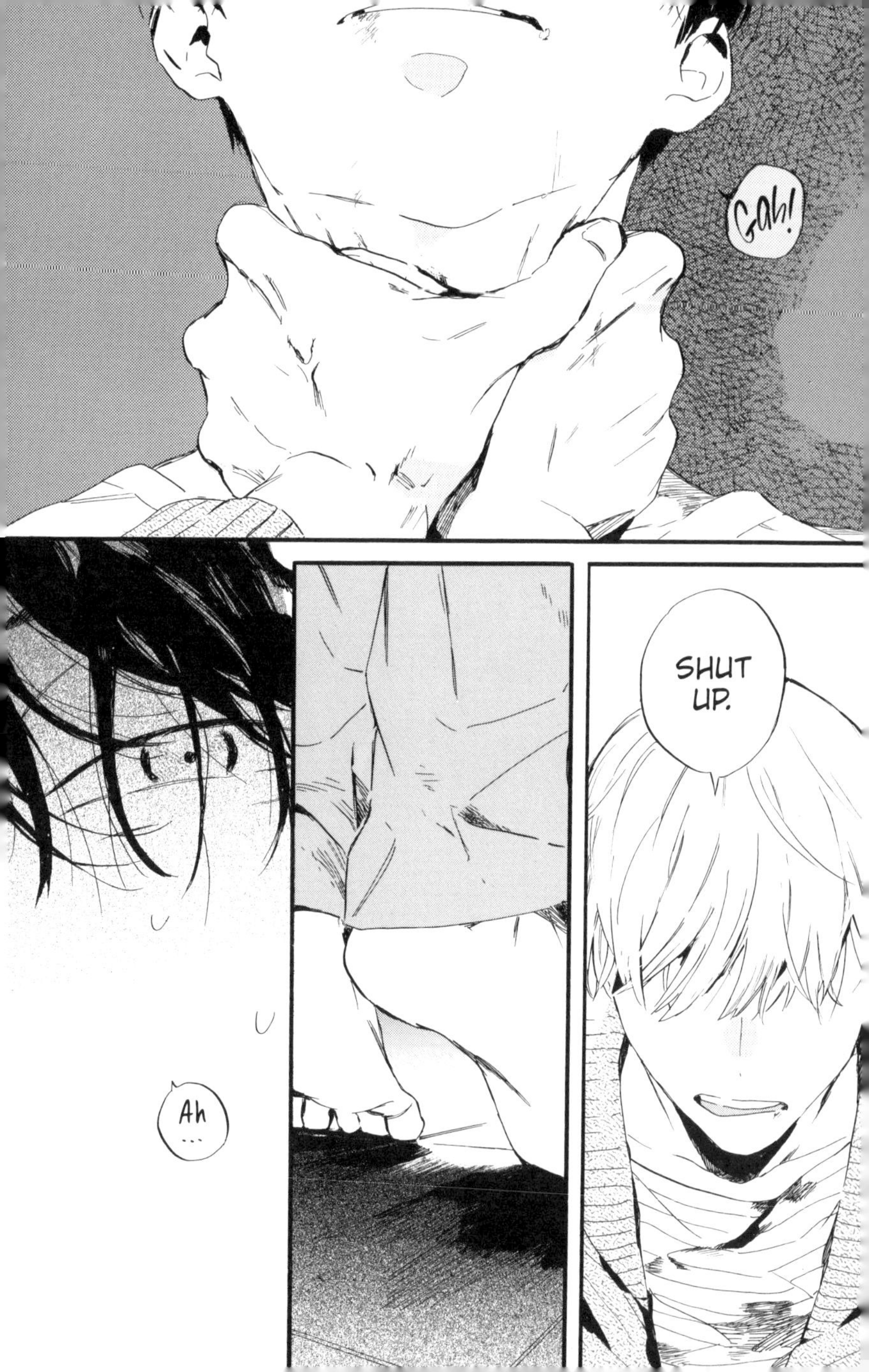
Gah!
SHUT UP.
Ah ...

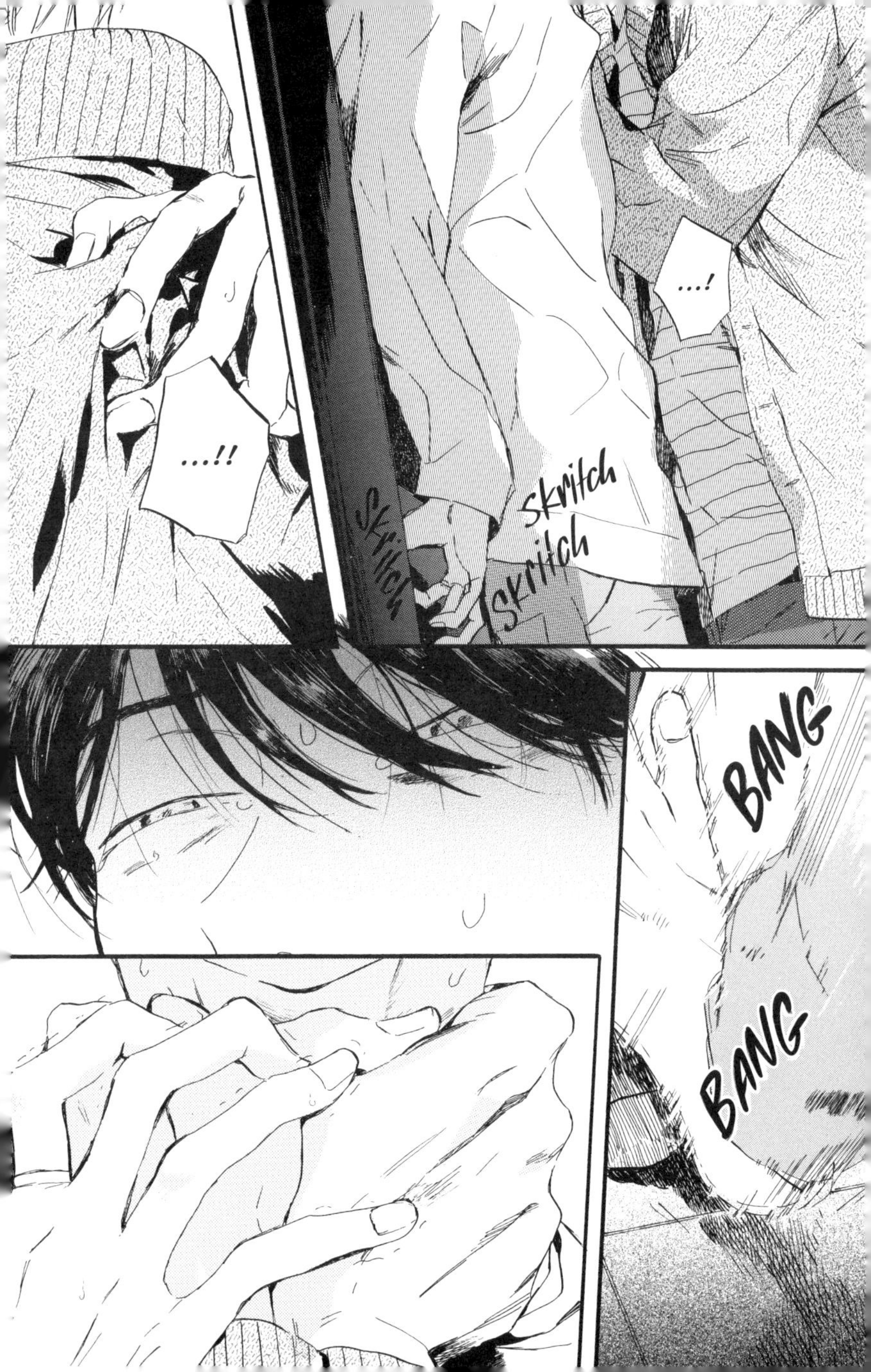

...!
skritch
skritch
skritch
...!!
BANG
BANG

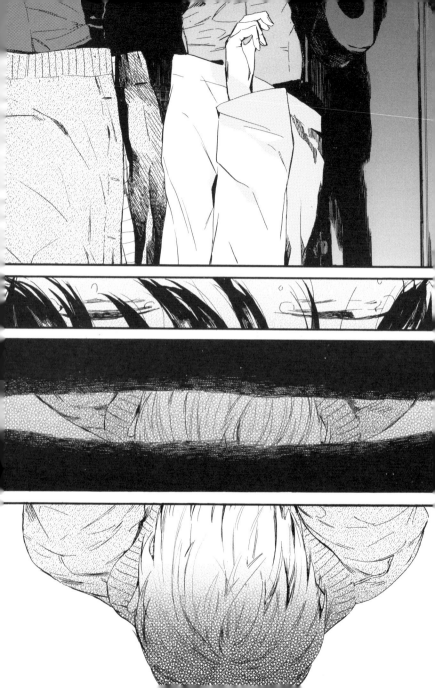

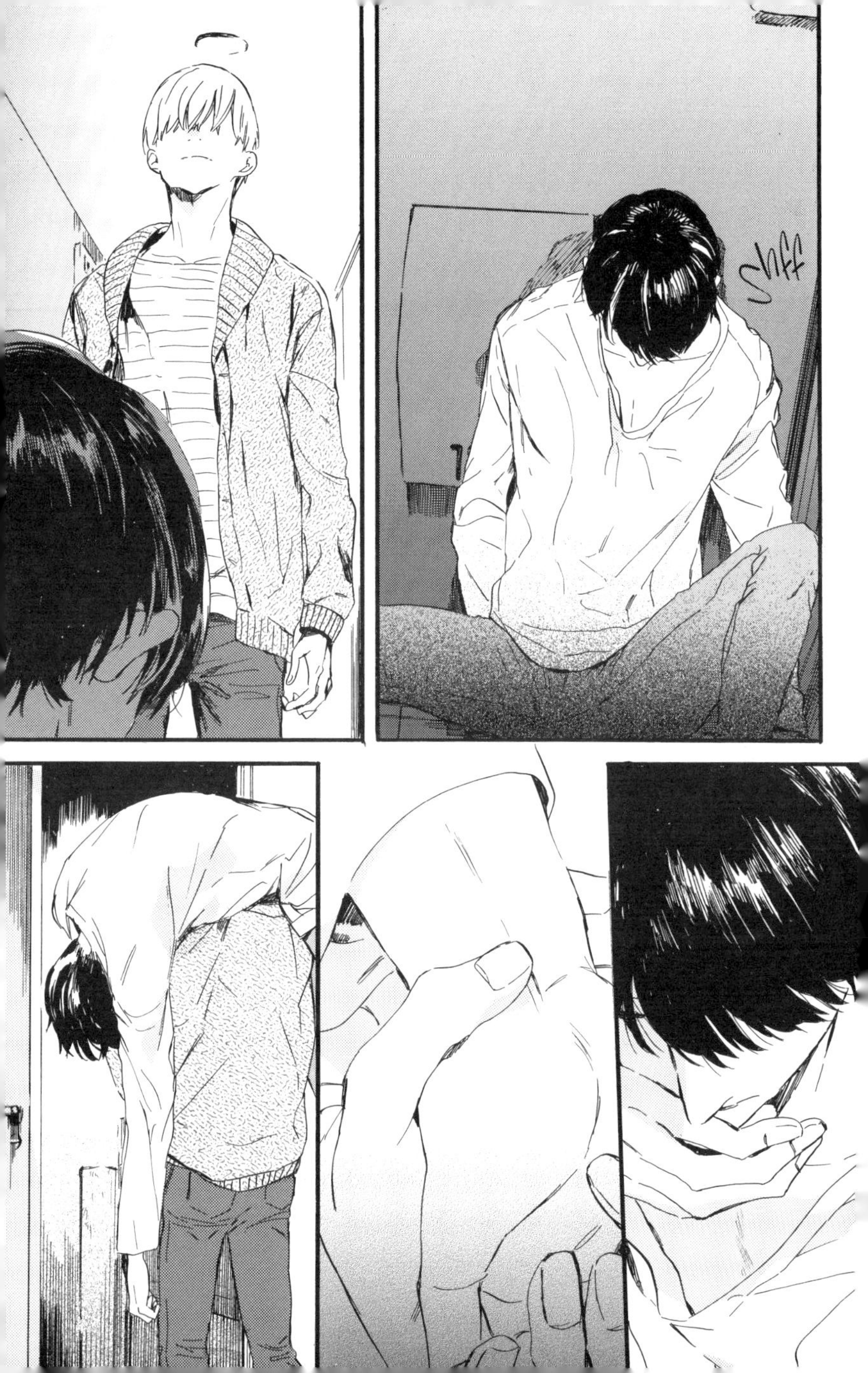
shff

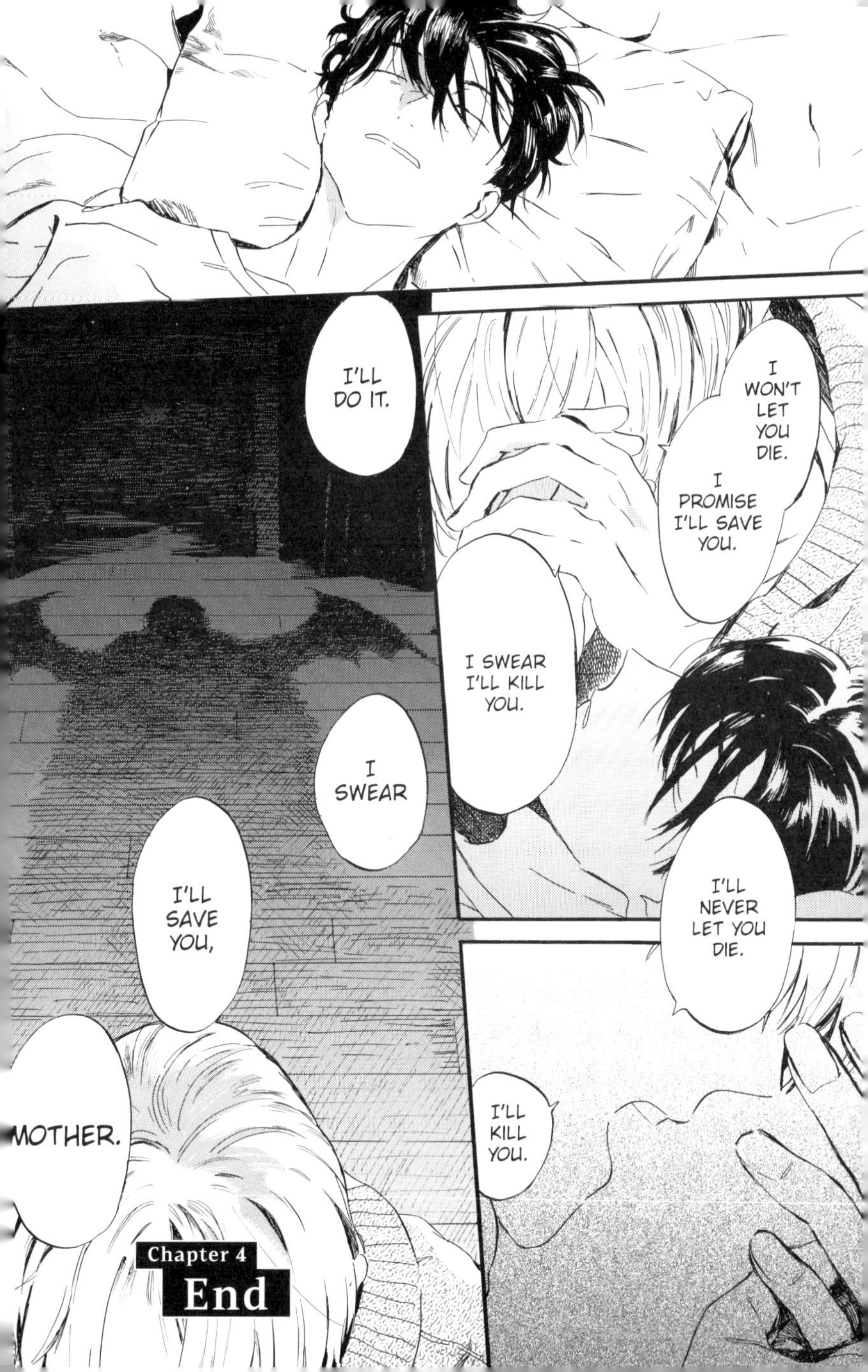
I WON'T LET YOU DIE.
I PROMISE I'LL SAVE YOU.
I SWEAR I'LL KILL YOU.
I'LL NEVER LET YOU DIE.
I'LL KILL YOU.
I'LL DO IT.
I SWEAR
I'LL SAVE YOU,
MOTHER.
Chapter 4 End

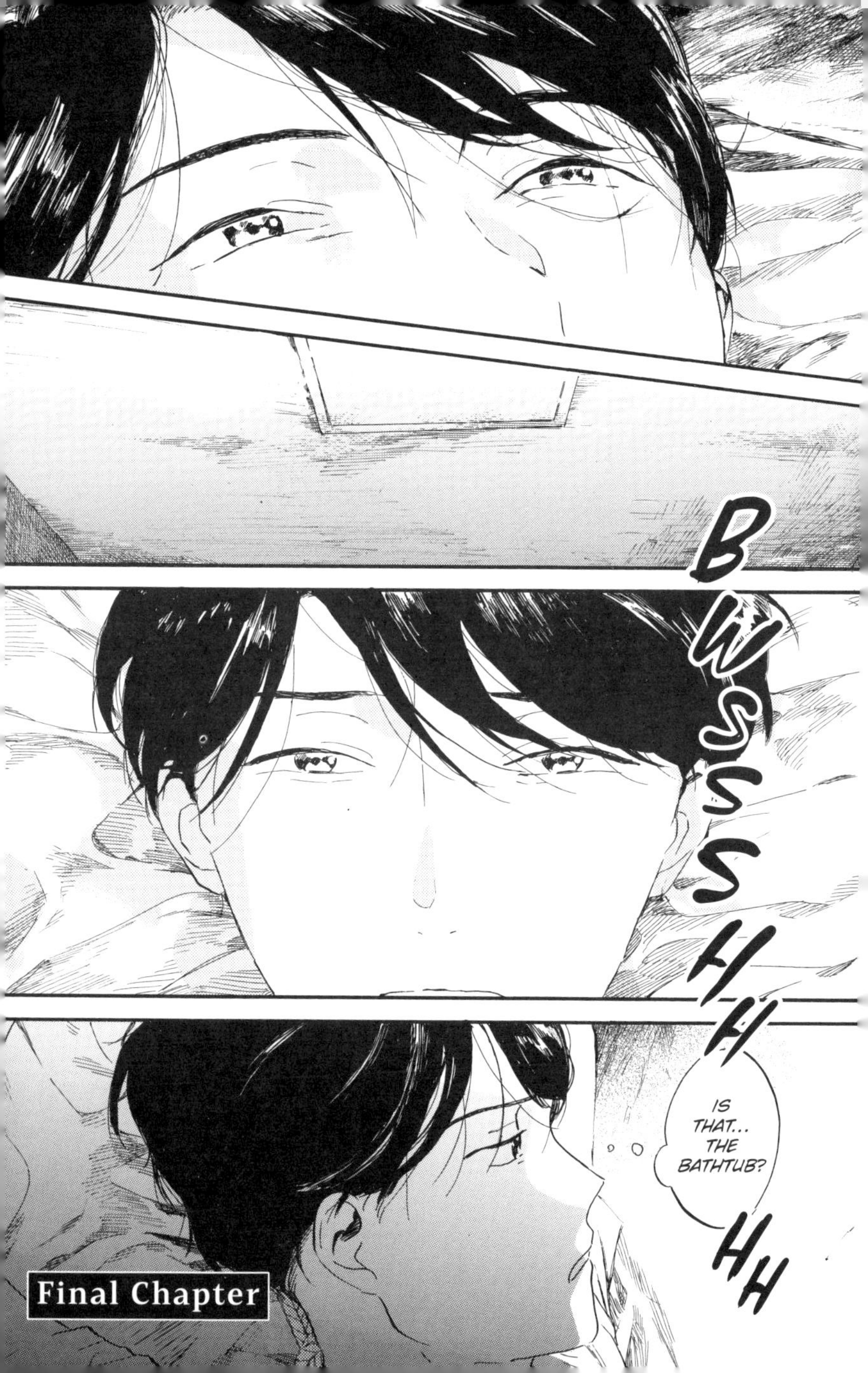
BWSSSHHHHH
IS THAT... THE BATHTUB?
Final Chapter

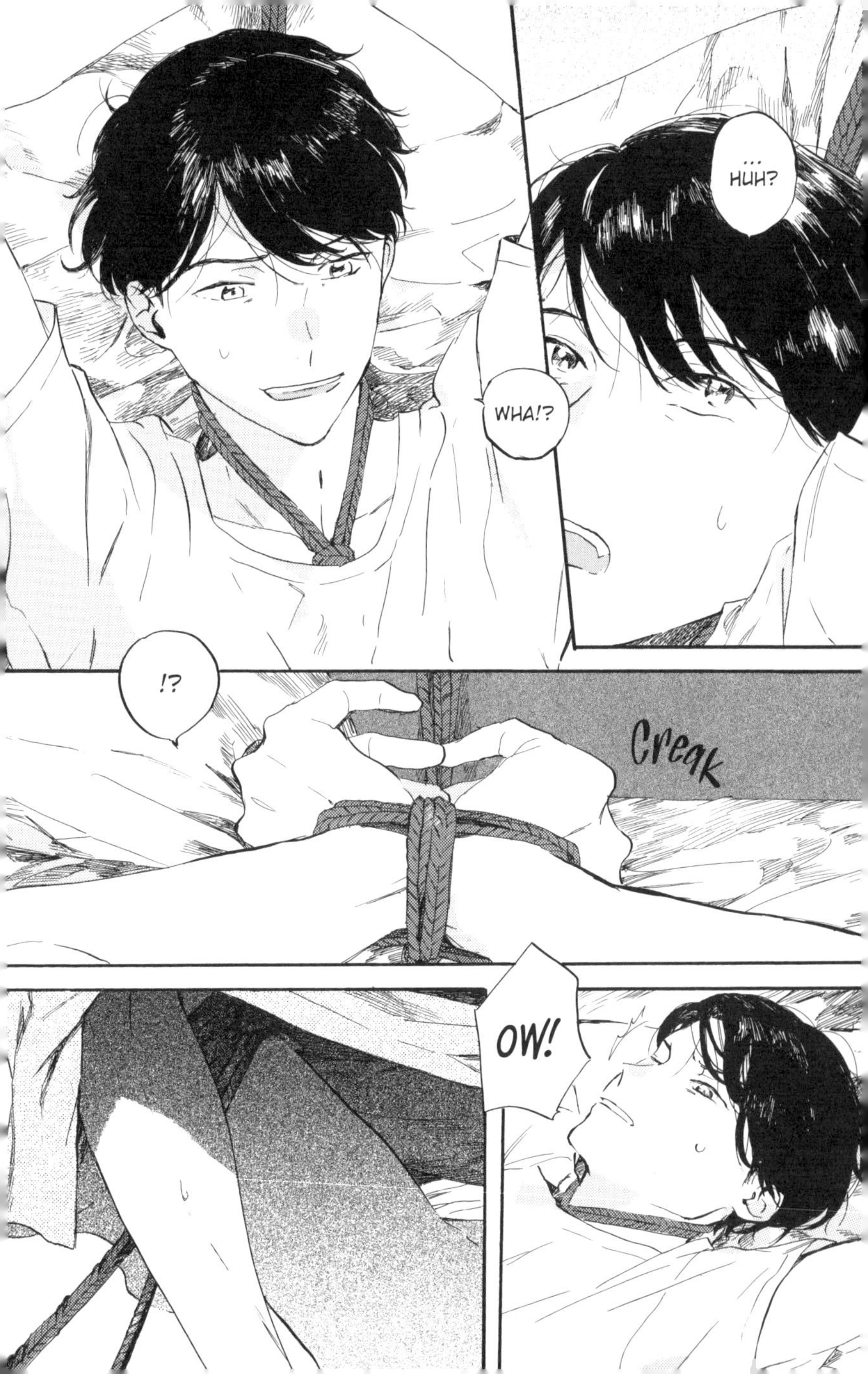
...HUH?
WHA!?
!?
Creak
OW!

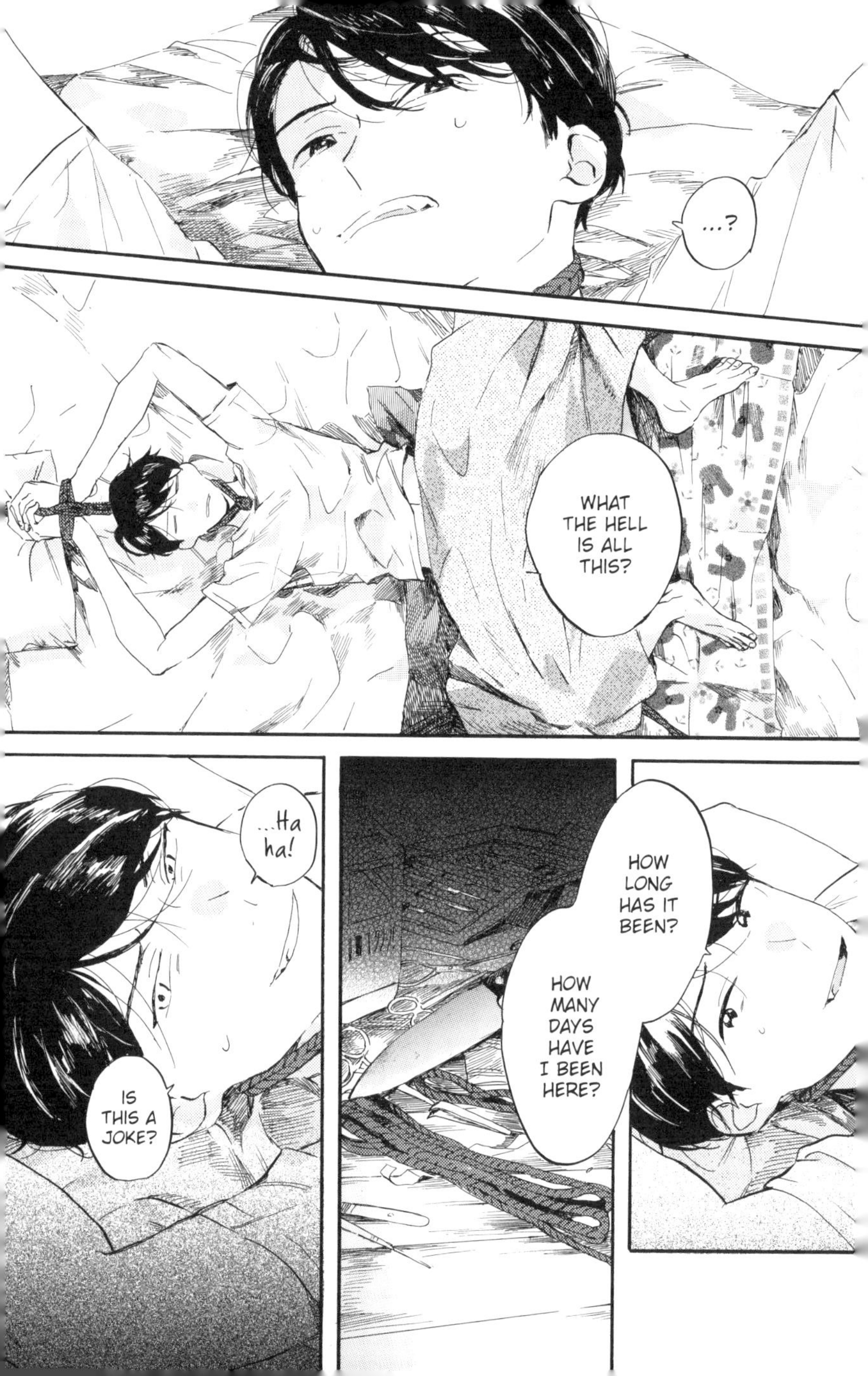
...?
WHAT THE HELL IS ALL THIS?
HOW LONG HAS IT BEEN?
HOW MANY DAYS HAVE I BEEN HERE?
...Ha ha!
IS THIS A JOKE?

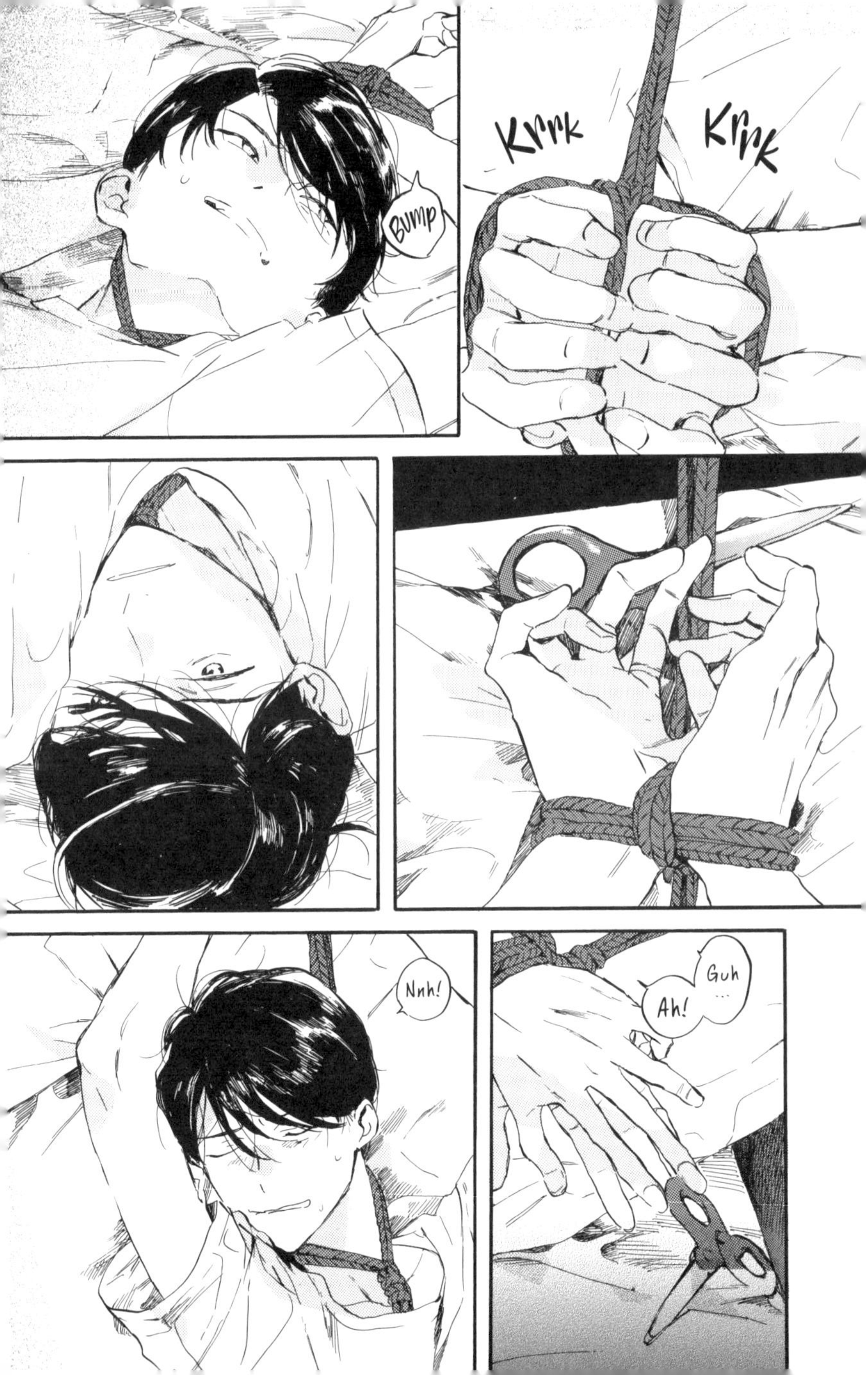
Krrk
Krrk
Bump
Guh…
Ah!
Nnh!

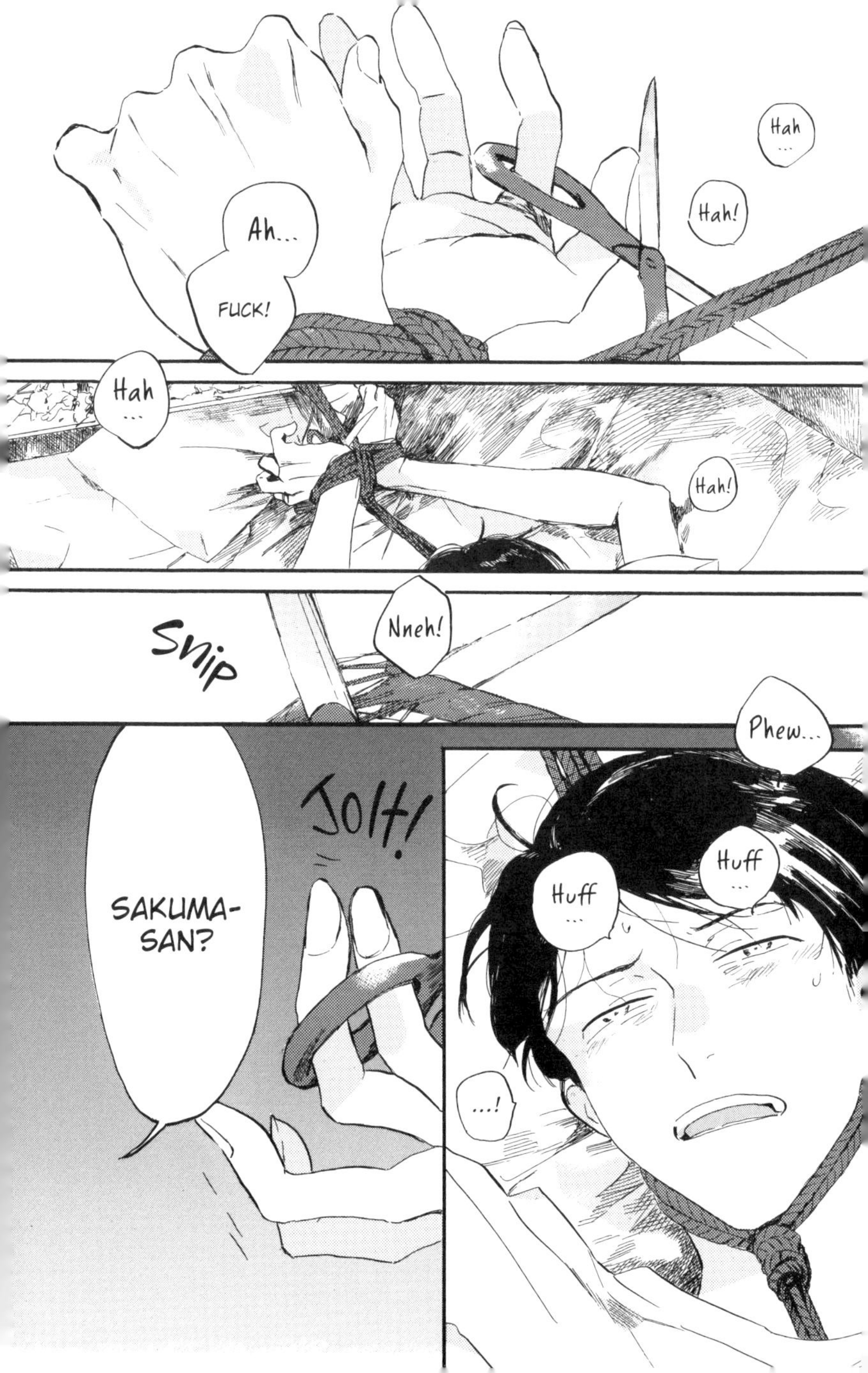
Hah...
Hah!
Ah...
FUCK!
Hah!
Hah...
Nneh!
Snip
Phew...
Huff...
Huff...
...!
Jolt!
SAKUMA-SAN?

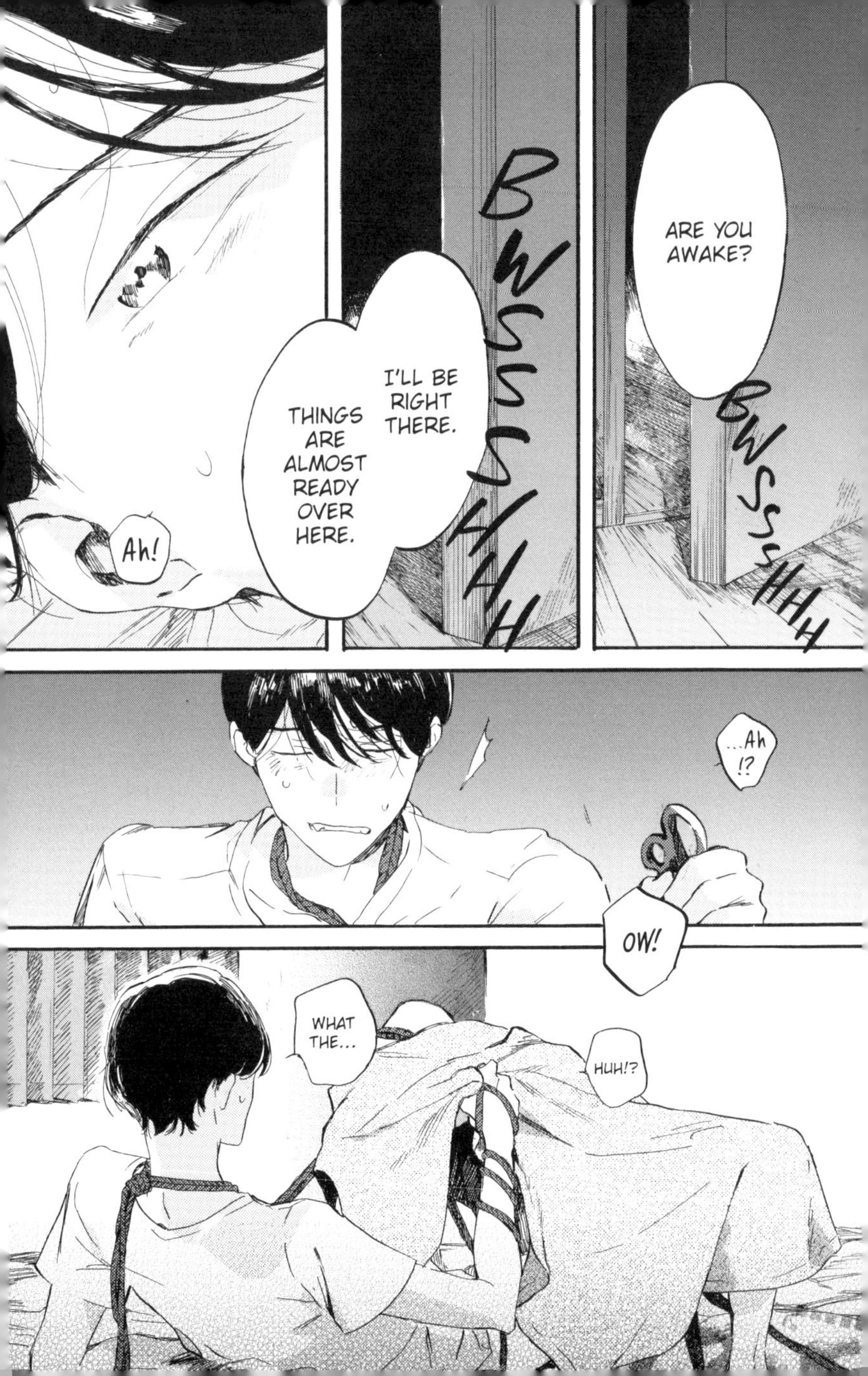
ARE YOU AWAKE?
BWSSSHHH
BWSSSHHH
I'LL BE RIGHT THERE.
THINGS ARE ALMOST READY OVER HERE.
Ah!
...Ah !?
OW!
HUH!?
WHAT THE...

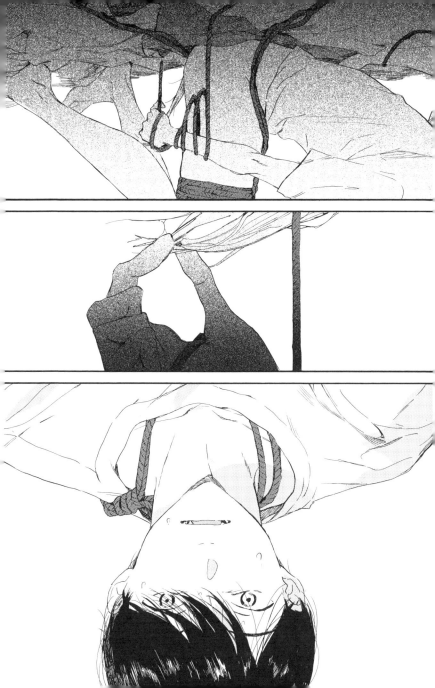

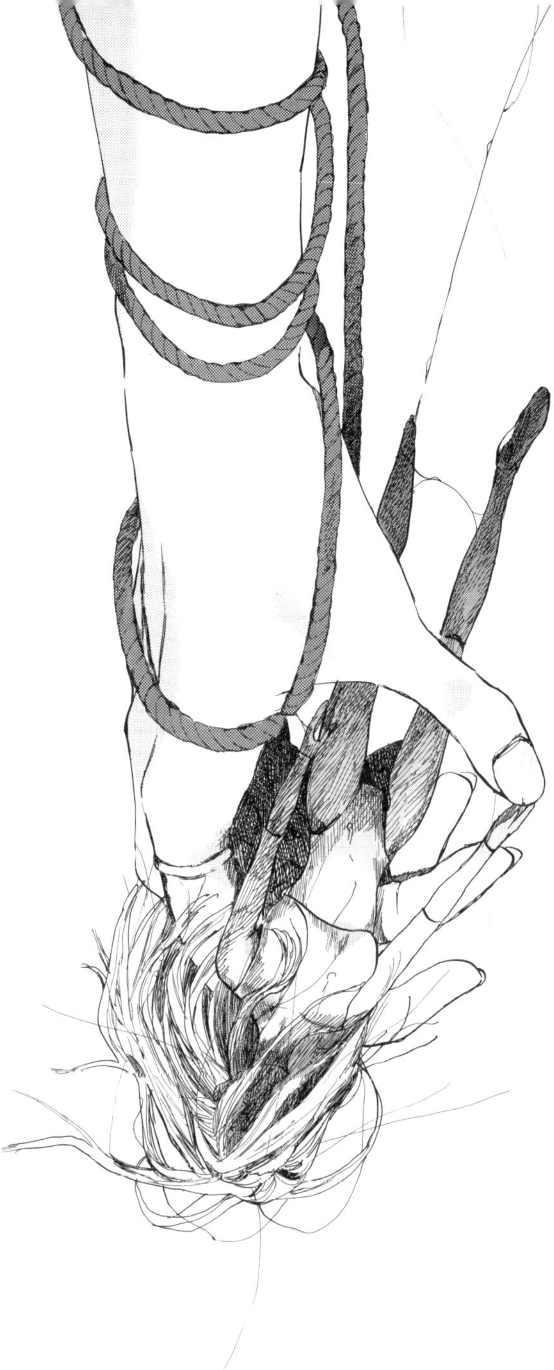

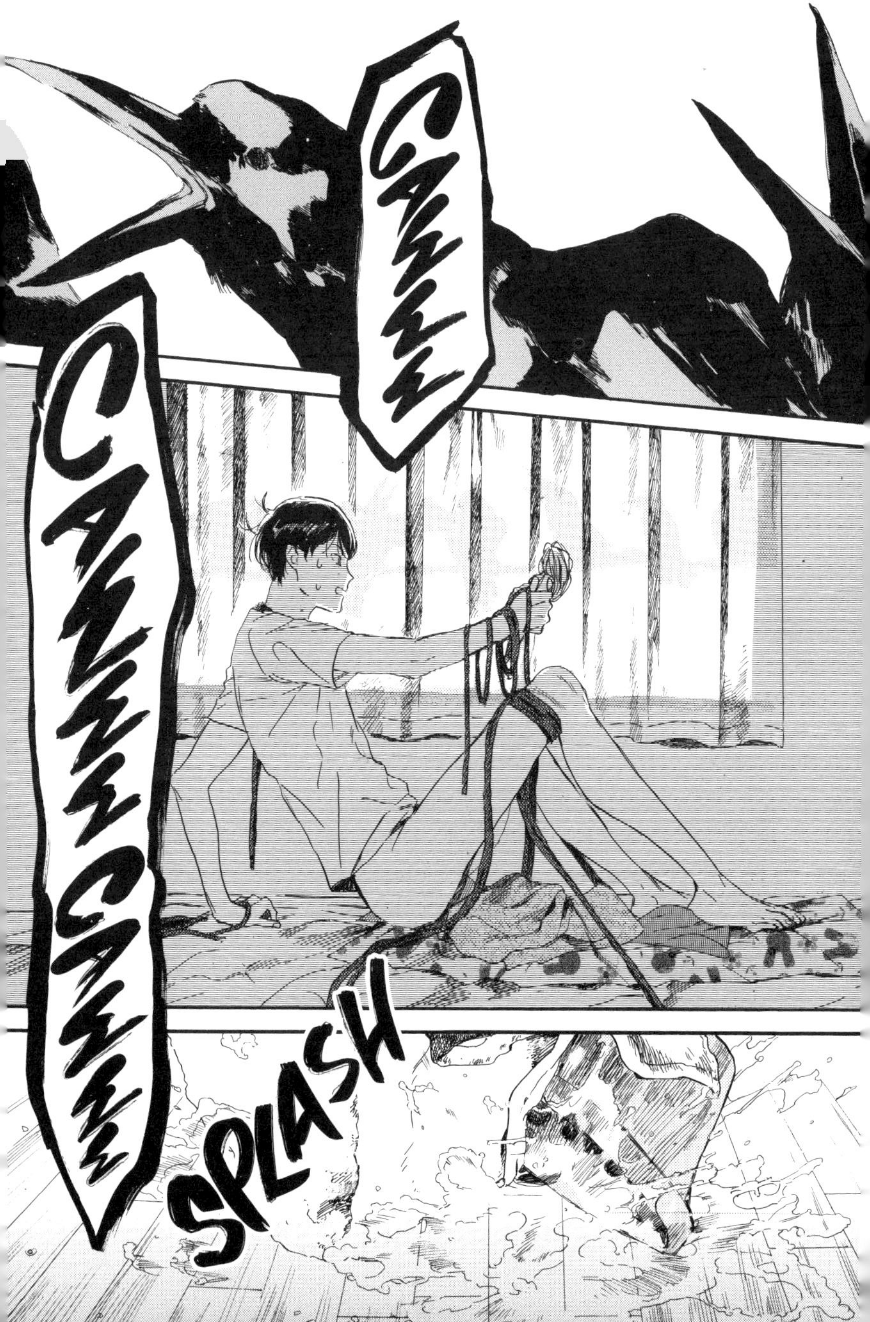
CAWWWW
CAWWWW CAWWWW
SPLASH

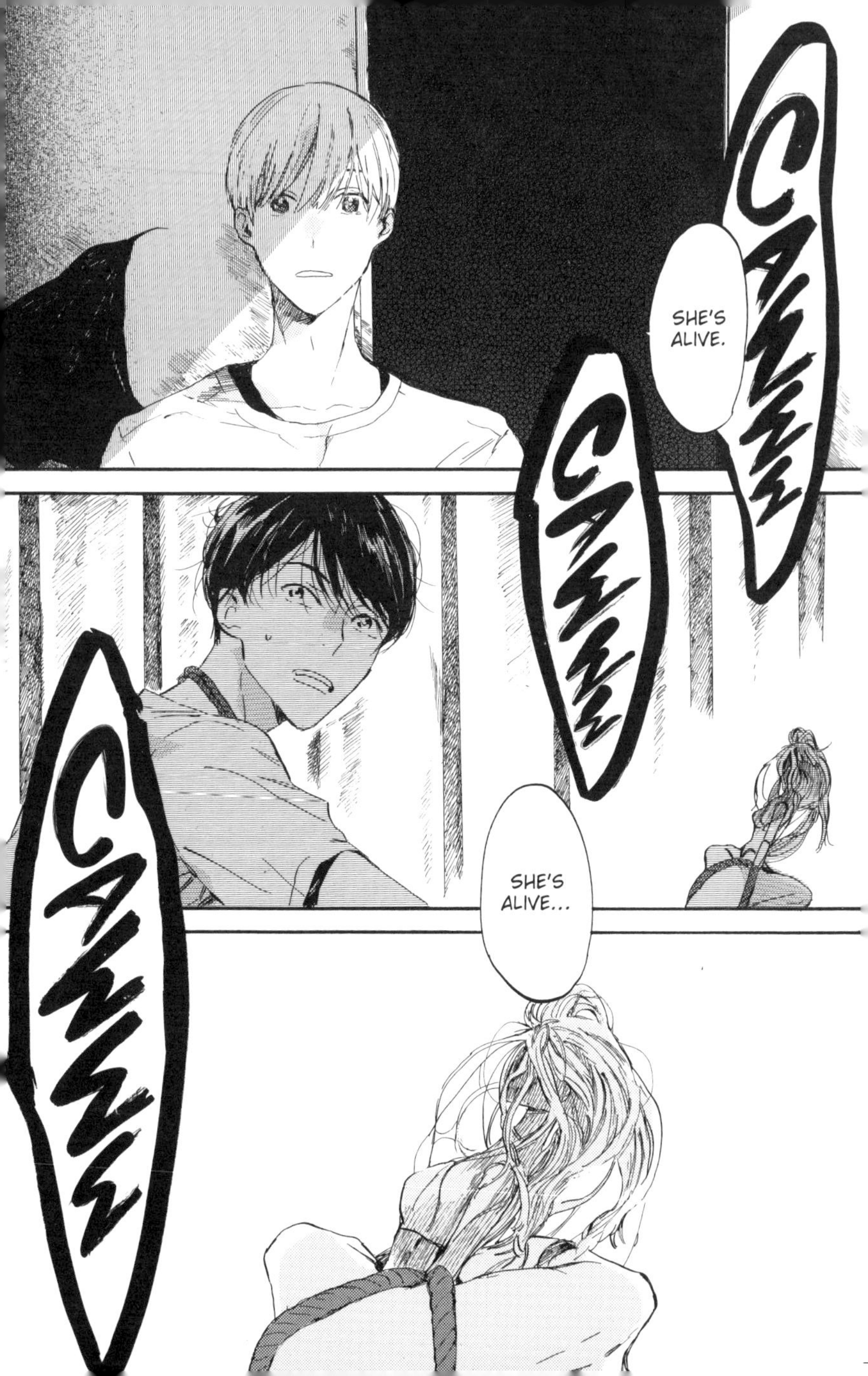
CAWWW
SHE'S ALIVE.
CAWWW
SHE'S ALIVE...
CAWWW

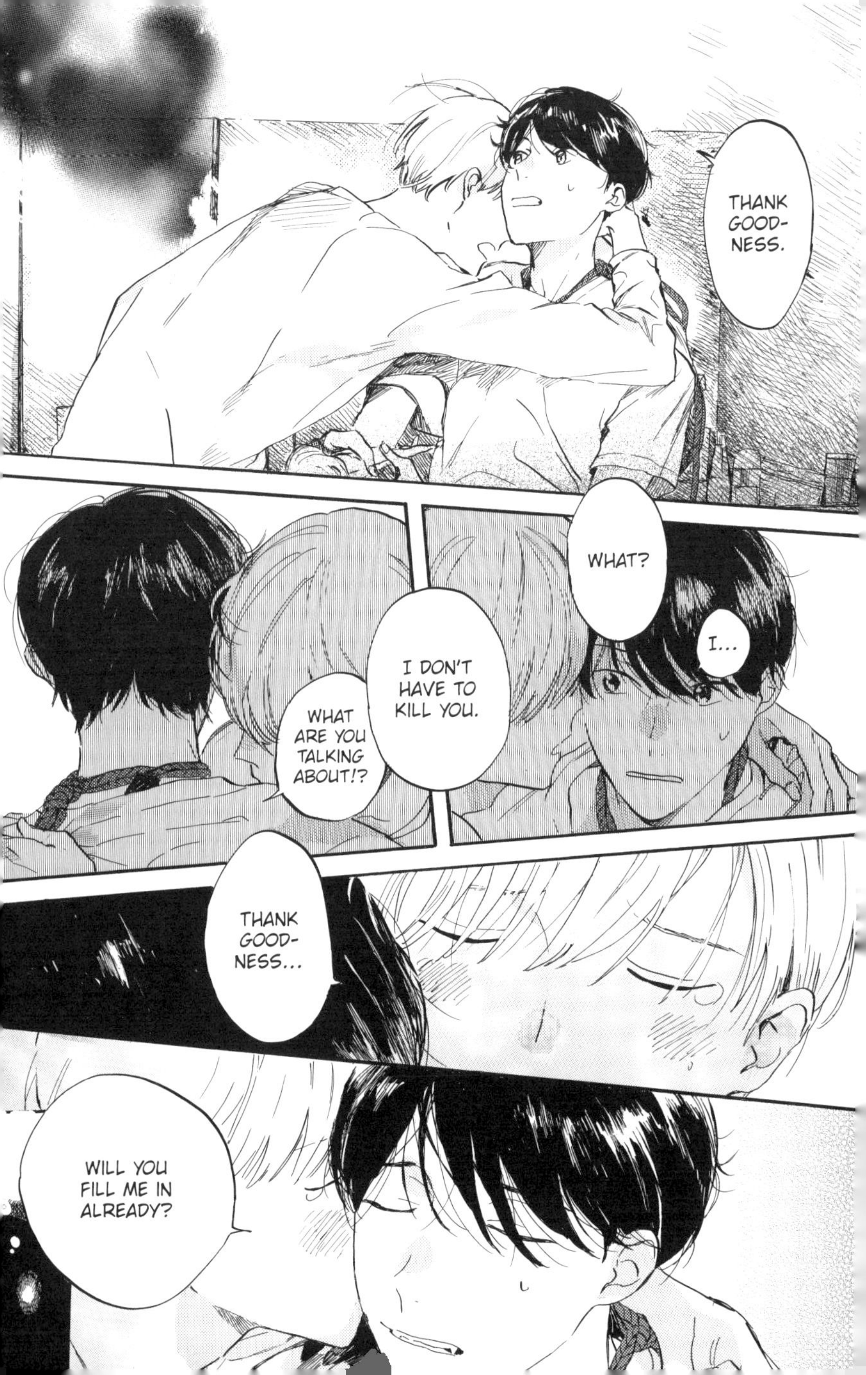
THANK GOOD-NESS.
WHAT?
I...
I DON'T HAVE TO KILL YOU.
WHAT ARE YOU TALKING ABOUT!?
THANK GOOD-NESS...
WILL YOU FILL ME IN ALREADY?

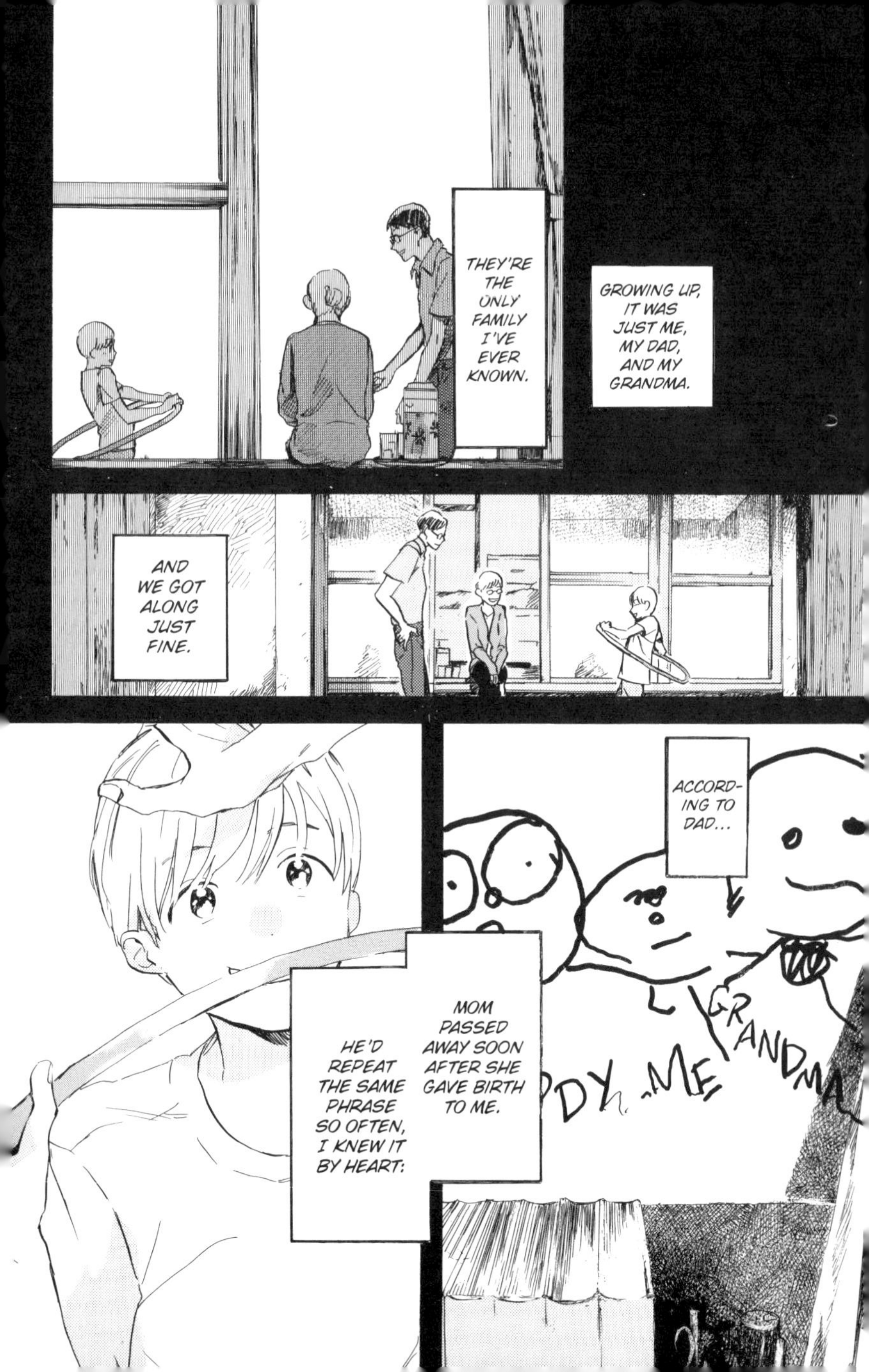
GROWING UP, IT WAS JUST ME, MY DAD, AND MY GRANDMA.
THEY'RE THE ONLY FAMILY I'VE EVER KNOWN.
AND WE GOT ALONG JUST FINE.
ACCORD-ING TO DAD...
GRANDMA
ME
MOM PASSED AWAY SOON AFTER SHE GAVE BIRTH TO ME.
HE'D REPEAT THE SAME PHRASE SO OFTEN, I KNEW IT BY HEART:

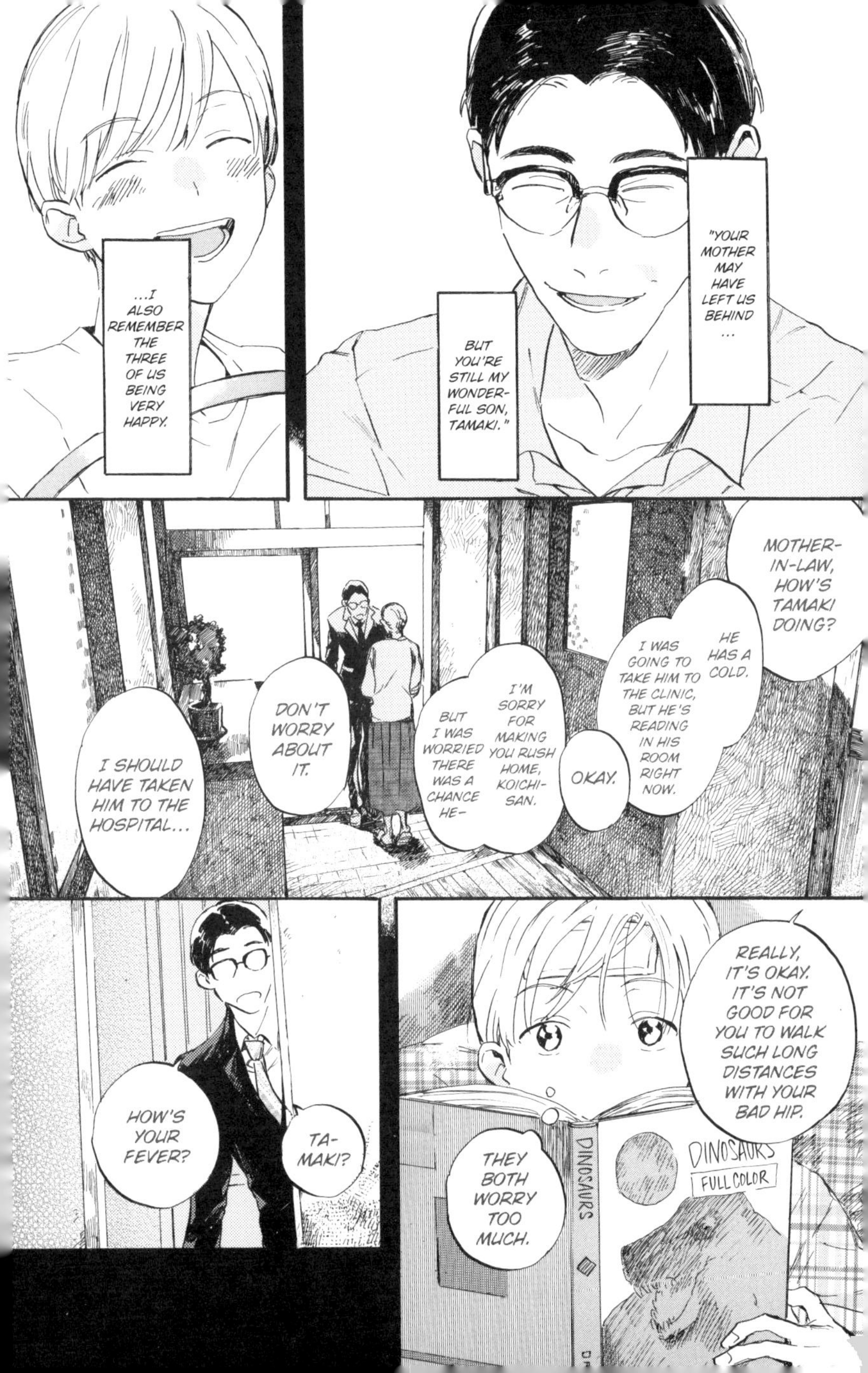
"YOUR MOTHER MAY HAVE LEFT US BEHIND ...
BUT YOU'RE STILL MY WONDERFUL SON, TAMAKI."
...I ALSO REMEMBER THE THREE OF US BEING VERY HAPPY.
MOTHER-IN-LAW, HOW'S TAMAKI DOING?
HE HAS A COLD.
I WAS GOING TO TAKE HIM TO THE CLINIC, BUT HE'S READING IN HIS ROOM RIGHT NOW.
OKAY.
I'M SORRY FOR MAKING YOU RUSH HOME, KOICHI-SAN.
BUT I WAS WORRIED THERE WAS A CHANCE HE-
DON'T WORRY ABOUT IT.
I SHOULD HAVE TAKEN HIM TO THE HOSPITAL...
REALLY, IT'S OKAY. IT'S NOT GOOD FOR YOU TO WALK SUCH LONG DISTANCES WITH YOUR BAD HIP.
THEY BOTH WORRY TOO MUCH.
DINOSAURS
FULL COLOR
DINOSAURS
TA-MAKI?
HOW'S YOUR FEVER?

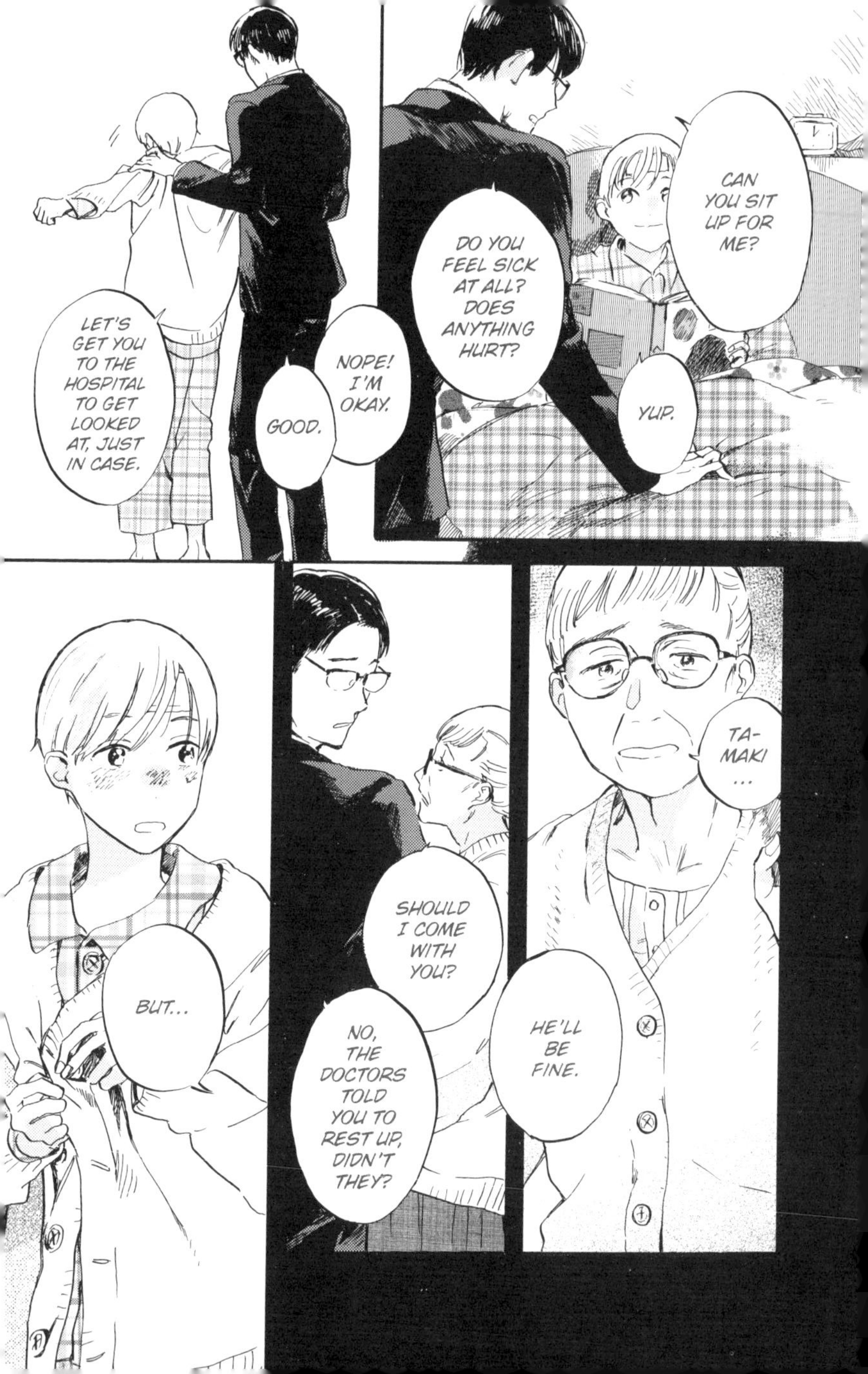
CAN YOU SIT UP FOR ME?
YUP.
DO YOU FEEL SICK AT ALL? DOES ANYTHING HURT?
NOPE! I'M OKAY.
GOOD.
LET'S GET YOU TO THE HOSPITAL TO GET LOOKED AT, JUST IN CASE.
TA-MAKI...
HE'LL BE FINE.
SHOULD I COME WITH YOU?
NO, THE DOCTORS TOLD YOU TO REST UP, DIDN'T THEY?
BUT...

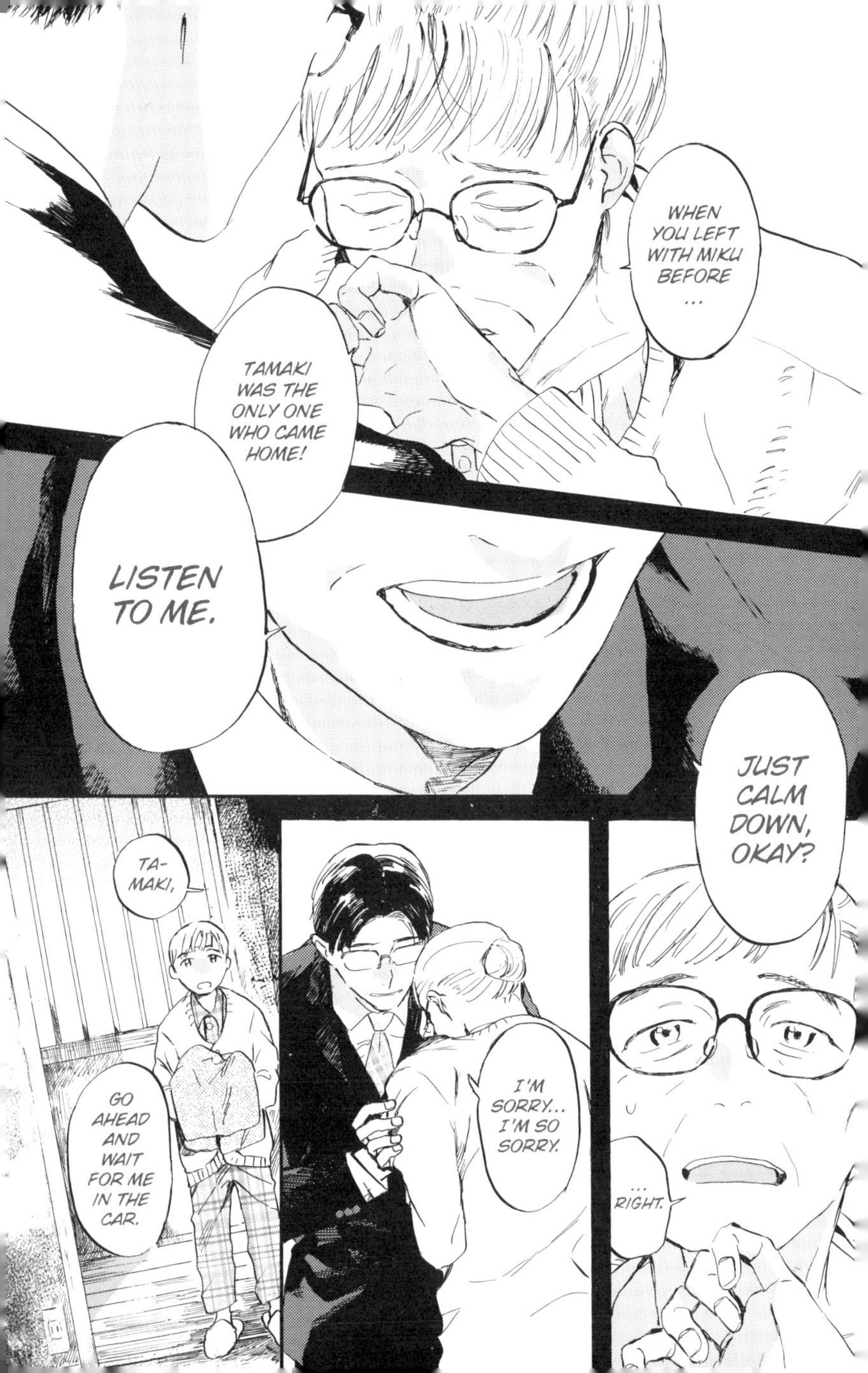
WHEN YOU LEFT WITH MIKU BEFORE ...
TAMAKI WAS THE ONLY ONE WHO CAME HOME!
LISTEN TO ME.
JUST CALM DOWN, OKAY?
... RIGHT.
I'M SORRY... I'M SO SORRY.
TA-MAKI,
GO AHEAD AND WAIT FOR ME IN THE CAR.

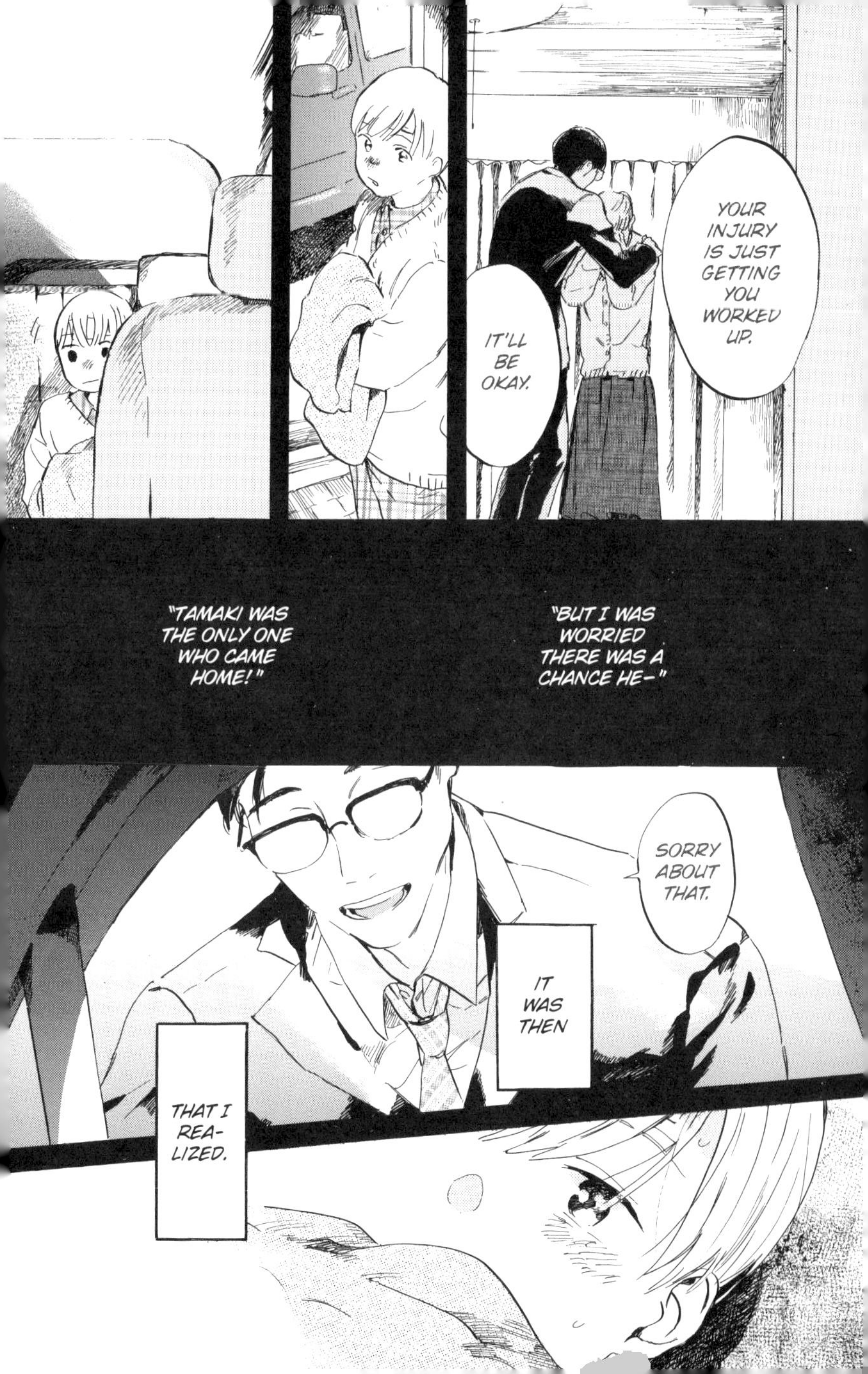
YOUR INJURY IS JUST GETTING YOU WORKED UP.
IT'LL BE OKAY.
"BUT I WAS WORRIED THERE WAS A CHANCE HE–"
"TAMAKI WAS THE ONLY ONE WHO CAME HOME!"
SORRY ABOUT THAT.
IT WAS THEN
THAT I REA-LIZED.

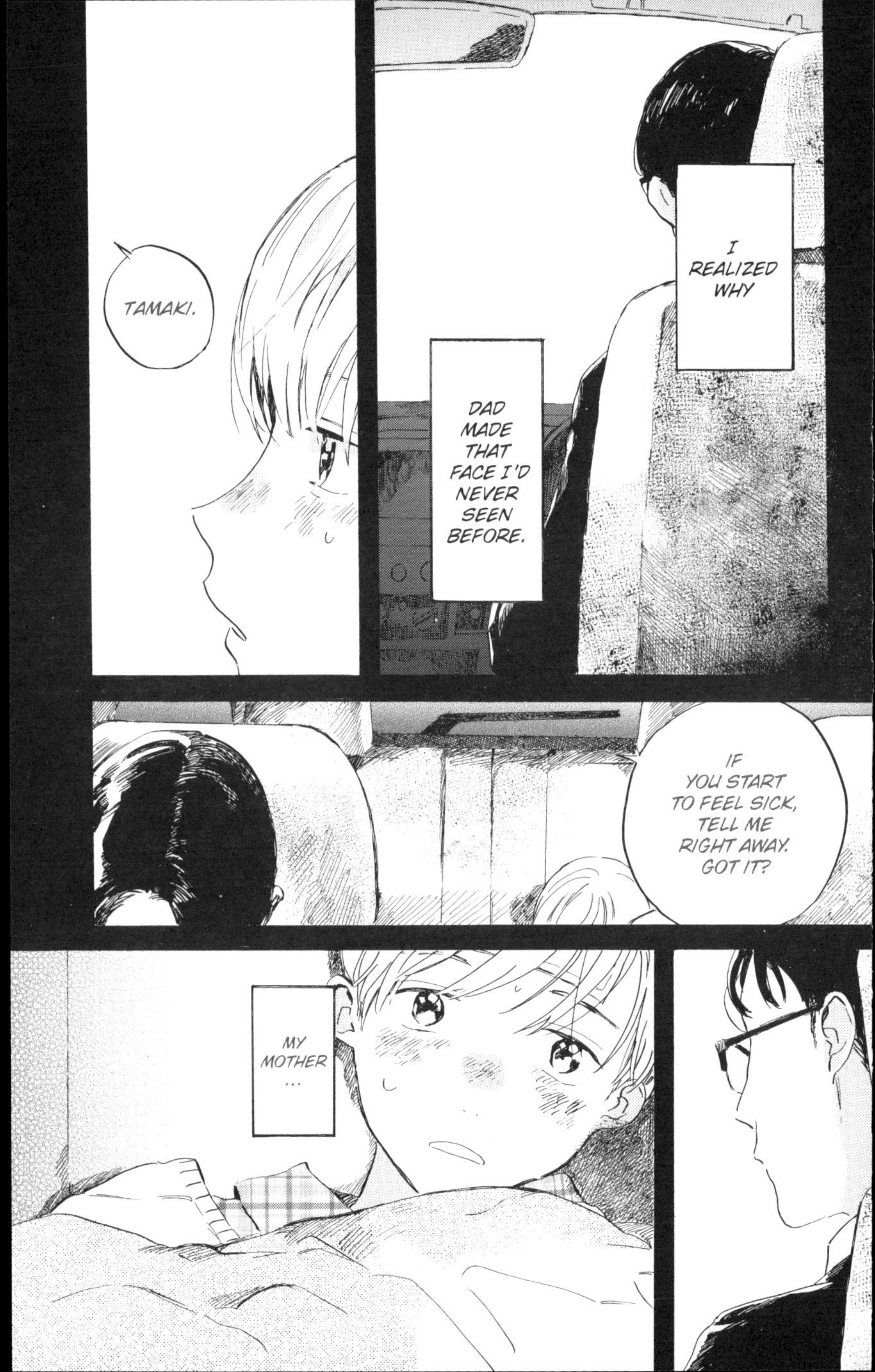
I REALIZED WHY
DAD MADE THAT FACE I'D NEVER SEEN BEFORE.
TAMAKI.
IF YOU START TO FEEL SICK, TELL ME RIGHT AWAY. GOT IT?
MY MOTHER ...

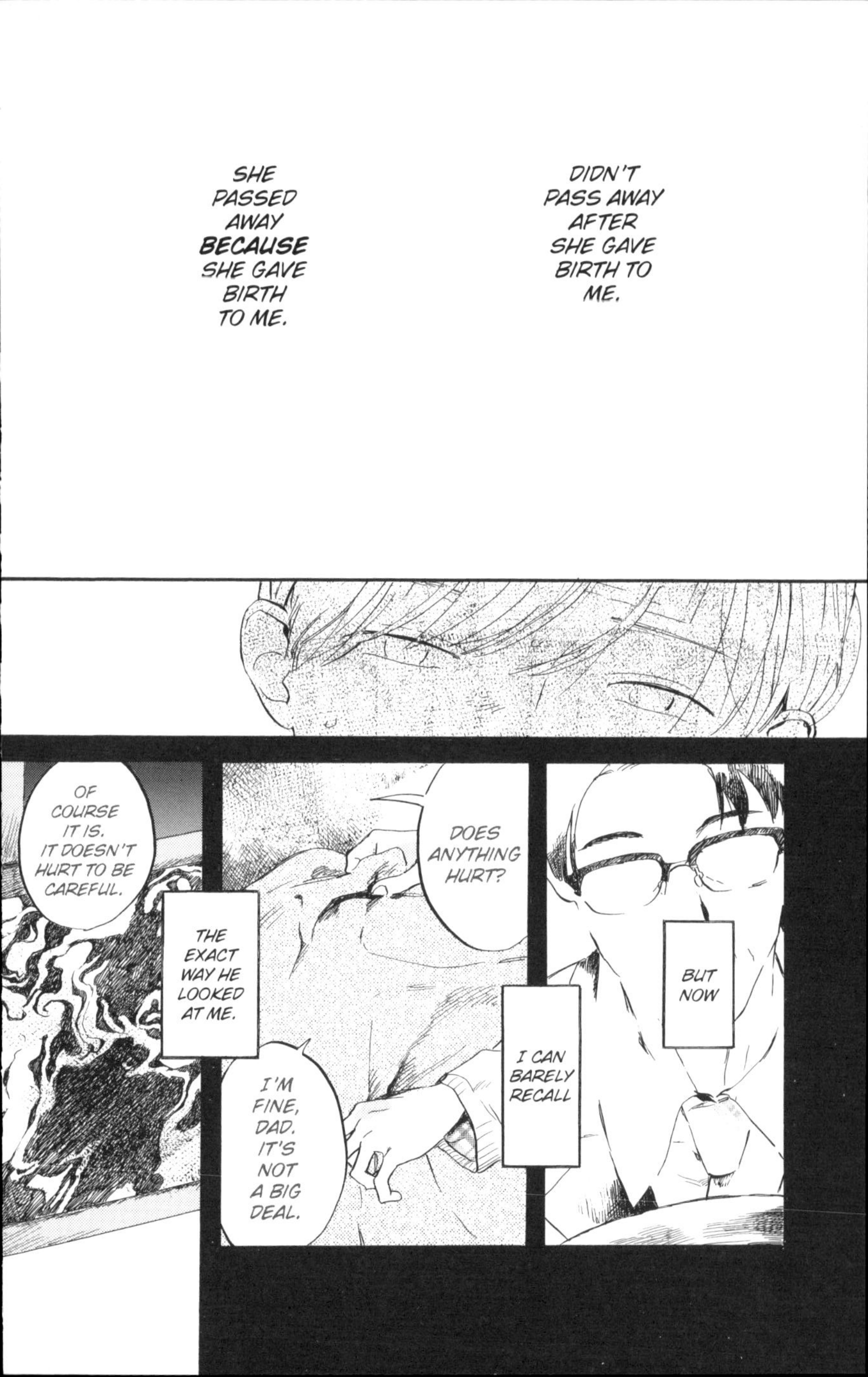
DIDN'T PASS AWAY AFTER SHE GAVE BIRTH TO ME.
SHE PASSED AWAY **BECAUSE** SHE GAVE BIRTH TO ME.
BUT NOW
I CAN BARELY RECALL
DOES ANYTHING HURT?
THE EXACT WAY HE LOOKED AT ME.
I'M FINE, DAD. IT'S NOT A BIG DEAL.
OF COURSE IT IS. IT DOESN'T HURT TO BE CAREFUL.

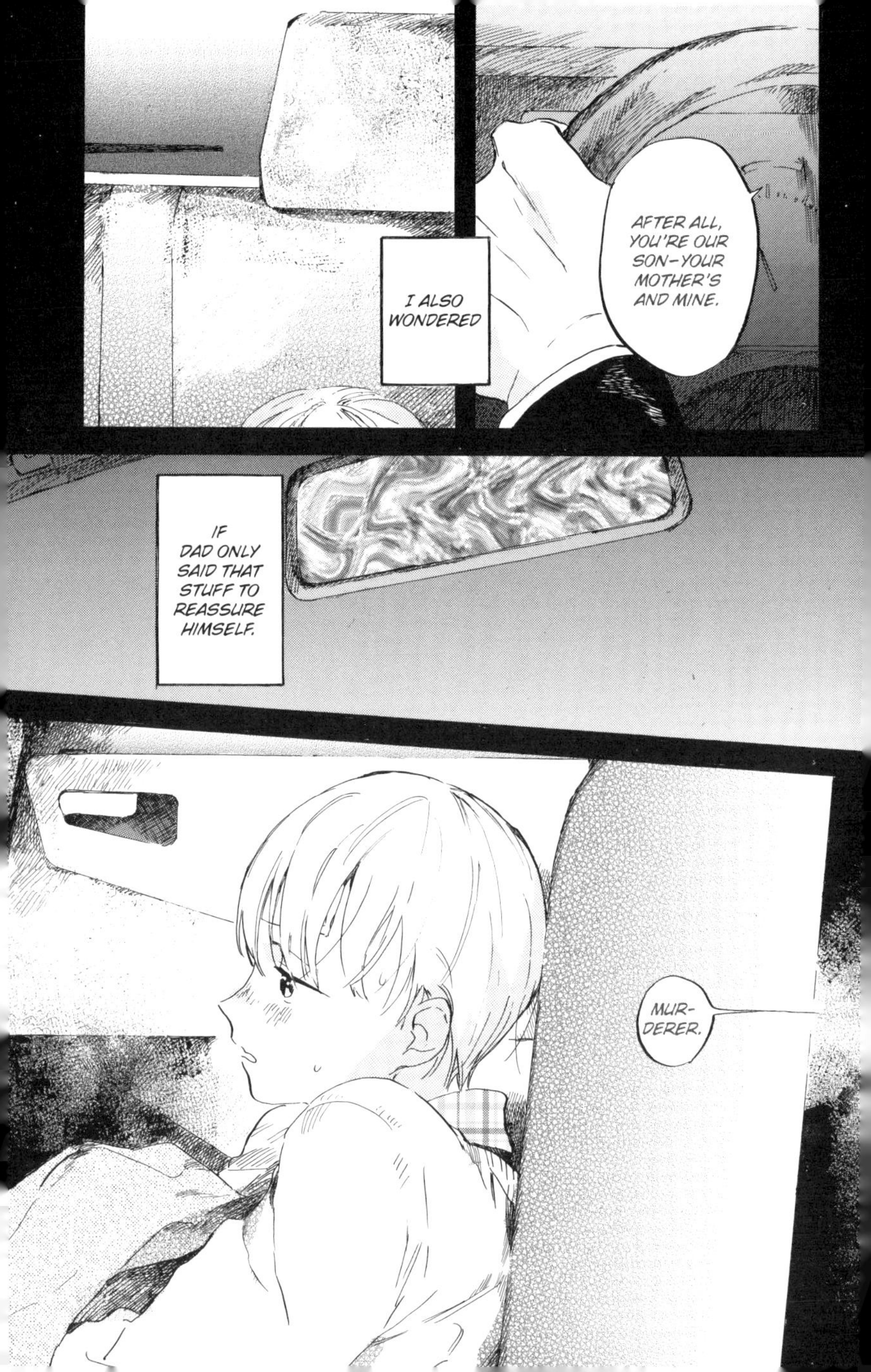
AFTER ALL, YOU'RE OUR SON—YOUR MOTHER'S AND MINE.
I ALSO WONDERED
IF DAD ONLY SAID THAT STUFF TO REASSURE HIMSELF.
MUR-DERER.

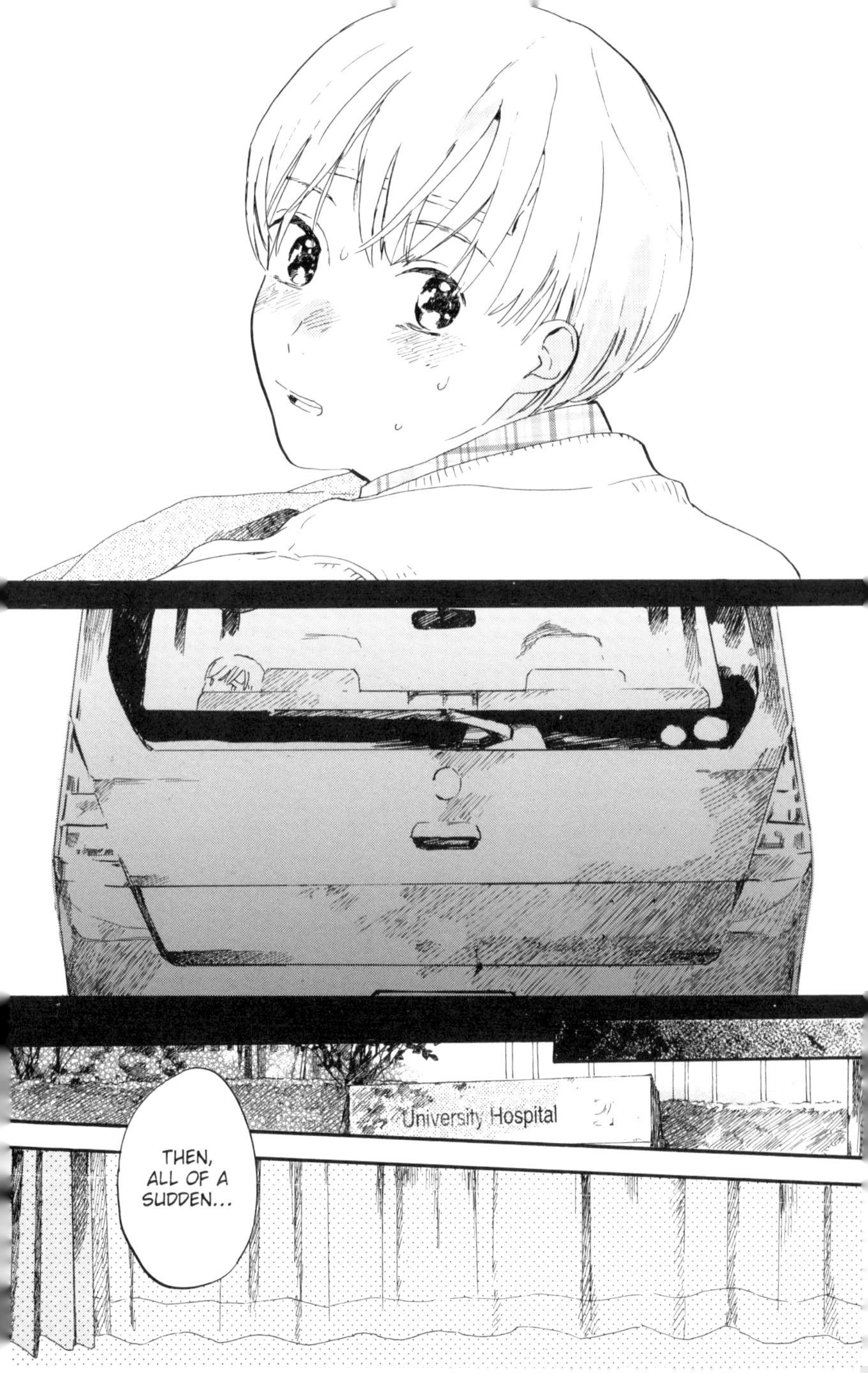
University Hospital
THEN, ALL OF A SUDDEN...

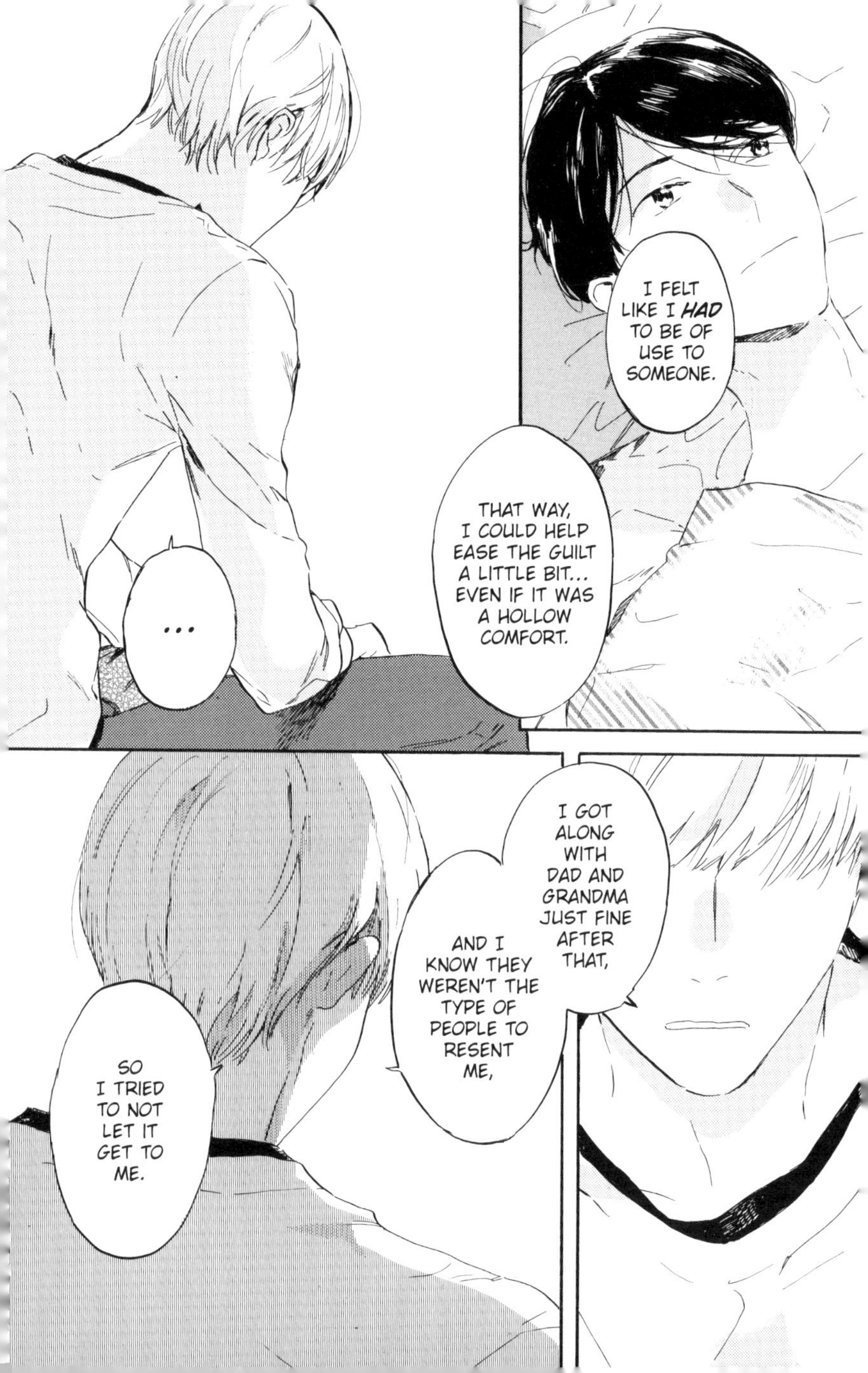
I FELT LIKE I ***HAD*** TO BE OF USE TO SOMEONE.
THAT WAY, I COULD HELP EASE THE GUILT A LITTLE BIT... EVEN IF IT WAS A HOLLOW COMFORT.
...
I GOT ALONG WITH DAD AND GRANDMA JUST FINE AFTER THAT,
AND I KNOW THEY WEREN'T THE TYPE OF PEOPLE TO RESENT ME,
SO I TRIED TO NOT LET IT GET TO ME.

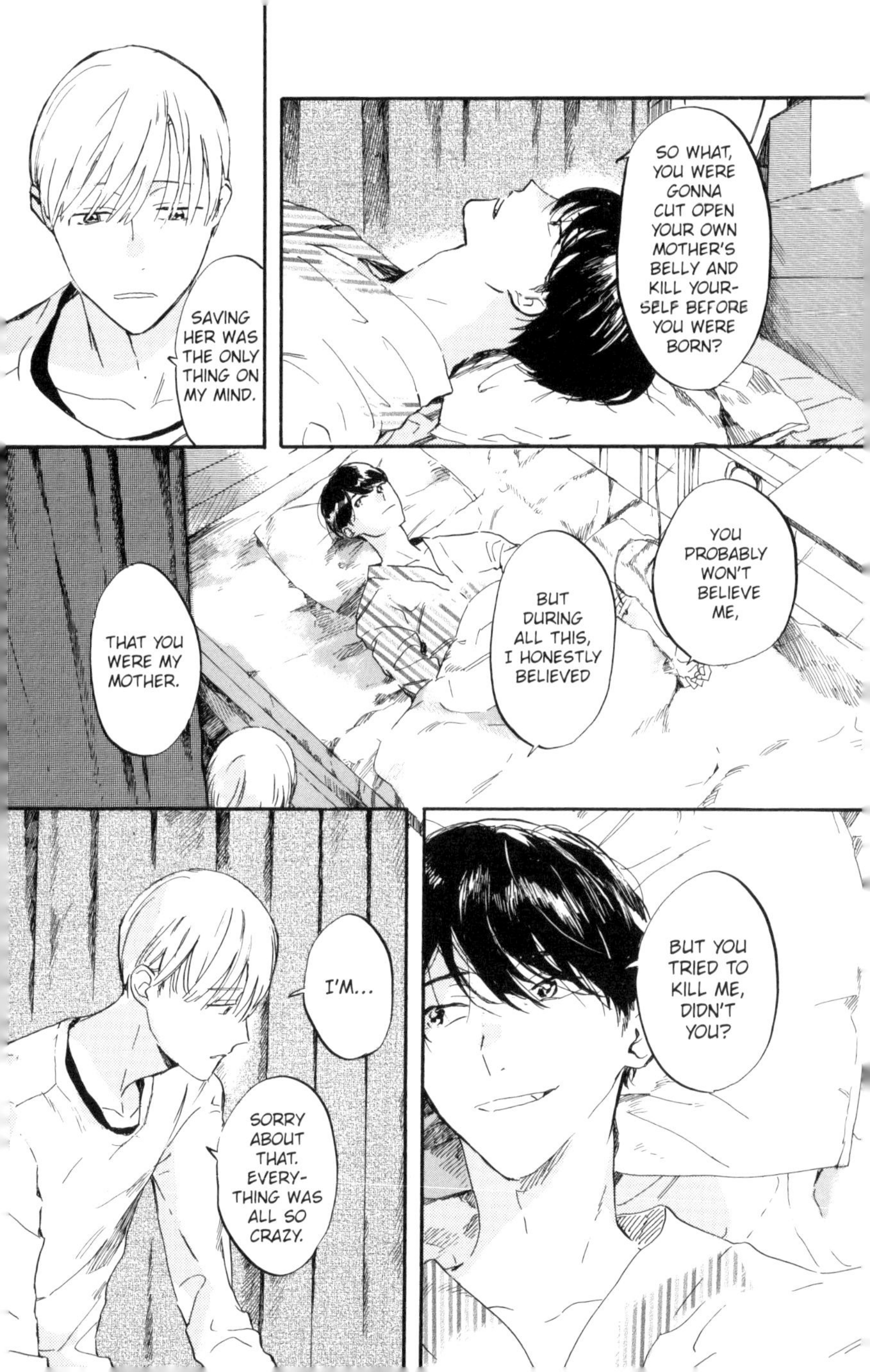
SO WHAT, YOU WERE GONNA CUT OPEN YOUR OWN MOTHER'S BELLY AND KILL YOURSELF BEFORE YOU WERE BORN?
SAVING HER WAS THE ONLY THING ON MY MIND.
YOU PROBABLY WON'T BELIEVE ME,
BUT DURING ALL THIS, I HONESTLY BELIEVED
THAT YOU WERE MY MOTHER.
BUT YOU TRIED TO KILL ME, DIDN'T YOU?
I'M...
SORRY ABOUT THAT. EVERYTHING WAS ALL SO CRAZY.

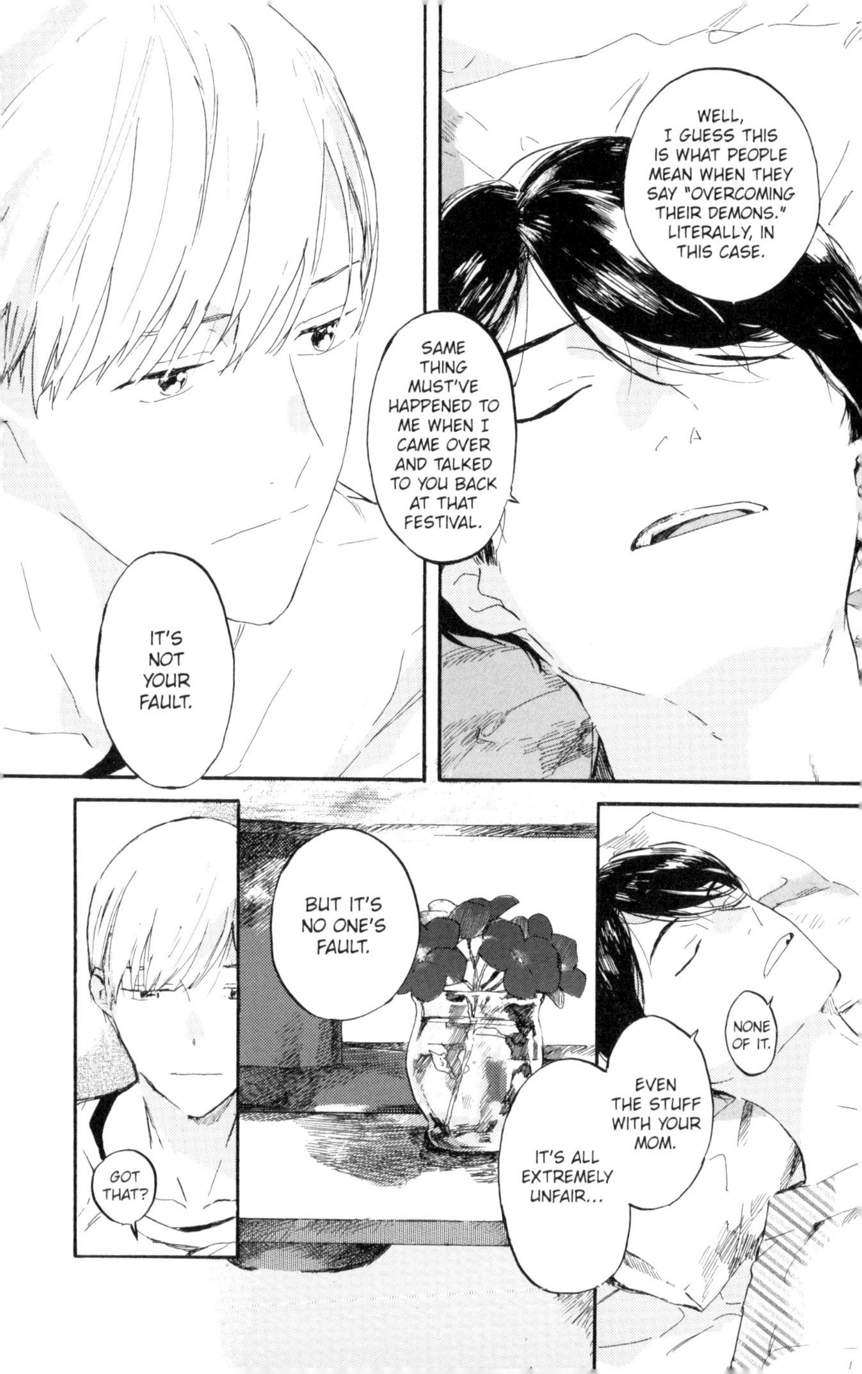
WELL, I GUESS THIS IS WHAT PEOPLE MEAN WHEN THEY SAY "OVERCOMING THEIR DEMONS." LITERALLY, IN THIS CASE.
SAME THING MUST'VE HAPPENED TO ME WHEN I CAME OVER AND TALKED TO YOU BACK AT THAT FESTIVAL.
IT'S NOT YOUR FAULT.
NONE OF IT.
EVEN THE STUFF WITH YOUR MOM.
IT'S ALL EXTREMELY UNFAIR...
BUT IT'S NO ONE'S FAULT.
GOT THAT?

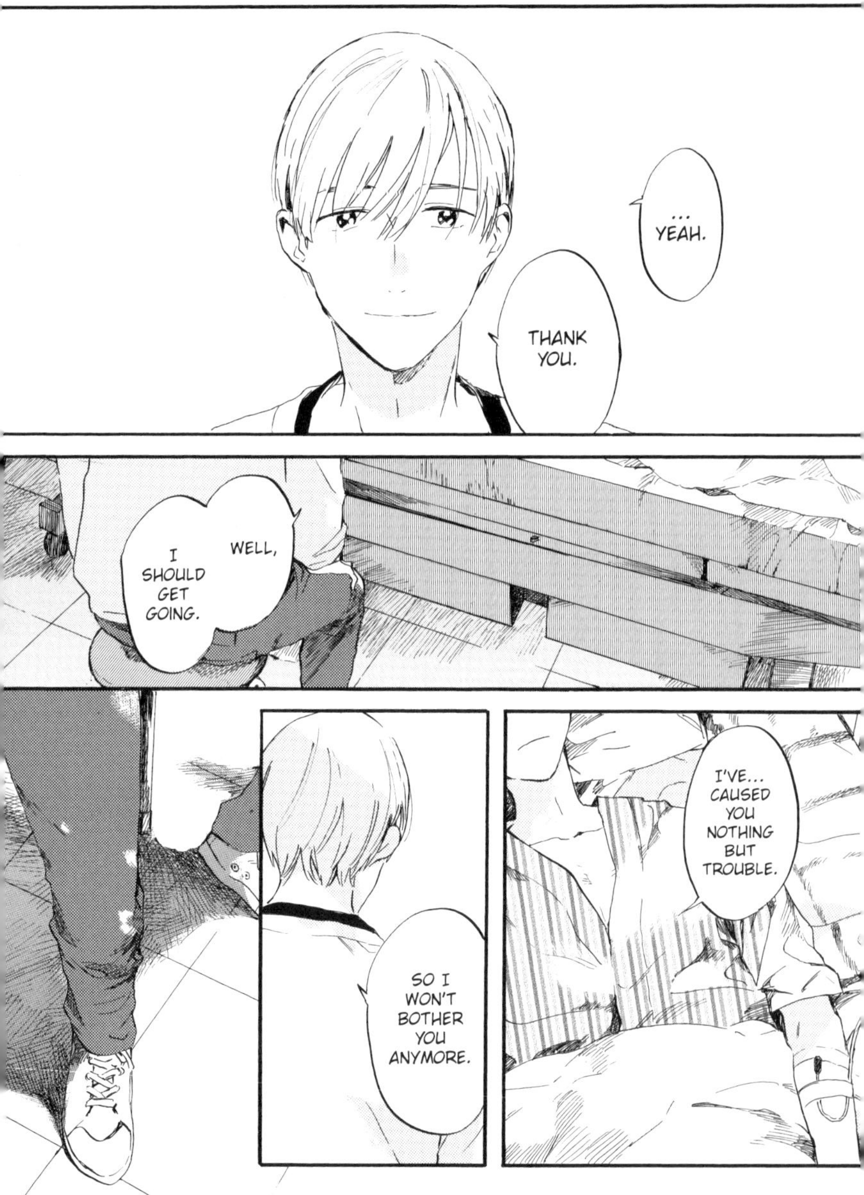
...YEAH.
THANK YOU.
WELL, I SHOULD GET GOING.
I'VE... CAUSED YOU NOTHING BUT TROUBLE.
SO I WON'T BOTHER YOU ANYMORE.

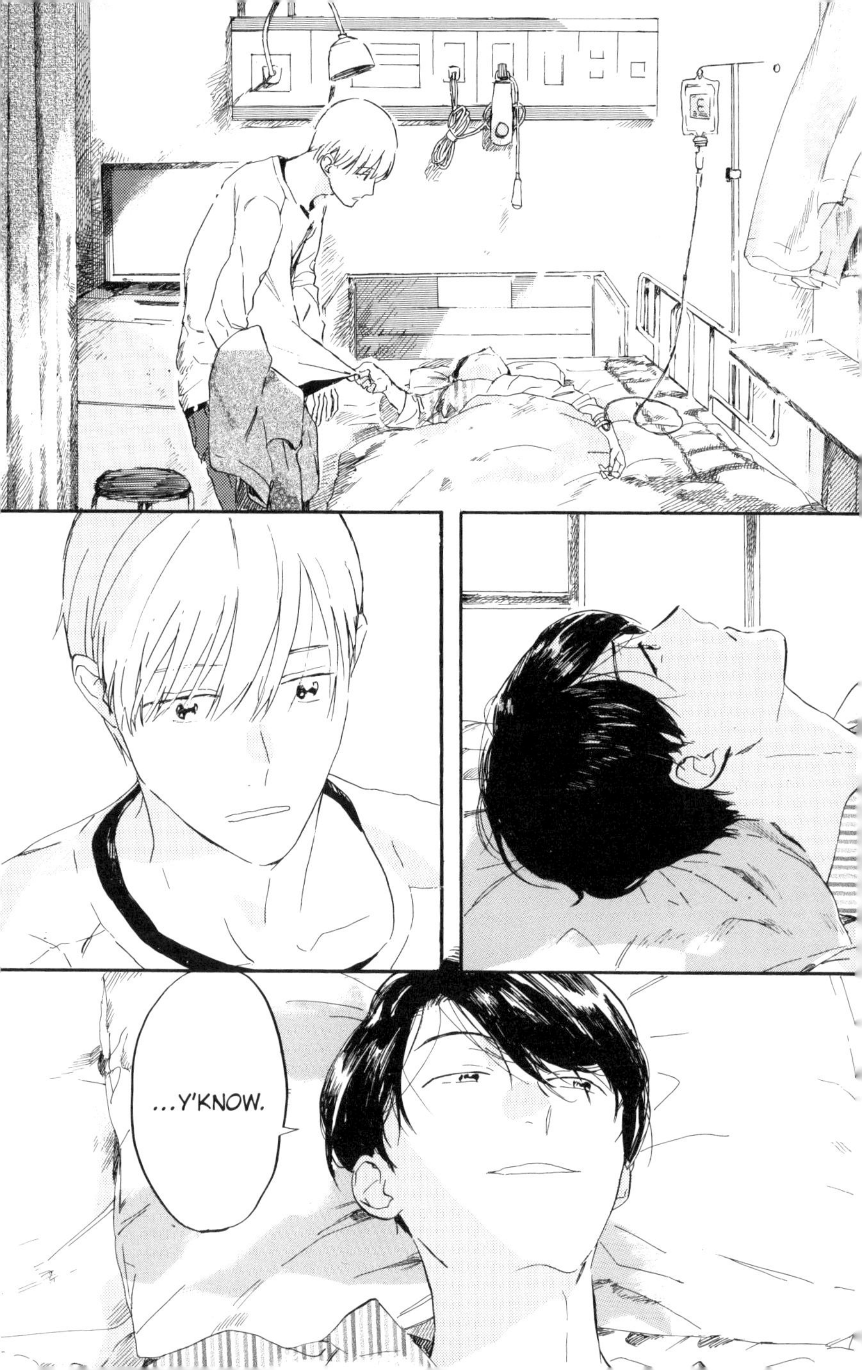
...Y'KNOW.

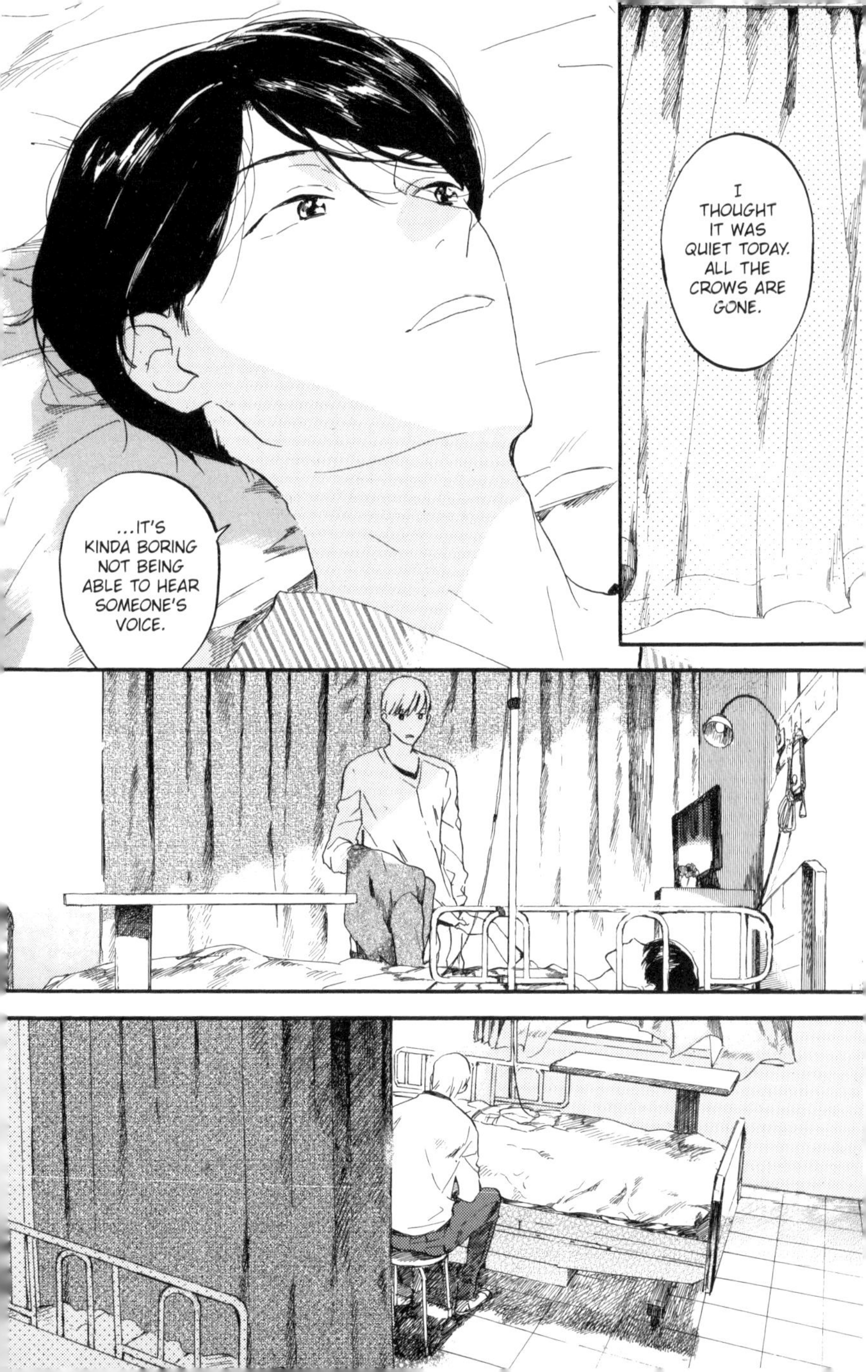
I THOUGHT IT WAS QUIET TODAY. ALL THE CROWS ARE GONE.
...IT'S KINDA BORING NOT BEING ABLE TO HEAR SOMEONE'S VOICE.

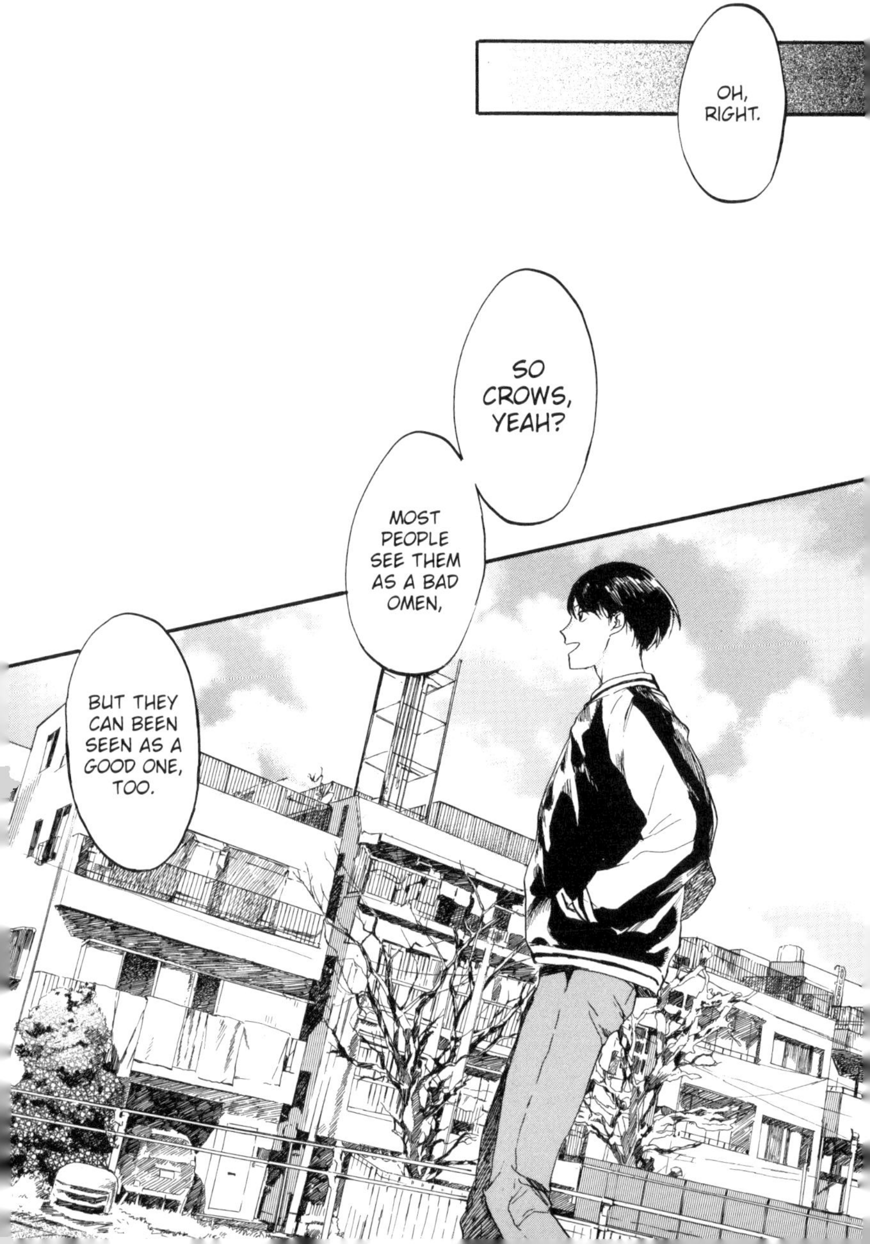
OH, RIGHT.
SO CROWS, YEAH?
MOST PEOPLE SEE THEM AS A BAD OMEN,
BUT THEY CAN BEEN SEEN AS A GOOD ONE, TOO.

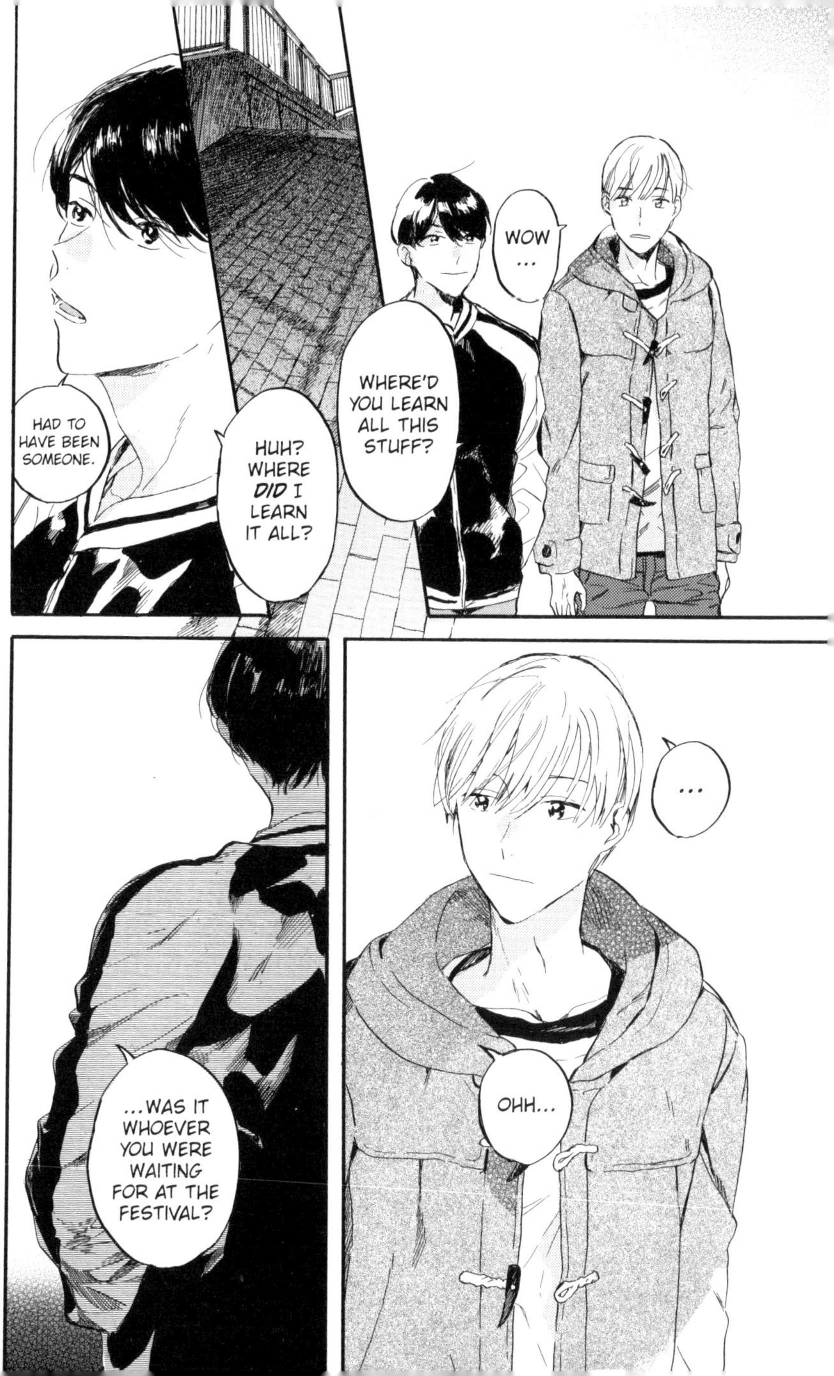
WOW ...
WHERE'D YOU LEARN ALL THIS STUFF?
HUH? WHERE *DID* I LEARN IT ALL?
HAD TO HAVE BEEN SOMEONE.
...
OHH...
...WAS IT WHOEVER YOU WERE WAITING FOR AT THE FESTIVAL?

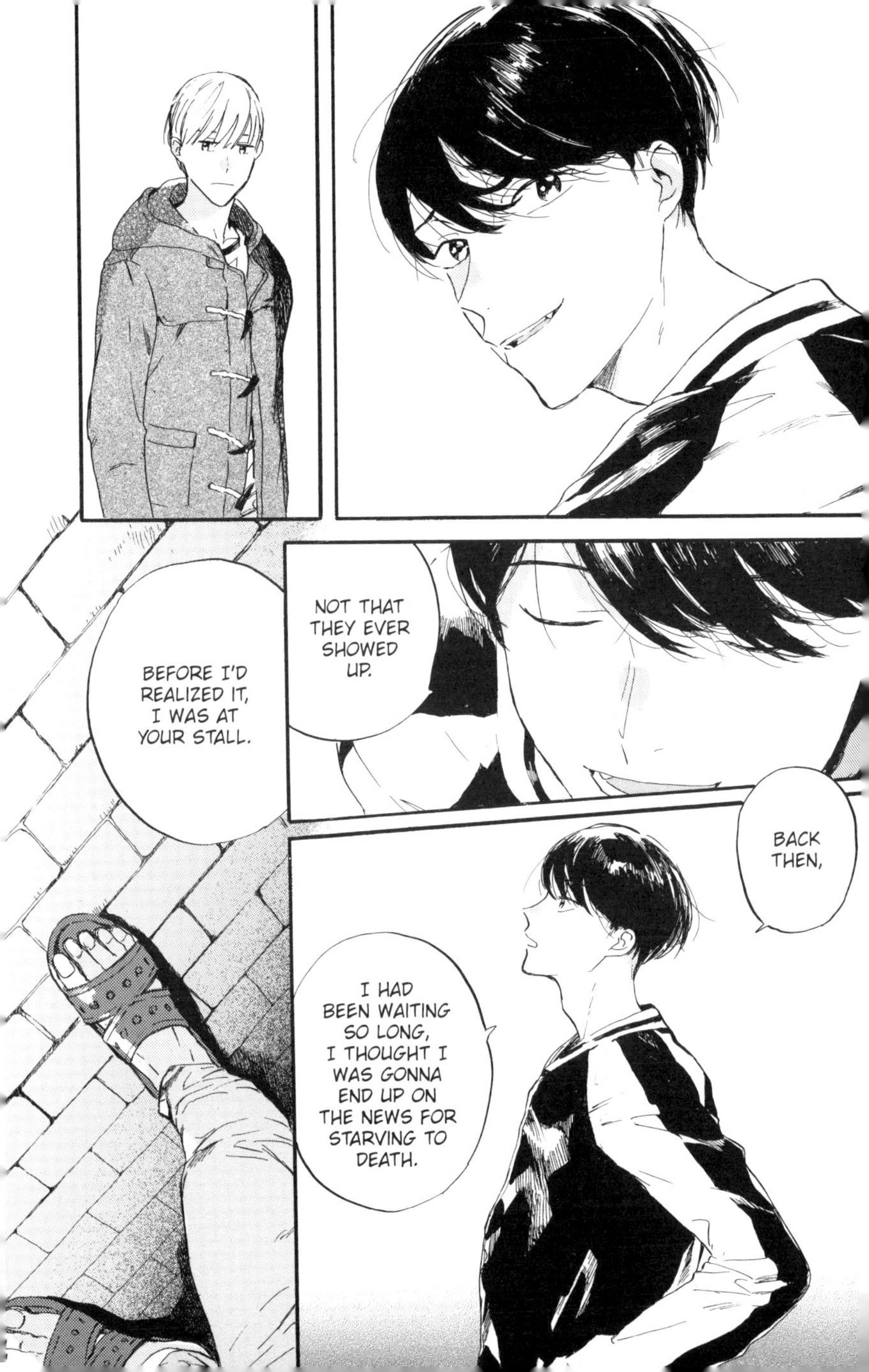
NOT THAT THEY EVER SHOWED UP.
BACK THEN,
I HAD BEEN WAITING SO LONG, I THOUGHT I WAS GONNA END UP ON THE NEWS FOR STARVING TO DEATH.
BEFORE I'D REALIZED IT, I WAS AT YOUR STALL.

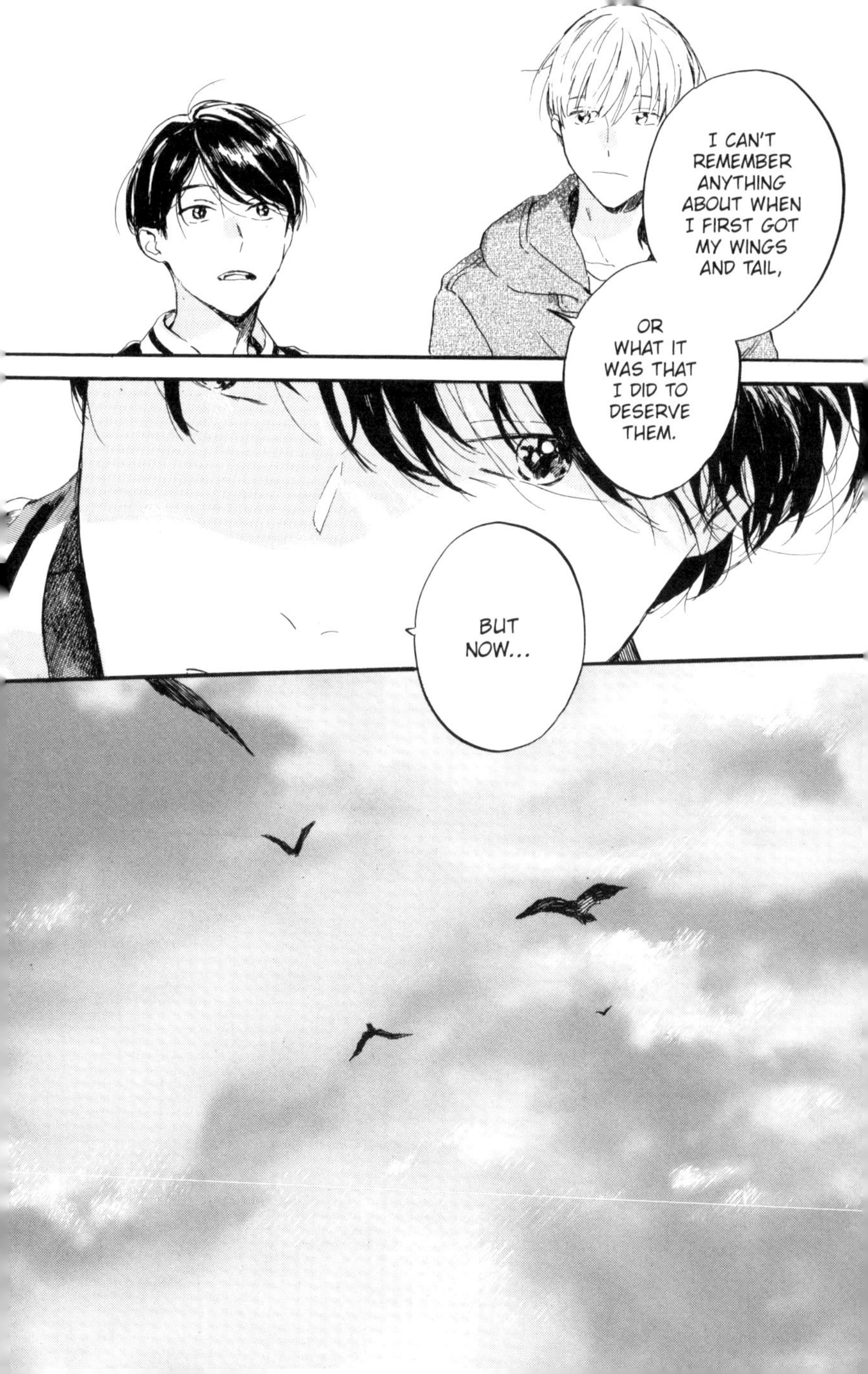
I CAN'T REMEMBER ANYTHING ABOUT WHEN I FIRST GOT MY WINGS AND TAIL,
OR WHAT IT WAS THAT I DID TO DESERVE THEM.
BUT NOW...

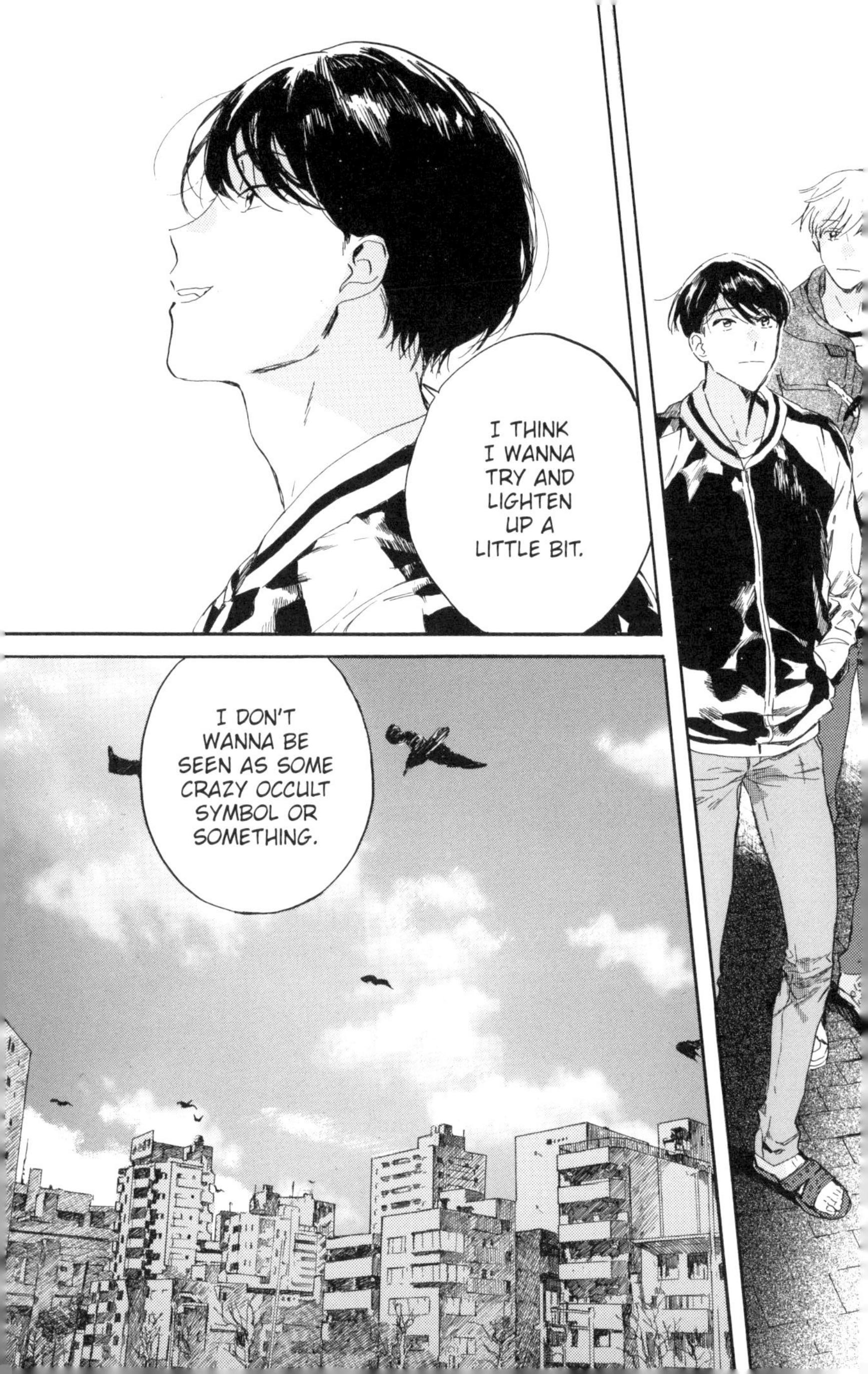
I THINK I WANNA TRY AND LIGHTEN UP A LITTLE BIT.
I DON'T WANNA BE SEEN AS SOME CRAZY OCCULT SYMBOL OR SOMETHING.

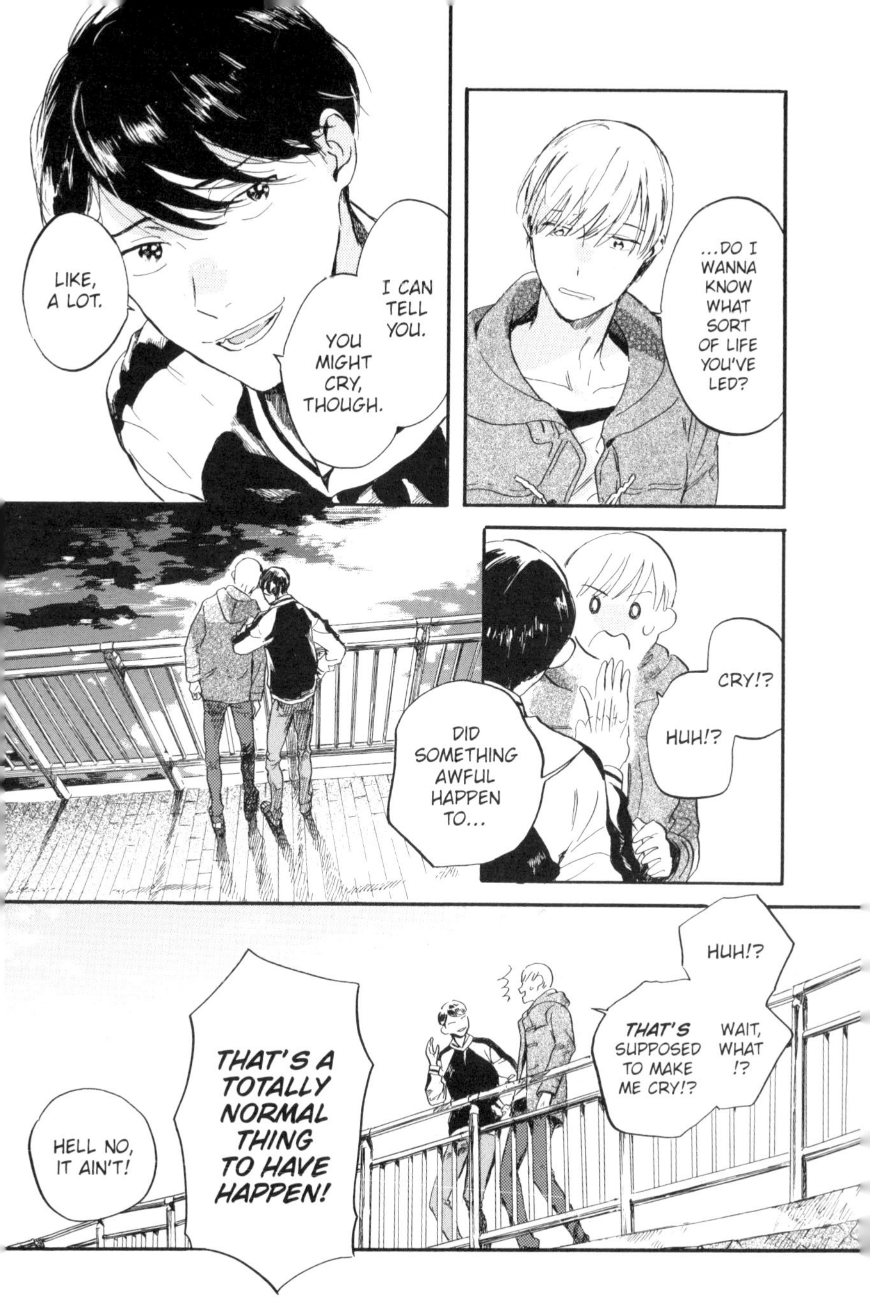
...DO I WANNA KNOW WHAT SORT OF LIFE YOU'VE LED?
I CAN TELL YOU.
YOU MIGHT CRY, THOUGH.
LIKE, A LOT.
CRY!?
HUH!?
DID SOMETHING AWFUL HAPPEN TO...
HUH!?
WAIT, WHAT !?
THAT'S SUPPOSED TO MAKE ME CRY!?
THAT'S A TOTALLY NORMAL THING TO HAVE HAPPEN!
HELL NO, IT AIN'T!

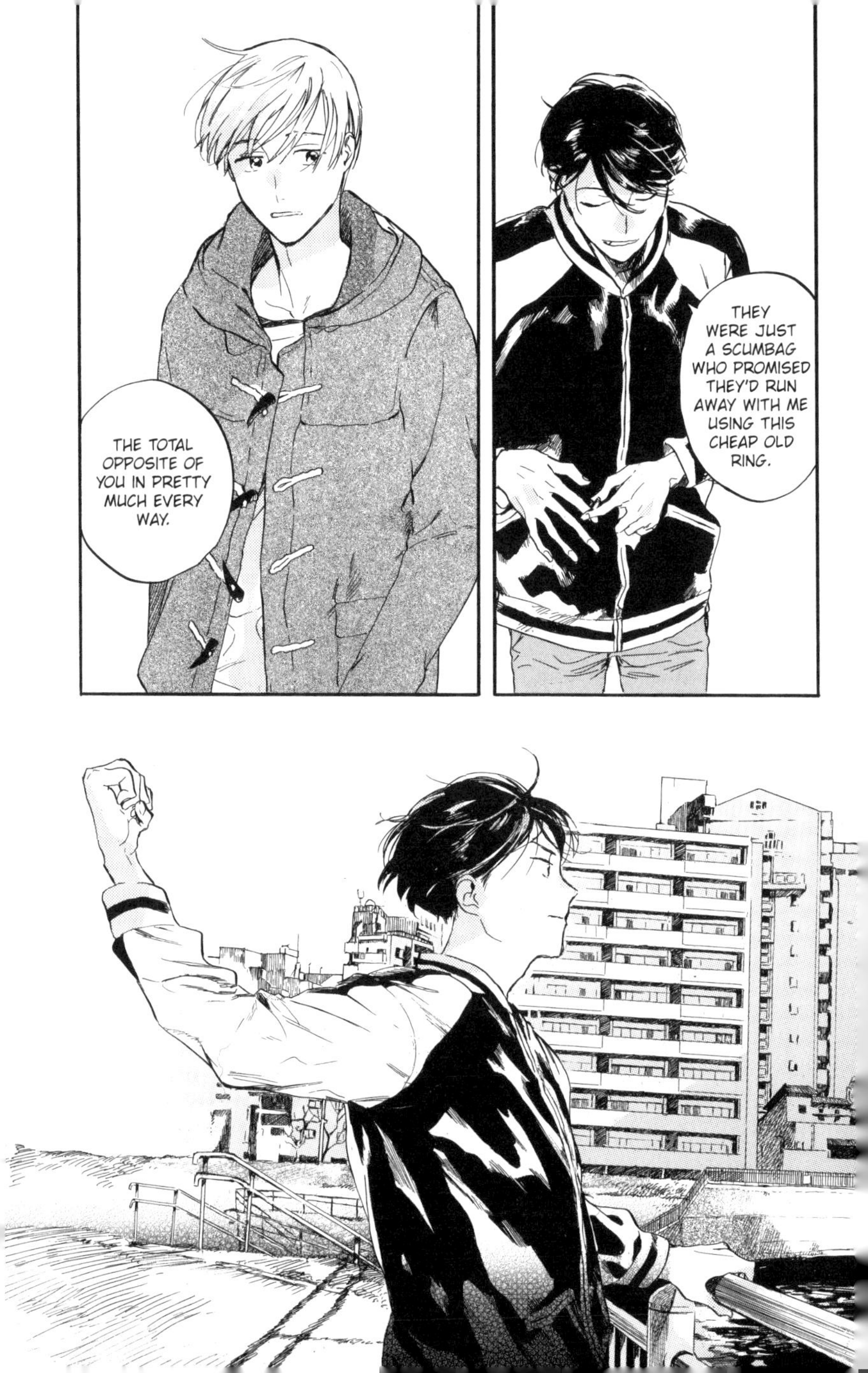
THEY WERE JUST A SCUMBAG WHO PROMISED THEY'D RUN AWAY WITH ME USING THIS CHEAP OLD RING.
THE TOTAL OPPOSITE OF YOU IN PRETTY MUCH EVERY WAY.

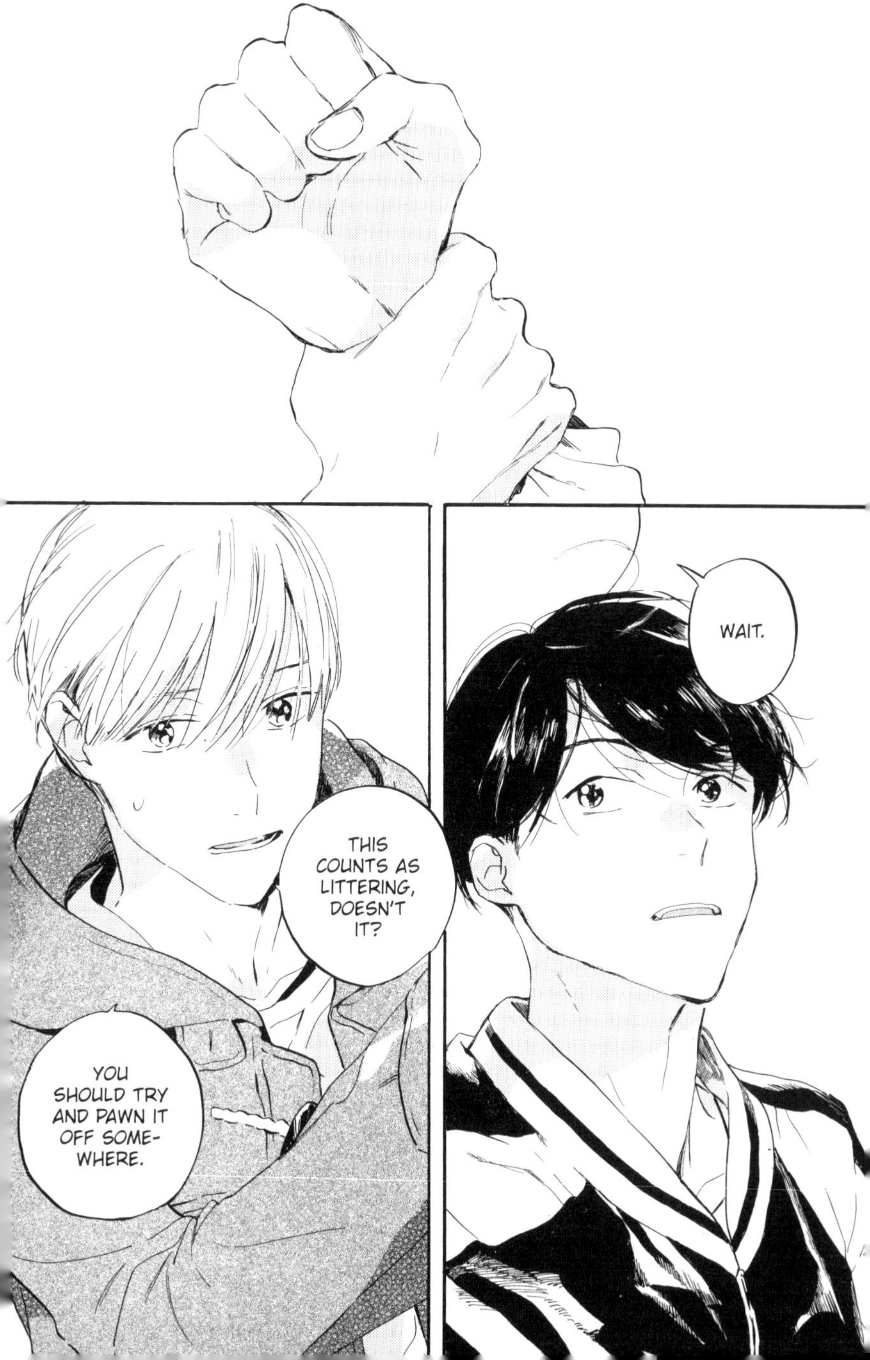
WAIT.
THIS COUNTS AS LITTERING, DOESN'T IT?
YOU SHOULD TRY AND PAWN IT OFF SOME-WHERE.

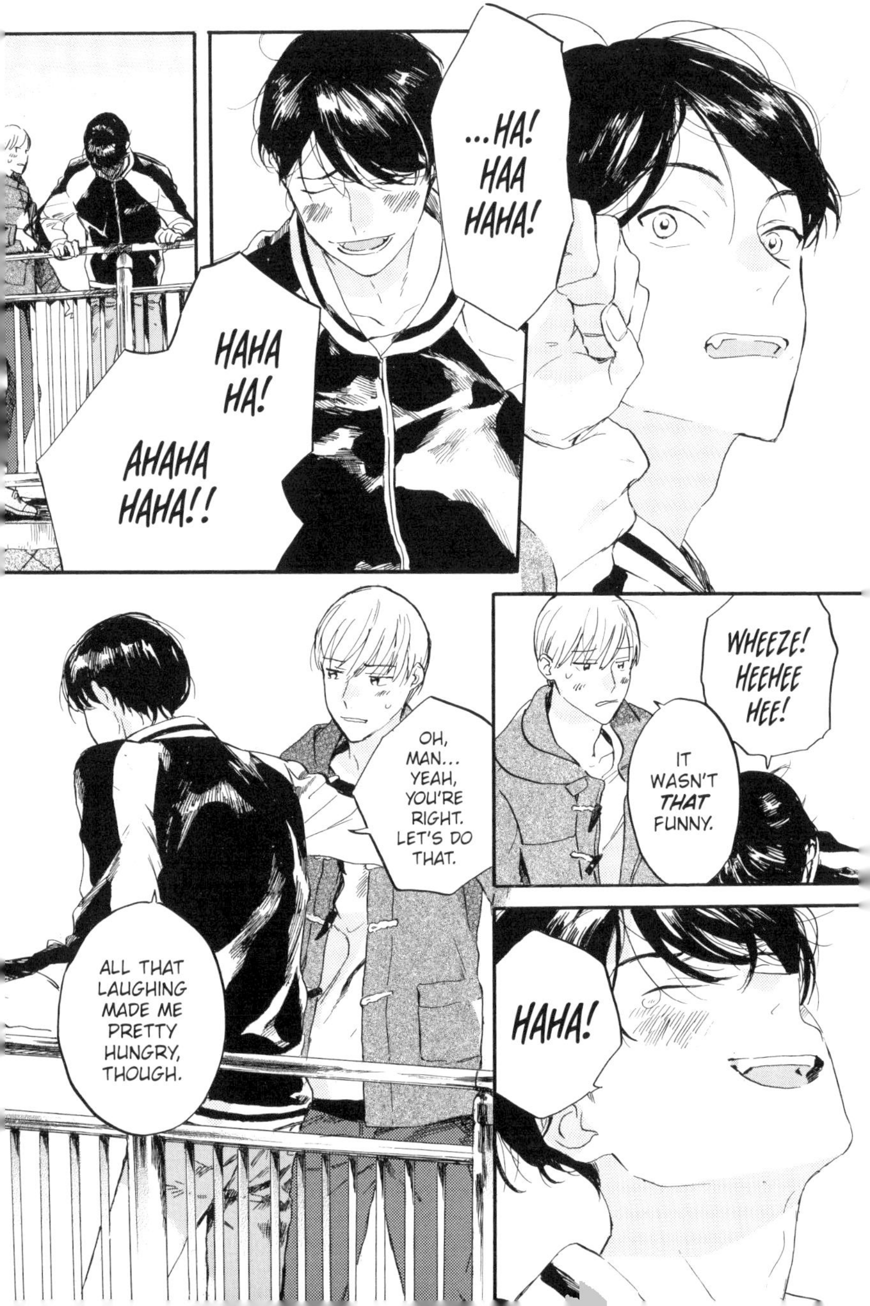
...HA! HAA HAHA!
HAHA HA!
AHAHA HAHA!!
WHEEZE! HEEHEE HEE!
IT WASN'T *THAT* FUNNY.
HAHA!
OH, MAN... YEAH, YOU'RE RIGHT. LET'S DO THAT.
ALL THAT LAUGHING MADE ME PRETTY HUNGRY, THOUGH.

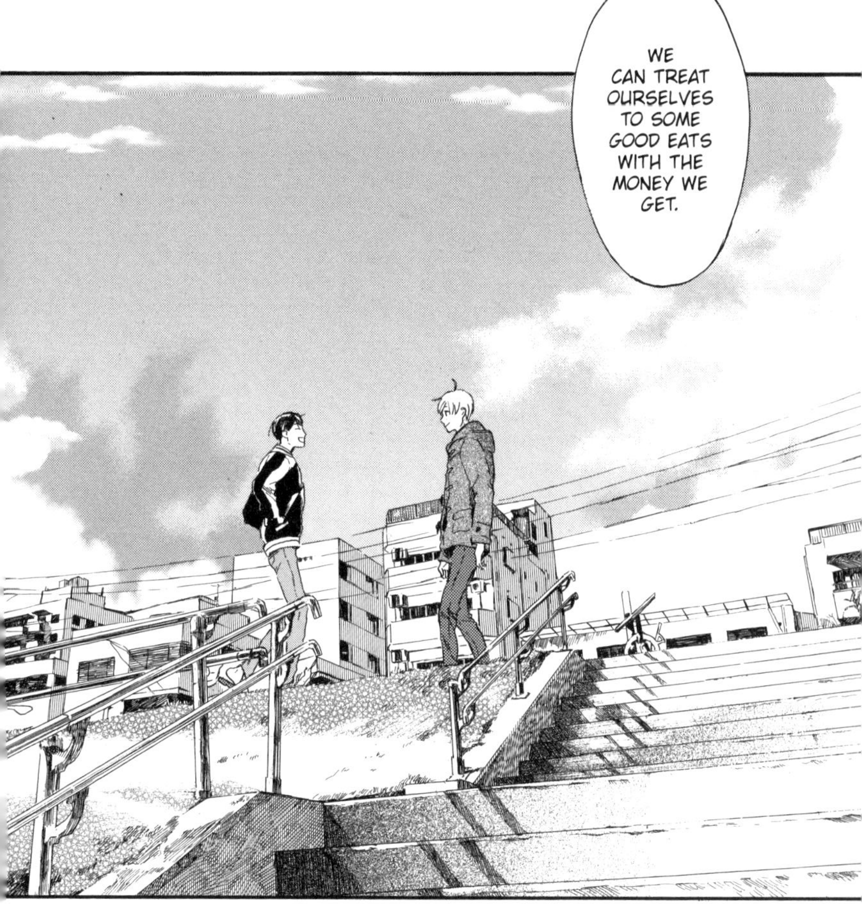
WE CAN TREAT OURSELVES TO SOME GOOD EATS WITH THE MONEY WE GET.

Final Chapter End

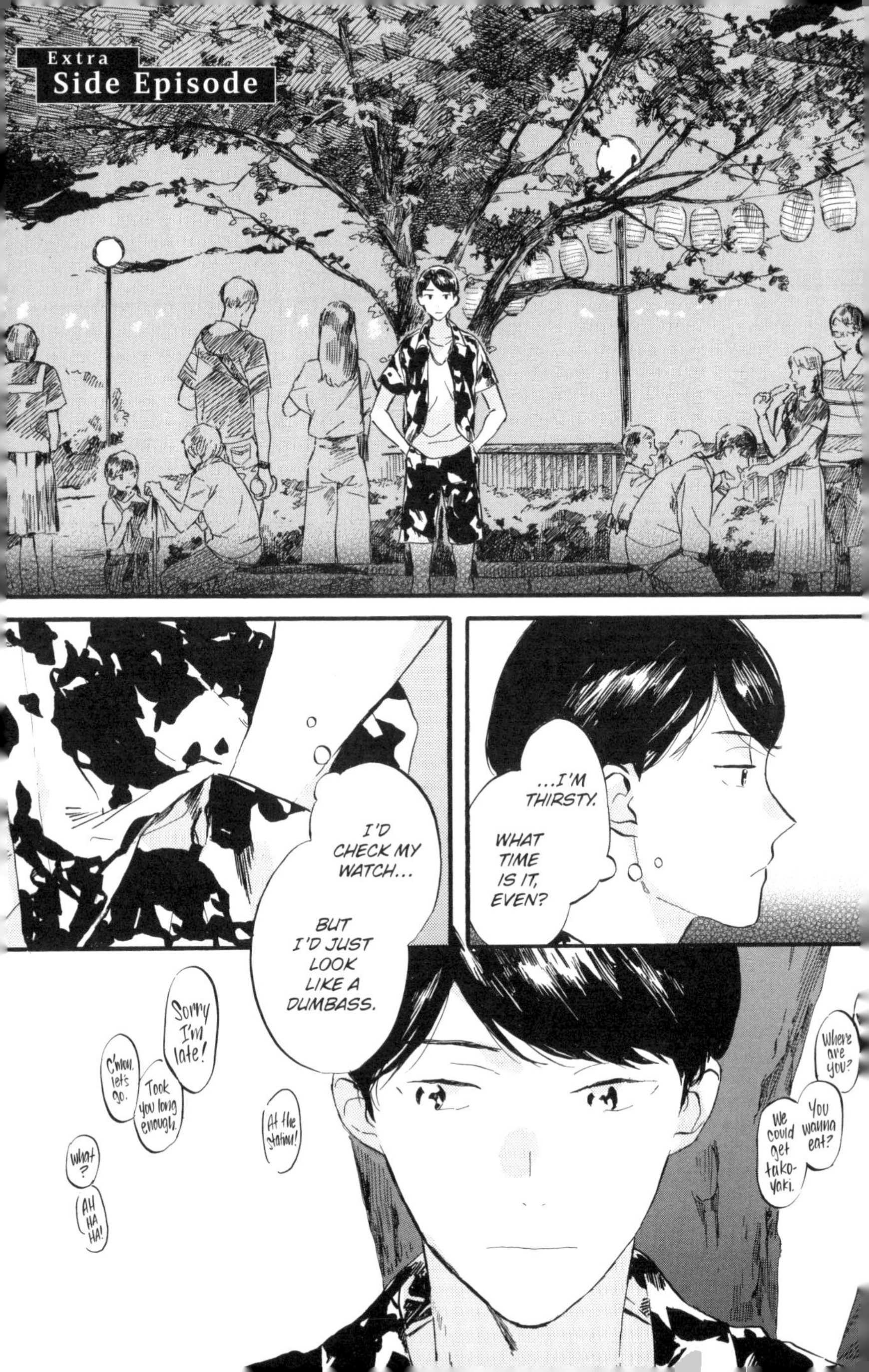
Extra
Side Episode
...I'M THIRSTY.
WHAT TIME IS IT, EVEN?
I'D CHECK MY WATCH...
BUT I'D JUST LOOK LIKE A DUMBASS.
Where are you?
You wanna eat?
We could get tako-yaki.
At the station!
Sorry I'm late!
Took you long enough.
C'mon, let's go.
what?
AH HA HA!

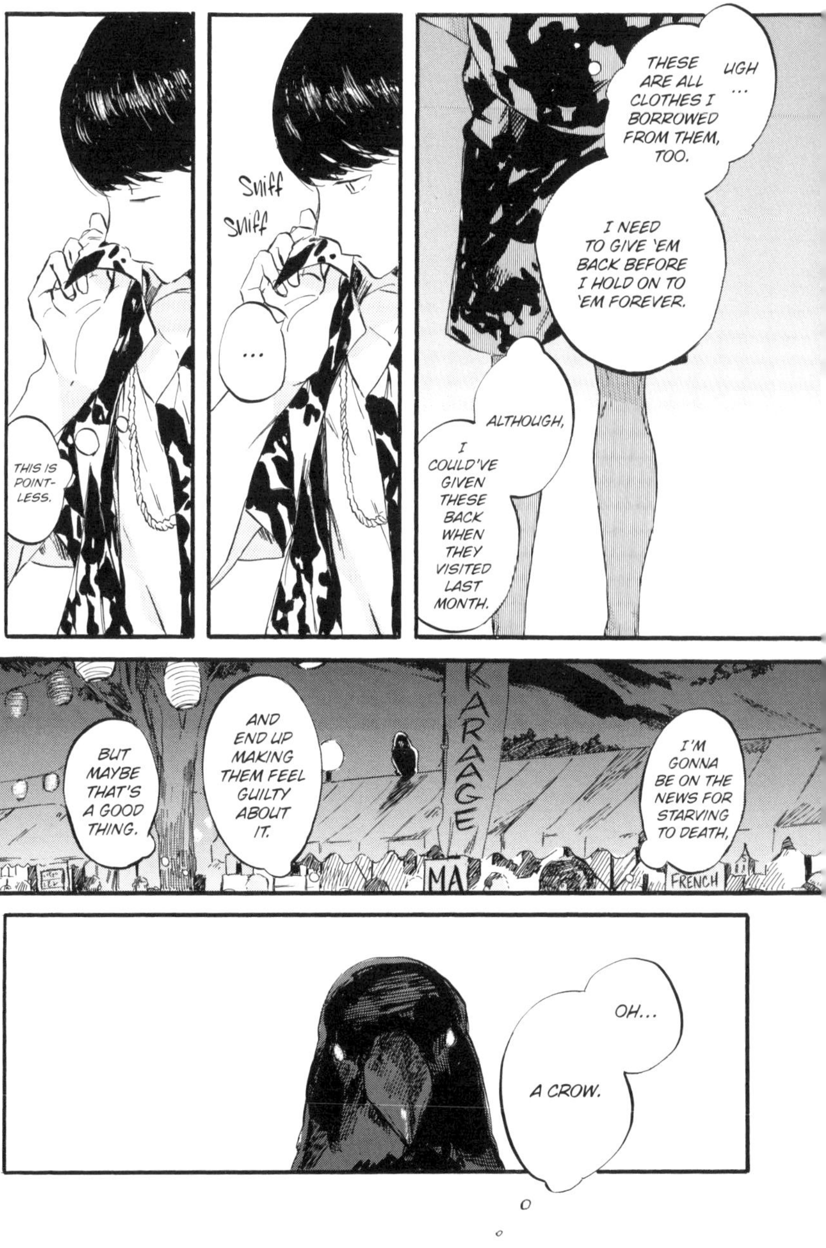
UGH…
THESE ARE ALL CLOTHES I BORROWED FROM THEM, TOO.
I NEED TO GIVE 'EM BACK BEFORE I HOLD ON TO 'EM FOREVER.
ALTHOUGH,
I COULD'VE GIVEN THESE BACK WHEN THEY VISITED LAST MONTH.
Sniff
Sniff
…
THIS IS POINT-LESS.
I'M GONNA BE ON THE NEWS FOR STARVING TO DEATH,
KARAAGE
MA
FRENCH
AND END UP MAKING THEM FEEL GUILTY ABOUT IT.
BUT MAYBE THAT'S A GOOD THING.
OH…
A CROW.

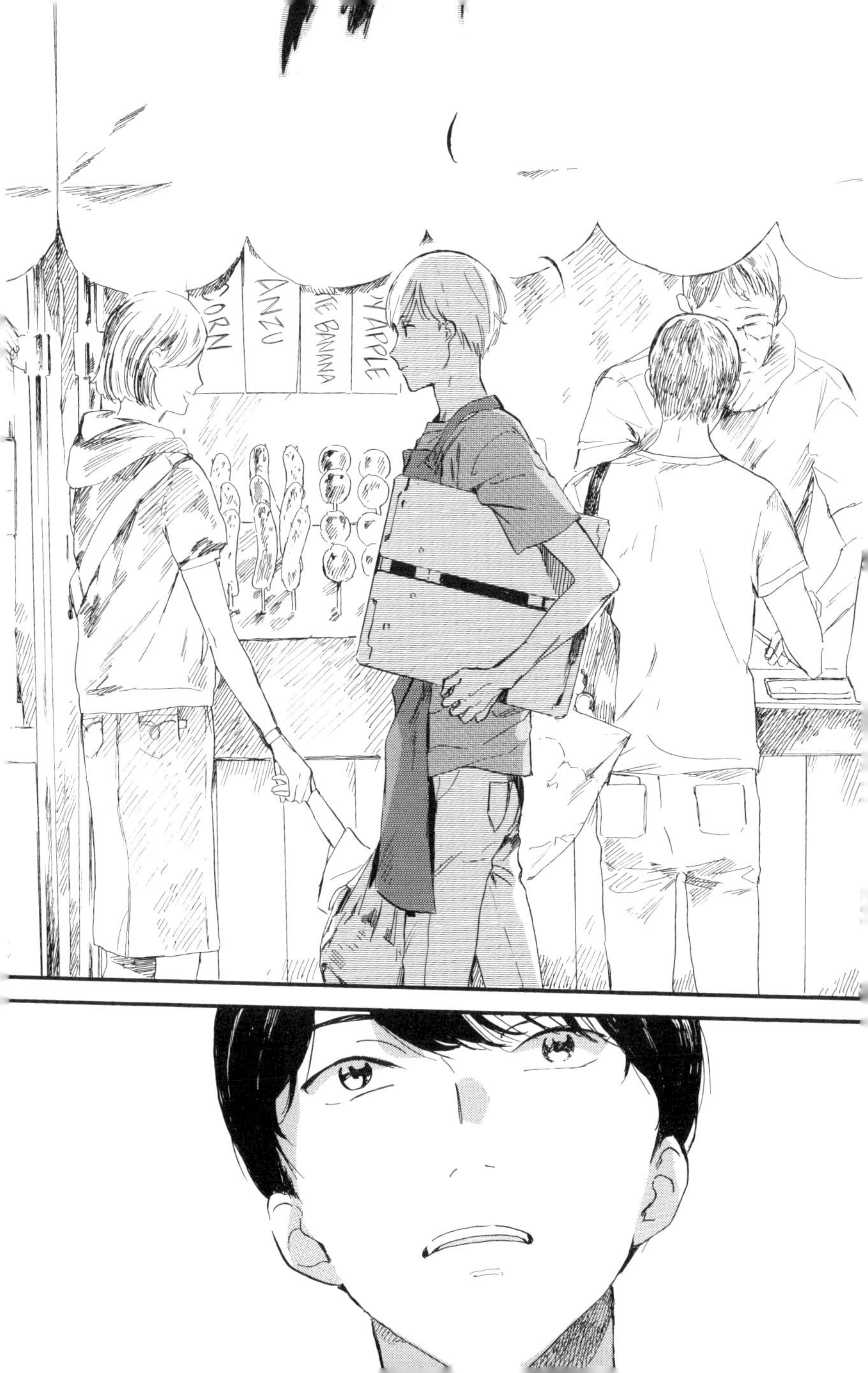
APPLE
BANANA
ANZU
CORN

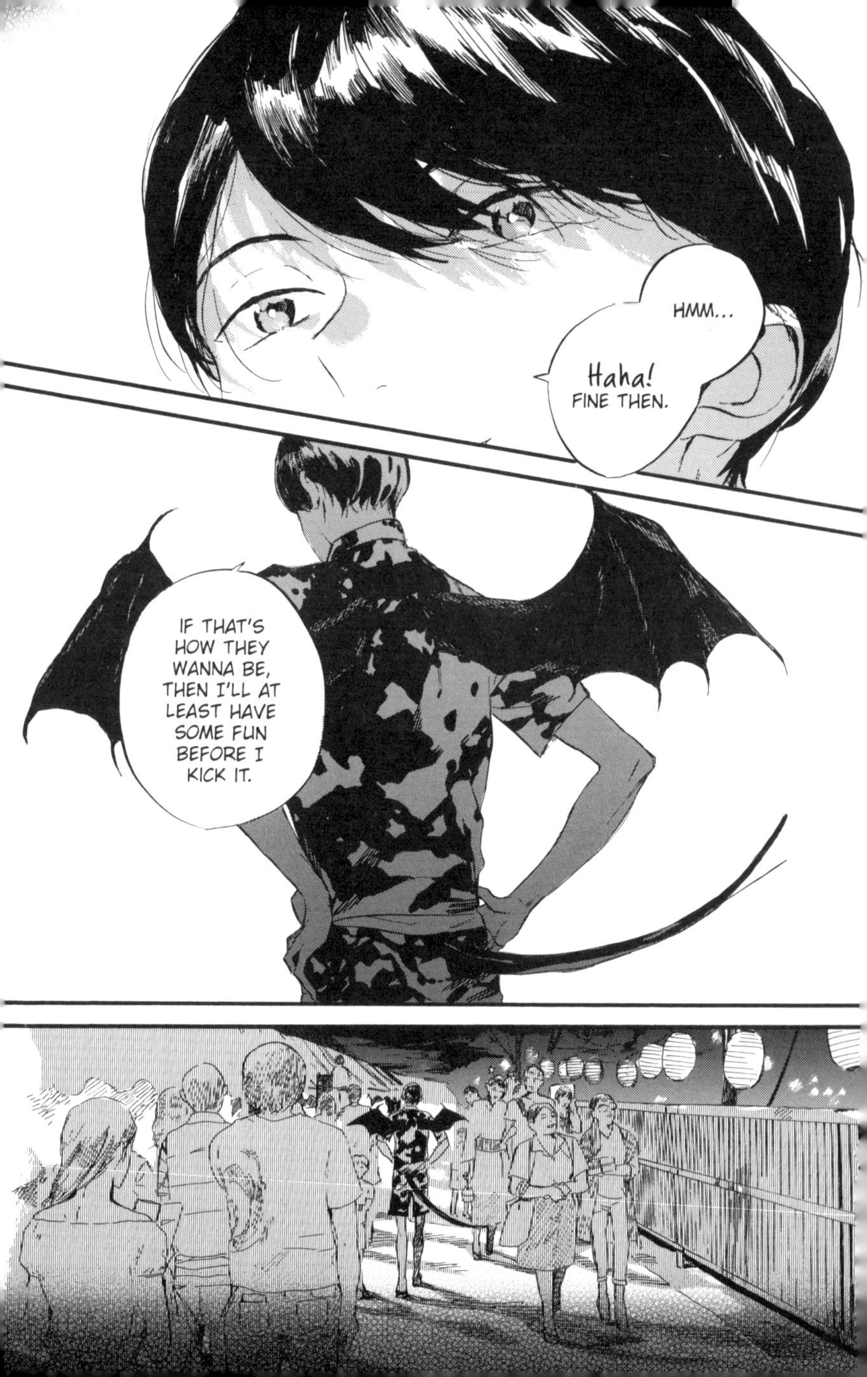
HMM...
Haha! FINE THEN.
IF THAT'S HOW THEY WANNA BE, THEN I'LL AT LEAST HAVE SOME FUN BEFORE I KICK IT.

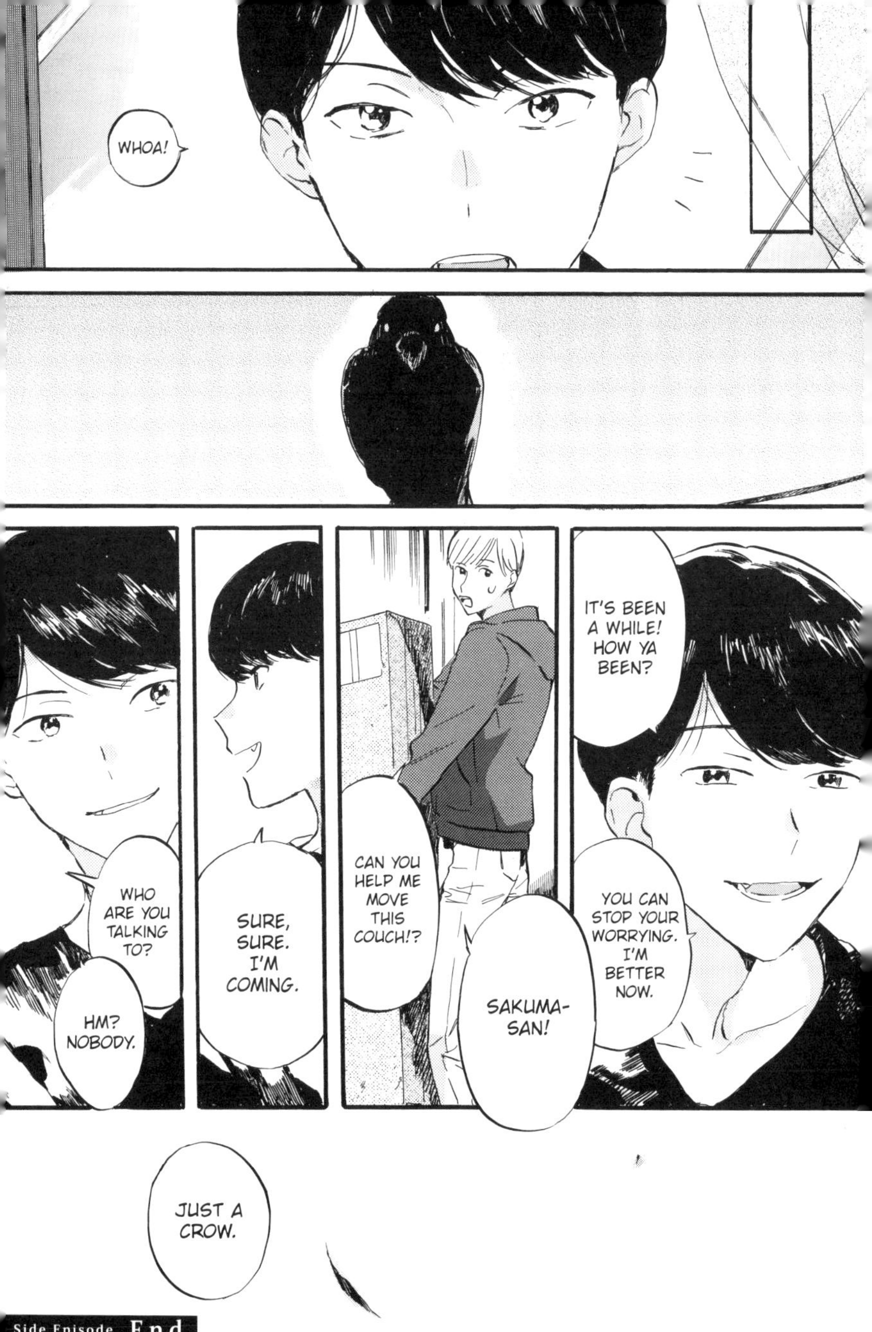
WHOA!
IT'S BEEN A WHILE! HOW YA BEEN?
YOU CAN STOP YOUR WORRYING. I'M BETTER NOW.
SAKUMA-SAN!
CAN YOU HELP ME MOVE THIS COUCH!?
SURE, SURE. I'M COMING.
WHO ARE YOU TALKING TO?
HM? NOBODY.
JUST A CROW.

Side Episode End

The River's Water Tastes Sweet

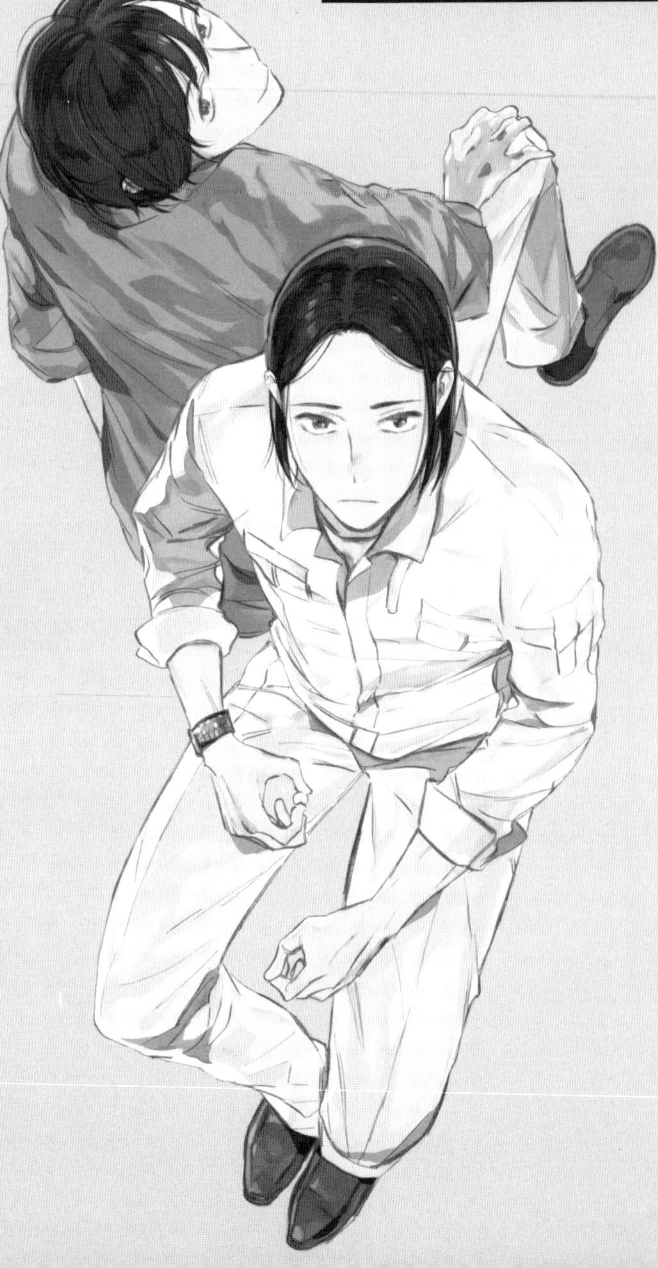

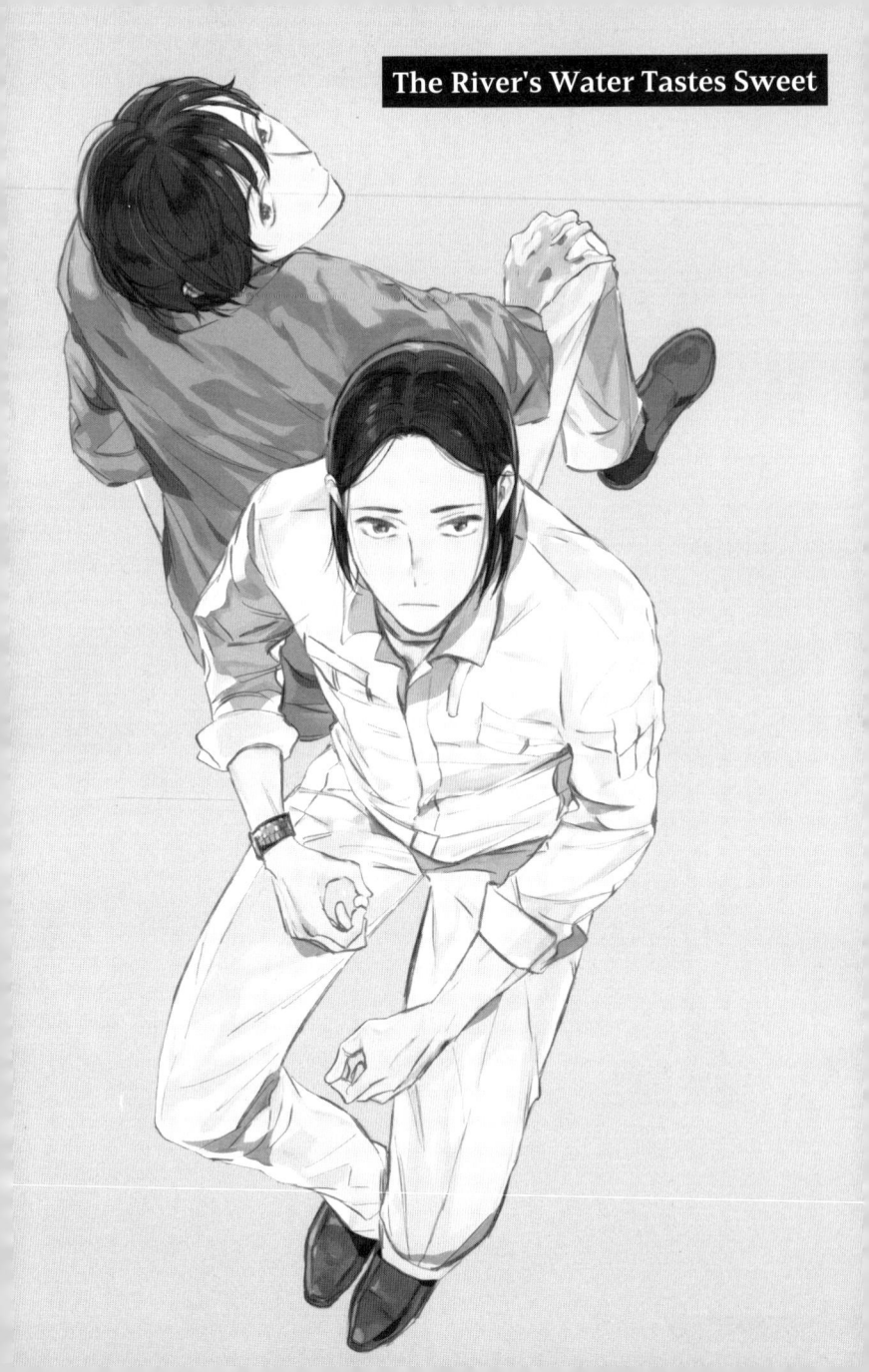

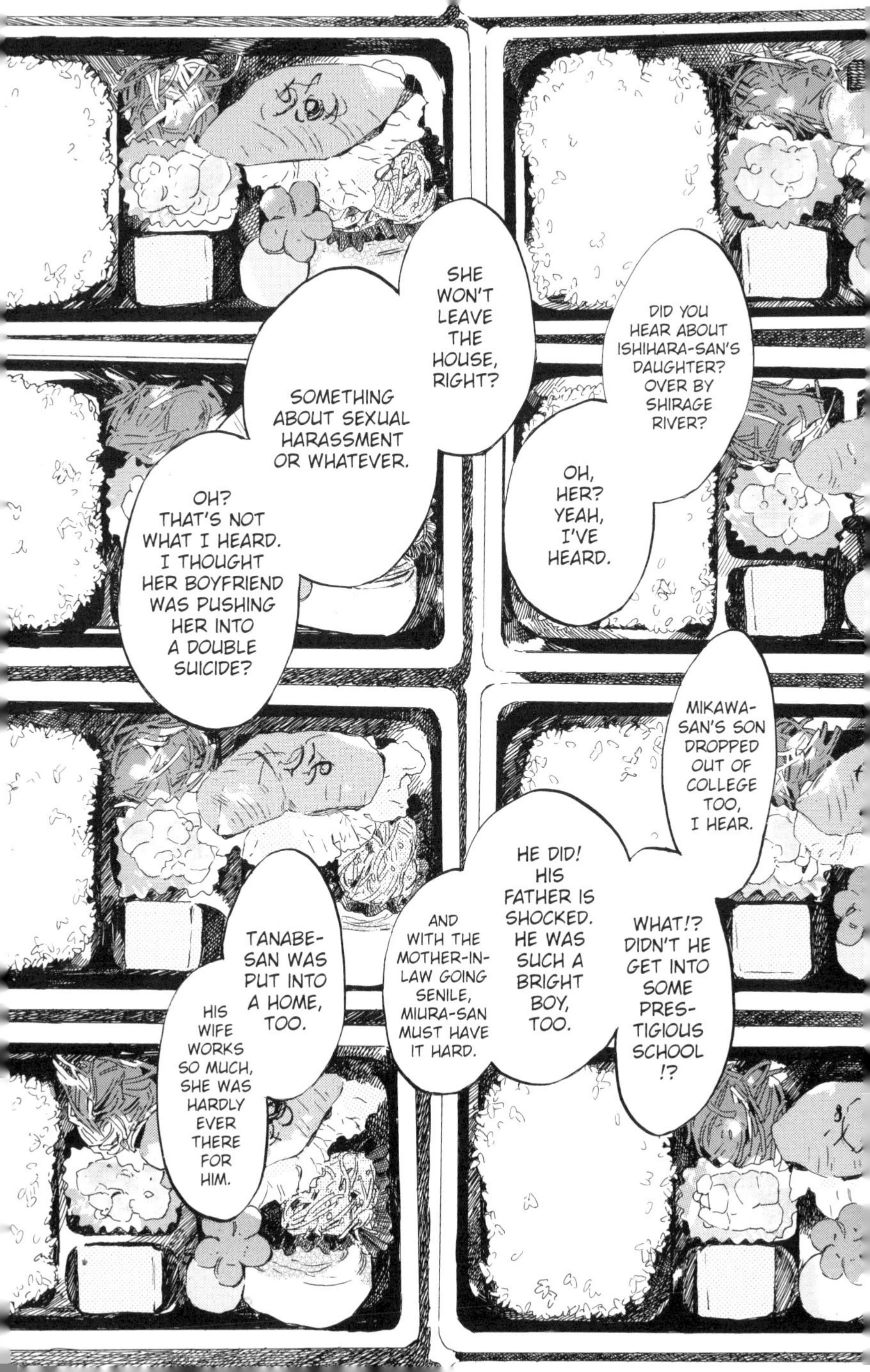
DID YOU HEAR ABOUT ISHIHARA-SAN'S DAUGHTER? OVER BY SHIRAGE RIVER?
OH, HER? YEAH, I'VE HEARD.
SHE WON'T LEAVE THE HOUSE, RIGHT?
SOMETHING ABOUT SEXUAL HARASSMENT OR WHATEVER.
OH? THAT'S NOT WHAT I HEARD. I THOUGHT HER BOYFRIEND WAS PUSHING HER INTO A DOUBLE SUICIDE?
MIKAWA-SAN'S SON DROPPED OUT OF COLLEGE TOO, I HEAR.
WHAT!? DIDN'T HE GET INTO SOME PRES-TIGIOUS SCHOOL !?
HE DID! HIS FATHER IS SHOCKED. HE WAS SUCH A BRIGHT BOY, TOO.
AND WITH THE MOTHER-IN-LAW GOING SENILE, MIURA-SAN MUST HAVE IT HARD.
TANABE-SAN WAS PUT INTO A HOME, TOO.
HIS WIFE WORKS SO MUCH, SHE WAS HARDLY EVER THERE FOR HIM.

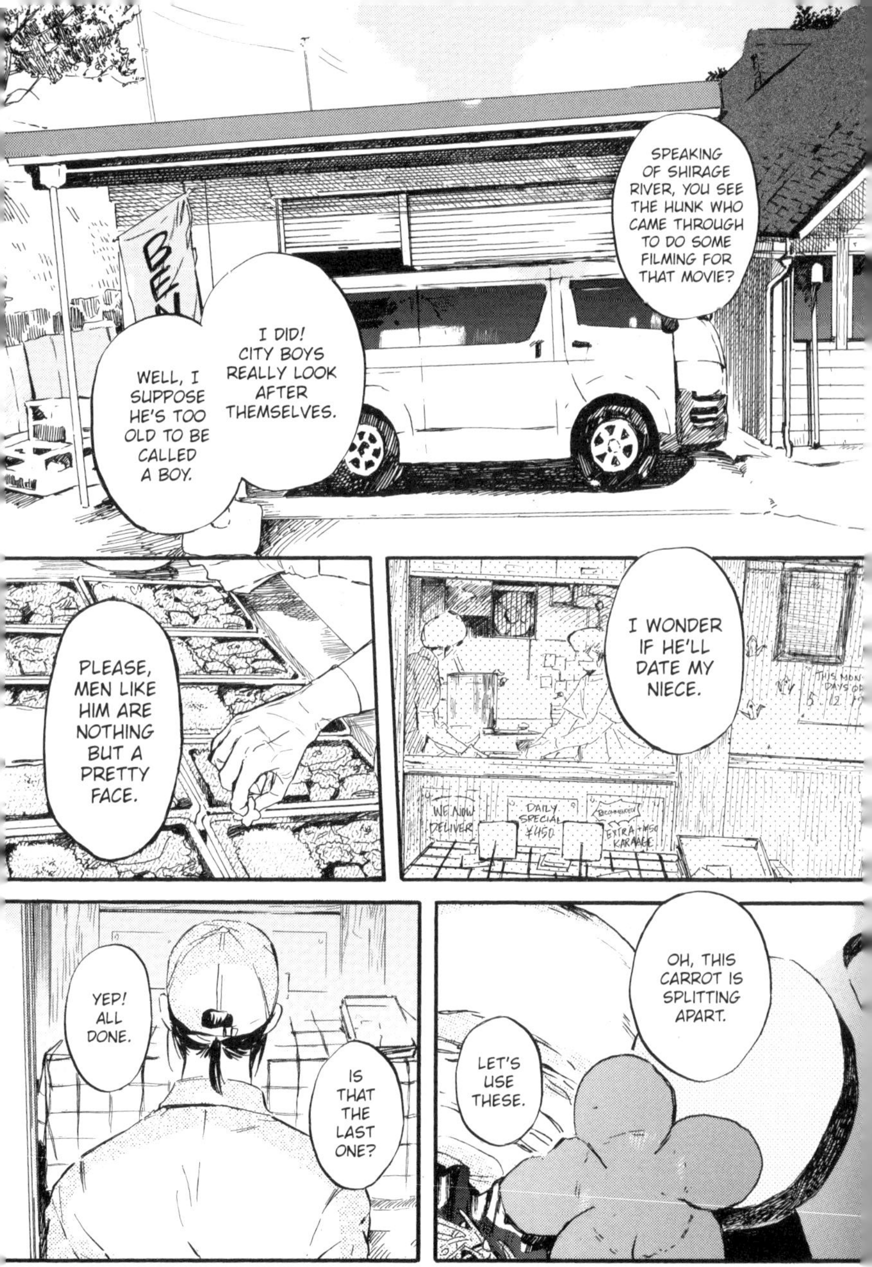
SPEAKING OF SHIRAGE RIVER, YOU SEE THE HUNK WHO CAME THROUGH TO DO SOME FILMING FOR THAT MOVIE?
I DID! CITY BOYS REALLY LOOK AFTER THEMSELVES.
WELL, I SUPPOSE HE'S TOO OLD TO BE CALLED A BOY.
I WONDER IF HE'LL DATE MY NIECE.
WE NOW DELIVER
DAILY SPECIAL ¥450
RECOMMENDED!
EXTRA +¥50 KARAAGE
PLEASE, MEN LIKE HIM ARE NOTHING BUT A PRETTY FACE.
OH, THIS CARROT IS SPLITTING APART.
LET'S USE THESE.
IS THAT THE LAST ONE?
YEP! ALL DONE.

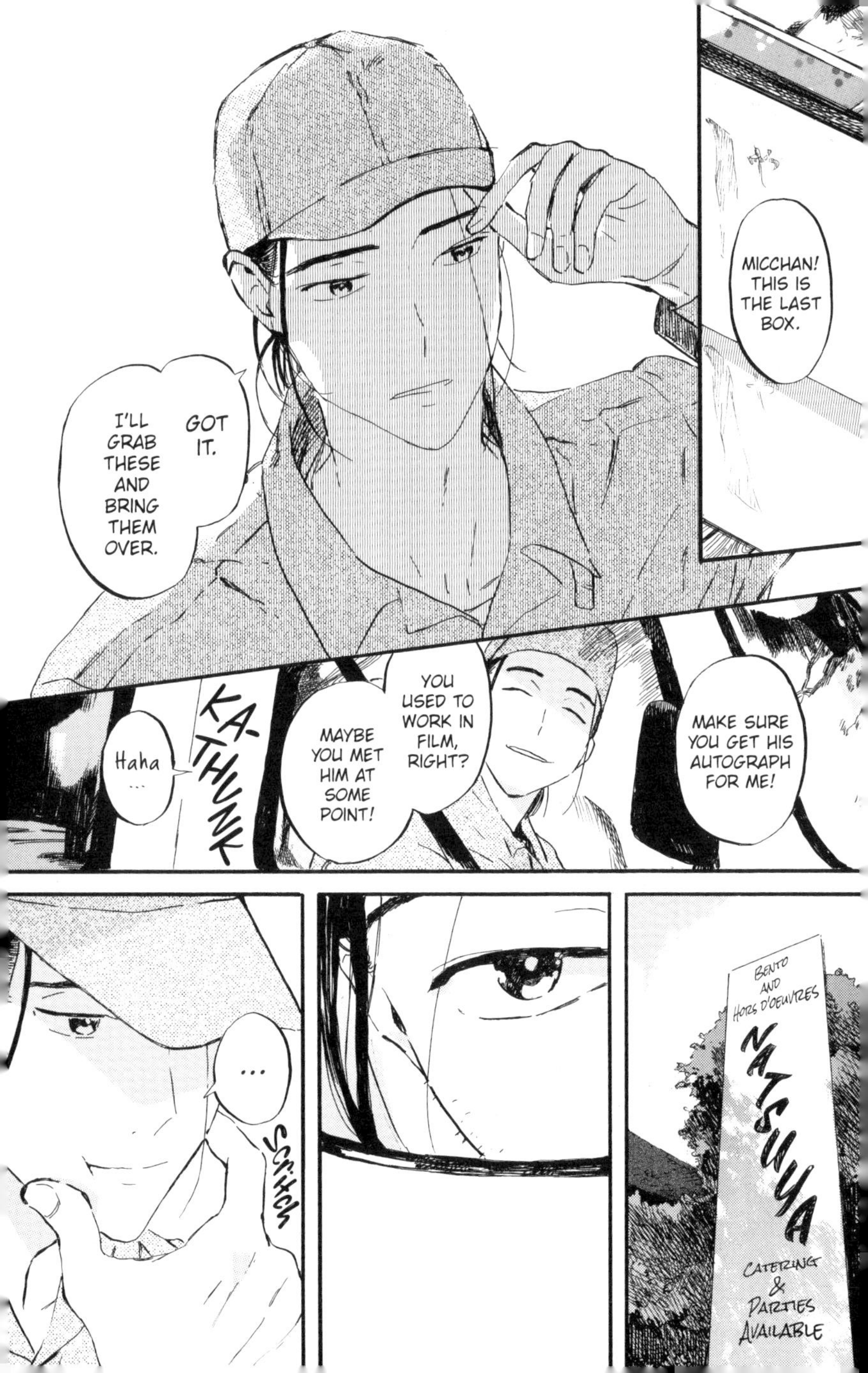
MICCHAN! THIS IS THE LAST BOX.
GOT IT.
I'LL GRAB THESE AND BRING THEM OVER.
MAKE SURE YOU GET HIS AUTOGRAPH FOR ME!
YOU USED TO WORK IN FILM, RIGHT?
MAYBE YOU MET HIM AT SOME POINT!
KA-THUNK
Haha ...
BENTO AND HORS D'OEUVRES
NATSUYA
CATERING & PARTIES AVAILABLE
...
SCRITCH

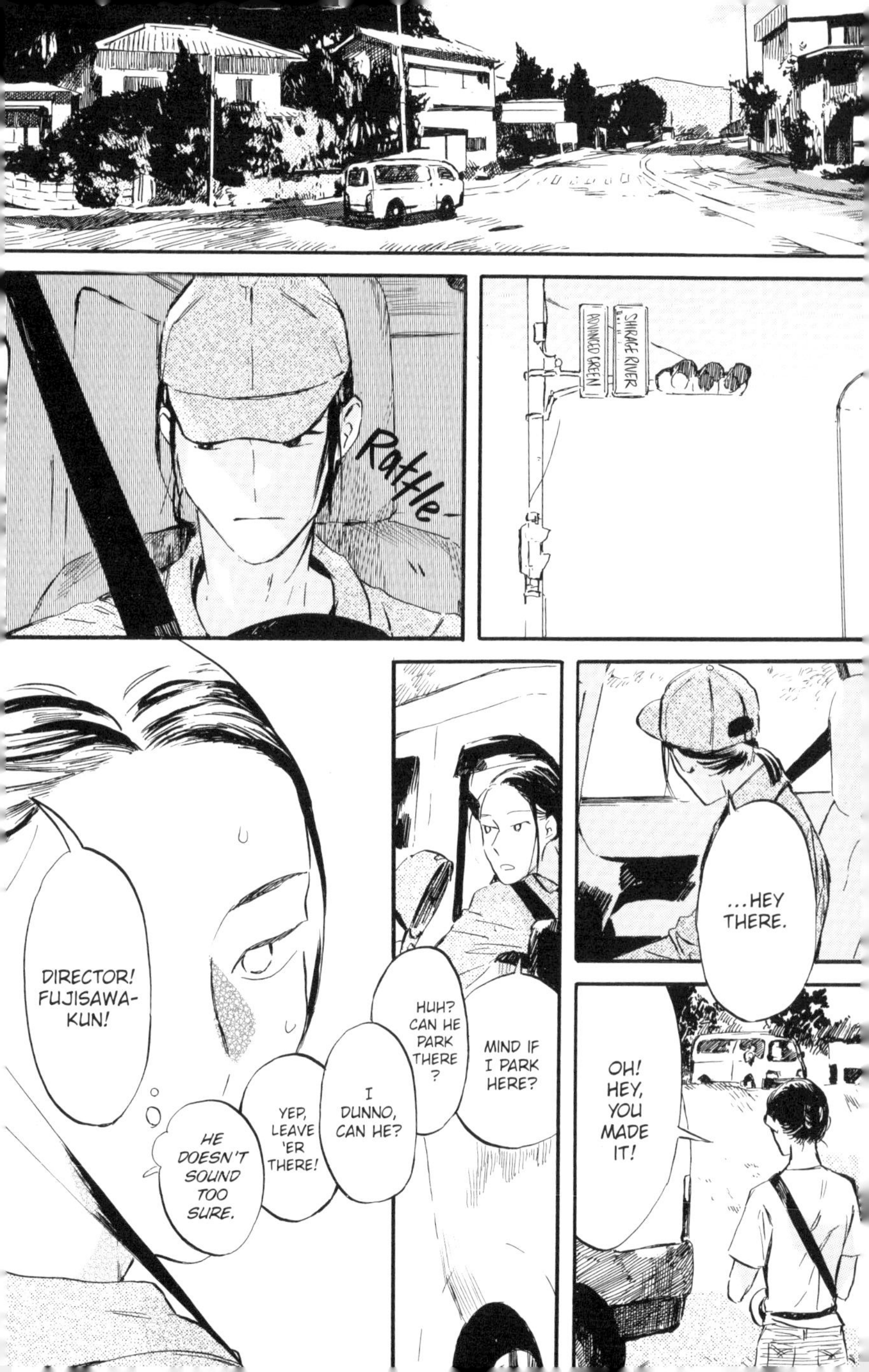
SHIRAGE RIVER
ADVANCED GREEN
Rattle
...HEY THERE.
OH! HEY, YOU MADE IT!
MIND IF I PARK HERE?
HUH? CAN HE PARK THERE?
I DUNNO, CAN HE?
YEP, LEAVE 'ER THERE!
DIRECTOR! FUJISAWA-KUN!
HE DOESN'T SOUND TOO SURE.

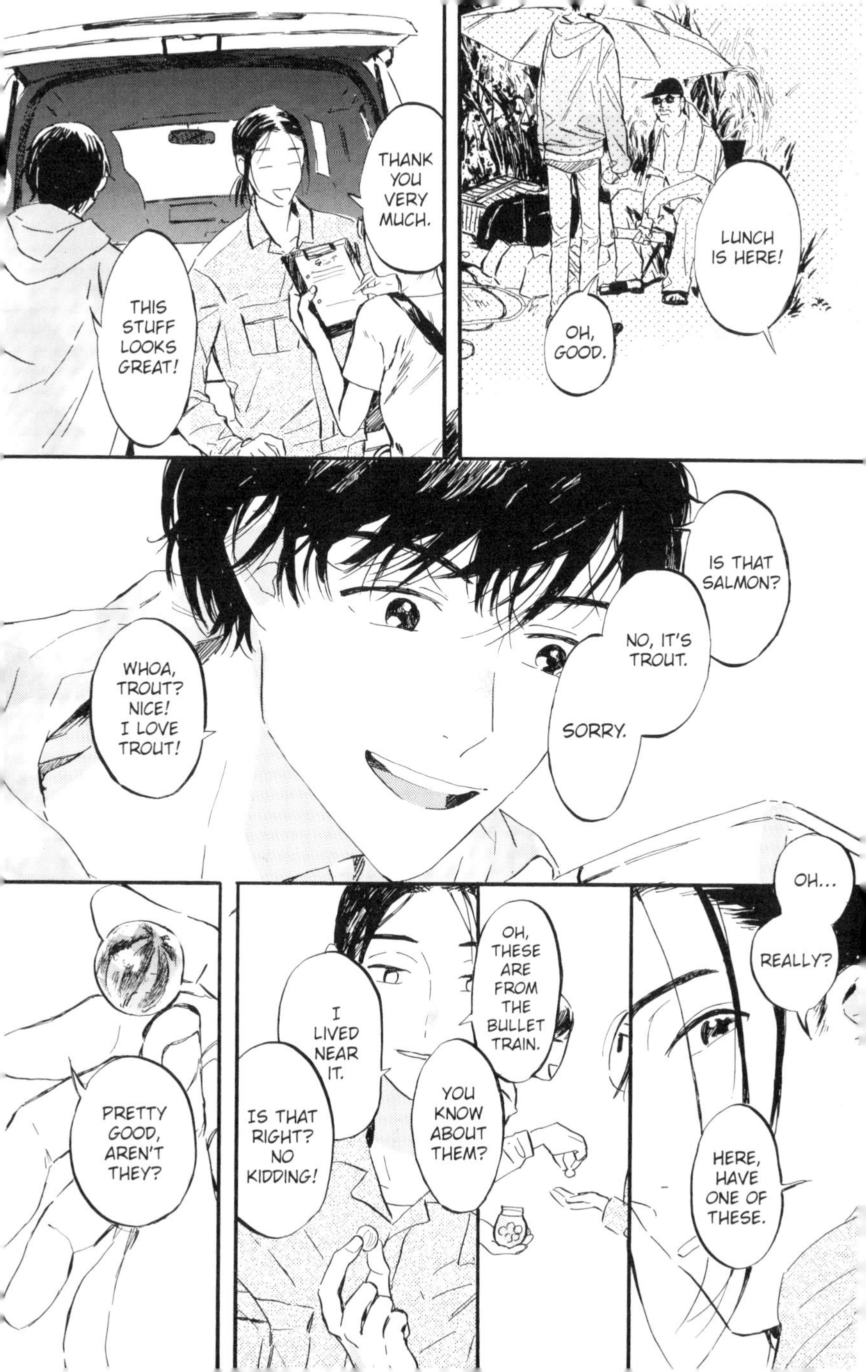
LUNCH IS HERE!
OH, GOOD.
THANK YOU VERY MUCH.
THIS STUFF LOOKS GREAT!
IS THAT SALMON?
NO, IT'S TROUT.
SORRY.
WHOA, TROUT? NICE! I LOVE TROUT!
OH...
REALLY?
HERE, HAVE ONE OF THESE.
OH, THESE ARE FROM THE BULLET TRAIN.
YOU KNOW ABOUT THEM?
I LIVED NEAR IT.
IS THAT RIGHT? NO KIDDING!
PRETTY GOOD, AREN'T THEY?

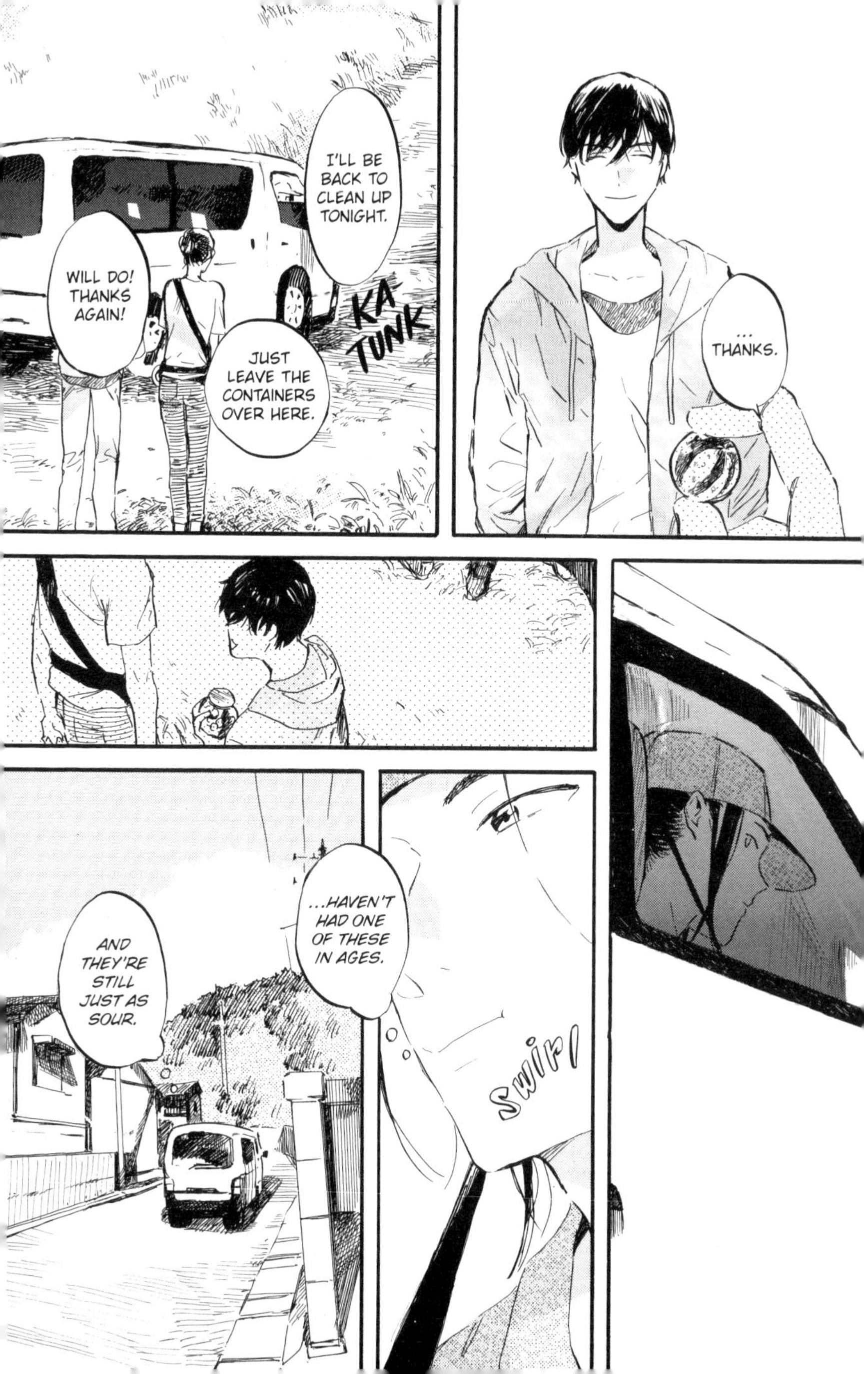
...THANKS.
I'LL BE BACK TO CLEAN UP TONIGHT.
KA TUNK
JUST LEAVE THE CONTAINERS OVER HERE.
WILL DO! THANKS AGAIN!
...HAVEN'T HAD ONE OF THESE IN AGES.
swirl
AND THEY'RE STILL JUST AS SOUR.

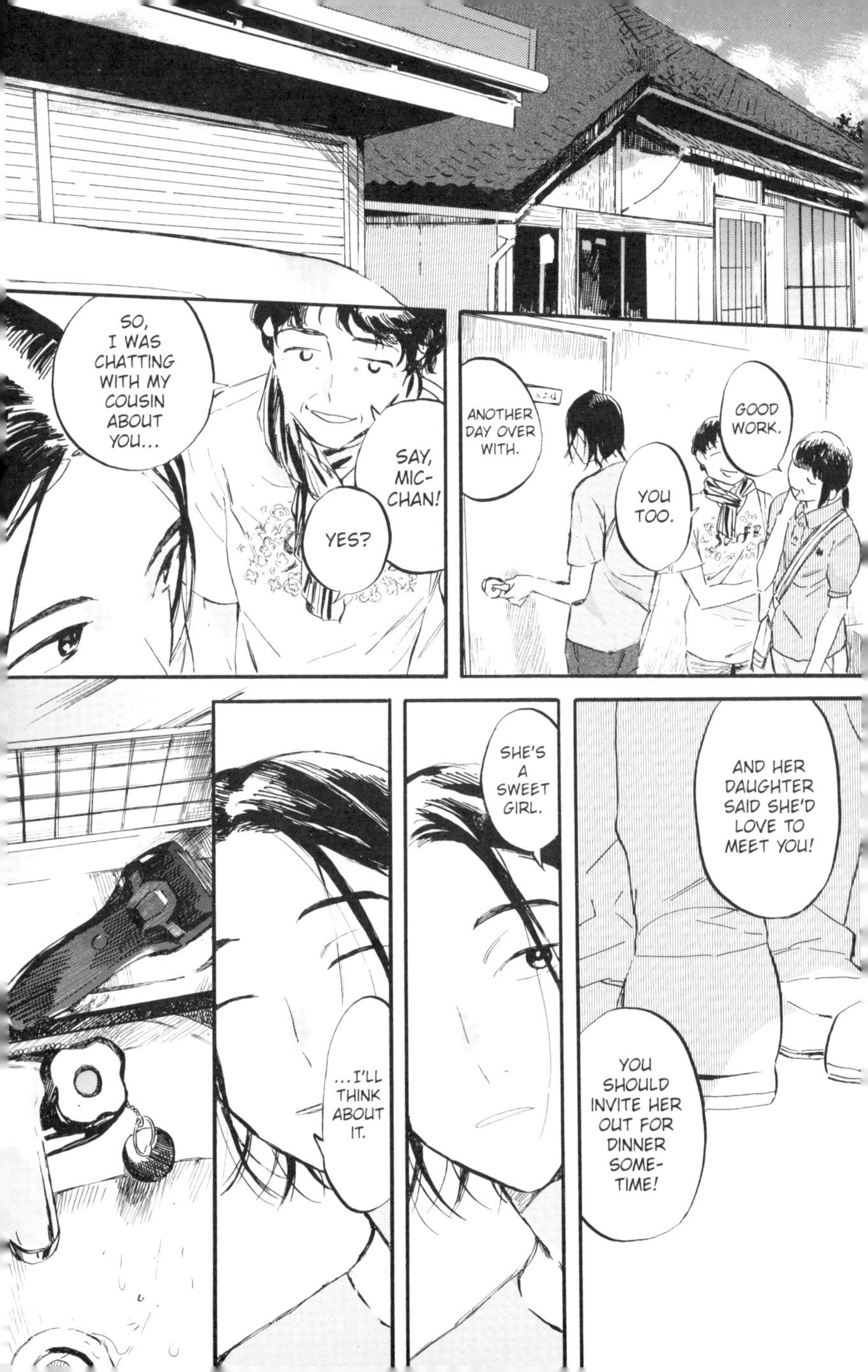
GOOD WORK.
YOU TOO.
ANOTHER DAY OVER WITH.
SAY, MIC-CHAN!
YES?
SO, I WAS CHATTING WITH MY COUSIN ABOUT YOU...
AND HER DAUGHTER SAID SHE'D LOVE TO MEET YOU!
YOU SHOULD INVITE HER OUT FOR DINNER SOME-TIME!
SHE'S A SWEET GIRL.
...I'LL THINK ABOUT IT.

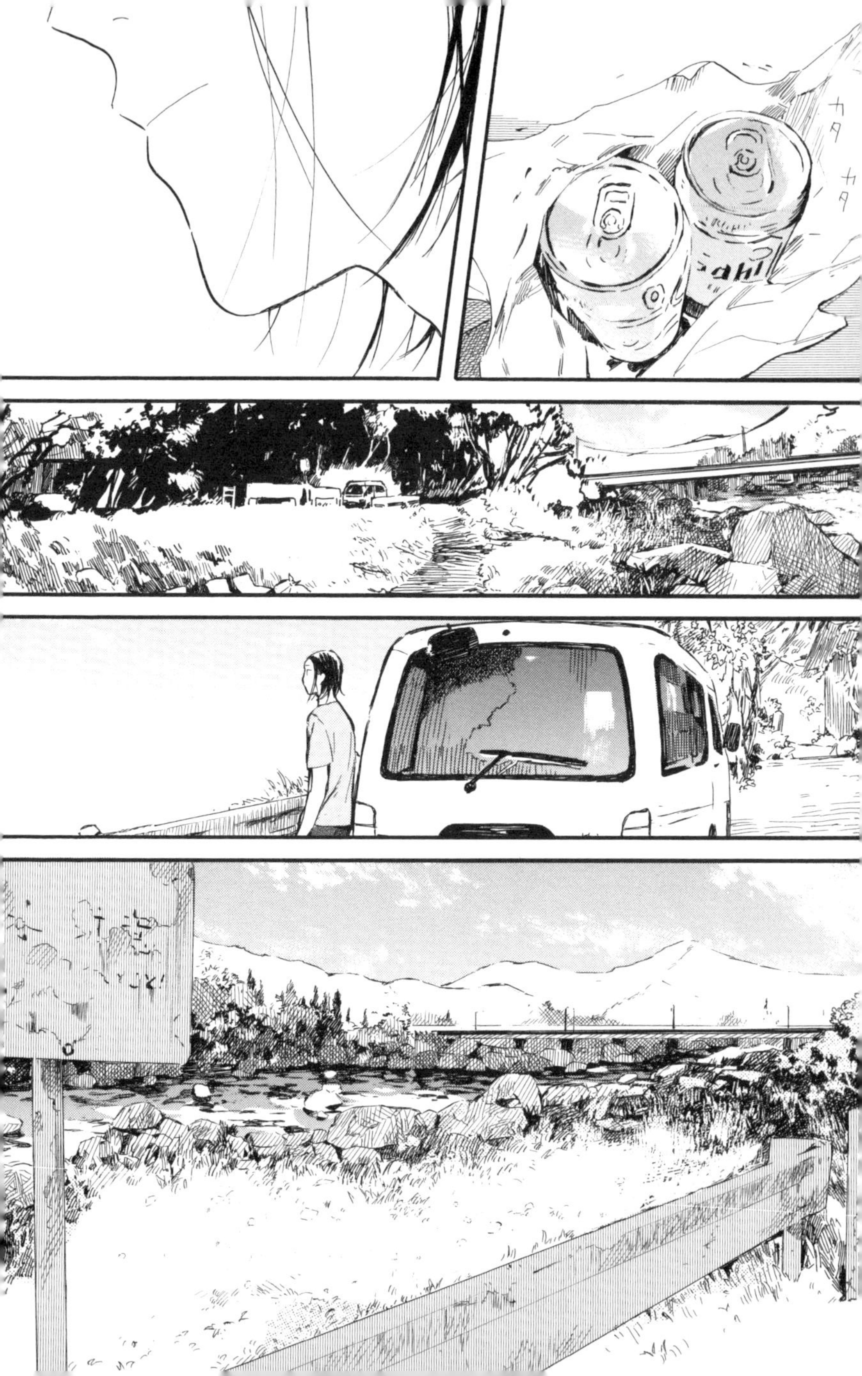
カタ
カタ

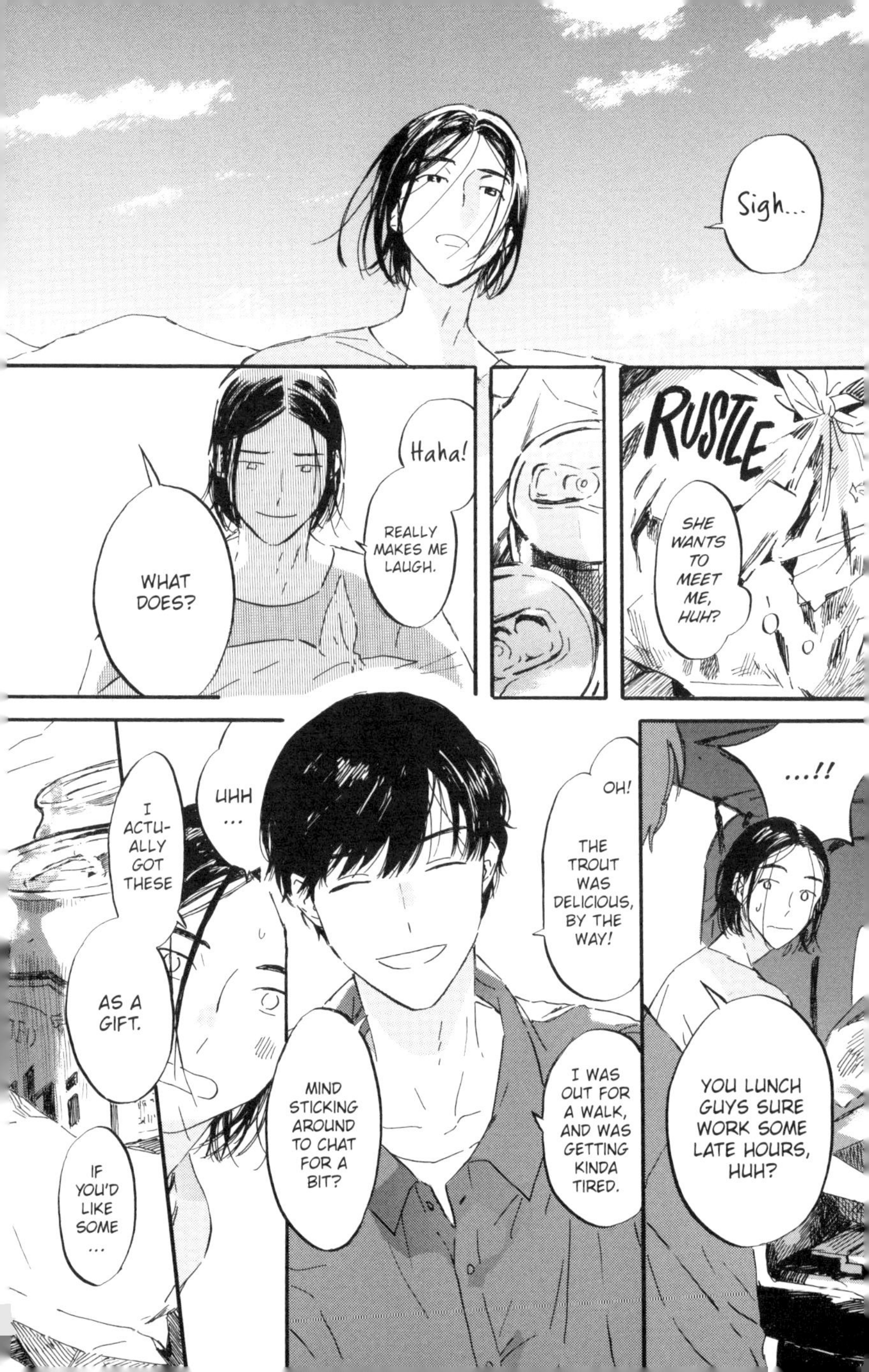
Sigh...
RUSTLE
SHE WANTS TO MEET ME, HUH?
Haha!
REALLY MAKES ME LAUGH.
WHAT DOES?
...!!
YOU LUNCH GUYS SURE WORK SOME LATE HOURS, HUH?
OH!
THE TROUT WAS DELICIOUS, BY THE WAY!
I WAS OUT FOR A WALK, AND WAS GETTING KINDA TIRED.
MIND STICKING AROUND TO CHAT FOR A BIT?
UHH ...
I ACTU-ALLY GOT THESE
AS A GIFT.
IF YOU'D LIKE SOME ...

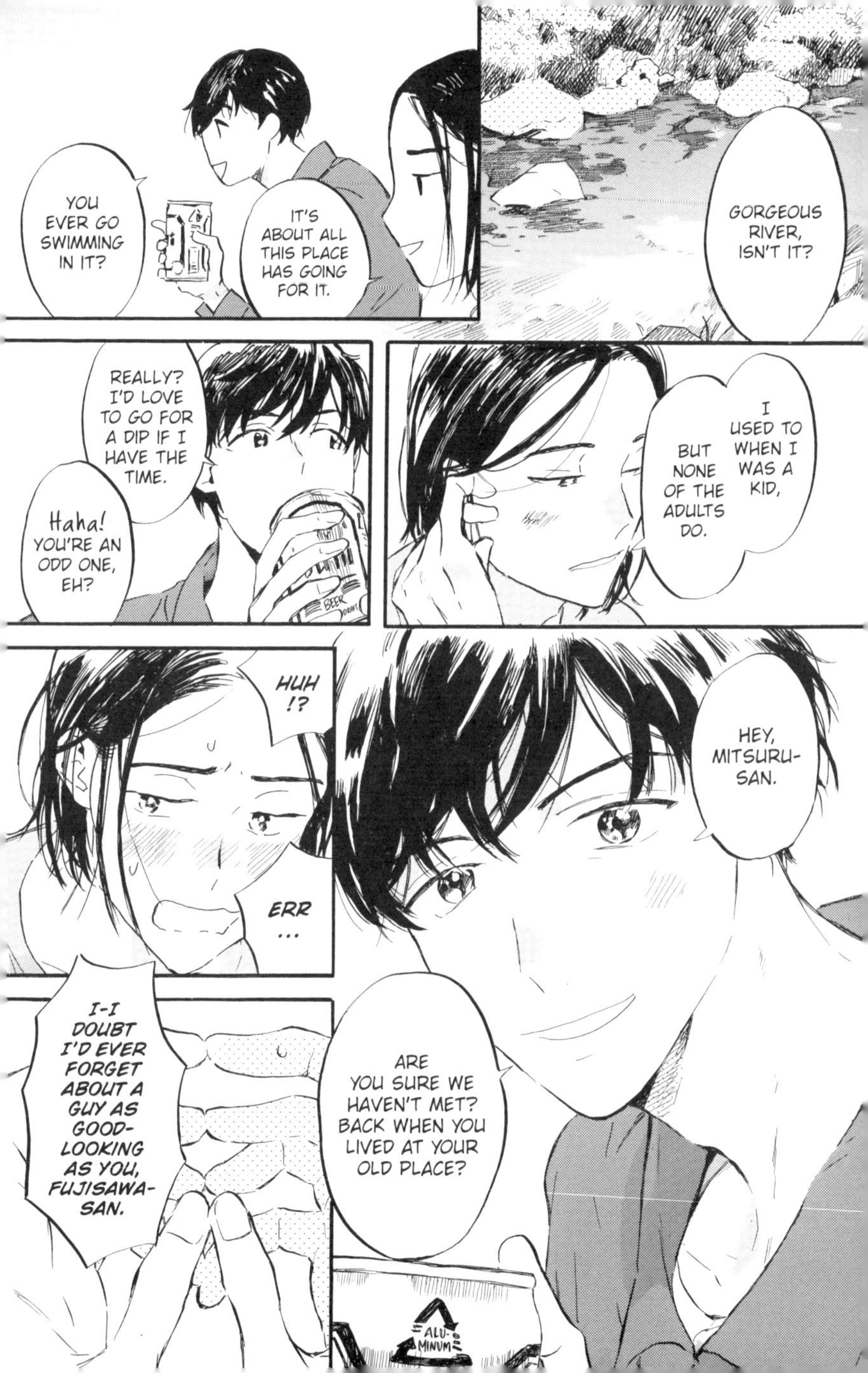
GORGEOUS RIVER, ISN'T IT?
IT'S ABOUT ALL THIS PLACE HAS GOING FOR IT.
YOU EVER GO SWIMMING IN IT?
I USED TO WHEN I WAS A KID,
BUT NONE OF THE ADULTS DO.
REALLY? I'D LOVE TO GO FOR A DIP IF I HAVE THE TIME.
Haha! YOU'RE AN ODD ONE, EH?
BEER DRAFT
HEY, MITSURU-SAN.
HUH !?
ERR ...
ARE YOU SURE WE HAVEN'T MET? BACK WHEN YOU LIVED AT YOUR OLD PLACE?
I-I DOUBT I'D EVER FORGET ABOUT A GUY AS GOOD-LOOKING AS YOU, FUJISAWA-SAN.
ALU-MINUM

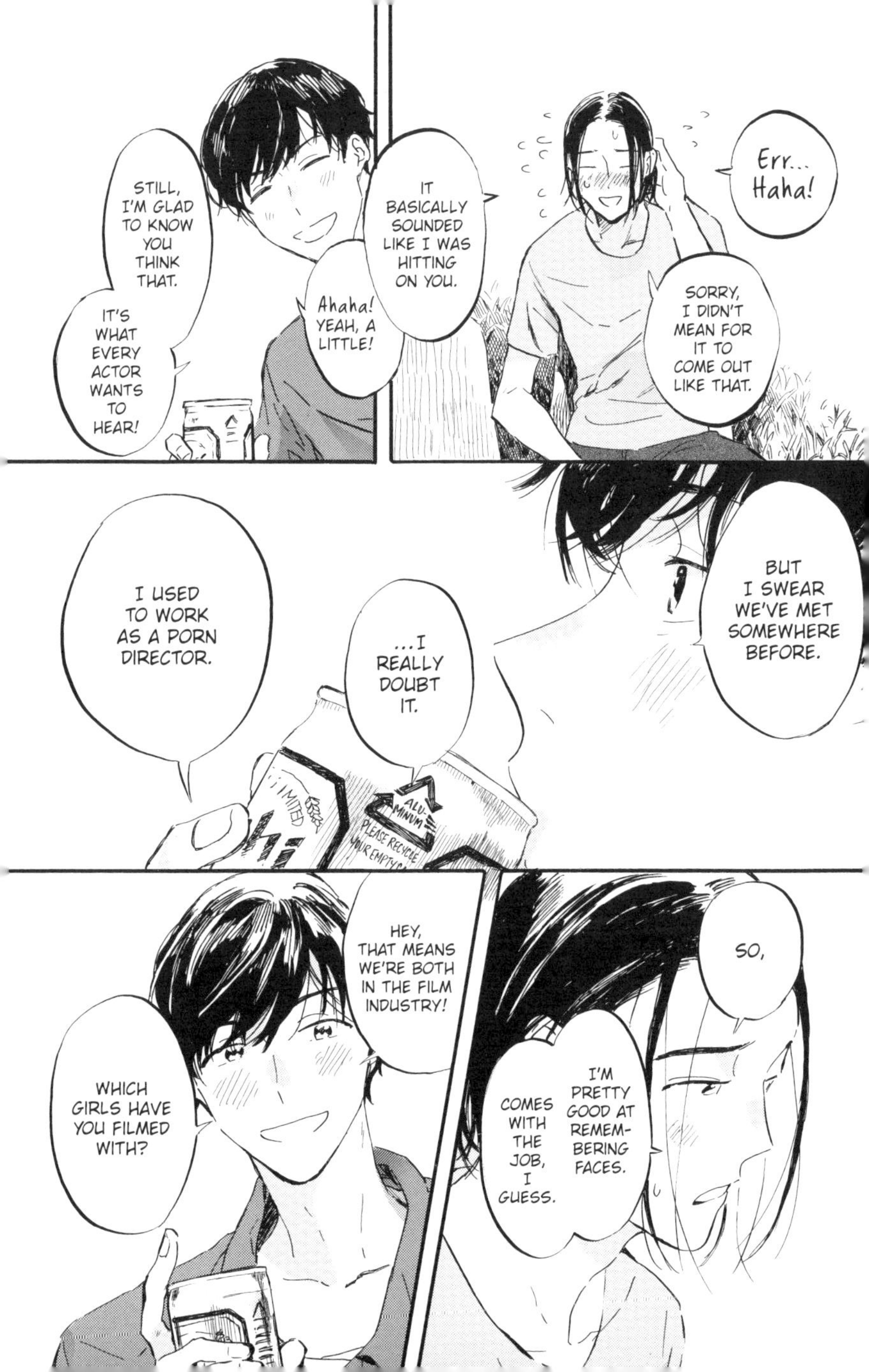
Err... Haha!
SORRY, I DIDN'T MEAN FOR IT TO COME OUT LIKE THAT.
IT BASICALLY SOUNDED LIKE I WAS HITTING ON YOU.
Ahaha! YEAH, A LITTLE!
STILL, I'M GLAD TO KNOW YOU THINK THAT.
IT'S WHAT EVERY ACTOR WANTS TO HEAR!
BUT I SWEAR WE'VE MET SOMEWHERE BEFORE.
...I REALLY DOUBT IT.
I USED TO WORK AS A PORN DIRECTOR.
ALU-MINUM
PLEASE RECYCLE YOUR EMPTY
LIMITED
SO,
I'M PRETTY GOOD AT REMEM-BERING FACES.
COMES WITH THE JOB, I GUESS.
HEY, THAT MEANS WE'RE BOTH IN THE FILM INDUSTRY!
WHICH GIRLS HAVE YOU FILMED WITH?

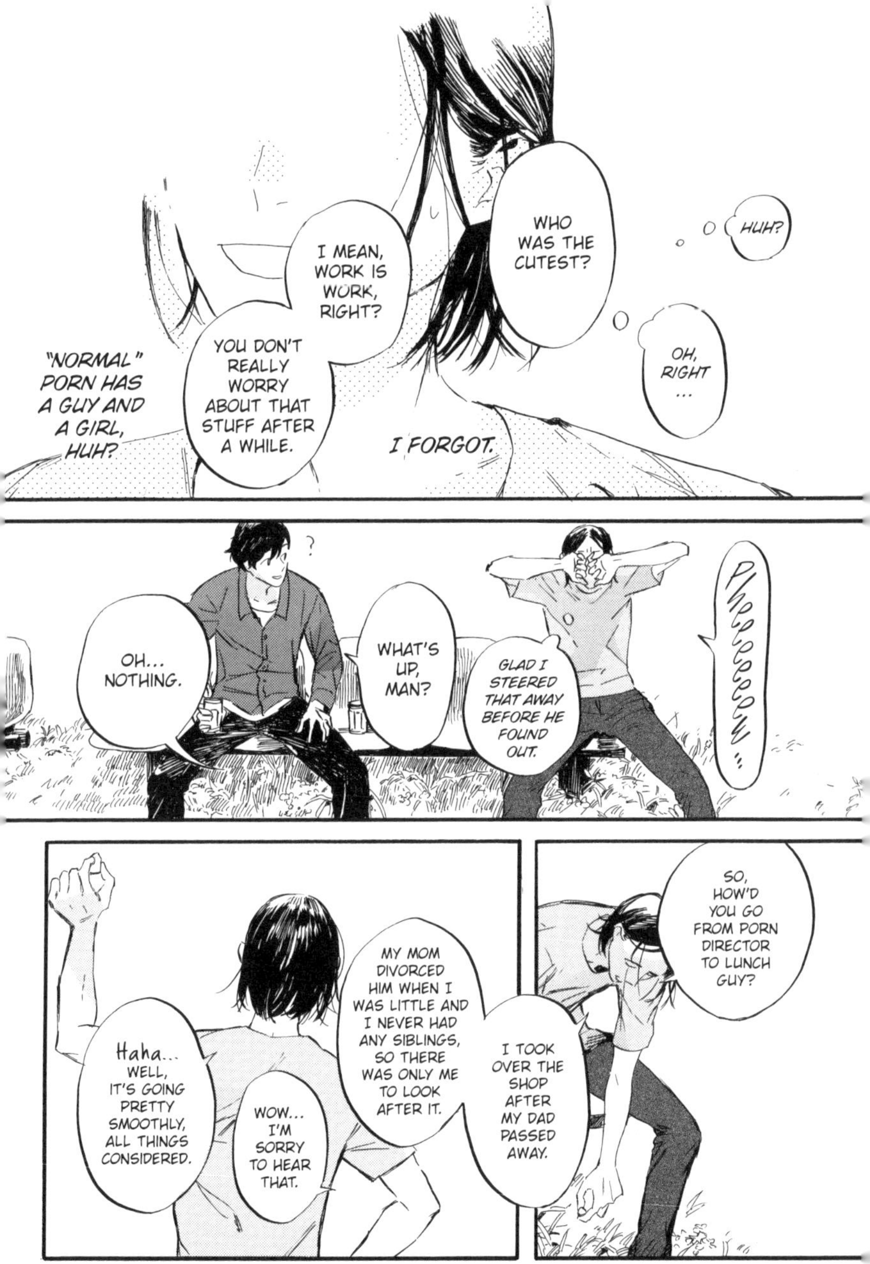
HUH?
OH, RIGHT ...
WHO WAS THE CUTEST?
I FORGOT.
I MEAN, WORK IS WORK, RIGHT?
YOU DON'T REALLY WORRY ABOUT THAT STUFF AFTER A WHILE.
"NORMAL" PORN HAS A GUY AND A GIRL, HUH?
Phheeeeew...
GLAD I STEERED THAT AWAY BEFORE HE FOUND OUT.
WHAT'S UP, MAN?
OH... NOTHING.
SO, HOW'D YOU GO FROM PORN DIRECTOR TO LUNCH GUY?
I TOOK OVER THE SHOP AFTER MY DAD PASSED AWAY.
MY MOM DIVORCED HIM WHEN I WAS LITTLE AND I NEVER HAD ANY SIBLINGS, SO THERE WAS ONLY ME TO LOOK AFTER IT.
WOW... I'M SORRY TO HEAR THAT.
Haha... WELL, IT'S GOING PRETTY SMOOTHLY, ALL THINGS CONSIDERED.

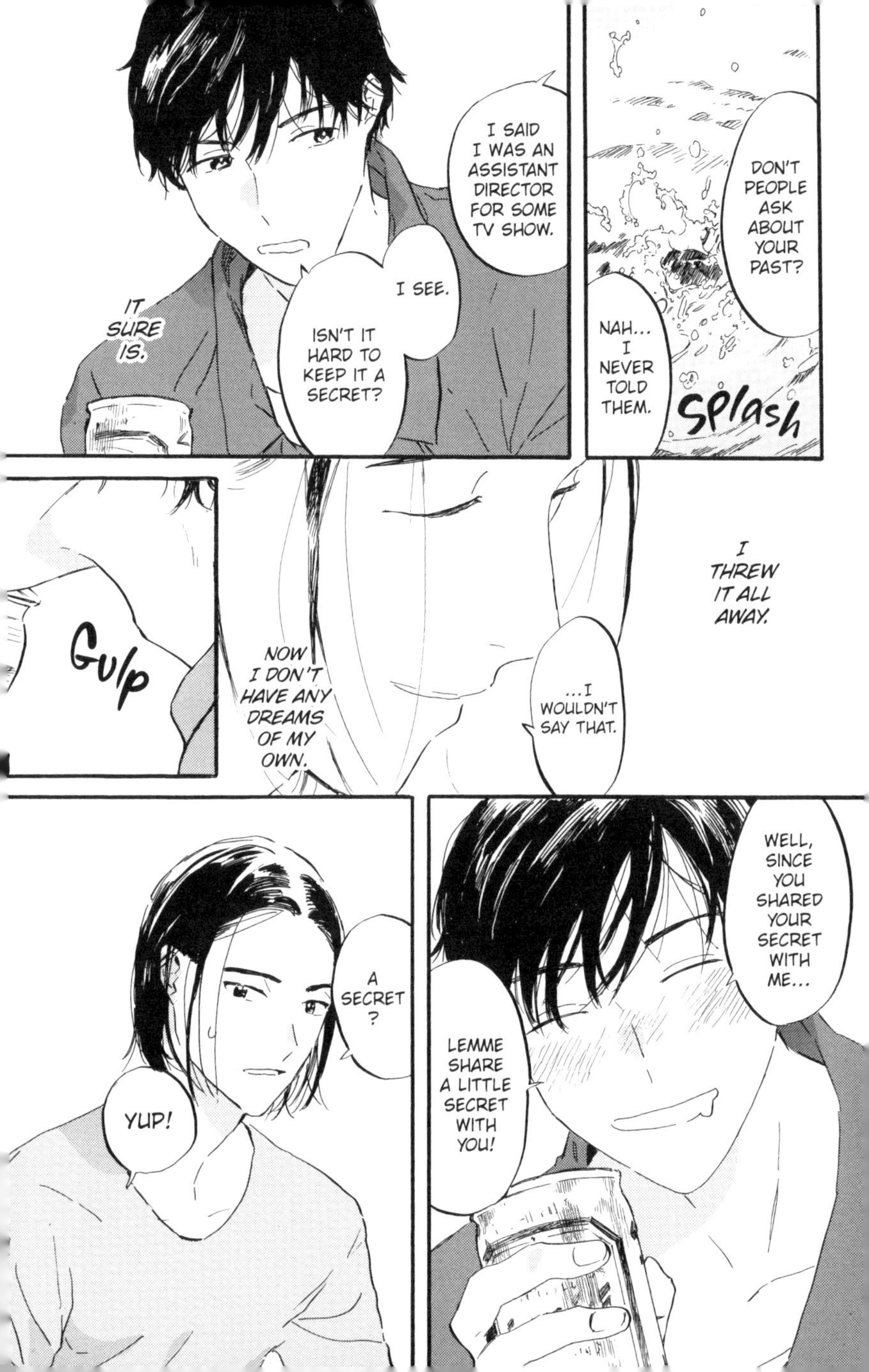
DON'T PEOPLE ASK ABOUT YOUR PAST?
NAH... I NEVER TOLD THEM.
SPLASH
I SAID I WAS AN ASSISTANT DIRECTOR FOR SOME TV SHOW.
I SEE.
ISN'T IT HARD TO KEEP IT A SECRET?
IT SURE IS.
I THREW IT ALL AWAY.
...I WOULDN'T SAY THAT.
NOW I DON'T HAVE ANY DREAMS OF MY OWN.
GULP
WELL, SINCE YOU SHARED YOUR SECRET WITH ME...
LEMME SHARE A LITTLE SECRET WITH YOU!
A SECRET?
YUP!

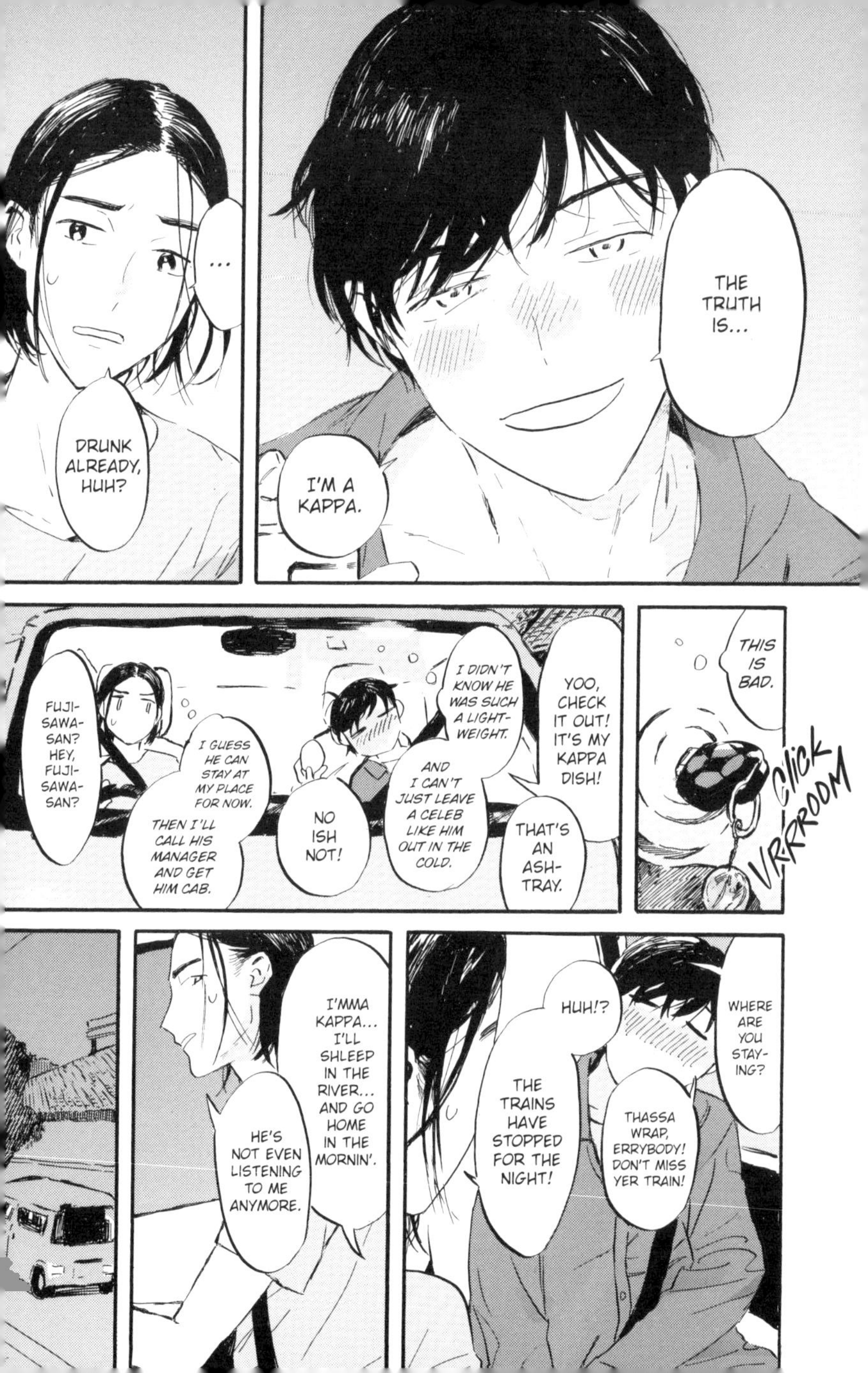
THE TRUTH IS...
I'M A KAPPA.
...
DRUNK ALREADY, HUH?
THIS IS BAD.
CLICK
VRRROOM
YOO, CHECK IT OUT! IT'S MY KAPPA DISH!
THAT'S AN ASH-TRAY.
I DIDN'T KNOW HE WAS SUCH A LIGHT-WEIGHT.
AND I CAN'T JUST LEAVE A CELEB LIKE HIM OUT IN THE COLD.
NO ISH NOT!
I GUESS HE CAN STAY AT MY PLACE FOR NOW.
THEN I'LL CALL HIS MANAGER AND GET HIM CAB.
FUJI-SAWA-SAN? HEY, FUJI-SAWA-SAN?
WHERE ARE YOU STAY-ING?
THASSA WRAP, ERRYBODY! DON'T MISS YER TRAIN!
HUH!?
THE TRAINS HAVE STOPPED FOR THE NIGHT!
I'MMA KAPPA... I'LL SHLEEP IN THE RIVER... AND GO HOME IN THE MORNIN'.
HE'S NOT EVEN LISTENING TO ME ANYMORE.

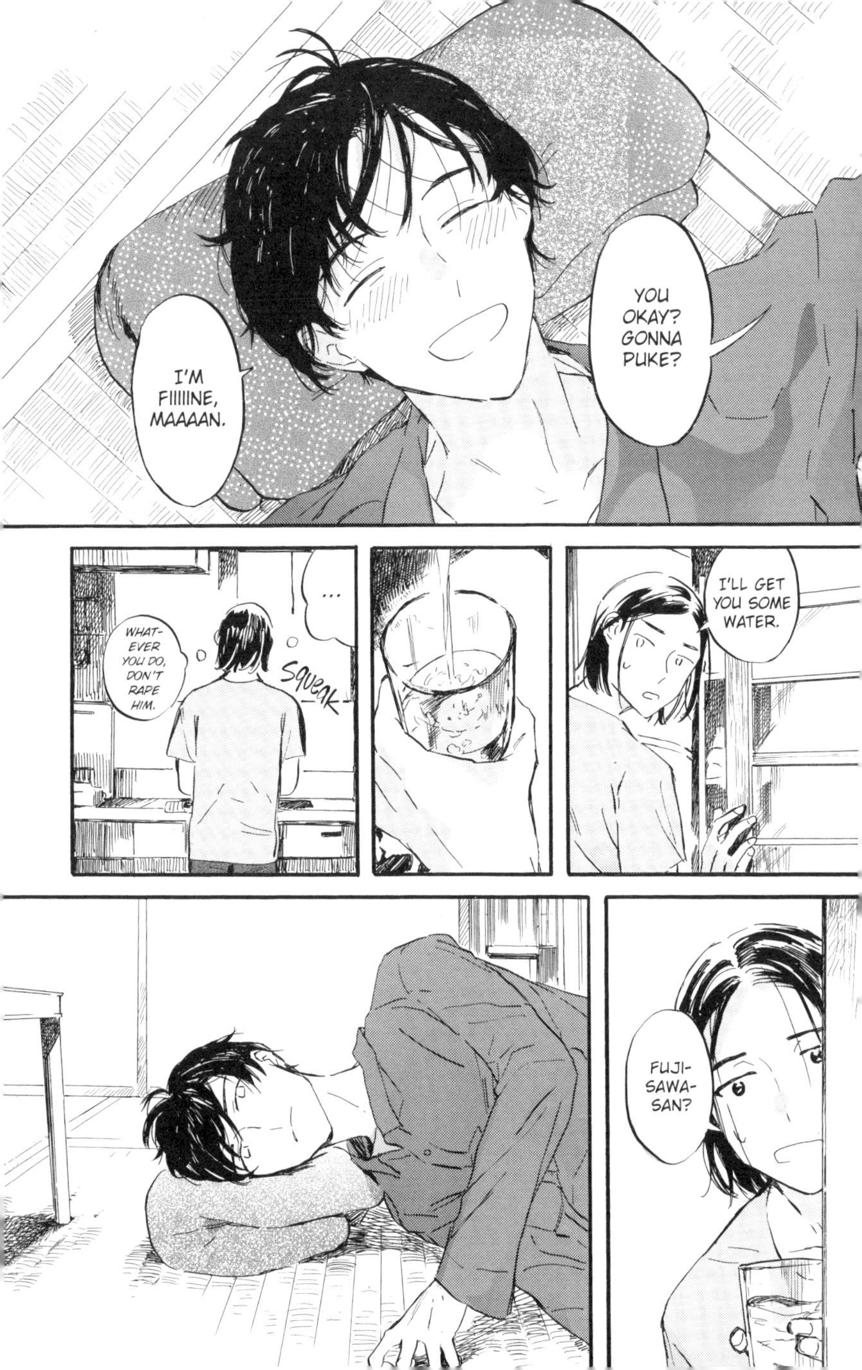
YOU OKAY? GONNA PUKE?
I'M FIIIIINE, MAAAAN.
I'LL GET YOU SOME WATER.
...
WHAT-EVER YOU DO, DON'T RAPE HIM.
SQUEAK
FUJI-SAWA-SAN?

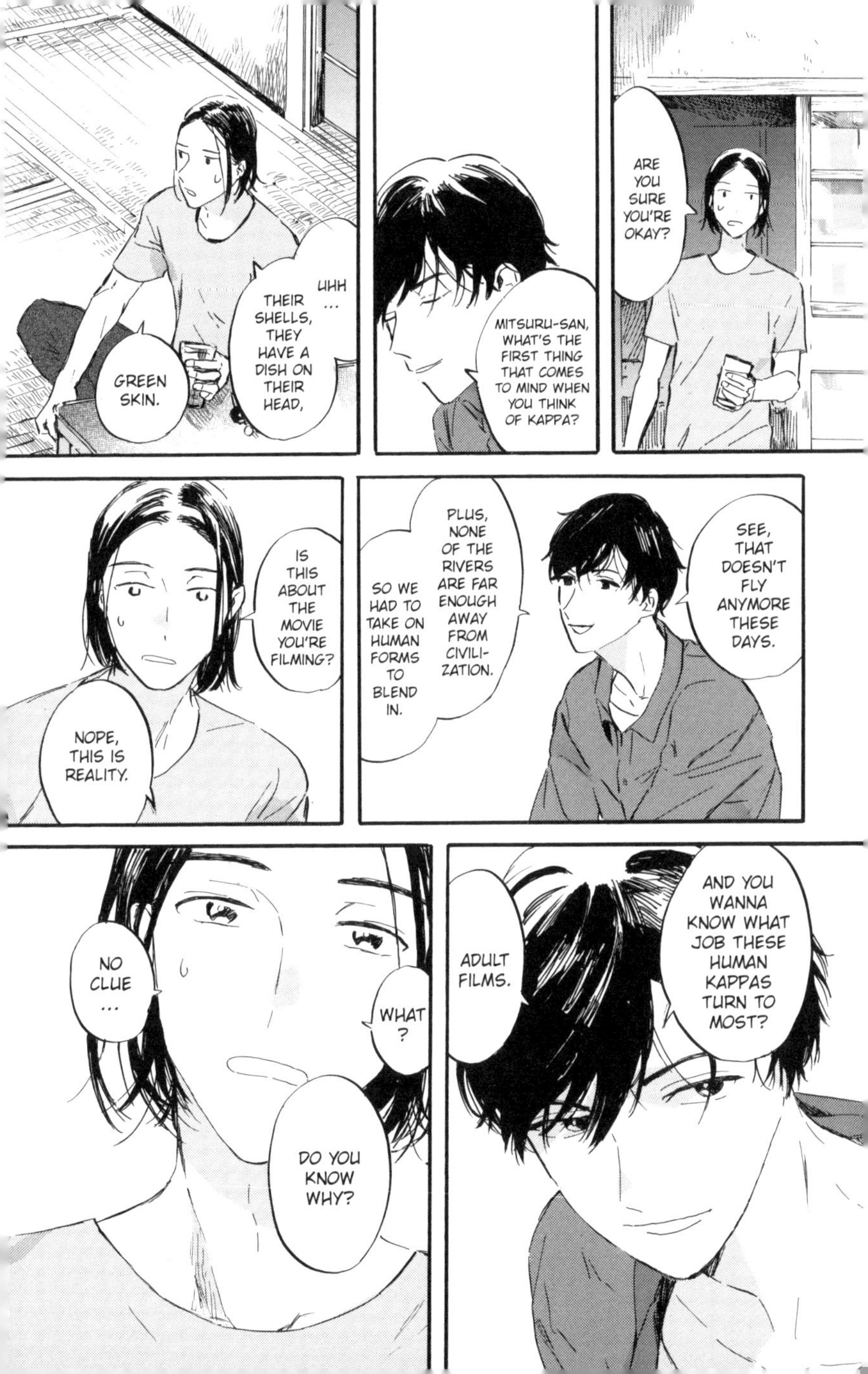
ARE YOU SURE YOU'RE OKAY?
MITSURU-SAN, WHAT'S THE FIRST THING THAT COMES TO MIND WHEN YOU THINK OF KAPPA?
UHH ...
THEIR SHELLS, THEY HAVE A DISH ON THEIR HEAD,
GREEN SKIN.
SEE, THAT DOESN'T FLY ANYMORE THESE DAYS.
PLUS, NONE OF THE RIVERS ARE FAR ENOUGH AWAY FROM CIVILI-ZATION.
SO WE HAD TO TAKE ON HUMAN FORMS TO BLEND IN.
IS THIS ABOUT THE MOVIE YOU'RE FILMING?
NOPE, THIS IS REALITY.
AND YOU WANNA KNOW WHAT JOB THESE HUMAN KAPPAS TURN TO MOST?
ADULT FILMS.
WHAT ?
NO CLUE ...
DO YOU KNOW WHY?

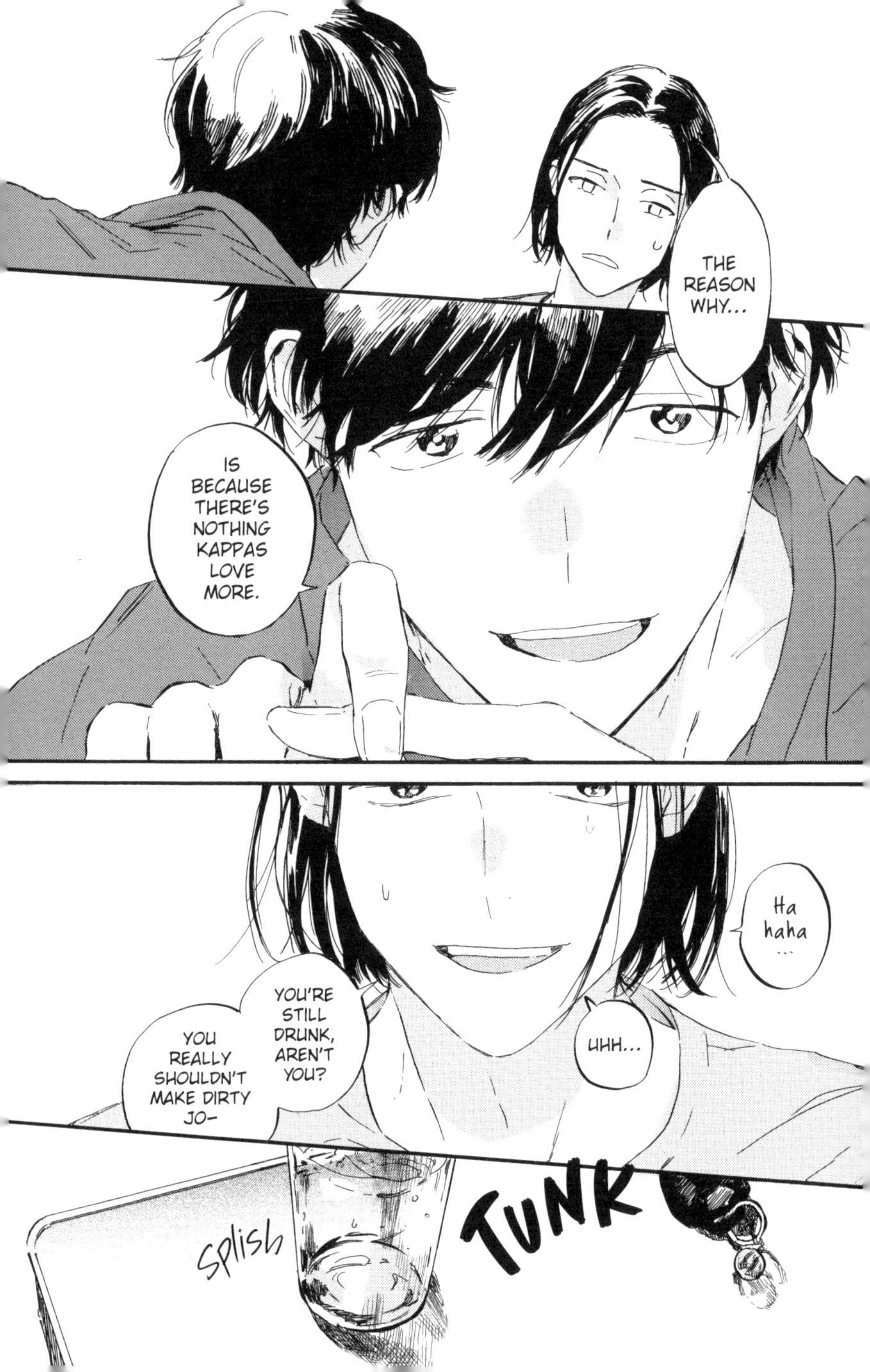
THE REASON WHY...
IS BECAUSE THERE'S NOTHING KAPPAS LOVE MORE.
Ha haha ...
UHH...
YOU'RE STILL DRUNK, AREN'T YOU?
YOU REALLY SHOULDN'T MAKE DIRTY JO-
TUNK
splish

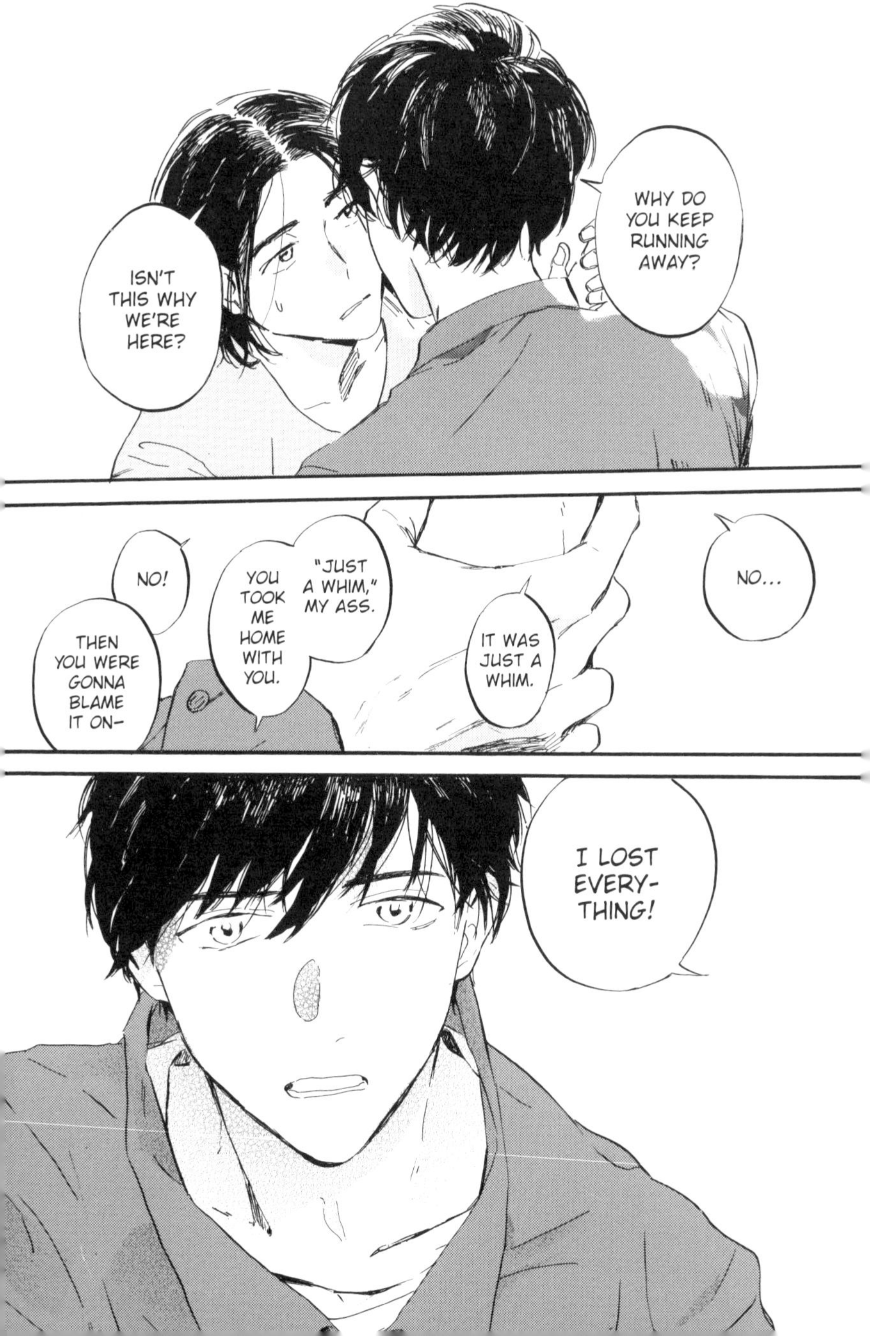
WHY DO YOU KEEP RUNNING AWAY?
ISN'T THIS WHY WE'RE HERE?
NO...
IT WAS JUST A WHIM.
"JUST A WHIM," MY ASS.
YOU TOOK ME HOME WITH YOU.
NO!
THEN YOU WERE GONNA BLAME IT ON–
I LOST EVERY-THING!

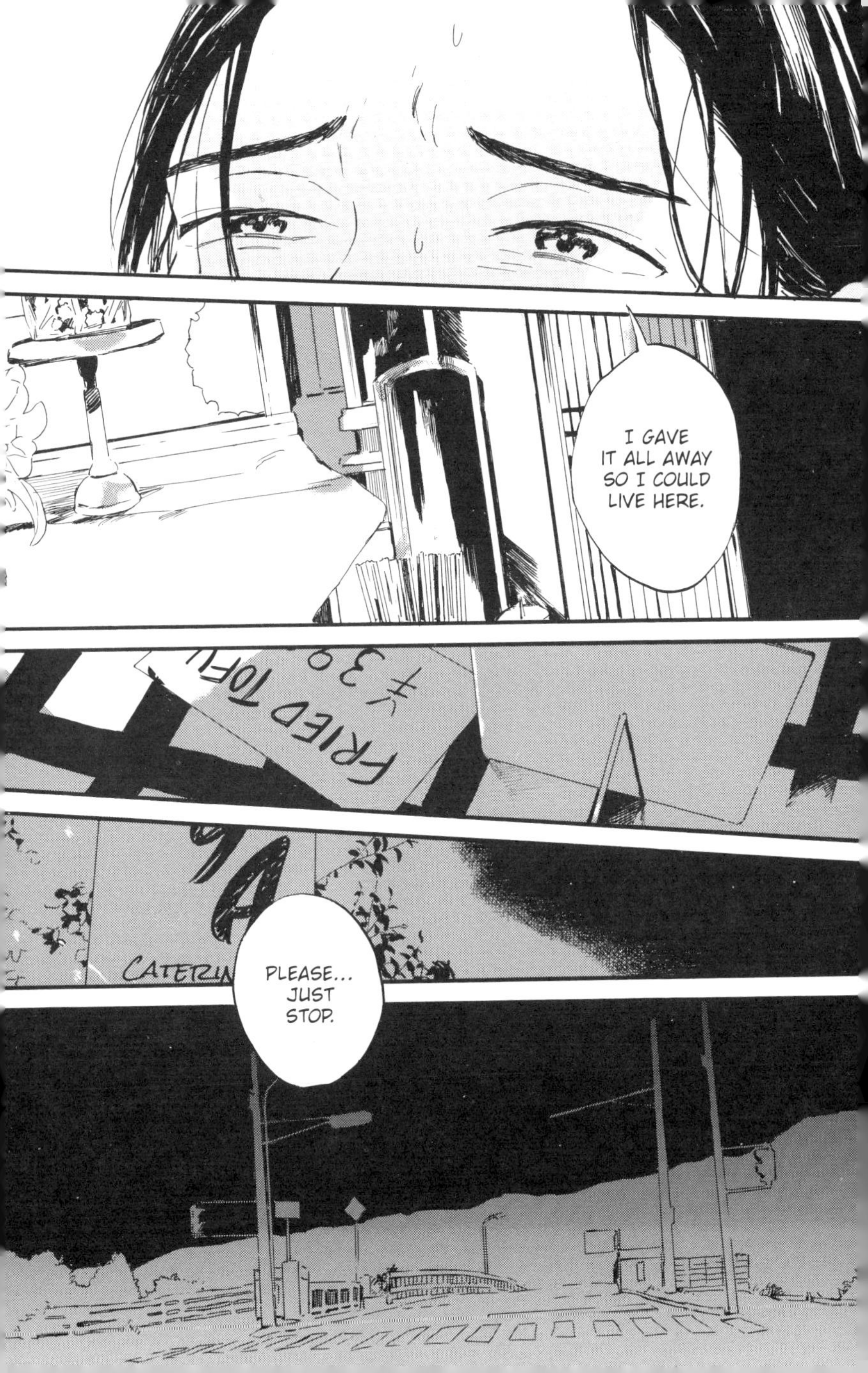
I GAVE IT ALL AWAY SO I COULD LIVE HERE.
FRIED TOFU
PLEASE... JUST STOP.

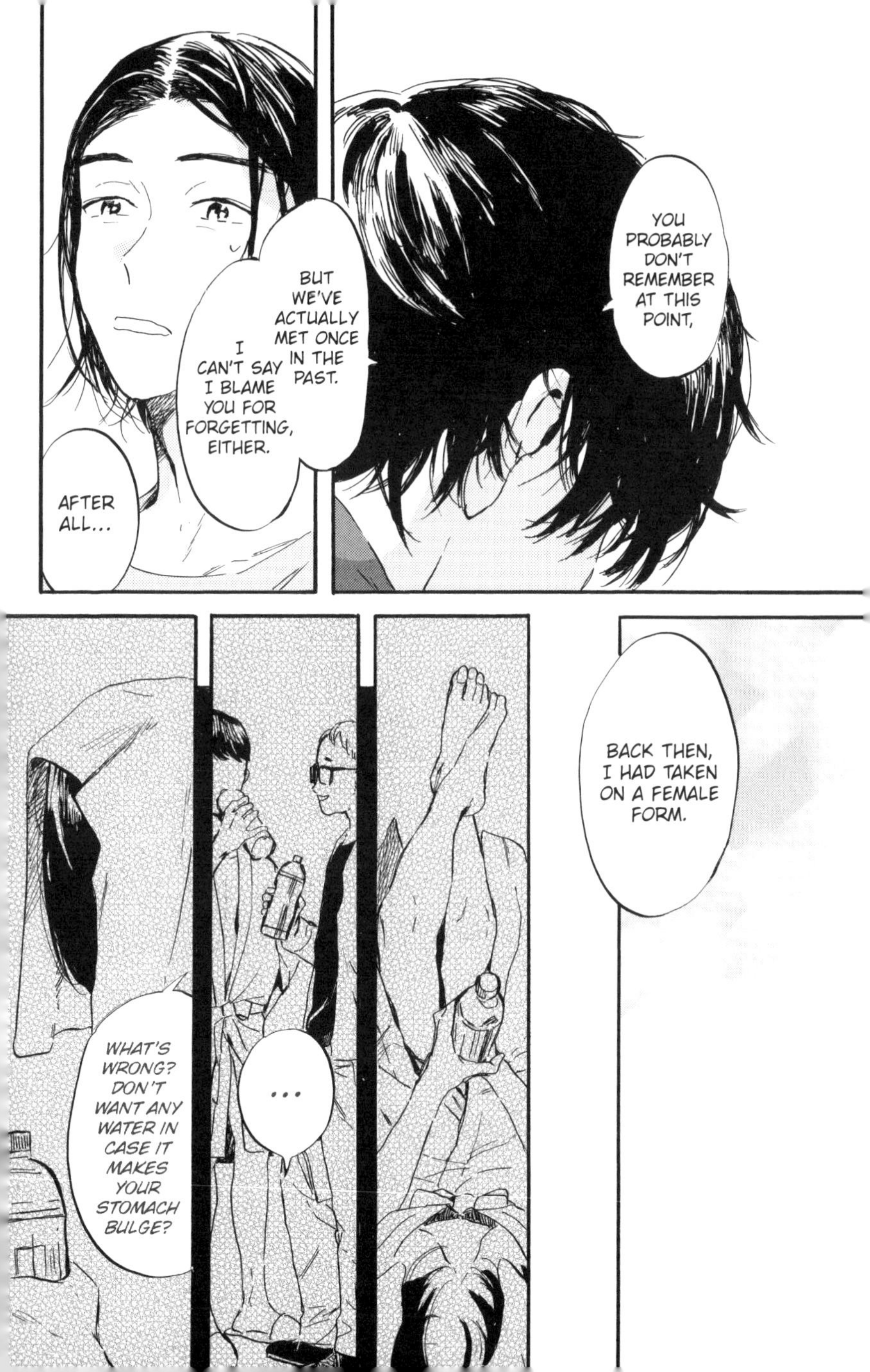
YOU PROBABLY DON'T REMEMBER AT THIS POINT,
BUT WE'VE ACTUALLY MET ONCE IN THE PAST.
I CAN'T SAY I BLAME YOU FOR FORGETTING, EITHER.
AFTER ALL...
BACK THEN, I HAD TAKEN ON A FEMALE FORM.
...
WHAT'S WRONG? DON'T WANT ANY WATER IN CASE IT MAKES YOUR STOMACH BULGE?

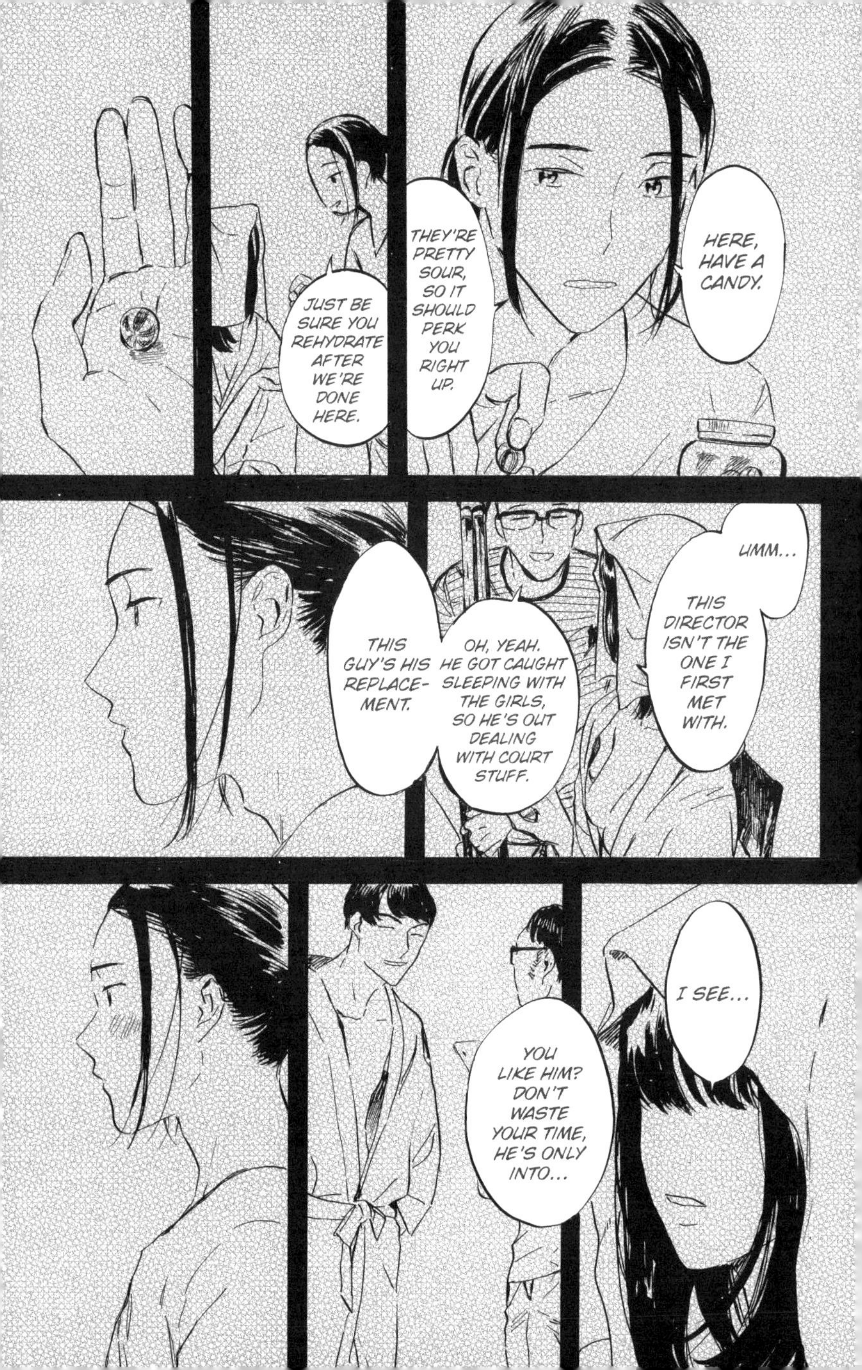
HERE, HAVE A CANDY.
THEY'RE PRETTY SOUR, SO IT SHOULD PERK YOU RIGHT UP.
JUST BE SURE YOU REHYDRATE AFTER WE'RE DONE HERE.
UMM...
THIS DIRECTOR ISN'T THE ONE I FIRST MET WITH.
OH, YEAH. HE GOT CAUGHT SLEEPING WITH THE GIRLS, SO HE'S OUT DEALING WITH COURT STUFF.
THIS GUY'S HIS REPLACEMENT.
I SEE...
YOU LIKE HIM? DON'T WASTE YOUR TIME, HE'S ONLY INTO...

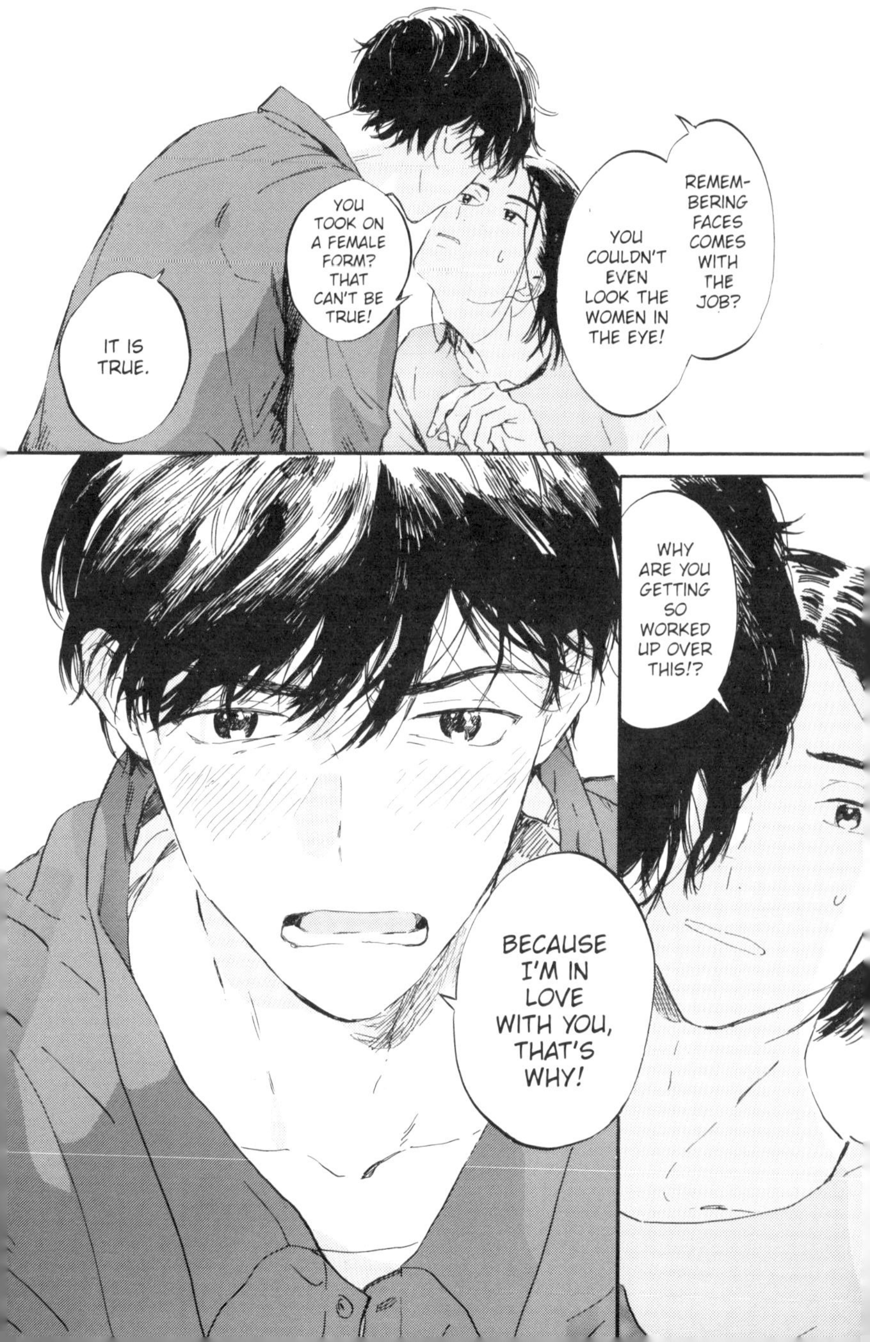
REMEMBERING FACES COMES WITH THE JOB?
YOU COULDN'T EVEN LOOK THE WOMEN IN THE EYE!
YOU TOOK ON A FEMALE FORM? THAT CAN'T BE TRUE!
IT IS TRUE.
WHY ARE YOU GETTING SO WORKED UP OVER THIS!?
BECAUSE I'M IN LOVE WITH YOU, THAT'S WHY!

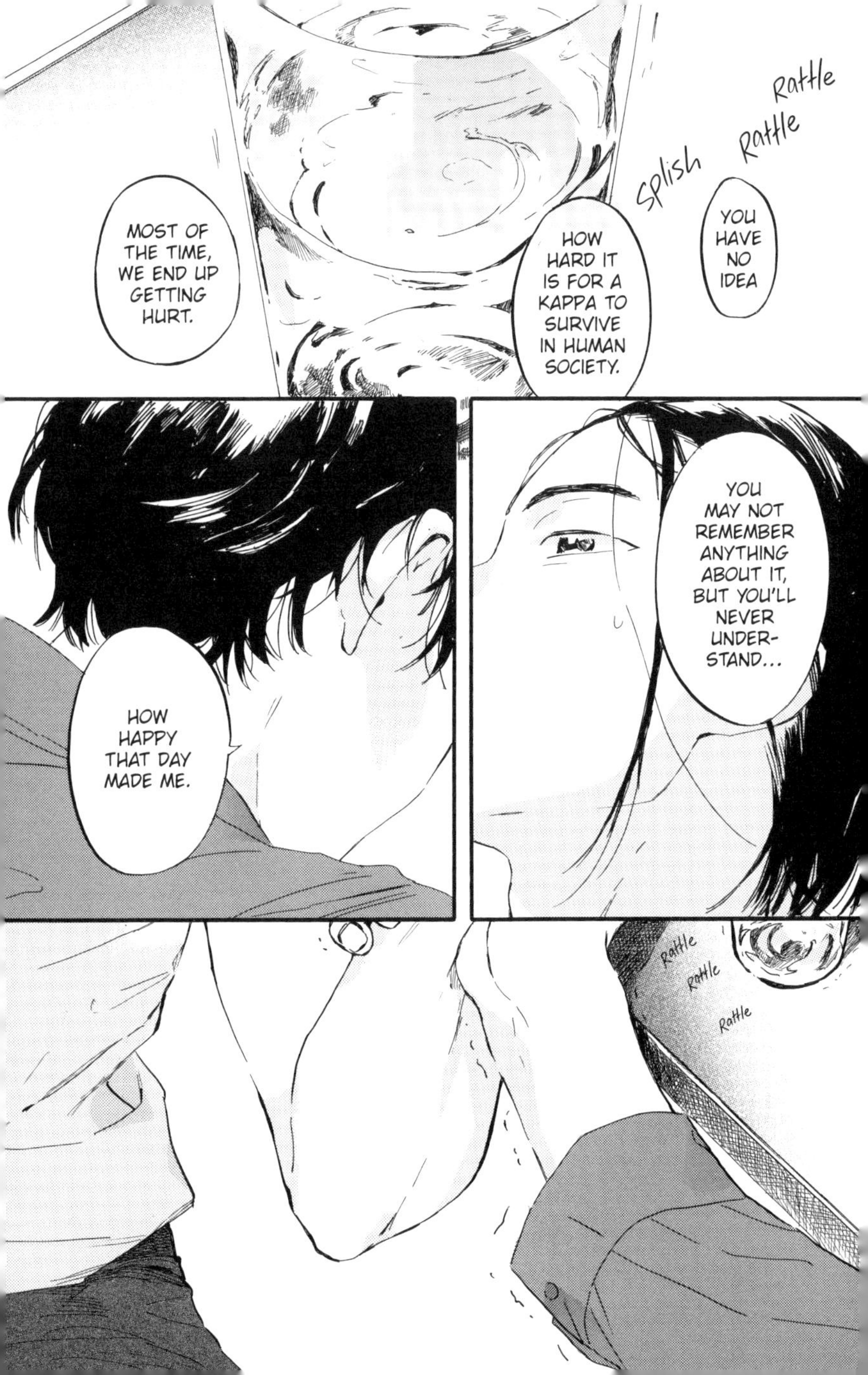
Rattle
Rattle
Splish
YOU HAVE NO IDEA
HOW HARD IT IS FOR A KAPPA TO SURVIVE IN HUMAN SOCIETY.
MOST OF THE TIME, WE END UP GETTING HURT.
YOU MAY NOT REMEMBER ANYTHING ABOUT IT, BUT YOU'LL NEVER UNDER-STAND...
HOW HAPPY THAT DAY MADE ME.
Rattle
Rattle
Rattle

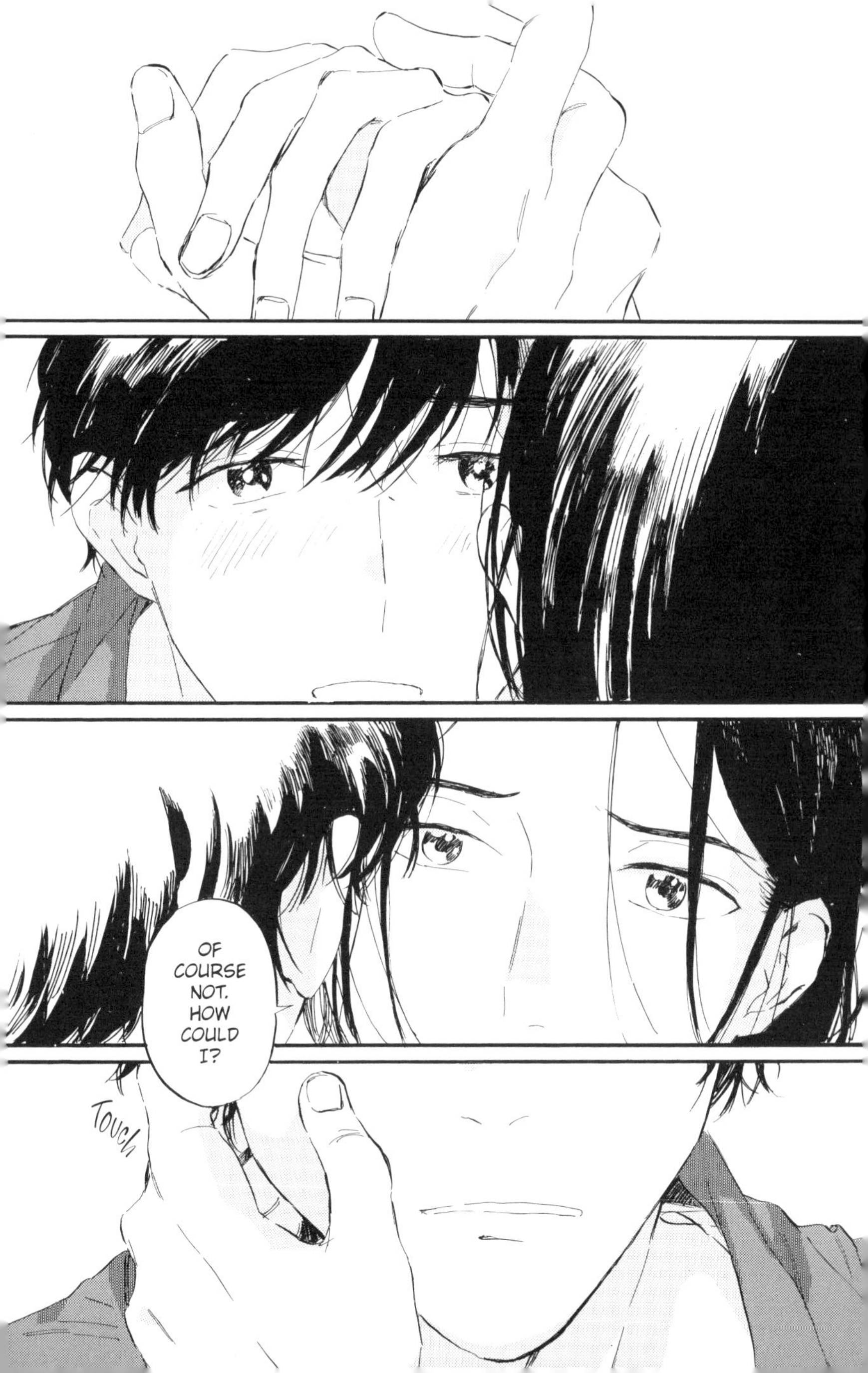
OF COURSE NOT. HOW COULD I?
TOUCH

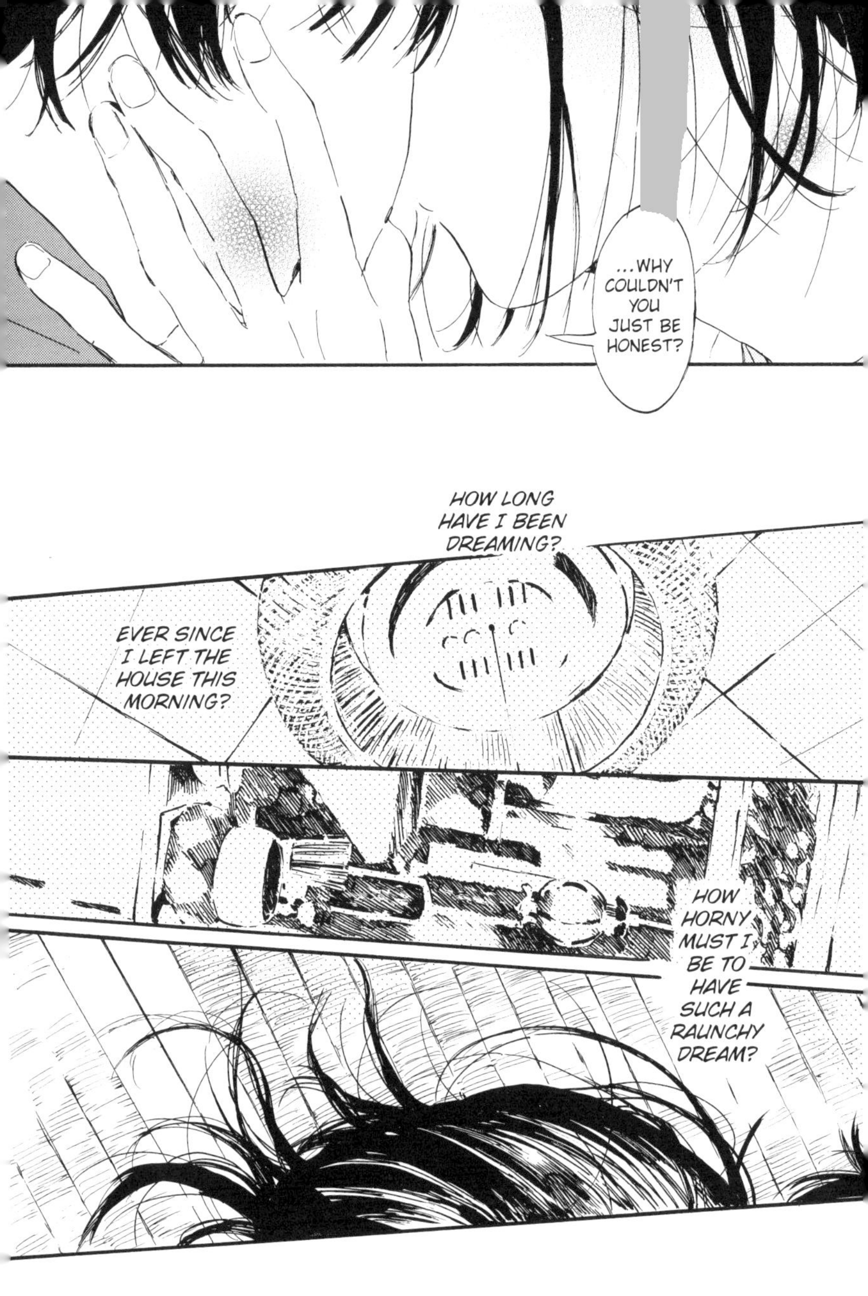
...WHY COULDN'T YOU JUST BE HONEST?
HOW LONG HAVE I BEEN DREAMING?
EVER SINCE I LEFT THE HOUSE THIS MORNING?
HOW HORNY MUST I BE TO HAVE SUCH A RAUNCHY DREAM?

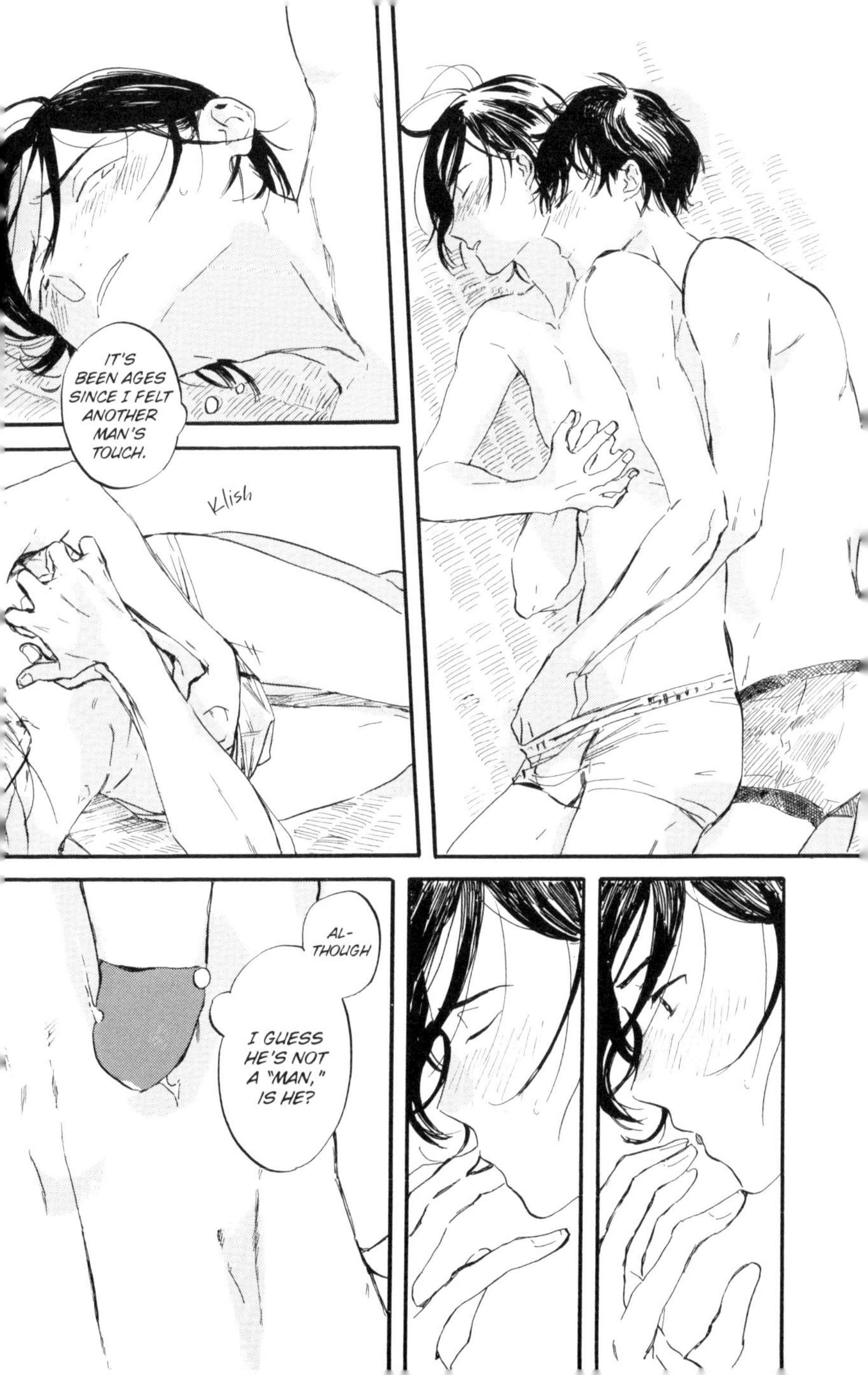
IT'S BEEN AGES SINCE I FELT ANOTHER MAN'S TOUCH.
Klish
AL-THOUGH
I GUESS HE'S NOT A "MAN," IS HE?

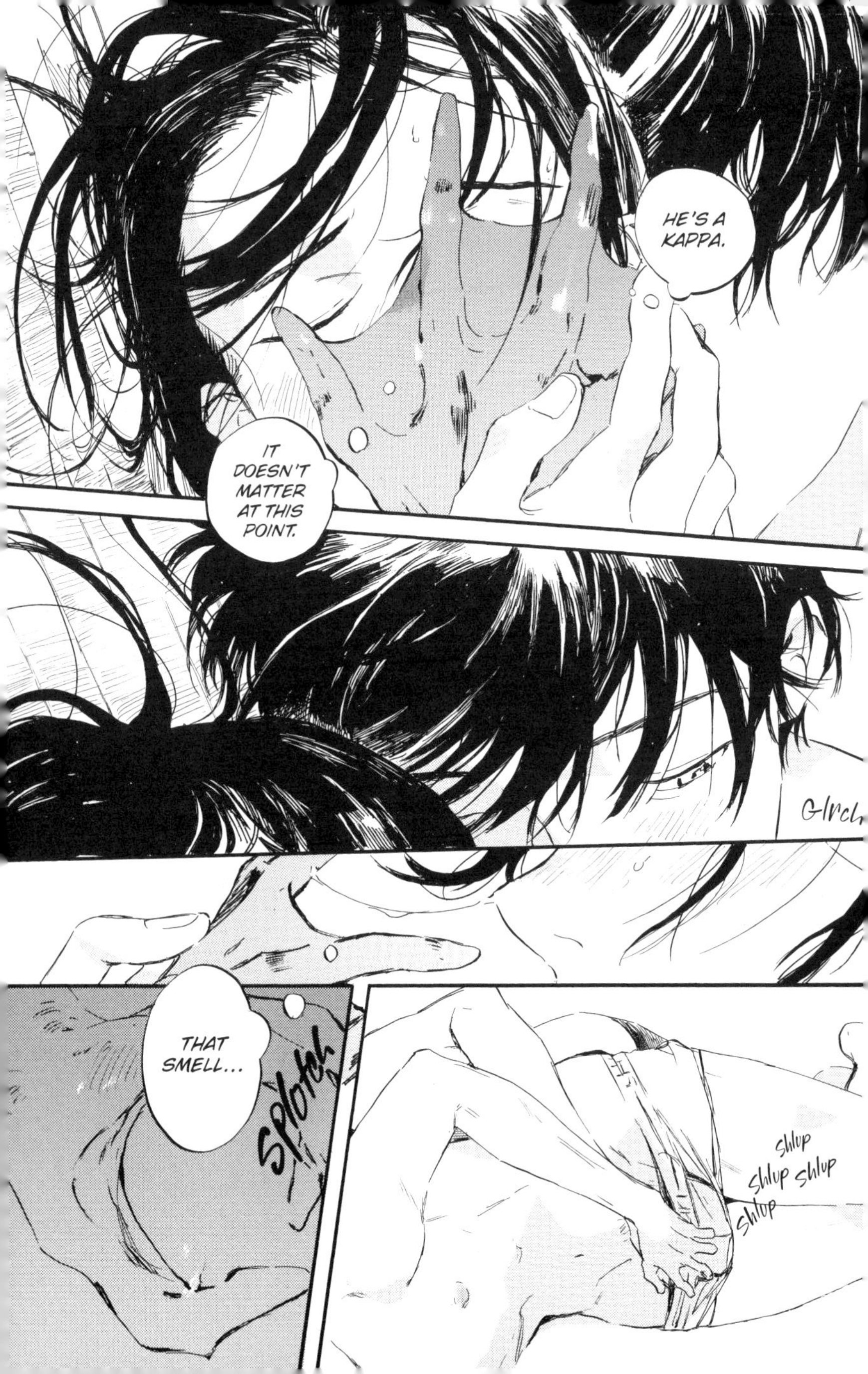
HE'S A KAPPA.
IT DOESN'T MATTER AT THIS POINT.
Glrch
Shlup Shlup Shlup Shlup
Splotch
THAT SMELL...

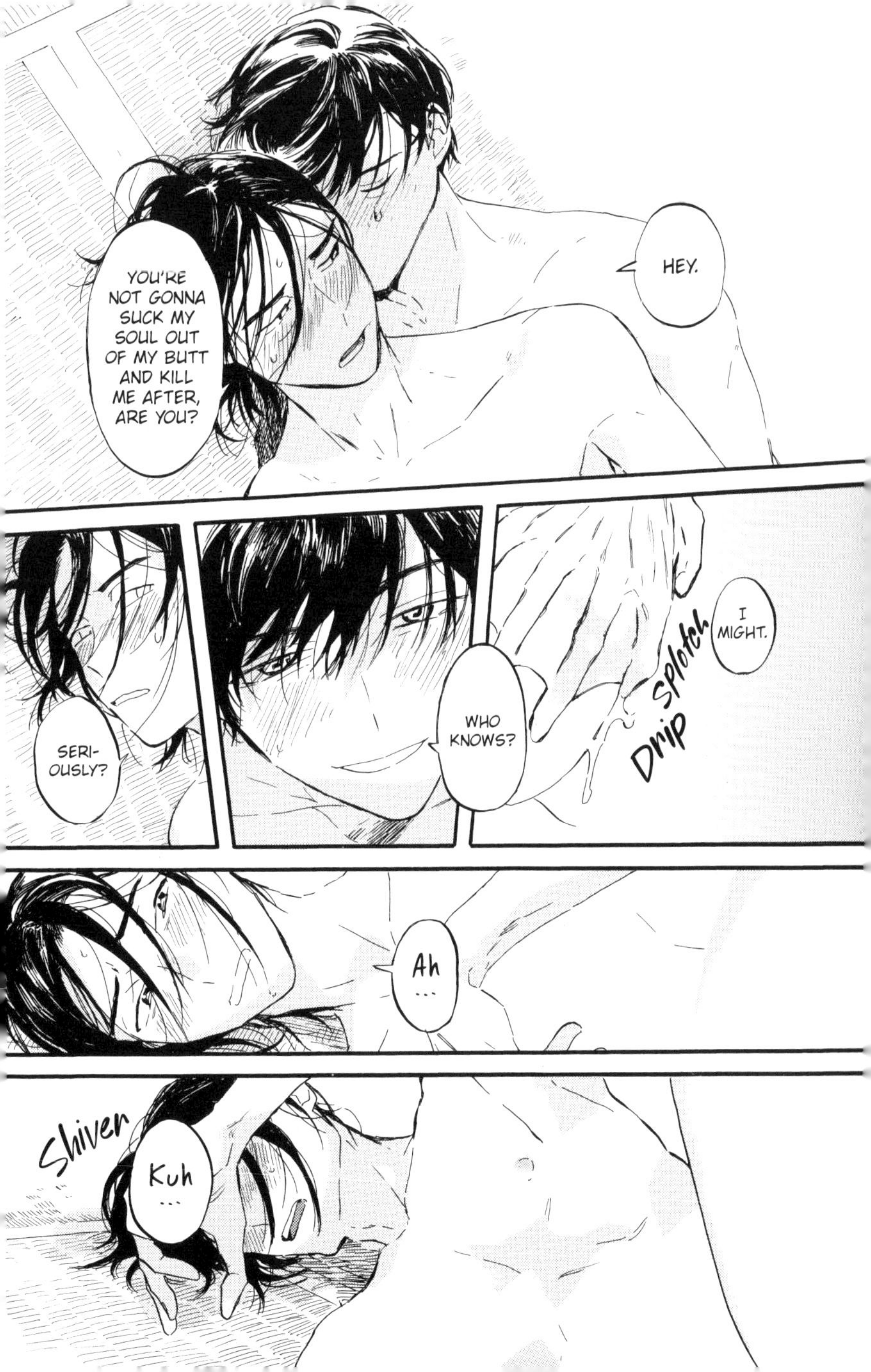
HEY.
YOU'RE NOT GONNA SUCK MY SOUL OUT OF MY BUTT AND KILL ME AFTER, ARE YOU?
I MIGHT.
Splotch
Drip
WHO KNOWS?
SERI-OUSLY?
Ah ...
Shiver
Kuh ...

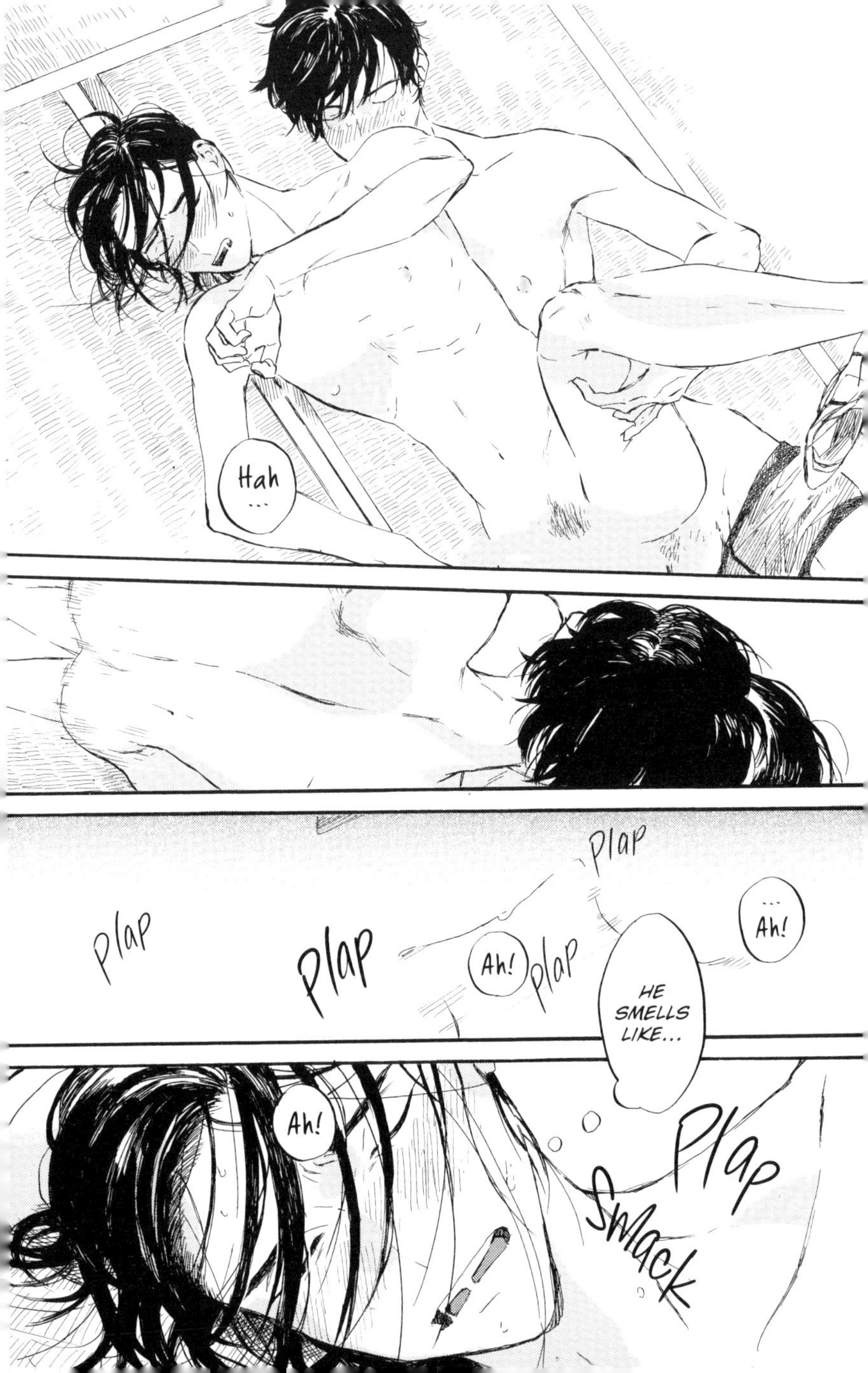
Hah
...
Plap
...
Ah!
He smells like...
Ah!
Plap
Plap
Plap
Ah!
Plap
Smack

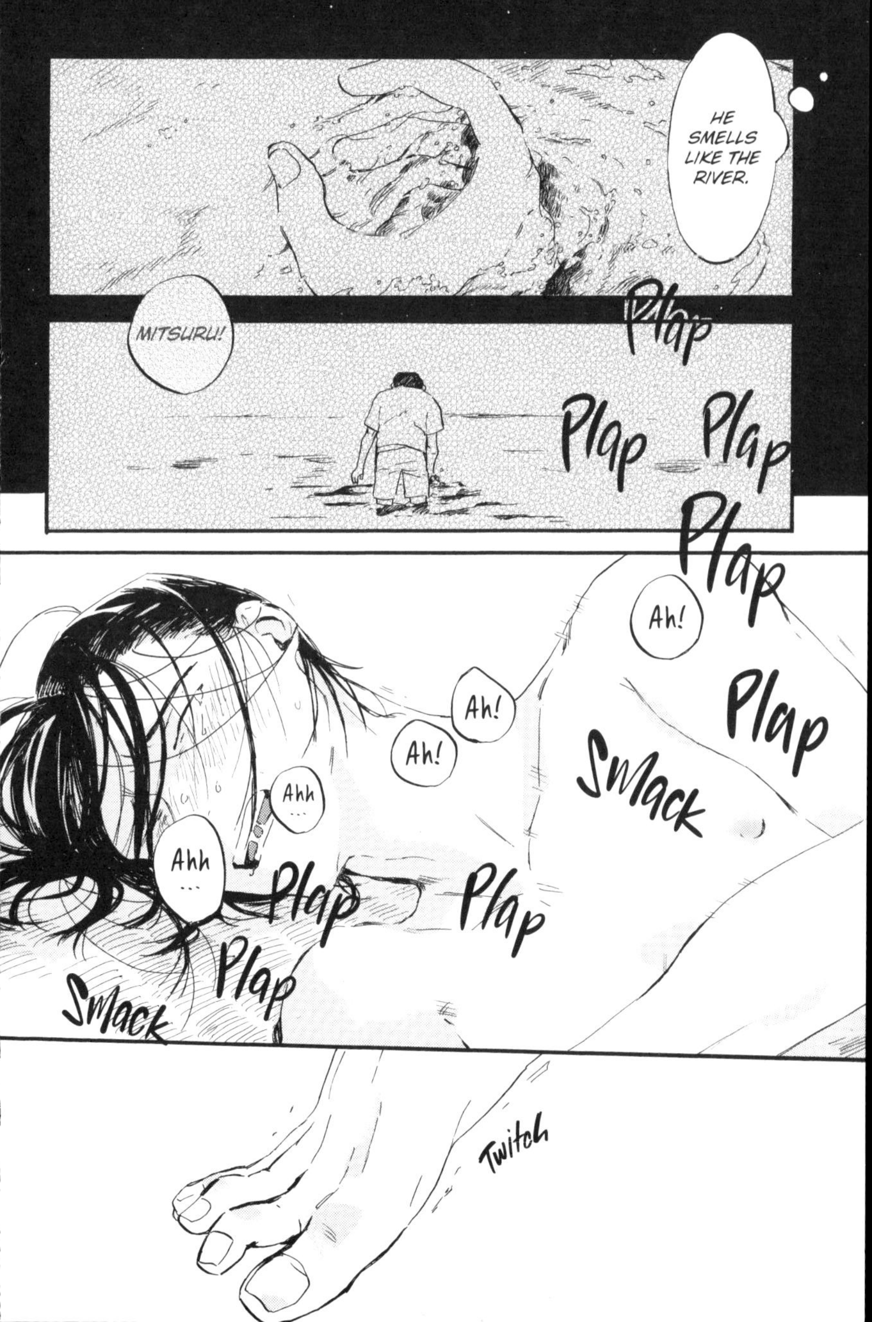
HE SMELLS LIKE THE RIVER.
Plap
MITSURU!
Plap
Plap
Plap
Plap
Ah!
Plap
Smack
Ah!
Ah!
Ahh ...
Ahh ...
Plap
Plap
Plap
Smack
Twitch

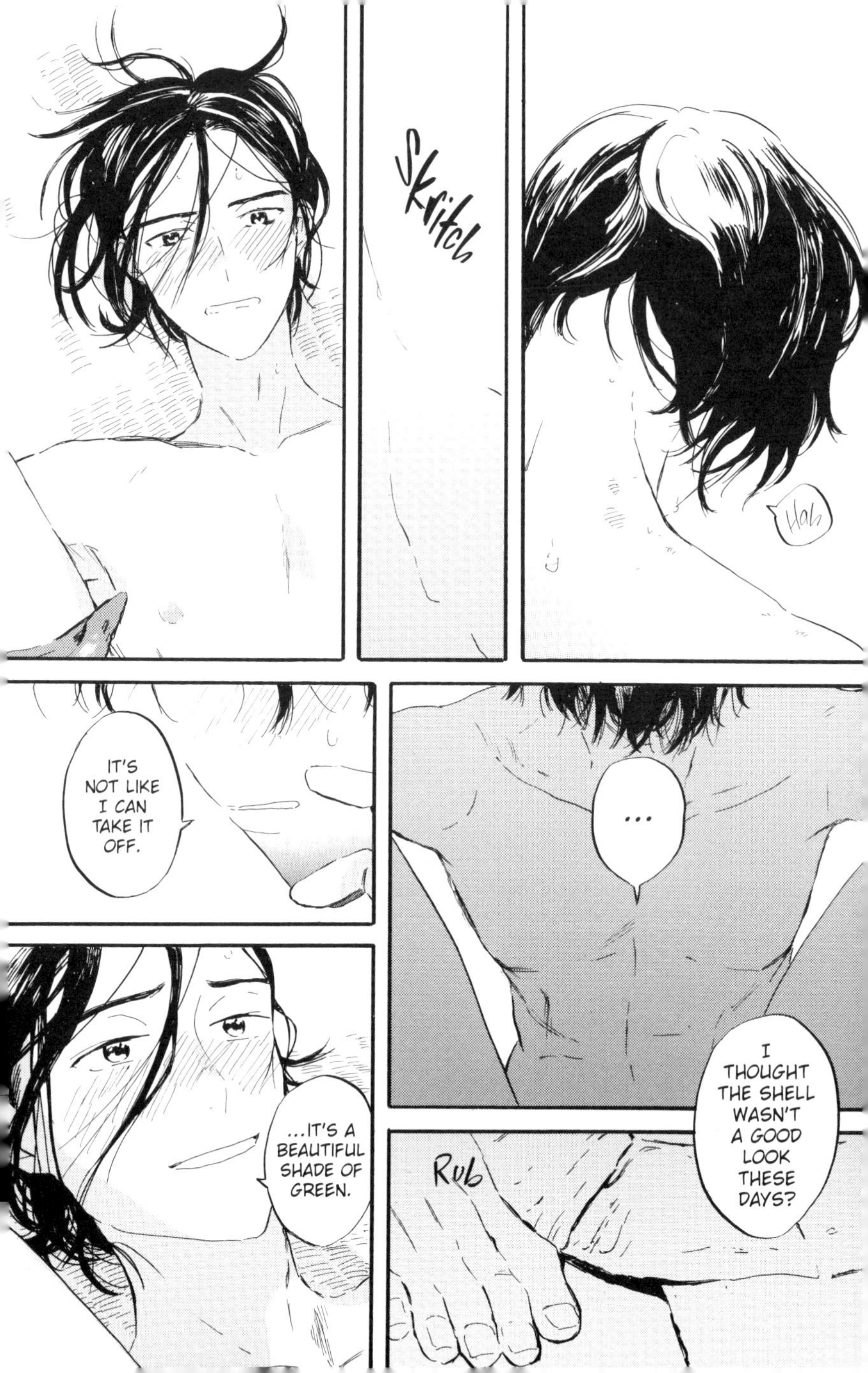
Hah
Skritch
...
I THOUGHT THE SHELL WASN'T A GOOD LOOK THESE DAYS?
Rub
IT'S NOT LIKE I CAN TAKE IT OFF.
...IT'S A BEAUTIFUL SHADE OF GREEN.

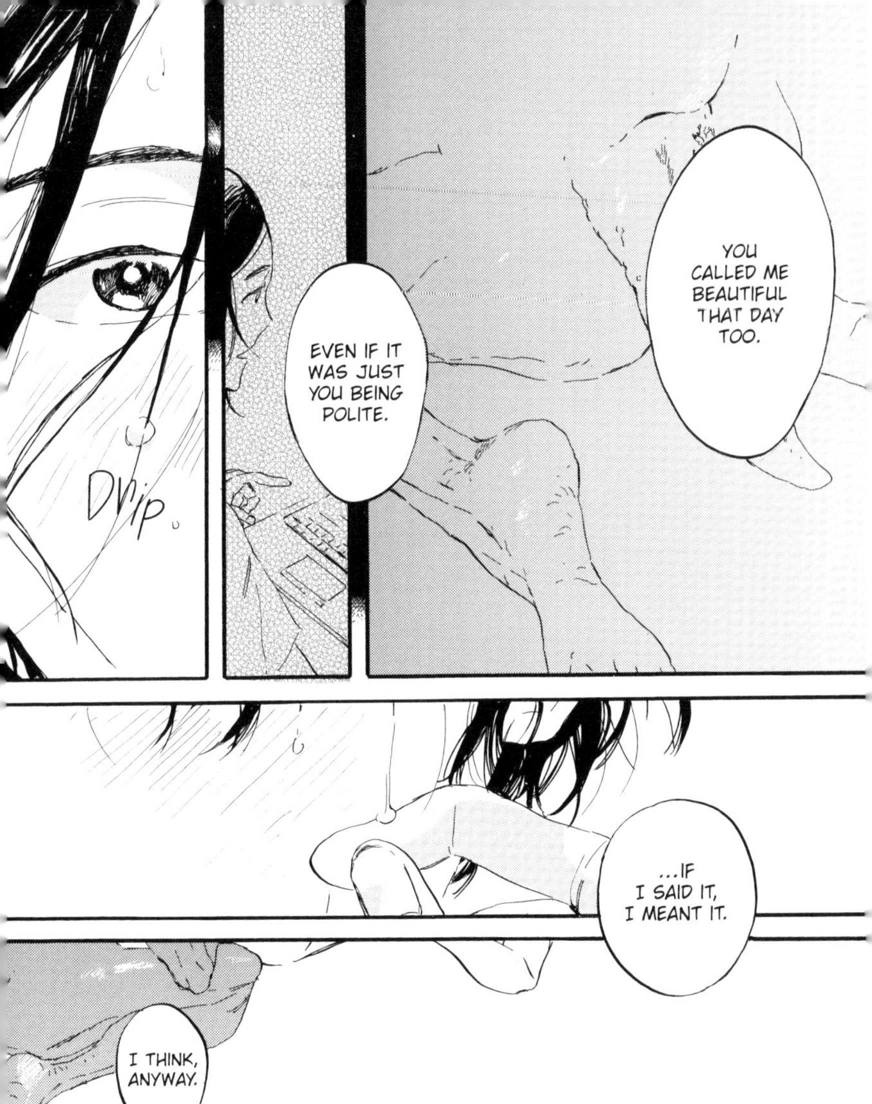
YOU CALLED ME BEAUTIFUL THAT DAY TOO.
EVEN IF IT WAS JUST YOU BEING POLITE.
Drip
...IF I SAID IT, I MEANT IT.
I THINK, ANYWAY.

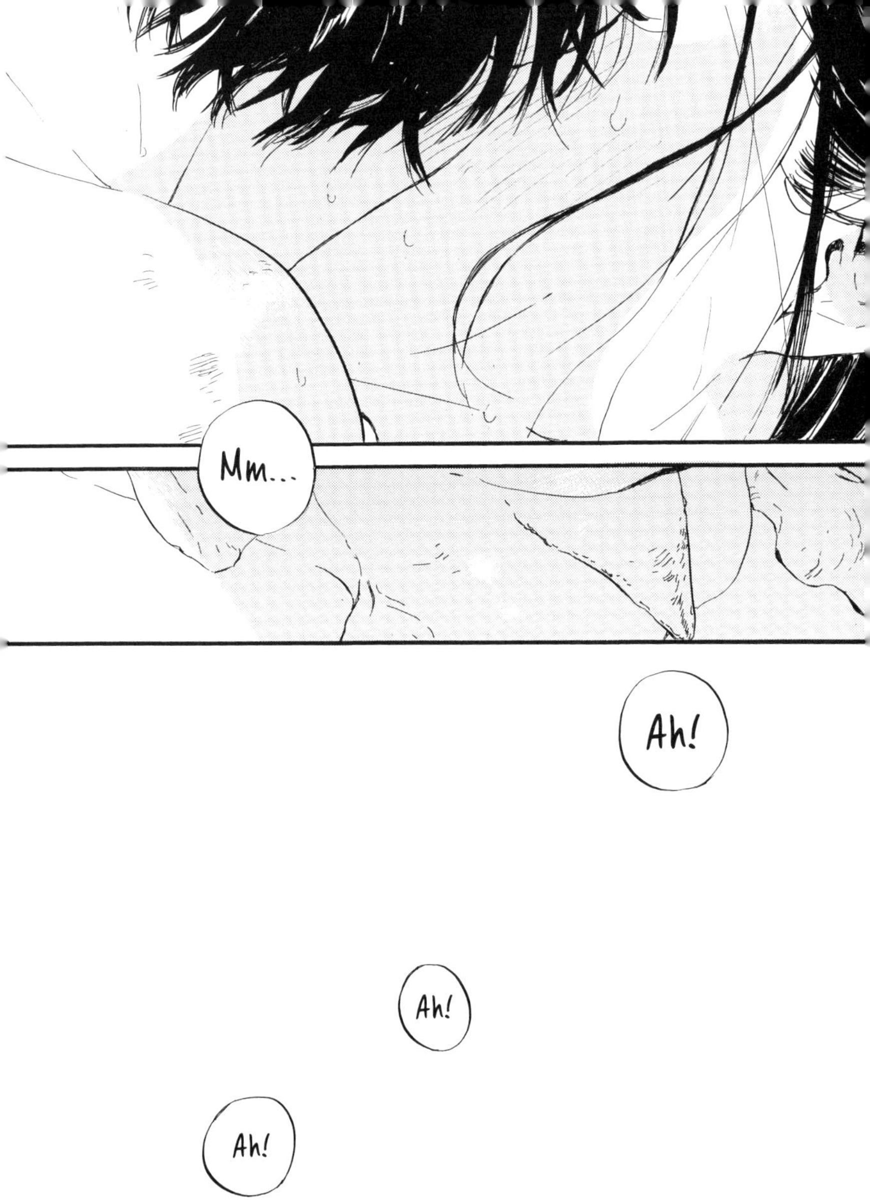
Mm...
Ah!
Ah!
Ah!

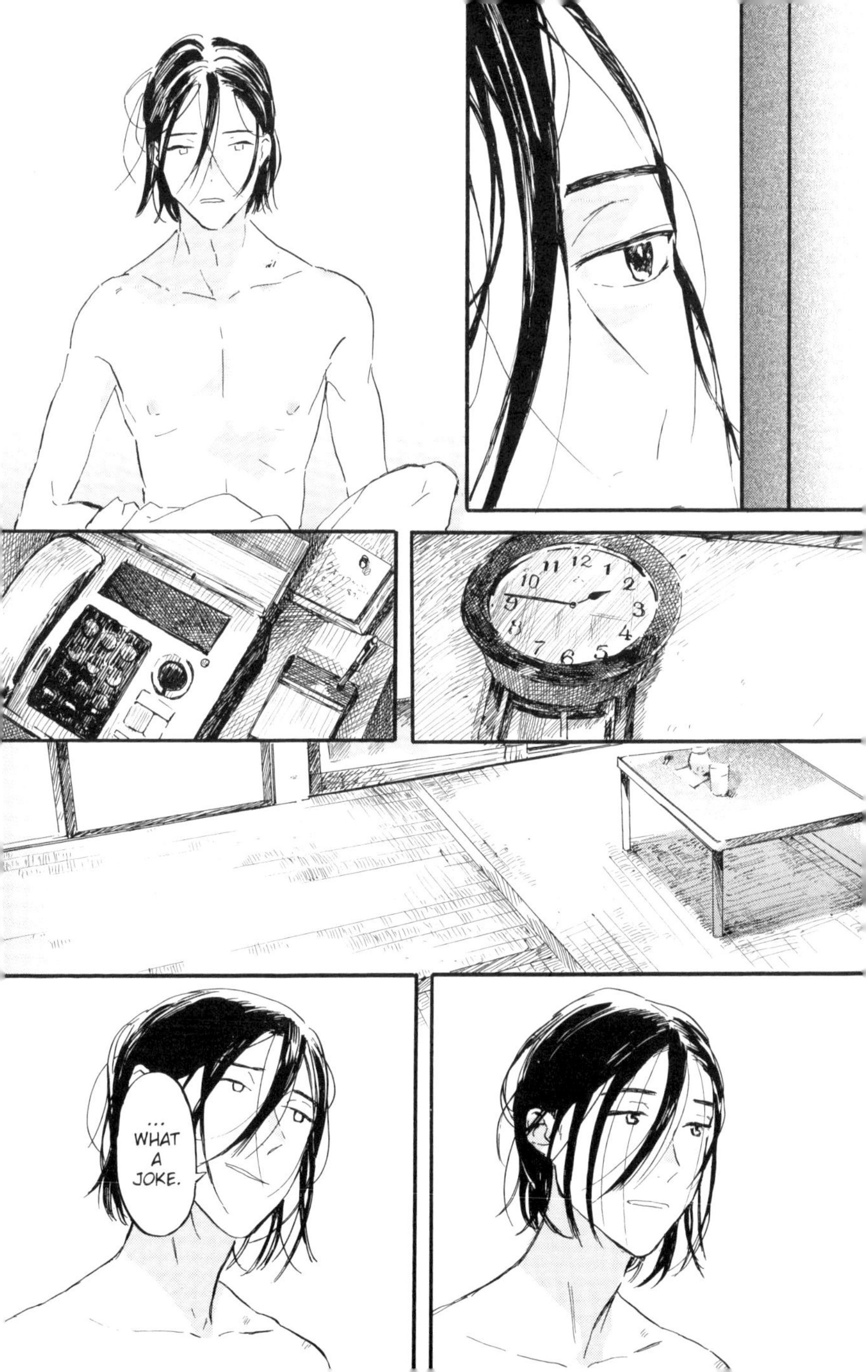
... WHAT A JOKE.

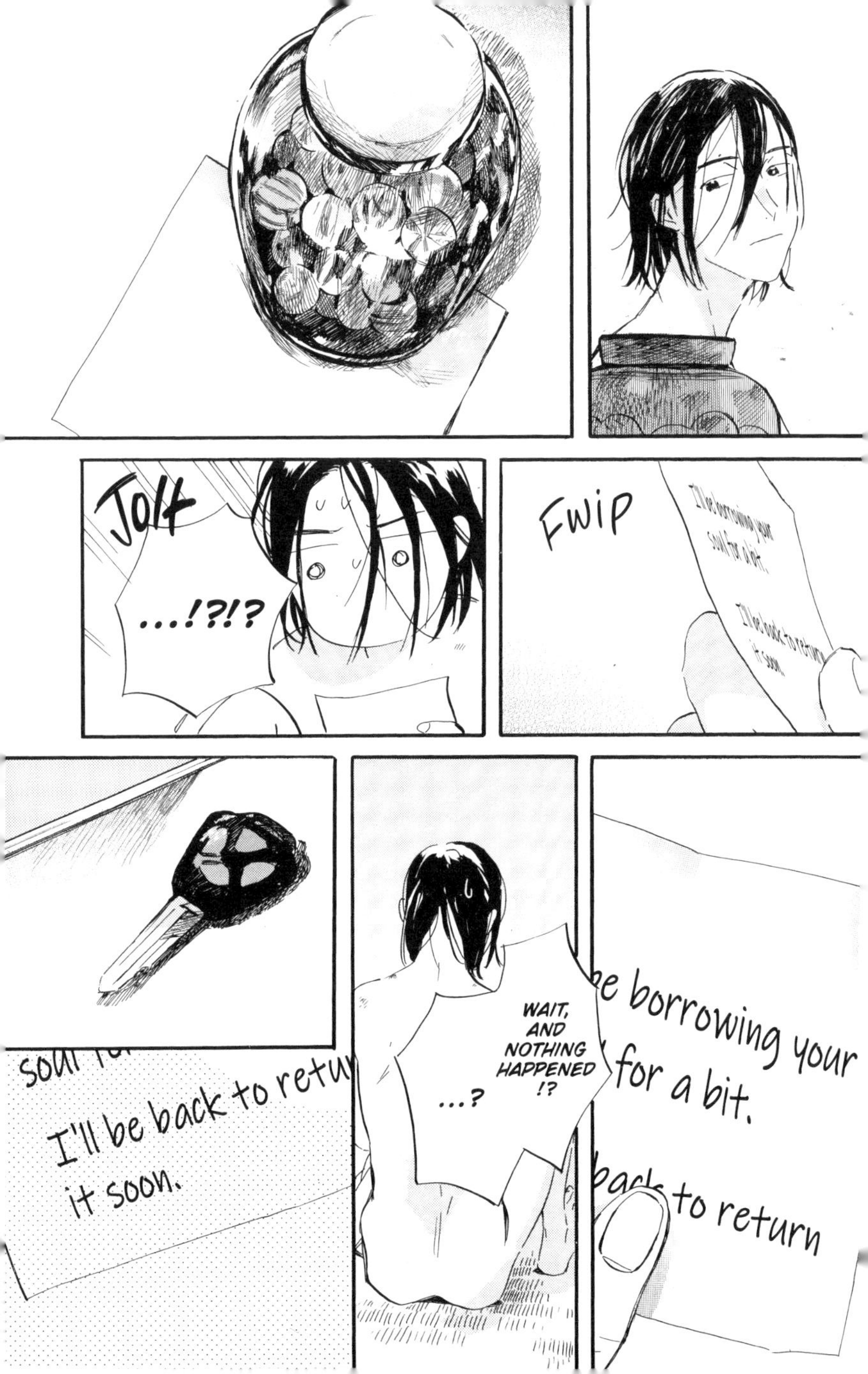
Fwip
I'll be borrowing your soul for a bit.
I'll be back to return it soon.
Jolt
...!?!?
e borrowing your
for a bit.
back to return
WAIT, AND NOTHING HAPPENED !?
...?
I'll be back to retu
it soon.

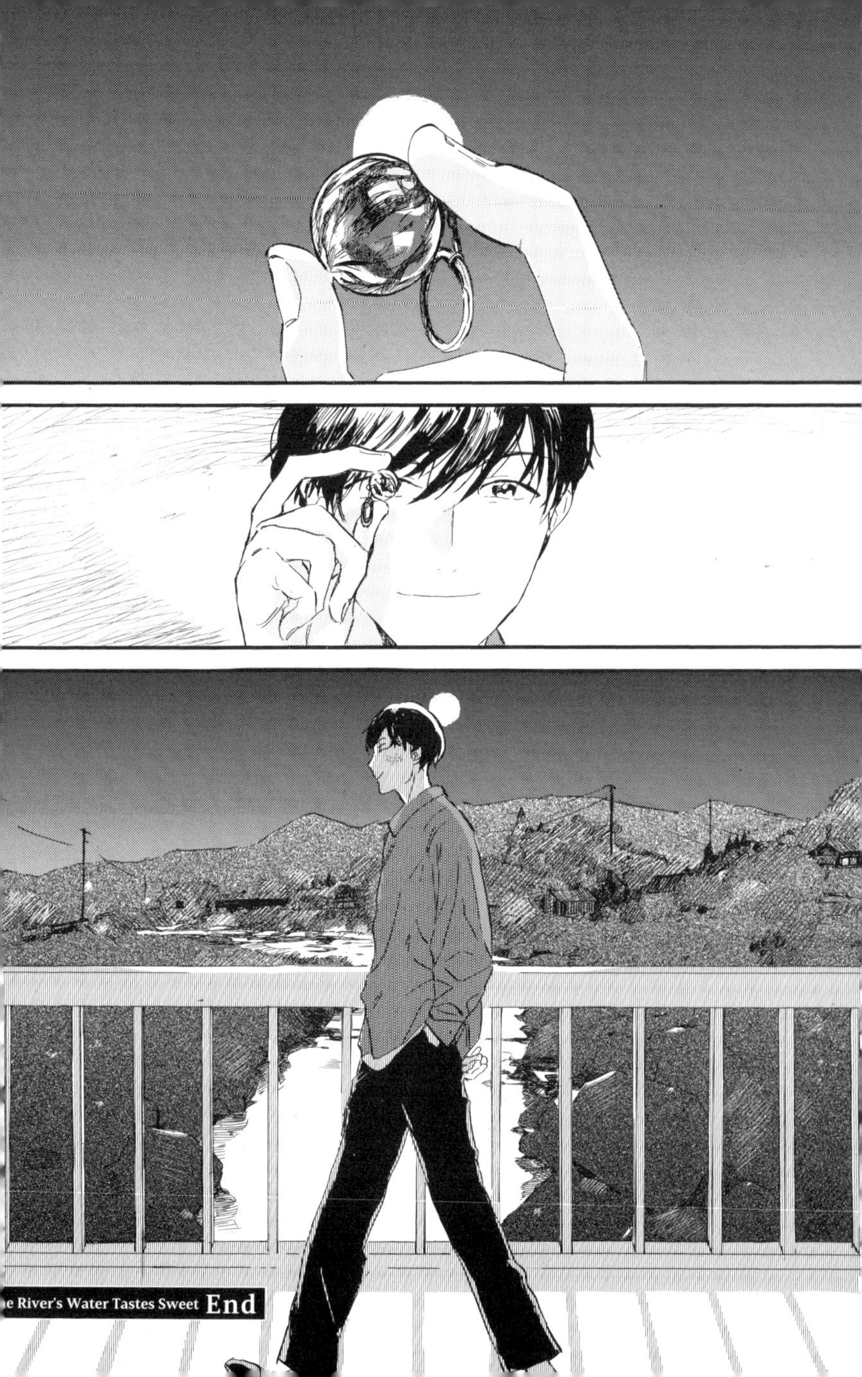
e River's Water Tastes Sweet End

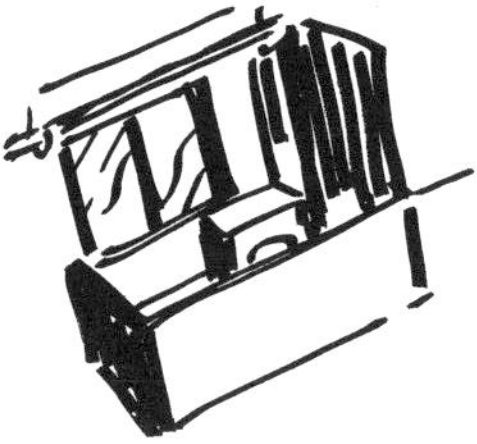

YOU ARE MY HAPPINESS

Originally, this was intended to be a horror comic, but after forgetting about it for three years, I redesigned it for BL. I was going for more of a Japanese horror feel, but I think most of the people into that genre don't really have a thing for demon wings and tails. I should've added horns too...

The balcony on their apartment was pretty big, but I only drew the window looking out onto it. Like you couldn't actually go outside onto it... Why?

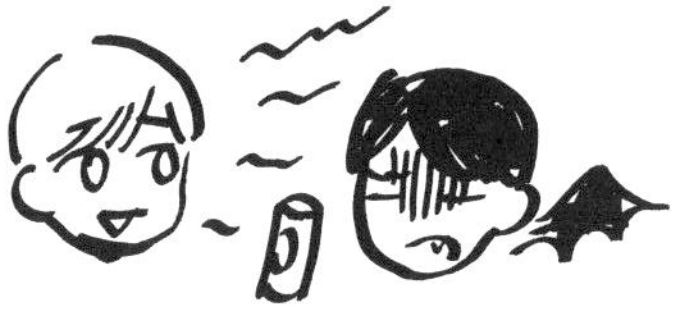

THE RIVER'S WATER TASTES SWEET

I always wanted to do a BL comic set in the countryside. I wanted to choose a monster that most people thought was kinda lame, and that's when it hit me. "Aha! A kappa!" And so, I chose a that.

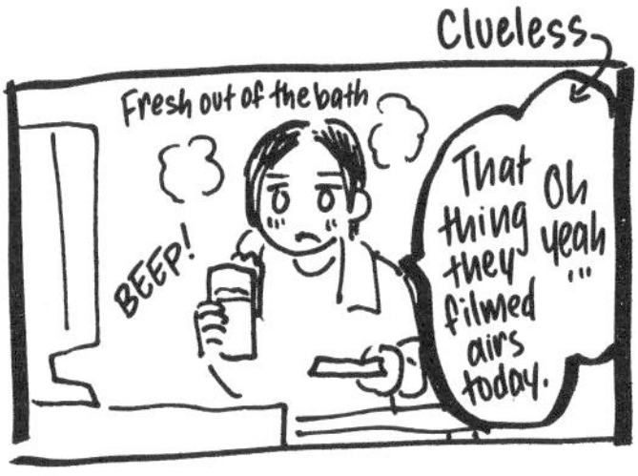
Clueless
Oh yeah... That thing they filmed airs today.
Fresh out of the bath
BEEP!

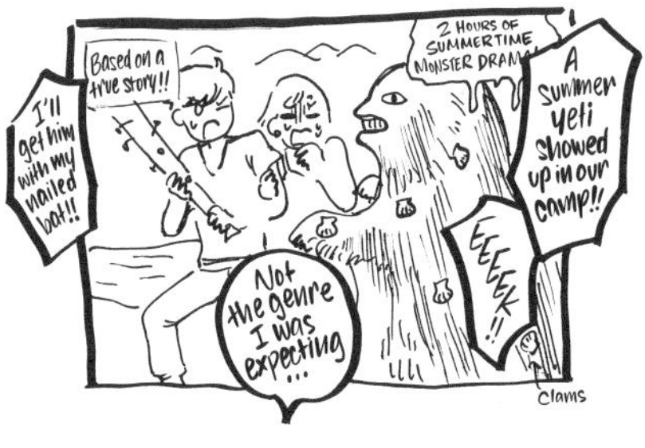
A summer yeti showed up in our camp!!
2 HOURS OF SUMMERTIME MONSTER DRAM
EEEEK!!
Clams
Not the genre I was expecting...
Based on a true story!!
I'll get him with my nailed bat!!

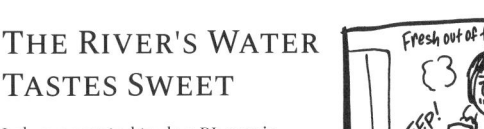

You are my Happiness

© Bukuro Yamada 2018
First published in Japan on June 10th, 2019
by Futabasha Publishers Ltd.
English version published by DENPA, LLC.,
Portland, Oregon, 2021

First Appearances

You Are My Happiness:
Comic Marginal Volumes
19 (09-07-2018),
21 (11-02-2018),
23 (01-04-2019),
24 (02-01-2019),
and 26 (04-05-2019)

You Are My Happiness Side Episode:
Book Exclusive

The River's Water Tastes Sweet:
Comic Marginal
Volume 16 (06-01-2018)

Publishing Team:

Translation:
Mike Wolfe

Proofreading:
Seanna Hundt

Lettering:
Kai Kyou,
Andrea Donohue

Production:
Jacob Grady,
Andrea Donohue,
Letty Chung

KUMA

Printed in China
ISBN-10: 1-63442-289-9
ISBN-13: 978-1-63442-289-5